Special Education in Canada

FIRST EDITION

Alan Edmunds
University of Western Ontario

Gail Edmunds
University of Western Ontario

McGraw-Hill Ryerson

Toronto   Montréal   Boston   Burr Ridge, IL   Dubuque, IA   Madison, WI   New York
San Francisco   St. Louis   Bangkok   Bogotá   Caracas   Kuala Lumpur   Lisbon   London
Madrid   Mexico City   Milan   New Delhi   Santiago   Seoul   Singapore   Sydney   Taipei

Special Education in Canada
First Edition

ISBN-13: 978-0-07-098191-1
ISBN-10: 0-07-098191-4

1 2 3 4 5 6 7 8 9 10 CCI 0 9 8

Printed and bound in the United States of America

Editorial Director: Joanna Cotton
Publisher: Nicole Lukach
Sponsoring Editor: Lisa Rahn
Director of Marketing: Jeff MacLean
Managing Editor, Development: Jennifer DiDomenico
Associate Developmental Editor: Alison Derry
Editorial Associate: Marina Seguin
Supervising Editor: Joanne Limebeer
Copy Editor: Tracey Haggert
Senior Production Coordinator: Paula Brown
Cover Design: Dianna Little Design
Cover Image: © Masterfile
Interior Design: Dave Murphy, Valid Design & Layout
Page Layout: SR Nova Pvt Ltd., Bangalore, India
Printer: Courier Companies, Inc.

Library and Archives Canada Cataloguing in Publication Data

Edmunds, Alan Louis, 1956-
        Special education in Canada/Alan Edmunds, Gail Edmunds. -- 1st ed.

Includes bibliographical references and index.
ISBN 978-0-07-098191-1

        1. Special education--Canada. I. Edmunds, Gail, 1956-
II. Title.

LC3984.E35 2008   371.9'0971   C2007-904871-4

Dedication

We dedicate this book to Andrea and Lindsey; they continue to inspire us as they follow their dreams with determination and passion.

About the Authors

Alan L. Edmunds, PhD (Alberta), is Associate Professor of Special Education and Educational Psychology at the Faculty of Education, University of Western Ontario. While his current research interests include behaviour management, learning disabilities, and the education of students who are profoundly gifted, his long-standing dedication has always been to the betterment of educational practices for all students. For more than twenty years he has examined the educational factors that make significant differences in the lives of students with exceptionalities and in the lives of their teachers and parents. These critical factors are the fundamental bases for his pre-service and graduate courses in educational psychology, special education, learning disabilities, giftedness, and cognition and learning. Alan's commitment to exemplary instruction has garnered several university teaching awards and his research has produced numerous articles and books. He is currently co-editor for a multi-authored collaborative text aimed at enhancing the connections between inclusion and educational leadership.

Gail A. Edmunds, M.Ed., studied educational psychology at the University of Alberta and subsequently began a career as an education/research consultant. She has over twenty years of experience working on projects with schools, colleges, universities, governments, and non-profit organizations across the country. Most recently, she was the researcher for the four-year Esso Family Math Program at the University of Western Ontario. In addition, she has been writing and editing supplementary materials for many education and psychology textbooks. Gail has also published numerous peer-reviewed articles in the areas of student writing skills, deaf education, family math, and gifted education.

Brief Contents

Contents

Preface

Welcome to the First Edition of *Special Education in Canada*. This book tells the stories of six unique Canadian students for whom very specialized forms of education were implemented. We featured these real-life case studies because they richly contextualize the educational realities that are faced by students, their teachers, and their families. We also included other professionals' perspectives on these stories to provide a uniquely insightful dimension not found in many other texts.

You will find our detailed pedagogical rationale for the book in Chapter 1; as this text will be used by teachers of teachers and by aspiring teachers, we felt strongly that its pedagogy could not be separated from its content. Please consult pages xii–xiv for a preview of the unique pedagogical support found within *Special Education in Canada*.

The Structure of the Text

The first three chapters provide an introduction to the domain of special education and lay out the guiding principles that govern our discussion of: (a) its historical and current perspectives; (b) its identification, assessment, and IEP process; and, (c) the creation and maintenance of exemplary teaching and learning environments.

Each of the next six chapters contains a story about a student who was identified under one of six categories of exceptionality: learning disability, behavioural disorder, gifted and talented, autism, intellectual disability, and multiple disabilities. We use each student's story as a lens through which his or her particular category of exceptionality is examined.

The last chapter in the text builds on the previous ten by providing students with ample opportunities to write their own special stories, thereby putting all their new-found theories into practice.

Student Resources

Visit the Online Learning Centre at **www.mcgrawhill.ca/olc/edmunds** to access practice quizzes with instant feedback and other learning and study tools.

Instructor Resources

Your **Integrated Learning Sales Specialist** is a McGraw-Hill Ryerson representative who has the experience, product knowledge, training, and support to help you assess and integrate any of our products, technology, and services into your course for optimum teaching and learning performance. Whether it's using our test bank software, helping your students improve their grades, or putting your entire course online, your *i*Learning Sales Specialist is there to help you do it. Contact your local *i*Learning Sales Specialist today to learn how to maximize all of McGraw-Hill Ryerson's resources!

At McGraw-Hill Ryerson, we take great pride in developing quality textbooks while working hard to provide you with the tools necessary to utilize them. We want to help bring your teaching to life using our products and services. We do this by integrating technology, events, conferences, training and more into services surrounding the textbook. We call it *i*Services. For additional information, visit **www.mcgrawhill.ca/college/iservices/overview.php**.

The **Instructor's CD-ROM** contains the Instructor's Manual, Test Bank in Rich Text Format, and Computerized Test Bank. The Instructor's Manual for *Special Education in Canada* was specifically designed to be consistent with the proven constructivist methods espoused in the text. Content from each chapter acts as a teaching or evaluation catalyst for the instructional elements suggested, all of which require higher order thinking. Not only will students have to "know," but they will have to provide a rationale as to why they know. The breadth and variety of activities (Pre-Class Student Assignments, Lecture and Discussion Ideas, and Classroom Activities) are so comprehensive that instructors will need to do very little extra preparation, other than developing some personal instructional choices. The purposeful consistency between the Instructor's Manual and the text will make for meaningful and interesting teaching and learning. The Instructor's Manual will also be available for download from a password-protected section of the Online Learning Centre at **www.mcgrawhil.ca/olc/edmunds**.

Acknowledgements

Obviously, we could not have written this text without the amazing contributions of the six students and their families. We came to realize that telling and retelling such an intimate family story is not as easy as it seems. While they remain anonymous, they know who they are and we are deeply grateful.

It also took considerable courage for Carol and Clayton Eaton to step back into the public spotlight after all these years and re-live Emily's story for us. It was truly uplifting to learn that despite the court's pronouncement, Emily's subsequent educational experiences were wonderful, fulfilling, and appropriate. Her graduation a few years ago was a very proud moment for Carol and Clayton. Many thanks.

We are also indebted to our colleagues Dr. Elizabeth Nowicki, Dr. Louise Larose, Lois Armstrong, and Richard Gilmore for their critical eye and sage advice. It's nice to have experts on your side.

We would also like to thank the reviewers, who offered helpful feedback on the manuscript in various stages of development:

Derek H. Berg, Mount Saint Vincent University
Paul Colini, University of Windsor
R. Marc Crundwell, University of Windsor
Kathryn Goldsmith, Malaspina University College
Gina Harrison, University of Victoria
Randy Hill, Brock University
Elizabeth Jordan, University of British Columbia
Corinne Kowalchuk, Lakehead University
Tim Loreman, Concordia University College of Alberta
Mike Parr, Nipissing University
Jae Patterson, Brock University
Allison Petrie, Acadia University
Nat Reed, Trent University
Sandra Reid, Nipissing University
Katreena Scott, OISE University of Toronto
E. Smyth, OISE University of Toronto
Gaby van der Giessen, Laurentian University

Last, but certainly not least, a sincere thanks to the whole McGraw-Hill Ryerson family who helped us throughout this exciting process. In particular, thank you to Marcie Mealia who got us started and to James Buchanan who first listened to our inventive idea, and then agreed to it! Karen Ritcey was highly instrumental in keeping the ball rolling, Lisa Rahn was our tireless advocate who won important battles on our behalf, and Jennifer DiDomenico, Tracey Haggert, and Joanne Limebeer were of immeasurable help in their attention to all the details that go into a project of this magnitude. Although they had no direct involvement in this endeavour, Joe Saundercook and Marlene Luscombe provided wonderful moral support.

What We Know...

Fragile X Syndrome

Fragile x syndrome is the most common form of inherited mental impairment. It involves changes in the x chromosome that affect the FMR1 gene. Because males have only one x chromosome, the syndrome usually affects them more severely than it does females. While the syndrome can affect individuals in a variety of ways, the most common characteristics include: intellectual disability, hyperactivity, short attention span, tactile defensiveness, hand-flapping, hand-biting, poor eye contact, speech and language disorders, long face, large or prominent ears, large testicles, Simian crease or Sydney line, connective tissue problems, and a family history of intellectual disability.

Individuals with fragile x syndrome often display autistic-like behaviours. While the syndrome is a cause of autism (15-33 percent of individuals with fragile x have autism), many individuals with the syndrome do not have autism despite the manifestation of these behaviours. Because they are interested in social interactions, they do not meet the diagnostic criteria for autism.

Source: National Fragile X Foundation, www.fragilex.org/html/home.shtml.

What We Know...boxes present aspects of exceptionality that do not necessarily apply to the student's story being told, and bring the professional literature into every chapter.

Imagine that you are a teacher in an inclusive classroom. Two of your students have an intellectual disability and require a slower pace of instruction. On occasion, they can be somewhat disruptive. Several parents approach you with their concerns. They feel that their children are not getting the best possible educational experiences because of the time and attention paid to these two "special" students. One parent states that disruptive children should be in a special class where they cannot annoy "regular" students. How would you respond to the concerns of these parents?

Something To Think About...

Something to Think About...boxes pose very specific questions that encourage critical thinking about educational issues.

From The Psychologist's Notebook...

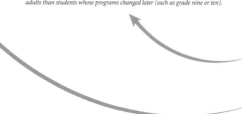

The coaching and support that David receives during his work placements are absolutely crucial to the quality of life he will lead once he gets out of school. The more independent he can become, the more fulfilling his day-to-day activities will be. Unfortunately, many teachers and parents are reluctant to change a student's curricular path away from academic subjects stating that this "seals their fate" and puts a glass ceiling on the student's learning. This reluctance is even stronger if a student's academic abilities are better than David's. However, the reality is that even if a student can continue to progress academically, it is unlikely that his or her life after school will revolve around the ability to perform academic type skills. Rather, the lives of students with intellectual disabilities are very probably going to revolve around their proficiency with skills that allow them to work and participate in society. Given that these students learn slowly and need lots of help when learning new things, the earlier their schooling focuses on life skills, work skills, social skills, and functional academics the better. In my experiences with the Canadian Association for Community Living (CACL), students whose programs included learning these types of living skills in grades five or six have had many more successful work experiences as adults than students whose programs changed later (such as grade nine or ten).

Canadian Association for Community Living
A Canada-wide association of family members and others working for the benefit of persons of all ages who have an intellectual disability.

From the Psychologist's Notebook...boxes feature a professional's insightful observations about the chapter content and/or student case study. These observations facilitate a deeper understanding of the student who has special needs.

Additional terms are defined in the margins.

Learning More About Students with Intellectual
Disabilities

Academic Journals

American Journal on Mental Retardation
Education and Training in Mental Retardation and Developmental Disabilities
Journal of Applied Research in Intellectual Disabilities
Journal of Intellectual Disabilities
Journal of Intellectual Disability Research
Journal on Developmental Disabilities
Mental Retardation
Research in Developmental Disabilities

Books

Taylor, R., Richards, S., & Brady, M. (2005). *Mental retardation.* Boston: Pearson
   Education, Inc.
B.C. Ministry of Education. (2001). *Students with intellectual disabilities: A resource
   guide for teachers.* www.bced.gov.bc.ca/specialed/sid.

Web Links

• *Canadian Association for Williams Syndrome*
   http://caws.sasktelwebhosting.com/
   CAWS was formed by a group of parents with the intent of raising awareness of
   Williams syndrome. Their Web site reflects their goal of supporting research that
   examines the educational, behavioural, social, and medical aspects of this syndrome.

Learning More About…sections offer print and online selections for further reading and research.

Tests of Achievement

Age at Time of Assessment: 15 years, 6 months

Test Administered: Woodcock-Johnson III Tests of Achievement

Test Results:

Cluster/Test	Age Equivalent	Percentile Rank
Basic Reading Skills	6–9	<0.1
Academic Skills	6–8	<0.1
Academic Knowledge	4–2	<0.1

Additional Tests	Age Equivalent	Percentile Rank
Letter-Word Identification	6–8	<0.1
Calculation	7–1	<0.1
Spelling	6–2	<0.1
Word Attack	6–9	<0.1
Picture Vocabulary	3–8	<0.1

Test Observations:
David's conversational proficiency seemed very limited for his age level. He was
cooperative, appeared at ease, and was attentive to tasks. David responded
promptly, but carefully, to test questions. He gave up easily when attempting
difficult tasks.

Test Summary:
When compared to others at his age level, David's academic knowledge and skills
are both within the very low range. This includes his basic reading skills.

David Robertson

Chapter opening "file folders" in Chapters 5–10
provide actual source documents pertaining to the
student case study (such as test results and excerpts
from IEPs and school reports).

Taking It Into Your Classroom...

Including Students who have Intellectual Disabilities

When a student who has an intellectual disability is first placed in my classroom, I will:

- review what I know about intellectual disabilities and locate resource materials
- read the student's file
- consult with the student's previous teachers
- consult with the student's parents
- meet with the school-based team to discuss the student's current school year

Other: _____

_____

When I suspect a student in my classroom has an intellectual disability, I will:

- review what I know about intellectual disabilities and locate resource materials
- collect information about the student through classroom interventions
- consult with other school personnel who are familiar with the student
- consult with the student's parents
- meet with the school-based team to present the information I have collected

Other: _____

_____

Key points to remember in my daily interactions with a student who has an intellectual disability:

- the student may have a short attention span
- the student may have both short-term and long-term memory problems
- the student may have a limited ability to express and understand language
- the student may need information delivered to them in short, simple chunks
- the student may have a decreased ability to generalize information across settings
- the student may exhibit behaviour problems, including aggression

Other: _____

_____

Taking It Into Your Classroom…sections conclude Chapters 5–10 with a synopsis of the important points from the chapter. The feature encourages readers to add their own points that they feel will be important to remember when teaching students with exceptionalities in their classrooms.

CHAPTER 1

Meaningful Stories: Meaningful Learning

From The Authors' Notebook...

We would like to welcome you to the first edition of "Special Education in Canada." We hope you find our book as interesting and as educational as we intended it to be. This exciting project came about for three reasons: (1) we felt a different kind of special education textbook was needed, (2) McGraw-Hill Ryerson had the foresight and conviction to break away from the traditional textbook mold, and (3) both parties wanted a textbook that made special education come to life.

Over the last twenty years, we have been working with students with exceptionalities, helping teachers and parents, and conducting research and publishing the findings. As well, we have been involved in the conception, revision, and editing of several textbooks, instructor's manuals, and teacher aide curricula. Along the way, we have read and examined several very good texts but we cannot say that any of these books are really all that different. Most books of this genre are presented in a similar, if not identical, fashion and despite excellent and comprehensive information about exceptionalities and teaching methodologies, there still seems to be something missing. The more we talked, the more we realized that what they lack is the authentic context of "the stories" that education students love to hear when studying special education. From our experience, when we talk about children with exceptionalities and provide examples of their school-related endeavours, students ask lots of questions and seek out additional readings or Web sites. This regularly happens from course to course and from year to year. Unfortunately, the same level and amount of interest does not occur when students are simply assigned textbook readings to discuss in class, even though the very same information is addressed. It has also been our experience that most people remember "the basic story" when presented with a complete case rather than a multitude of facts, even if they do not remember all the specific details. For example, many in education are aware of the Emily Eaton decision in 1997 in which the Supreme Court of Canada ruled that the Brant County Board of Education had the right to judiciously place Emily in a specialized classroom, despite the legal protest of her parents (Eaton v. Brant, 1997). However, because Emily's story was mostly presented from a legal (factual) perspective and little emphasis was placed on Emily's life situation, few people remember that this eleven-year-old girl had cerebral palsy and experienced considerable difficulty when trying to communicate with others. Further, many in education may not even be aware that up until the time the legal issues began, Emily was a member of the regular classroom where she had the full-time support of an educational assistant. We contend that providing more information regarding Emily and her school experiences would have made the details surrounding her situation more memorable and, therefore, more accurately discussed at a later date.

This keen level of curiosity regarding the lives of students with special needs is not only limited to those who are involved in the field of education. We have noticed that when we informally share children's stories with people who are not even remotely connected to our field, their interest is piqued. We have a friend who, even after three years, always asks about Geoffrey (Chapter 7) because he finds "Geoffrey's story" fascinating. Our friend has learned more about students who are gifted and talented than he probably ever cared to know but it is because he is curious and wants more information, not because we push it on him. We became convinced that if this approach could have such a positive learning effect on a non-educator, it would be invaluable for aspiring and experienced teachers. We know there is something very special about compelling stories, therefore, it made sense to write a book about students with exceptionalities that was first and foremost a collection of stories that people would want to read.

But, as educators, we also know that gripping stories do more than merely spark curiosity, they also set the stage for excellent learning by association. The reason stories are so riveting is because individuals immediately identify with the characters and their particular circumstances. This does not readily happen if information is presented without a compelling context. It is likely that every person who reads this book will know of children with exceptionalities and many will have witnessed or will have heard about the lives of these children. This instant association will enable readers to easily expand upon what they already know about special education.

A Constructivist Approach

While the beginning chapters of this book serve as an introduction to special education issues, the latter chapters present the stories of students with exceptionalities. Each of the student's stories is presented as an in-depth and comprehensive case study. The case study is an effective teaching and learning method that has been around ever since people started sharing educational information and it has certainly become the instructional method of choice in law, business, engineering, and medicine. Recently, there has been considerable research evidence that effective teacher preparation programs are using well developed case studies more and more often (Kuntz & Hessler, 1998).

Cases addressing educational issues can be developed from typical or atypical portrayals of students and/or they can be centered on common and recurrent themes or problems that students and teachers encounter in schools every day. The intrinsic learning value of cases is that they allow the reader to vicariously participate in the experiences of the story being told. Jay's (2004) research clearly demonstrated that an instructor's use of different types of cases provides students with a deeper understanding of complex issues. According to Kuntz and Hessler (1998), the most important feature of the case study is that it provides educators with opportunities to have their students: (1) employ higher-order thinking skills, (2) generalize learning to actual classrooms, (3) question assumptions about the theories presented, (4) engage in self-analysis, and (5) become aware of and understand the complex nature of teaching.

As you can see, the effects that cases can have on student thinking are consistent with the fundamental tenet of *constructivism* which advocates that individuals should actively and meaningfully construct their own knowledge and understanding in light of their own experiences (Palincsar, 1998). This is what happens when readers compare Emily Eaton to someone they know. However, the cases in this book are not just meant to be read and understood. They are meant to be analyzed, discussed, and debated by both instructors and students as they engage in interactive dialogue. Interactive dialogue is an effective *social constructivist approach* to teaching and learning because it emphasizes the value of the context within which learning strategies and knowledge are mutually constructed. With this emphasis, all students gain a better personal understanding of the topics at hand because their representations are distilled from, and compared to, what their peers and instructors think and say. Rather than assuming that learning takes place in the minds of individuals, it is better to assume that learning is more efficient and knowledge is better constructed when it is the result of interactions between people. In an extended fashion, students' representations are also formed by mutually comparing Emily's social milieu to their own, thus bringing their personal context to bear on their new-found knowledge.

In addition, the cases in this book are real-life accounts of existing Canadian children who are operating under real-world circumstances. Learning about the facts of these cases, and then comparing and contrasting them to their own lived experiences, enables students to experience *situated cognition* — thinking and learning that becomes located and enhanced by the specific context of each case (King, 2000). However, the cases in this book will extend students beyond typical applications of situated cognition because they will be expected to extrapolate and transfer their knowledge and their thinking to their real world — their classrooms. The ultimate goal of this text is to present thought-provoking cases that will stimulate discussion. We want each learner to contribute to their own understanding of students with exceptionalities as they interpret and make meaning of their own learning through the cases presented here. We are convinced that these special stories, in the form of comprehensive case studies, will result in enhanced learning.

 # The Framework of the Text

What Does the Text Include?

After explaining how we designed this book to facilitate meaningful learning (this chapter), we continue with a brief introduction to special education (Chapter 2) followed by a discussion of the identification of students with exceptionalities (Chapter 3) and the need for exemplary learning environments for these students (Chapter 4). In chapters 5 to 10, we tell the stories of the following six children: Karl, a student with learning disabilities who is in grade five (Chapter 5); Lindsey, a student with a behavioural disorder who is in grade seven (Chapter 6); Geoffrey, a student who is gifted and in grade four (Chapter 7); David, a student with an intellectual disability who is in grade eleven (Chapter 8); Zachary, a student with autism who is in kindergarten (Chapter 9); and, Monique, a student with multiple disabilities who is in grade eight (Chapter 10). Each of these chapters begins with the presentation of information extracted from the student's actual school file. The reader is then given more details about the student and his or her school life. We conclude our story-telling in chapter 11, and offer advice as to how you, as an educator, can best assist the students who will become the stories in your classroom.

How Were the Six Special Stories Chosen?

You may be wondering why we chose to tell the stories of the particular students included in this text; after all, there are endless fascinating stories available. First of all, we wanted to focus on the high-incidence categories of exceptionality because these categories represent the vast majority of students with exceptionalities that occur in the general population and, therefore, are those students mostly frequently encountered by regular classroom teachers. *High-incidence exceptionalities*, also commonly referred to as mild disabilities, typically include learning disabilities, behavioural disorders, giftedness, and intellectual disabilities. In addition, this text also provides an introduction to *low-incidence exceptionalities* in two of the stories because many teachers will likely have students like Zachary (Chapter 9) or Monique (Chapter 10) in their classroom at some point in their careers given the current emphasis on inclusionary practices. Low-incidence exceptionalities usually refer to the more moderate and severe disabilities that occur less frequently in the general population such as autism, hearing and visual impairments, serious health impairment, and multiple disabilities.

Other reasons for choosing the particular stories presented in this text included the need to cover a wide range of grade levels (i.e., students who are currently enrolled in the lower elementary grades, middle level grades, and secondary grades) and the need to reflect the fact that in the general population there are more boys with exceptionalities than girls. As well, we had to choose the stories of students whose parents were willing to share the details of their children's lives. It is interesting to note that every parent who was approached was more than willing to have their child's story included in this text. They were very excited that teachers would have the opportunity to learn from the experiences of real children. As one parent stated, "…the problems we faced within the school system have a better chance of being fixed if teachers are able to objectively examine what happened to our child…we can all learn by looking back at what worked and what didn't work."

Having obtained permission to write about these children and their families, we respected the need to preserve the confidentiality of all the individuals involved. Therefore, names have been changed and in some instances, alterations were made to the children's stories. Nonetheless, in an effort to retain contextual authenticity, we have remained true to each individual's special story as much as professionally possible. We chose to do this because even though these real-life educational stories are less than perfect depictions of what "should happen," we, like the parents, are convinced that much can be learned from educational situations, decisions, and actions that are sometimes less than exemplary.

What Do These Special Stories Have to Offer Students and Instructors?

We sincerely believe that our unique and innovative approach will make the topic of students with exceptionalities come alive for both students and instructors. If you are a student, we want you to be fully engaged in each story while you learn about this exciting domain and we want you to take away valuable information that will positively affect your teaching for years to come. If you are an instructor, we offer you each story as a starting point for the specific topics that you want to teach. We presume you will use modified and adapted perspectives of each story to suit the emphases of your course. Our overall intention is that the themes of the stories will evoke probing questions from students and instructors alike, questions such as:

- Why did the Supreme Court decide in the School Board's favor in the Eaton case? (Chapter 1)
- How can students who are disruptive be properly managed in the classroom? (Chapter 4)
- Why did the Cognitive Credit Card learning strategy work for Karl when other strategies did not? (Chapter 5)
- What are the different ways that students can be identified as being gifted and talented? (Chapter 7)
- How can a student with autism cope with all the sensory input that occurs in a regular classroom? (Chapter 9)

Does the Text Only Address the Learning Experiences of Six Students?

We recognize that not all aspects of an exceptionality apply to any one child regardless of their exceptional condition or the life situations they experience. The obvious question for us was, "How will the textbook portray all the different aspects of an exceptionality if the focus is on one child's story?" We accomplish this in each chapter with *What We Know* boxes. The information contained in these boxes presents aspects of an exceptionality that do not necessarily apply to the child's story being told. This special feature brings the rest of the professional literature into every chapter and it expands the comprehensiveness of each category of exceptionality. Once readers become comfortable with the complete picture, they can then have more reasoned and informed discussions about the exceptionality at hand. For example, now that you know that Emily was a student with a physical disability and struggled considerably with communication, you can readily compare and contrast her traits, characteristics, and school conditions with those of other students with similar conditions to understand the broader spectrum of all students with intellectual and developmental disabilities. Even though Emily's case is not one of the focus cases in this book, we present more details of her story below in a *What We Know* box to demonstrate its form and purpose. The details in the box are excerpted from Bedgell & Molloy (1995) and The Learning Disabilities Association of Canada (2005).

What We Know...

Emily lives in Burford, Ontario. She has cerebral palsy and she is unable to communicate through speech, sign language or other communication systems. She also has a visual impairment and is mobility impaired, and therefore requires the use of a wheelchair. Although she was identified as an "exceptional student" upon her entry into school, Emily, at her parents' request, was placed in her age-appropriate kindergarten in her neighborhood school in the public system on a trial basis. As dictated by her high needs, Emily was assigned a full-time Educational Assistant (EA).

In Emily's grade three year, school personnel concluded that this placement was not in her best interest because of her lack of academic progress and a social environment she had great difficulty managing. Emily's parents refused to allow their daughter to be moved to a segregated class because they strongly believed that her needs could be met in the regular class, that she would be psychologically harmed in a segregated classroom, and that in order to be truly part of her community, Emily needed to go to her neighborhood school with her peers. Emily's parents were essentially arguing for the concepts that are at the heart of the philosophy of inclusion.

When the Identification Placement and Review Committee (IPRC) determined that Emily should be placed in a special education class, her parents appealed that decision to a Special Education Appeal Board, which confirmed the IPRC decision. The parents appealed again to the Ontario Special Education Tribunal, which also confirmed the decision. The parents then lost in Ontario's Divisional Court but the Ontario Court of Appeal found in favor of the parents stating that segregation violated Emily's equality rights under Section 15(1) of the Canadian Charter of Rights and Freedoms. The Court held that making distinctions on the basis of disability was discriminatory and that the Ontario Education Act itself violated the Charter in giving school boards the discretion to place children with disabilities in segregated classes against their parents' wishes.

The Brant County School Board appealed this judgment to the Supreme Court of Canada which set aside the decision of the Court of Appeal. The Supreme Court of Canada ruled that the educators and the Tribunal had not violated the equality rights of Emily Eaton, rather they had balanced her educational interests appropriately, taking into account her special needs. The Supreme Court observed that a disability, as a prohibited ground of discrimination, differs from other grounds such as race and gender, because of the vastly different circumstances of each individual and that, related to education, inclusion can be either a benefit or a burden depending on whether the child can profit from the advantages that inclusion provides. This meant that educational decisions affecting placement must be based on the child's best educational interests, not based on what adults want for their children.

Source: Excerpted from Bedgell & Molloy (1995) and The Learning Disabilities Association of Canada (2005).

Emily Eaton – Age 22.

As you can see, the information presented in the *What We Know* box enhances Emily's story and provides further insight to her case. You are now in a position to discuss and debate the placement of students in specialized settings versus their placement in the regular classroom. The discussion can be expanded to include an examination of the varying implications each placement scenario has for teachers and how each would affect their curricular choices and instructional methods. As you can see, the opportunities for learning are nearly endless but there is no doubt that they all emanate from the basic story of one child. For your information, most students with exceptionalities will not be educated in specialized settings, but that is not the point. The point is that Emily's story, even though only briefly presented here, has grabbed your attention. Imagine what a full blown story covering several years of schooling will do!

What Other Special Features Does This Text Include?

The *What We Know* boxes are just one component of a consistent framework that systematically supports each of the student's stories. Another special component is *From The Psychologist's Notebook*. These boxes provide a professional's insightful observations about the child and/or his or her situation. These types of observations are not often found in special education textbooks, yet they have much to offer in terms of facilitating a deeper understanding of the student who has special needs. An example of this type of box is presented on the next page. It refers again to the Emily Eaton story.

From The Psychologist's Notebook...

I interviewed Emily Eaton's parents in February of 2007 to find out more about Emily's special story. It had been ten years since the Supreme Court of Canada handed down its landmark decision. I met Clayton, Carol, and Emily at their family home in Burford. Emily was to turn 23 in a few weeks. She remains verbally uncommunicative and has limited use of her limbs. However, she uses gestures to indicate her likes and dislikes, and according to her parents, she does this quite often and quite clearly.

Both of Emily's parents described having had experience working in the education system. Clayton was once a teacher but, at the time of the interview, he was working for the Ontario Ministry of Education as a resource consultant for students with visual impairments. Carol had previously worked as a school counselor at W. Ross MacDonald School.

Emily graduated from high school when she was 21. Once out of school, Carol and Clayton designed a program for her that mostly involves participating in social activities and doing every day things like going to the dentist, getting groceries, etc… Emily still needs constant supervision and assistance to do most things. She has the services of a Personal Care Worker whose salary is paid by the Ontario government. Her current Worker is a young woman who is Emily's age. On the day that I visited, the two of them were off to see a movie with other friends.

At the beginning of the administrative wrangling over Emily's educational placement, the Eatons were confused by the school board's decision to place her in a segregated classroom. For two years previous, Emily was provided a full-time EA and she was fully included in all regular class activities. By Clayton and Carol's account, all went well for those two years and they were very pleased with Emily's overall schooling experiences. In her grade three year, the school board stipulated that Emily would only have EA support for half a day but provided no reason for this decision other than budgetary restraints. When the Eatons argued that this was contrary to the Board's previous decisions, and that Emily's educational needs had not changed enough to warrant such an action, the Board stated that if the Eatons wanted full-time support for Emily, she would have to be in a segregated class. This contentious position never changed throughout the legal process.

Immediately after the Special Education Tribunal's ruling in favor of a segregated placement, Clayton and Carol moved Emily to the local elementary school of the Catholic board. She continued her elementary education there and completed her secondary education at one of the Catholic high schools in nearby Brantford. For all of those years, until she was 21 years old, Emily had a full-time EA and was educated in regular classrooms with her peers. She only left the classroom for specialized interventions in speech, physical therapy, and occupational therapy. Clayton and Carol were extremely pleased with how it all turned out and could not say enough about the kindness and compassion of nearly all of Emily's teachers and classmates in both schools.

When asked why this seemingly obvious solution was not possible in the public system, Clayton and Carol explained how they had often suggested this very solution but were rebuked at every turn. They felt that once the battle lines had been drawn, the Board did not want to back off from their original position.

I asked if anyone or any of the ruling bodies involved in the entire case had ever suggested the above educational solution for Emily. They informed me that the Supreme Court ruling was not really about Emily, per se, rather the decision had more to do with ruling on the legitimacy of the school board policy. Therefore, nobody wanted to get into the details of Emily's specific case and no such suggestions were proposed, except by themselves. In a cruel twist of fate, after all they had been through, their local Catholic school said they would welcome Emily into the regular classroom. It was as simple as going down the road to another school. It could have been as simple as providing her with a full-time EA at her original school.

Carol and Clayton were emphatic that parents of students with exceptionalities need to be very vigilant about their child's schooling and not be afraid to advocate on their child's behalf whenever necessary. Despite their long ordeal, they found that constant diplomatic pressure, coupled with precise and copious documentation, made a significant difference in getting their point across. They also made it clear that, regardless of training or special expertise, teachers who are open minded about a child's condition, and kind and compassionate in their teaching of that child, make more of a difference than any specialized programs. While they admitted that not all of Emily's teachers were exemplary, the majority were appreciated because of the reasons stated above.

It is difficult to comment on Emily's case because it became more focused on policies and responsibilities than on Emily's education in particular. It is heartwarming that all went well for Emily eventually, but I think her parents paid an emotional price along the way. Currently, they are skeptical of what educational policy documents "say" about students with exceptionalities and place much more value on what educators "actually do" to support what is stated. While their position is understandable, it is not how we, as educators, want the public to view our roles in their children's lives. To prevent this perspective from becoming pervasive, we all have to "walk the talk."

Unfortunately, Emily and her parents were victims of their own time. I am convinced that if Emily's situation arose today, her case would never be argued beyond the jurisdiction of the governing school board, and it certainly would not make it to the Supreme Court. Educational decision-makers, aware of the prevailing research on the best educational practices and policies for students with exceptionalities, would make the appropriate accommodations. There is no question that the overarching objective for all students with exceptionalities must be that they have the most and best educational opportunities possible to be able to actualize their potential. It is only under the auspices of valid, reliable, and proven special educational practices and policies that this is possible.

Also included in this textbook are *Something To Think About* boxes which pose very specific questions that encourage critical thinking about educational issues that extend beyond each child's respective case. Each of the student's stories concludes with a section entitled *Taking It Into Your Classroom*, which presents a synopsis of the important points from the chapter. This box also allows the reader to add their own points, or reminders, that they feel will be important to remember when teaching students with exceptionalities in their classroom.

A Reminder

As you learn about special education through the meaningful stories presented in this text, keep in mind that it was never our intent to provide comprehensive information that would qualify you as an expert once you had read and discussed the material. In the field of special education, there are entire textbooks that cover many of the topics presented in the chapters of our book. It is our intention, therefore, to introduce you to these topics and pique your interest so that you continue to pursue knowledge in this area throughout your teaching career. We hope you come to realize that teaching students with exceptionalities is not as daunting as it is sometimes portrayed. While there are new teaching skills to learn, they are not that different from the skills you use to teach students without special needs.

Something To Think About...

As you begin to learn about special education, it is important to reflect on your current feelings about the field and the experiences you have had that have lead to the formation of these feelings. For example, you may have some negative thoughts about teaching students with exceptionalities and you can trace this back to your own school years when you were in classrooms where very disruptive students took all of the teacher's time. It may be helpful to express your feelings on paper and re-visit your writing after you have completed your coursework. It may be the case that more knowledge about the field will alter your feelings about special education. In any event, it is important to recognize the views you bring to your study of this topic.

CHAPTER 2

Introduction to Special Education

What is Special Education?

In every classroom, in every school, on any given day, teachers know they will face groups of students who have different abilities and behaviours. They fully expect that not all students will learn at the same rate, or act and react to their environment in the same manner. Teachers are known to frequently teach lessons while purposefully wandering around their classroom providing instructional prompts, extra help, and/ or guidance so that each child can better understand the topic. Teachers also seem to intuitively know when a particular look or verbal reminder is necessary to nip potentially problematic behaviour in the bud. As a result of their education and classroom experiences, teachers develop a wide range of teaching and classroom management strategies to accommodate the typical range of student diversity.

However, in these very same classrooms, there will also be students whose learning and behaviours differ considerably from the norm. Without specialized knowledge, their teachers will likely lack the educational tools that are needed to teach and manage these students properly. We refer to this group of children as *students with exceptionalities* — students who exhibit differences in learning and behaviour that significantly affect their educational potential and whose exceptional needs cannot be met by typical approaches to schooling. This group of students is just as varied and diverse as the rest of the school population and it includes those who require physical accommodations, behavioural interventions, specialized computers, particular learning strategies, modified curricula, and advanced placement university exams. *Special education*, then, is a particular type of schooling that is constructed and delivered to suit the specific strengths and needs of students with exceptionalities. It is founded on

A teacher learns to recognize and address students' needs.

the premise that if their education is properly differentiated, more and more of these children will reach their full potential.

The Modern History of Special Education

There is ample historical evidence that special types of educational services were provided for individuals with exceptionalities as far back as the eighteenth century, but the modern era of special education really began in the 1960s with the emergence of the civil rights movement in the United States. During that decade, nearly everyone associated with education rejected the existing practices of separately educating students who were different and housing them in institutions. As unpalatable as it may be, we have to remember that the early forms and types of special education were not designed with the best interests of children with exceptionalities in mind. Rather, they were designed as convenient measures to thwart perceived threats to the education of normal students (Taylor & Harrington, 2001). However, there was a strong movement across North America in the 1960s advocating that all individuals had the right to live, learn, and work with all other individuals. This represented a monumental change in our social consciousness. As a result, more and more educators of the day questioned the validity and effectiveness of the non-egalitarian approach that prevailed and special education came into its own.

Legislation Affecting Special Education

In Canada, education is the jurisdictional responsibility of the thirteen individual provinces and territories, while in the United States it is the Federal Office of Education that governs special education issues. It is not commonly known that some Canadian provinces were enacting legislation to ensure the education of students with exceptionalities as far back as 1969 (Goguen, 1993), and earlier. For example, "By 1955, the [British Columbia] provincial government introduced funding for programs for 'handicapped' children as part of the basic grant to school districts" (Siegel, 2000, p. 8). Another example occurred in Alberta where "… in 1950, there were 256 identified exceptional students, in 16 classrooms across the province, and there were three categories of student exceptionality that were recognized" (Lupart, 2000, p. 5).

The passage of wide-sweeping laws to change special education practices started in the late 1960s, had its heyday in the 1970s, and it carries on today as educational perceptions about best practices continually evolve. It is generally perceived that the ground breaking legislation for special education across North America occurred in 1975 with the signing of U.S. Public Law 94–142, the Education for All Handicapped Children Act. The most influential feature of this law was its emphasis on individualized instruction that emerged from a child's **individualized education program** or IEP (see Chapter 3 for full details). Along with individualized programs, PL 94–142

individualized education program
A legal document that describes a student's specialized learning expectations and the educational services that will be implemented to help the student meet these expectations.

also required that all students with special needs be educated in the *least restrictive environment* — the most appropriate classroom setting for each child's instructional needs. In addition, this landmark law contained provisions for the mandatory identification of students with exceptional needs, the use of non-discriminatory assessment criteria, and child and parental access to due process for dispute settlement. As well, it outlined and defined the ten specific *categories* under which students could be identified. These mandated features of PL 94–142 had to be implemented if states wanted to receive supplementary funding for the education of students with special needs. In 1978, PL 95–561, and later the Javits Gifted and Talented Students Act of 1988, were enacted to address the educational needs of students who are gifted and talented, thus bringing the number of identifiable categories to eleven. However, because PL 94–142 only mandated special education for children aged six to eighteen years, another law, PL 99–457, was passed in 1986 to provide services for infants (0–3 years) and for preschoolers (3–6 years). This legislation set the stage for early intervention services for young children with special needs. The next major revision of PL 94–142 occurred in 1990 with the introduction of the Individuals with Disabilities Education Act (IDEA). This legislation added traumatic brain injury and autism to the collection of identifiable categories thus resulting in the thirteen that are widely used today. As well, IDEA was the first law to implement a people-first approach, using terms like "children with disabilities" instead of "disabled children." IDEA was further refined in 1997 as Public Law 105–17 when it made teachers accountable for student progress relative to the regular curricula and required that the regular curricula be the preferred starting point for all student outcome measures. This change put the onus on classroom teachers to directly involve students with exceptionalities in the regular course of studies.

Something To Think About...

As well as implementing very good teaching methods in a particular way and for very particular purposes, special education, like all other professional disciplines, also requires the use of precise and professional terminology. You will note that throughout this book we use non-stigmatizing professional terms that emphasize a "people-first" approach, just as was implemented in the IDEA legislation. We speak of the child first and of their disabling condition second. We encourage you to immediately begin using terms like *students with learning disabilities* and *students who are gifted and talented*, rather than *LD students* and *gifted students*. Do you think it makes a difference to use this professionally accepted language? How might it affect both the student and those who work with the student?

The No Child Left Behind Act

The U.S. legislation that has had perhaps the most impact on special education over the last twenty years is the No Child Left Behind Act of 2001 (NCLB, P.L. 107–110). This act was signed into law in January 2002 and established a sweeping set of reforms for our discipline. Its primary objective was to improve the academic success of all students but especially for those who have exceptional learning and behavioural needs. According to the U.S. Department of Education (2002), this act addresses four critical concerns: (1) accountability of educators for student academic achievement, (2) flexibility of specialized funding implementation to maximize student achievement, (3) the option for parents to change their child's school if the child's achievement is not at expected levels, and (4) the use of scientifically proven methods to have every child reading by the end of grade three. The NCLB also includes requirements that teachers be fully qualified, that non-English speaking children receive intensive instruction in English, and that schools be safe and drug free. The most significant implication of NCLB is that schools that do not enable students with exceptionalities to achieve appropriately may be subject to remedial action (we interpret this to mean the withholding of special education funding).

Is NCLB Making a Difference?

There has been much debate over the NCLB legislation. One of the major criticisms of the original law voiced frequently and strongly by teachers and researchers in special education was that the NCLB assessment requirements did not exempt students with exceptionalities from district-wide or state-wide yearly achievement tests. Measuring these students against the general curricula goes against everything that speaks to the individualized nature of special education and it may serve to undermine their access to programming based on their IEPs. The U.S. Department of Education recently changed the law and allowed a flexibility option:

> *The newly released proposed regulations for the 2 Percent Flexibility Option give states and districts more leeway in assessing students with disabilities. States can develop modified assessments for 2 percent of their students with disabilities who do not meet grade-level standards despite high quality instruction, including special education services. Though the modified assessments must be aligned with grade level content standards, they may differ in breadth or depth from the achievement standards for non-disabled students. The proposed regulations make it clear that high expectations will be held for students with disabilities who take modified assessments. The students must have access to grade-level instruction, and the modified standards cannot preclude the students from receiving a regular diploma. Further, the students must be appropriately*

assessed on modified achievement standards. The IEP team will play a critical role in determining not only which students will take modified assessments, but also the type of modified assessment individual students will take.

(Council for Exceptional Children, 2006)

charter school
An independent, publicly funded school that operates under provincial law and is governed by a charter (agreement) with a school district sponsor.

Other criticisms of NCLB include the lack of funding available under the law and the potential for cost savings for the government via virtual charter schools. There are also a wide variety of educators who are worried about NCLB's apparent narrowing of the scope of the overall curricula (and assessments thereof) that places more focus on math and reading at the expense of other curricular topics (McKenzie, 2003).

From our perspective, the NCLB ambitions are laudable, especially given the recent inclusion of a flexibility option. However, the NCLB legislation will not affect special education practice or legislation in Canada in immediate or obvious ways. Nonetheless, as time goes on and Canadian teachers, researchers, and policy makers share ideas with our U.S. colleagues, it is probable that the elements of NCLB that prove to be improvements on current practice will find their way into Canadian policies and classrooms. One of the organizations that is most involved in an ongoing detailed analysis of NCLB, and the provision of recommendations for change, is the Council for Exceptional Children (CEC). You can get up-to-date information on the latest developments regarding NCLB on their Web site at **www.cec.sped.org**.

How is Special Education in Canada and the United States Similar?

The practice of educating students with exceptionalities in Canada is so similar to that of practices in the United States that not many individuals, even educators, would be able to tell the difference between the jurisdictions if they walked into comparable schools or classrooms. This is because the basic practices of special education follow the same conceptual models reported in literature worldwide; these are models that know no political boundaries.

However, there is one major difference between special education in Canada and the United States and that is in the way in which it is governed. The U.S. operates under the federally-mandated laws described previously and while each Canadian province and territory has their own respective education legislation that governs the education of students with exceptionalities, these provisions are not laws per se. The closest that Canada comes to having a federal law regarding special education is the previously mentioned Canadian Charter of Rights and Freedoms. Section 15 of the Charter states that "Every individual is equal before and under the law and has the right to the equal protection and equal benefit of the law without discrimination and, in particular, without discrimination based on race, national or ethnic origin, colour, religion, sex, age or mental or physical disability" [s. 15 (1)]. To date, the Supreme Court of Canada has consistently interpreted Section 15 of the Charter to mean that the best interests of the individual child must be considered when determining a child's educational placement and intervention program. As you will see in the following *What We Know* box, the Court has been consistent in that decisions regarding the provision of special education made thus far have been determined on a child-by-child basis. While the Elwood case below was not decided at the Supreme Court level (the parties reached an out-of-court settlement), it was the very first challenge to segregated educational placements under section 15 of the Charter. The parents of the child used Charter sections 15 (equality), 2 (freedom of expression), and 7 (right to life, liberty, and security) to negotiate for their child's placement in the regular classroom.

What We Know...

Elwood v. The Halifax County-Bedford District School Board

Luke Elwood of Halifax, Nova Scotia was nine years old and in a special education class for the 'trainable mentally handicapped' until 1986 when his parents enrolled him in a regular class in nearby Lawrencetown, N.S. for the coming year. The Halifax County-Bedford District School Board asked his parents, Maureen and Rick Elwood, to place him back in his special education class in Halifax. When they refused, the Board held a formal meeting where they decided that Luke would continue in his special education placement.

After many legal maneuvers wherein the parents attempted to keep their child in a regular class and the Board attempted to not let that happen, an injunction was granted to allow Luke to stay in a regular classroom until the dispute was resolved. The Board's basic argument was that if the parents had the right to choose their child's educational placement, the Board would be obliged to develop a new and different education program. They had no way of providing an appropriate education for Luke other than in his segregated and specialized classroom. Immediately prior to the deciding court date of June 1997, the Board and the parents came to an out-of-court settlement.

The important point here is that the parents used Charter sections 15 (equality), 2 (freedom of expression), and 7 (right to life, liberty, and security) to: (a) secure the injunction while awaiting the court date, and (b) successfully negotiate with the Board for their child's placement in the regular classroom. The Board was unsuccessful in arguing that education was a provincial matter as defined by statutes and regulations and as directed by educational administrators.

Source: MacKay (1987).

Thus, while the Supreme Court did not render a decision in the Elwood case, the Charter shaped educational policy in favor of the best interests of the child, like it did soon after in its decision regarding Emily Eaton. It is expected that all similar future decisions will be decided in the same manner. This is a highly significant development for special education because it means that the interpretations of the Charter were not precedent setting, as is usually the case with legal decisions of such magnitude. It is perhaps even more significant because the highest court in our land is adhering to the most fundamental tenet of special education: that educational decisions are to be made in the best interests of each and every individual child who is exceptional. On one hand, this means that not all students with exceptionalities will be included in regular classrooms, but on the other, it also means that children will not be excluded from the regular classroom unless their situation warrants it.

Prevalence of Students with Exceptionalities

When discussing students with exceptionalities, many aspiring teachers want to know how likely it is that they will have these students in their classrooms and/or how many students fall under the broad definition of "exceptional student." The fact is that the vast majority of classrooms now include students with exceptionalities and nearly all teachers are required to teach and manage these students on a daily basis.

Exact statistics regarding the inclusion of students with exceptionalities in the regular classroom are difficult to acquire in Canada. Canada does not have a process that parallels the federal function of the United States Department of Education which, through its mandated annual report to the U.S. Congress, tracks the number of students with disabilities who receive special education funding and services. Despite the slightly different criteria used in some states, these reports are the most complete and accurate information on how many students in the United States have exceptionalities. It is important to note that students who are identified as gifted and talented are not included in this report as it only deals with students who are considered disabled. The generally accepted percentage of students identified as gifted and talented is two to five percent depending on the jurisdiction and the criteria used. We have extracted some of the pertinent statistics and descriptions from the 2000–2001 school year report (U.S. Department of Education, 2002) to provide you with a general indication of what teachers can expect in regards to special education:

- in every year since 1976–77, more students have received special education services
- the number of students receiving special education services increases to age 9, then slowly decreases to age 17
- about twice as many males as females are identified as exceptional
- in 2001/02, students with exceptionalities aged 6 to 17 represented 8.8 percent of the student population [not including preschoolers aged three to five (1%) or gifted (2–5%)]

- in 2001/02, 88 percent of all children receiving special education services fell into four categories – learning disabilities (50%), speech and language impairment (18.9%), intellectual disability (10.6%), and behavioural and emotional disturbances (8.2%)
- in 2001/02, approximately 85 percent of students with exceptionalities had mild disabilities
- the "typical" child receiving special education services is an elementary age boy with learning disabilities who spends part of each school day in the regular classroom and part of the day in a resource room getting extra help

In Canada, it is generally agreed that the percentage of students who are considered exceptional ranges from 12 to 16 percent of all school aged children ("Prevalence…", 1995). Of course, this range will vary slightly from jurisdiction to jurisdiction depending on the criteria for designation. While country-wide statistics are not available, it is useful to consider the statistics of one of the larger jurisdictions, such as British Columbia, to determine if the numbers are comparable to those reported by the United States. In 2006, the British Columbia Ministry of Education reported statistics for the period 2001/02–2005/06 in their document *Students with Special Needs: How Are We Doing?* (2006). Some of their findings included:

- in 2005/06, 61,277 students where identified as having special educational needs
- in 2005/06, the proportion of students with special needs in the total B.C. public schools student population was approximately 10.2 percent
- in 2005/06, males were twice as prevalent as females in both the learning disabilities category and the behaviour disabilities category
- in 2005/06, the number of students reported in the gifted and talented category represented 2 percent of the total provincial enrolment
- between 2001/02 and 2005/06, the number of students reported in the Learning Disabilities Performance Reporting Group increased by 13 percent
- between 2001/02 and 2005/06, the number of students reported in the Behaviour Disabilities Performance Reporting Group decreased by 11 percent
- between 2001/02 and 2005/06, the number of students with Moderate to Severe/Profound Intellectual Disability has not changed significantly
- between 2001/02 and 2005/06, the number of students with Physical Disability/Chronic Health Impairment increased 29 percent
- between 2001/02 and 2005/06, the number of students with autism increased by 70 percent (in 2002/03, the Ministry of Education revised its identification criteria for these students to be more aligned with B.C. Ministry of Health Standards and Guidelines for the Assessment and Diagnosis of Young Children with Autism Spectrum Disorder)

In general, these statistics are not unlike those presented by the U.S. Department of Education. Based on this consistency, we can assume that they are fairly representative of what is happening across Canada.

What We Know...

Special Education in Canada

In 2001, the Canadian Council on Social Development published the results of a study conducted by Gibson-Kierstead and Hanvey on the state of special education in Canada. Seventeen special education experts from across the country, including individuals from all provinces and territories, were interviewed.

Eighty-eight percent of the experts reported that their education systems had gone through major restructuring over the last five years. Most of these experts indicated that this restructuring had impacted upon the delivery of special education services. Eighty-two percent reported that funding for special education was inadequate.

Nineteen percent of the experts said that the children with special needs in their region were having their learning needs met. Eighteen percent reported that their province or territory was capable of providing special education services to all children likely to benefit from such services.

Eighty-seven percent of the experts reported that the needs of children in their regions were not met consistently across urban and rural centres. Children who lived in urban centres were much more likely to receive better levels of service than children who resided in rural centres. Despite location, children with physical disabilities were the most likely to receive acceptable levels of service while children with ADHD were unlikely to receive the services needed.

Ninety-four percent of the experts indicated that the need for special education services had increased in their region. Eighty-eight percent stated that there were not enough specialists available to provide these services to children nor were there nearly enough teachers' aides and assistants.

Source: Gibson-Kierstead and Hanvey (2001).

Inclusionary Practices

Until the early to mid 1980s, most special education services in Canada were traditionally provided via specialized programming which was delivered in classrooms and other settings that were wholly or partially separated from the regular classroom. Today, because nearly all Canadian provinces have adopted the philosophy of inclusion, most students with exceptionalities receive their specialized programs in regular classroom settings.

It is important to understand that inclusion does not simply mean educating all students with exceptionalities in the regular classroom with their age-appropriate peers. Students must still be provided with appropriate educational programming in the most appropriate educational environment possible. Therefore, while it is preferred that the regular classroom be the first placement option for students with exceptionalities (perhaps with instructional methods and curricula that are considerably modified) it would be inappropriate to say that this arrangement is the only alternative. It is essential that educators clearly recognize that in order to properly meet the specific needs of some students, these students may need specialized assistance via pull-out programs and/or resource teacher support, or they may require the help of highly specialized teachers in specialized and separate classrooms. To think that the regular classroom is the only option for students with exceptionalities is an abuse of the fundamental tenet of inclusion which is to provide an appropriate education for all students.

What We Know...

The Concept of Inclusion in Canadian Jurisdictions

In an extensive review of the history of special education in Canada, the province of Saskatchewan (Saskatchewan Education, 2000) provided a synopsis of how most jurisdictions in the country have adopted the concept of inclusion in their statements of philosophy for special education [we have added the Newfoundland and Labrador (Newfoundland and Labrador Department of Education, 1997), Northwest Territories (Education, Culture and Employment, 2004), Nunavut (Nunavut Department of Education, 2003), and Yukon (Governmentof Yukon, 2002) perspectives as they were not in the Saskatchewan document].

Alberta:
  '...regular classrooms in neighbourhood schools...first placement option...'

British Columbia:
  '...equitable access to learning by all students...'

Manitoba:
  '...students with special learning needs in regular classroom settings...'

New Brunswick:
  '...with same age peers in most enabling environments...'

Newfoundland and Labrador:
  '...programming is delivered with age peers except where compelling reasons exist...'

Northwest Territories:
  '...whenever possible, access to an education program in a classroom setting...'

Nova Scotia:
  '...within regular instructional settings with their peers in age...'

Nunavut:
  '...equal access for all students to educational programs offered in regular classroom settings with their peers...'

Ontario:
> '...integration as the first consideration...'

Prince Edward Island:
> '...most enabling environment that allows opportunities to interact with peers...'

Quebec:
> '...a view to facilitating their learning and social integration...'

Saskatchewan:
> '...students with exceptional needs...should experience education...in inclusive settings...'

Yukon:
> '...in the least restrictive and most enabling environment to the extent that is considered practicable...'

integration
The process of integrating students with exceptionalities back into the regular classroom, if possible.

mainstreaming
The selective placement of students with exceptionalities in regular classrooms on a part-time basis where possible (dependent on ability).

To date, inclusion is the best philosophical approach we have had to direct the education of students with exceptionalities; however, Lupart and Webber's (2002) analysis of decades of changes in the implementation of regular and special education concluded that much work needs to be done to make inclusion the norm in Canadian schools. Inclusion is a better system than **integration** or **mainstreaming** because it seeks to change educational systems and classroom environments to suit the needs of the child rather than trying to "fix the child" to suit the system (FSU Center for Prevention & Early Intervention Policy, 2002). Nonetheless, the term *special education* cannot simply be replaced with the term *inclusion*, as has occurred in some Canadian provinces and territories. Inclusion is primarily an overarching philosophy that advocates for the regular classroom as the first placement option for students with exceptionalities but it does not provide specific definitions as to how that implementation is supposed to take place. Without effective implementation principles, inclusion runs the risk of being perceived as an ivory tower concept that has no credence with educators in everyday classrooms. This has been consistently evidenced in numerous studies of educators' perceptions of inclusion. These studies have revealed that educators support the philosophical tenets of inclusion but they are concerned about its lack of procedures for implementation (Bunch, Lupart & Brown, 1997; Edmunds, 2003; 1999; Edmunds, Halsall, MacMillan & Edmunds, 2000; Garvar-Pinhas & Schmelkin, 1989; Houck & Rogers, 1994; King & Edmunds, 2001; Scruggs & Mastropieri, 1996). Therefore, the specifics of implementation still have to come from the effective and proven procedures that have served special education so well for so long.

It should be noted that when educators use the term special education, some incorrectly emphasize the word "special" resulting in special education being construed as something magical and mystical that only a limited number of teachers know how to deliver. We feel that the emphasis needs to be on the word "education" so that special education is seen as nothing more than very good teaching that happens to be applied differently for very special students. With this understanding and emphasis, special education becomes something that many more teachers can expect to deliver effectively.

What We Know...

Canadian Teachers' Views of Inclusion

In 2003, *Exceptionality Education Canada* produced a special edition of their journal that focused on the issues surrounding the preparation of Canadian teachers for inclusion. The following research findings were presented:

- Teacher candidates expressed a need for extended, mandatory studies in special education within preservice teacher education programs. They also emphasized the importance of having opportunities to work with knowledgeable associate or mentor teachers during their practicums and having this mentoring continue once they become practicing teachers (Woloshyn, Bennett, & Berrill, 2003).
- While regular classroom teachers' attitudes towards inclusion were positive, many reported that they felt unprepared to teach students with special needs. They stated that they do not feel confident regarding their skills to adapt curricula to meet the needs of these students. They also reported that inclusion has increased their teaching workload considerably. They expressed a desire to have the opportunity to acquire the skills that will allow them to be good teachers in an inclusive setting (Edmunds, 2003).
- For the most part, teachers indicated their support of the educational soundness of a full inclusion model. Attitudes were most positive at the elementary level. However, teachers did express concerns regarding the implications inclusion has on their workload. They also reported significant concerns about the relationship between teachers and support staff (Pudlas, 2003).

Imagine that you are a teacher in an inclusive classroom. Two of your students have an intellectual disability and require a slower pace of instruction. On occasion, they can be somewhat disruptive. Several parents approach you with their concerns. They feel that their children are not getting the best possible educational experiences because of the time and attention paid to these two "special" students. One parent states that disruptive children should be in a special class where they cannot annoy "regular" students. How would you respond to the concerns of these parents?

Something To Think About...

The Categorical Model

The intent of special education is to modify educational approaches to suit the educational requirements of children with exceptionalities. To properly and professionally accomplish this goal, students' abilities and needs must first be defined and then identified, classified, and categorized. Therefore, the *categorical model* of special education is the one adhered to in this text because, in our estimation, it is the most logical and systematized way of identifying and defining the specialized and diverse needs of children. This approach also clearly establishes the full parameters of each category so that educators do not confuse one with the others, even though children in different categories may exhibit similar skills or needs. This does not mean that overlap amongst the categories is ignored or dismissed, because we know that many instructional interventions are applicable to a wide range of students who are categorized differently. Rather, it means that the complete scope and criteria of a category are fully considered when providing educational interventions. By paying close attention to the specific criteria that apply to each particular child, effective educational interventions can be designed to suit the child's unique and special situation. Furthermore, by clearly illustrating how one category can apply to a wide variety of children, all of whom are distinctly different, educators will refrain from overgeneralizing the characteristics of a specific category to any one child. As you will see in the case studies presented in this text, each child meets the identifying criteria of their respective category of exceptionality, but not all other students who fit into each of the categories are like the children we have written about here.

The categorical model of special education is the most widely used and accepted approach because it provides distinct definitions for each of the categories of exceptionality. These definitions allow educators to separate and classify students according to their unique abilities and needs. As well as facilitating the design and implementation of specific programs for specific children, this systematic approach also provides the basis for specialized training for teachers and for consistency across research studies that investigate the effectiveness of special education interventions. In addition, the categorical model provides a reliable and consistent manner of communicating about exceptionalities. Students often must be described as belonging to specialized categories in order for educational jurisdictions to be eligible for designated funding and services. Furthermore, the categorical model has had a significant impact on education in Canada as it is through this approach that more students have been identified as having special needs and, consequently, funding for special education has increased (Lupart & Odishaw, 2003).

In contrast, there are others who prefer a *non-categorical* approach to special education. The non-categorical model evolved as a reaction to the perception that the categorical model emphasized a reliance on labelling to guide testing, assessment, and placement. Advocates of the non-categorical approach claim that the defining labels of the categories are pejorative. They feel that these labels frequently stigmatize, isolate, and stereotype individuals with learning, behavioural, or physical differences. They also claim that the categories are arbitrary and that the categorical model has too much of a diagnostic emphasis and not enough of a functional service purpose. They contend that a better approach is to remove the emphasis on assessment processes. The non-categorical approach examines student performance relative to expectations, identifies instructional needs, and monitors and evaluates progress in response to intervention, thus resulting in a data-based approach to instructional planning rather than reliance on specific labels (National Association of School Psychologists, 2002). Some who support the non-categorical perspective suggest that global efforts towards more effective instructional planning, classroom organization, and adapting teaching and assessment procedures are preferred to individualizing education to suit the specific needs of learners with special needs (Hutchinson, 2002).

To summarize, then, the non-categorical approach is primarily premised on two arguments. The first speaks to the perceived injustices that can arise from the potential misuse of the labels associated with special education. This is a problematic argument with no foreseeable solution because no one can control the intention that makes a term pejorative regardless of the word used to label a category. The second argument typically presented is that the non-categorical approach is better because it is more concerned about functional educational services than the placement outcome of the referral-assessment-placement emphasis attributed to the categorical model. This argument has been rendered moot by the advent of inclusion, wherein most students with exceptionalities will be educated in the regular classroom. The current focus of inclusion is on serving students based on their specific educational needs, not based on a special delivery model. There is no doubt that inclusion places more responsibility on all teachers to understand and properly respond to students with exceptionalities, something that they did not do well in the past, mostly because they did not have to do it. In the final analysis, the categorical model offers a classification mechanism that can consistently identify a student's educational needs and abilities and it provides educators with a systematized way of thinking about and evaluating educational interventions; the non-categorical model does not.

Despite the delivery of similar special education services across the ten provinces and three territories of Canada, there are differences in the process used to identify, assess, and program for students with exceptionalities. As Dworet and Bennett (2002) pointed out, these differences include the use of varying labels and descriptors to describe exceptionality categories. In fact, some jurisdictions do not use any labels at all. How do you think this might affect a student with an exceptionality who moves from one jurisdiction to another?

Something To Think About...

This book was written with an overarching categorical perspective for a second fundamental reason: teachers need to know the criteria that are used to identify students with exceptionalities and how the identifying criteria vary across categories. In nearly all instances, these criteria provide beneficial insights as to how curricula, teaching methods, and evaluation can be differentiated to suit the specific needs of each child. In addition, knowing the specific criteria allows teachers to readily notice problems that a child may be having and, therefore, more timely referrals for interventions are made. If teachers know what a particular child's needs and abilities are, they can easily make numerous and varied changes to their teaching to help that child. With non-categorical approaches to special education, teachers do not know the identifying criteria and they do not know the differences between the criteria for the various exceptionalities. Within this model, we do not feel that teachers are in as strong a position to intervene.

Let's examine both models in light of the case of a student who has great difficulty reading. Using the categorical model, this child is referred and assessed and someone, usually a special education specialist or a psychologist, explains the reasons why the child cannot read as well as he or she needs to in order to complete academic tasks. The assessor then offers suggestions as to how the classroom teacher can adapt or modify teaching methods to suit the child's abilities. For example, the student may have sight word recognition problems, problems decoding, and/or he or she may struggle so much with reading the words on the page that his or her working memory is unable to process the meaning of the sentences being read (typically called an inability to comprehend). There are several other reasons why individuals do not read well, but the point is that each of them requires a specific type of reading intervention because there is no one general reading intervention that can effectively remediate all of the above problems. This common classroom situation also has significant but different instructional implications if the reading problem is identified when the child is learning to read (up to grade three or four) as opposed to being identified when the child is expected to read to learn (grade three or four onward). More importantly, because the assessment process will have also identified the child's specific learning strengths, the teacher can use these assets to help the child overcome the reading difficulty. In most instances, specific reading interventions that suit the diagnosed problem, perhaps with some trial-and-error and/or slight modification, will prove beneficial.

In comparison, the non-categorical model tends to eschew the diagnostic tone of the referral and assessment procedure, preferring to answer the question "How do I adapt my teaching to include these exceptional individuals?" (Hutchinson, 2002, p. xvi). This is an excellent question. Following this model, however, the teacher only knows that the child cannot read adequately and he or she is left to try to adapt instruction without any idea as to the nature of the child's specific problem. Without knowing what the child's specific needs and abilities are, the teacher can only guess at how to meet the child's learning objectives. Worse yet, the teacher runs a very high risk of doing things that are inappropriate. It is not uncommon for teachers and special education teachers, who operate under such a mandate, to try something that seems to work one day, yet have it prove extremely ineffective the following day, and not know why. What is even more troubling is that these teachers will not even know why some instructional methods worked because they do not have access to the necessary diagnostic information.

We believe that the categorical approach advocated here will go a long way towards eliminating this confusing and frustrating approach to teaching students with exceptionalities. As we are fond of saying, we never met a teacher who did not know how to modify their curriculum or their teaching or their classroom environment to suit any child's *known* situation; however, no teacher can make modifications for even one child's *unknown* situation.

Learning More About Special Education in Canada

- Council of Ministers of Education Canada
  www.cmec.ca/index.en.html
  The CMEC is an intergovernmental body founded in 1967 by ministers of education to serve as a forum to discuss policy issues; a mechanism through which to undertake activities, projects, and initiatives in areas of mutual interest; and a means by which to consult and cooperate with national education organizations and the federal government.

- Government Education Research Network
  www.cmec.ca/gern/indexe.asp
  The aim of GERN is to make education research conducted by provincial/territorial governments more accessible for both the public and other governments. The GERN Web site facilitates this by providing links to Canadian education research.

- Departments and Ministries Responsible for Education in Canada

Alberta	**www.education.gov.ab.ca**
British Columbia	**www.gov.bc.ca/bced**
Manitoba	**www.edu.gov.mb.ca**
New Brunswick	**www.gnb.ca/0000/index-e.asp**
Newfoundland and Labrador	**www.gov.nl.ca/edu**
Northwest Territories	**www.ece.gov.nt.ca**
Nova Scotia	**www.ednet.ns.ca**
Nunavut	**www.gov.nu.ca/education/eng**
Ontario	**www.edu.gov.on.ca**

Prince Edward Island   www.gov.pe.ca/education
Quebec   www.mels.gouv.qc.ca
Saskatchewan   www.aee.gov.sk.ca
Yukon   www.education.gov.yk.ca

● Statistics Canada
www.statcan.ca/start.html

Please visit the Online Learning Centre for *Special Education in Canada* at
www.mcgrawhill.ca/olc/edmunds for additional learning and study resources.

CHAPTER 3

The Assessment and IEP Process

Special Education: The Implementation of Exemplary Teaching Practices

As we described in Chapter 2, special education is a particular type of schooling that is constructed and delivered to suit the specific strengths and needs of students with exceptionalities. In this light, special education is a necessary and fundamental part of our educational system because students with exceptionalities, like all other students, have the right to an appropriate education. We also previously described how special education is not something that should be viewed as being highly complex, secretive or mystical, nor should it be perceived as something that can only be practiced by a select few teachers. Rather, special education is best viewed as nothing more than exemplary teaching practices that all teachers can easily implement or make adjustments to with some experience, wherein these teaching practices are designed and implemented based on specific types of information. While this perspective may contradict what you have previously heard about special education being "so specialized," read on and you will see what we mean when we say that all teachers can effectively engage in special education, given the right conditions.

If special education is simply the implementation of good classroom teaching practices in an effort to provide specialized programming for students with exceptionalities, there are three obvious questions:

- How do we determine how students with exceptionalities are different from their non-exceptional peers?
- What specialized programming is needed to meet the needs of students with exceptionalities and how does it get constructed?
- What do teachers have to know and do differently to properly implement specialized programming?

The two short answers to these important questions are: (1) a proper and comprehensive assessment reveals how students with exceptionalities are different from their peers, and (2) from these assessments, specialized programming is constructed according to identified strengths and weaknesses, thus providing teachers with what they specifically need to know about these students and what they can do (or attempt to do) in terms of educational interventions. These brief answers are provided here to give you an overarching conceptual framework to think about as you read the rest of the chapter. In it, you will find detailed and comprehensive descriptions of what these seemingly simplistic answers truly mean. By the time you finish reading the chapter, you will see that there clearly is a viable and effective process called special education that can effectively serve students with exceptionalities, their teachers, and their parents. Once you understand what this course of action entails, you will be in an excellent position to modify the process to suit whatever teaching situations you will encounter in your career.

What is Assessment?

Before we go any further, let's carefully examine the word assessment so that we are clear as to what it means. If you were to mention *assessment* at a social gathering, many people, regardless of whether they were connected to education or not, would immediately think of "testing someone," perhaps on a variety of topics. Only rarely would someone think of assessment as having a variety of different formats when applied in educational settings. In fact, most individuals would be able to tell you little about what kinds of assessment tools are available or exactly how an assessment is carried out. Instead, their comments would probably be focused on the secrecy and specialness that is often associated with assessment (e.g., they had some kind of special test in school but no one ever told them what it was for or what the results were). Another common perception of assessment is that it is a one-time process based on one test, a sort of snap-shot in time that sets a student's course for many, if not all, his or her school years. While these perceptions are not totally inaccurate, they are mostly erroneous and they outline the misperceptions that many individuals have about assessment, both within and outside of education.

In general, the term *assessment* refers to a comprehensive process of collecting a variety of data for the purpose of making educational decisions about individuals (and sometimes groups). In special education, the term *psycho-educational assessment* is more often used because the data gathered usually includes a variety of indices of social and psychological variables as well as measures of academic achievement so that comprehensive educational decisions can be made for students with exceptionalities. While this process invariably identifies areas of need and deficits in abilities, the predominant emphasis of assessment focuses on a student's current level of functioning so that proper instructional interventions can be designed. Psycho-educational assessment is best viewed as a dynamic process that, as necessitated by the student's abilities and/or learning environment, involves the gathering of data from multiple sources, across a variety of settings, using various measures, and is done on multiple occasions so that informed and reliable decision-making can occur. It is only from this professional perspective that teachers can begin to alter their teaching or the curricula to suit a student's educational needs.

The assessment process is vital to special education because it provides education professionals with objective, valid, and reliable data upon which suitable and appropriate educational programming can be based. Specialized programming for students with exceptionalities can range from minor modifications to the regular curricula and/or the typical teaching methods used in the regular classroom, to fully specialized programs that include completely different curricula and/or teaching methods implemented in a congregated classroom or school. The type and extent of changes that educators make to curricula and/or teaching methods is entirely dependent upon each individual student's strengths and needs. Therefore, students with exceptionalities are best served by accurate assessments of their abilities and needs as this type of information makes for the most meaningful educational outcomes (Salvia & Ysseldyke, 2004). By contrast, approaches to special education that do not utilize a formalized assessment process run the risk of making inappropriate educational decisions (or no decisions) that usually exact a high human cost from students. In an effort to emphasize the importance of the assessment process and the diagnostic and decision-making ability it affords us, we reiterate our statement from Chapter 2: we never met a teacher who did not know how to modify their curriculum or their teaching or their classroom environment to suit any student's *known* situation; however, no teacher can make modifications for even one student's *unknown* situation. It is clear that if teachers are going to make the right kinds of changes to help students who have a variety of educational needs that are different than their classmates, education professionals need to gather and interpret the kind of information that only a proper assessment can provide.

It is worth noting at this juncture that the vast majority of educators, and the psychologists and **psychometrists** who conduct psycho-educational assessments, are not as concerned today as they were in the past about what causes the majority of differences in student learning (McLoughlin & Lewis, 2005). Most *learning differences* are caused by variables that educators cannot control or remediate. The field has come to realize that except in very few cases, knowing the causes of learning differences has limited effects on how educators design and implement effective learning interventions. On the other hand, educators are quite concerned about the causes of *behavioural differences* because the vast majority of problematic behaviours are caused by learned behaviours or learned reactions, and educators have far greater control over them (Johnson & Edmunds, 2006). The causes of behaviour, commonly referred to as **antecedents**, are important pieces of information to understand and consider when designing effective behavioural interventions to help children in classrooms. They may not be obvious nor appear to be directly linked to the observed behaviour, therefore, assessments of the abilities of students with exceptionalities must be comprehensive.

By now, you are probably wondering just how many students require formal assessments and how many of these students are eventually classified as having an exceptionality. Salvia and Ysseldyke's (2004) ninth edition of their gold standard text *Assessment: In Special and Inclusive Education* details the process by which proper assessments of students with exceptionalities are conducted. According to their research and experience, they estimate that:

> . . . *approximately 40 percent of all students will experience difficulty during their school careers, and approximately 10 to 12 percent of all students who actually enter school will experience sufficient difficulty to be identified as*

psychometrist
A certified specialist who administers educational, psychological, and psychometric tests under the supervision of a psychologist.

antecedents
Behaviors that occur immediately before an identified problematic behaviour; often cause the behaviour.

handicapped at some time during their school careers. Most of the students identified as disabled will receive special education services because they need special instruction (p. 262).

The Assessment and IEP Process

Fundamental Principles

The referral, assessment, and educational intervention procedure that we are about to describe depicts the most common procedure currently used throughout Canada and the United States (and in many other countries such as Great Britain and Australia). It is widely understood that the various provinces, territories, and states of North America have slightly different steps or processes that they follow in their particular assessment procedure, but they all adhere to the following fundamental principles and purposes of educational assessment:

> *The assessment process determines the student's learning and behavioural strengths and needs, the degree to which the student's particular strengths and needs differ from those of his or her peers, and the adjusted educational programming that will be implemented to give the student an excellent opportunity to fulfill his or her educational potential.*

The vast majority of students with exceptionalities receive specialized educational programming outlined in a document called an *individualized education program* or IEP. Across Canada, there are a variety of names and definitions for this document, none of which are used universally. For example, it is referred to as an IEP or individual education plan in Manitoba and Ontario (Manitoba Education, Citizenship and Youth, 2006; Ontario Ministry of Education, 2004), as an IPP or individual program plan in both Alberta and Nova Scotia (Alberta Education, 2006; Nova Scotia Department of Education and Culture, 1996), a PPP or personal program plan in Saskatchewan (Saskatchewan Education, 2000), and a ISSP, or individual services support plan in Newfoundland and Labrador (Newfoundland and Labrador Department of Education, 2005), to name a few. For the purpose of being consistent throughout this text, we chose *individualized education program* because it is the universal term used by the Council for Exceptional Children (CEC, 2004) and it is the official term of the IDEA legislation (U.S. Department of Education, 2000a).

Given the differences in terminology used across the regions of Canada, it is not surprising to find that the definitions used to describe the IEP are equally different from jurisdiction to jurisdiction. However, they all tend to adhere to the following fundamental principles:

> *The IEP is the legal document that outlines a student's individualized educational goals, the services that a student with exceptionalities will receive, the*

methods and strategies that will be used to deliver these services to ensure that goals are met, and the placement in which all of these will be provided.

You will find more details on the contents and construction of the IEP later in this chapter.

Something To Think About...

What assessment process is followed in your province or territory? What is the IEP definition that is used? Compare your findings to the fundamental principles presented in this text.

An Overview of the Process

The assessment and IEP process often gets started when a teacher notices a child struggling with school work. The following is a common scenario:

I have observed that James finds it difficult to learn some concepts and even though he is a conscientious student, he seems to struggle to get his work done on time. He is falling further and further behind in his grade 7 social studies class. I have talked to another one of James' teachers and he has noticed similar problems. His parents have expressed similar concerns and told me that James is showing signs of frustration when doing his homework. I'm not sure if he has a disability but it seems like a definite possibility. What can I do to get someone to investigate my concerns?

As in James' situation, teachers may be unsure about how procedures in special education are carried out. In the following pages we will walk you through the detailed process that often begins with this very type of teacher observation.

There are usually six major phases involved in the process of evaluating a student's educational situation and determining what changes are needed. These phases include: (1) identification, (2) diagnostic instruction, (3) referral, (4) assessment/IEP, (5) educational intervention, and (6) evaluation of student progress. In some cases, the complete process takes very little time and only minor changes to a student's schooling are required. In other instances, the process takes longer and results in major changes to the way things are done. Regardless of how much time it will take, it is time well spent.

The purpose of this six-phase systematized process is to provide educators with a consistent and comprehensive method of coming to reasoned conclusions about the fate of a student's future educational path. We have included a schematic figure of the overall process in Figure 3.1. As you will note, there is a cyclical nature to the process that involves an ongoing review and evaluation of the student's situation.

FIGURE 3.1
**The Six
Phases of the
Assessment
and IEP Process**

**PHASE 1
Identification**

Teacher becomes
aware that a student is
having difficulty with
learning and/or
behaviour.

**PHASE 6
Evaluation of Student
Progress**

Teacher uses a variety of evaluation
tools to determine the student's
progress. The focus of evaluation is
to compare student performance
and/or behaviour with objectives
outlined in the IEP.
Evaluation results are used to
determine whether or not further
assessment or changes to the IEP
are needed.

**PHASE 2
Diagnostic Instruction**

Teacher adjusts instruction
or management methods
to determine if this will
alleviate the student's
difficulties.

**PHASE 5
Educational Intervention**

Based on the IEP, the teacher
takes action to provide the student
with appropriate
educational interventions.
Interventions range from minor
changes in teaching and curricula
to the use of completely different
teaching methods and/or curricula.

**PHASE 3
Referral**

When these adjustments do
not resolve the student's
difficulties, the teacher refers
the student to the school-
based team. The teacher
presents the team with all
relevant information
regarding the student.

**PHASE 4
Assessment/IEP**

Comprehensive data regarding
current level of functioning is
gathered via psycho-educational
testing.
The assessment results are used by
the school-based team to develop
an IEP, a specific blueprint of the
student's individualized education
program.

Phase One: Identification

As in the scenario presented above, students who do not learn readily, who do not express their learning efficiently, and/or who demonstrate problematic behavioural differences usually catch the attention of parents, caregivers or teachers. These adults become alerted to the fact that something is not quite right with the student based on their knowledge of children's typical demonstrations of learning or behaviour in particular contexts. For example, in a parent's case, it may be that a child seems to have a very limited vocabulary compared to the vocabulary an older sibling had at the same age. In a teacher's case, it may be that a student does not seem to be acquiring reading skills like all the other grade three students in the class, or a student appears overly aggressive towards her peers when on the playground. A high school guidance counselor may observe that a student seems particularly anxious during school social activities. These intuitive and educated hunches that something is amiss usually mark the beginning of the assessment process; these informal types of referrals account for approximately 15 to 20 percent of all referrals made for special education support or consideration (Lerner, Mardell-Czudnowski, & Goldenberg, 1981).

The remaining 80 to 85 percent of students who are eventually identified as having exceptional learning and behavioural needs are usually identified through screening assessments. *Screening assessments* are most often classroom activities carried out by teachers and/or other school personnel to determine which students may be at risk for learning or behavioural difficulties. These assessments may include the use of teacher-made investigative tools often used on an individual basis to investigate the educated hunches that parents and teachers have about a student's performance. Or, they may involve the implementation of commercially available tests that are administered to large groups of students such as entire classes, entire grades, or sometimes groups of grades. Regardless of the type of assessment tool used, screening assessments are most often implemented at critical junctures in the school curricula, usually at points where students are expected to engage in more complex and sophisticated thinking and learning and/or at grades where the curricula or teaching methods change dramatically. The most common critical junctures are: (a) entry to school to determine school readiness, (b) grade two/three/four where students make the transition from learning-to-read to the more complex school activity of reading-to-learn, (c) grade six/seven at the transition from elementary to junior high (or middle school) where students are taught by several different teachers, where the curricula become more demanding, and where students are expected to be **autonomous learners**, and (d) grade nine/ten at the transition from junior high to senior high school where curricular demands and student products are expected to be more sophisticated and adult-like.

An example of a screening assessment at a critical education juncture is the completion of a variety of spelling and reading exercises at the beginning of the grade three

autonomous learners
Students who learn how to learn, solve problems, or develop new ideas with minimal external guidance.

year to see which children may need special attention when tackling the more demanding language elements of the grade three curricula. When properly implemented and carefully evaluated, the results of these screening activities can be used to identify and eliminate minor problems that can be rectified by proper instruction. There is a vast difference between a student who simply cannot read and a student who cannot read because they did not receive adequate instruction. Both of these poor readers may score the same on the screening measure but their requirements for reading instruction will be quite different. In the first instance, special reading interventions will be required and the teacher may have to enlist the services of the school resource teacher. In the second instance, the teacher will simply do what he/she normally does when teaching reading, probably keeping a watchful eye on the student's progress being cognizant that the student has a lot of catching up to do.

Whether activated by a hunch or by a formal screening activity or test, the early identification of learning and/or behavioural differences is the important first step in a comprehensive assessment process that is typically used to determine whether a student may need special education services. Since Bloom's

In secondary classrooms, students are expected to learn more independently.

(1964) seminal work on the positive relationship between stimulating environments and intellectual growth and learning, there has been an abundance of research evidence that has consistently and clearly indicated that the sooner a student's difficulties are identified and the sooner proper educational interventions are provided, the more likely it is that the student will learn more, and learn more efficiently [for a comprehensive review see Shonkoff & Meisels' (2000) *Handbook of Early Childhood Intervention*]. With regards to behavioural and emotional disorders, McConaughy, Kay & Fitzgerald (2000) demonstrated the positive effects of early identification and recommended longer (two-year) rather than shorter (one-year) intervention models for teachers in classrooms. There is no doubt that an earlier rather than later identification and intervention process provides educators with a much better chance of both halting the progress of deficits and/or improving a student's ability to cope with their deficits (Shonkoff & Meisels, 2000).

The important point demonstrated above is that teachers play a variety of vital and necessary roles in the early identification process. We contend that the more teachers know about the specific traits of students with special needs and the identification processes that can have positive outcomes for these students, the more observant, diligent, and effective teachers can be in reacting to observed differences. While early identification is best and desirable, late identification is always better than no identification at all.

Phase Two: Diagnostic Instruction

The next step in the assessment process is called *diagnostic instruction*. Teachers are instructional experts and when it comes to understanding their curricula, they usually know many different and effective ways to present the same content. Therefore, diagnostic instruction is simply a very purposeful implementation of their best teaching skills. Any teacher who becomes aware that a student is having difficulty learning academic content can make adjustments to their instructional approach to determine whether these adjustments alleviate the student's learning difficulties. Often, students themselves (from grade two or three onward) can also provide suggestions on how teachers can better help them learn. The following is an actual example of a student's input into the diagnostic instruction process:

> *A grade seven teacher noticed that one of his students seemed to excel on some parts of most tests but also did very poorly on other parts of the same tests. This inconsistent performance led the teacher to talk to the student about the situation and check the student's class notes. In this instance, class notes were the primary information base that students studied from for their tests. The teacher discovered that the student had a hard time keeping up with his instruction and note-writing pace, and she was too embarrassed to ask classmates for their notes for fear that she would look incompetent. Upon further discussion, the teacher found out that while the student's notes were accurate and well organized, she simply could not write fast enough to keep up. The teacher and student agreed that the student would continue to take notes in class because the teacher knew the value of having students write their own notes from information they have processed. The teacher promised to be more aware of the speed at which he presented material. Through further discussion and observation, the teacher noted that the student did not necessarily have a writing speed problem as much as she appeared to need more time to process the information that was on the board before she could write the notes. The teacher decided that he would provide the student with photocopies of his teaching notes after his classes so that the student could be sure to get all the necessary information. As a result of this diagnostic process, the student performed exceptionally well on subsequent class tests.*

Unfortunately, the problem that this student is experiencing with note-taking is quite common. Numerous students with learning disabilities indicate that they learn a lot more in class by paying attention to the teacher's spoken comments rather than by writing notes. Another instructional option in this instance would be for the teacher to provide photocopies of the notes in **cloze format** so that the student has to only occasionally write down key words or phrases. This would allow the student to focus on learning rather than writing. In both of these instructional examples, the teacher is required to make slight adjustments so that the typical teaching method does not exacerbate the student's learning weaknesses. Instead, the adjustments take advantage of the student's strengths.

Here is another example that regularly occurs for students who have **simultaneous processing difficulties**:

> *A grade nine science teacher noticed that one of her students struggled considerably with some of the concepts presented in class. When she asked the student why this was the case, the student replied that she got very confused when the teacher used more than one example to explain a new concept. While this is an excellent teaching strategy employed by many teachers, it was not serving this student very well at all. The student also stated that she usually understood a new concept after the first explanation but she then had a very hard time relating the slightly different information in the extra examples to her newly acquired information. After discussing several options, they agreed that the teacher would indicate to the student when she had fully explained a new concept and this would be the student's signal to not pay attention to the extra examples (if applicable). They also agreed that the teacher would check with the student to make sure the process was working, and the student would approach the teacher if she felt that she did not fully grasp a particular concept.*

If teaching adjustments are successful like they were in the above-mentioned examples, the teacher should make note of them for three critical reasons: (1) for ongoing personal use and for future use by other teachers of that student, (2) for further modification if necessary, and/or (3) for consideration at the educational intervention phase of the assessment process (Phase 5) should the student have other difficulties that need to be addressed. The teacher's effective interventions may provide valuable insight into how other educational interventions should be designed for that student.

Unfortunately, unlike the scenarios already presented, it is more common that a teacher's initial instructional adjustments are not effective. After trying several adjustments, the teacher may decide that the student's needs cannot be met by simply changing the instructional approach. In this situation, the student needs to be referred for a more detailed diagnostic assessment. As previously mentioned, it is imperative that the teacher record what type of adjustments were attempted and the results realized by these efforts. This information is vital to the subsequent phases of the assessment process.

cloze format
A fill-in-the-blank activity where students use the context of other written or spoken words to comprehend the concept being conveyed.

simultaneous processing difficulties
A deficit in the ability to efficiently process multiple pieces of information at the same time.

Phase Three: Referral

The primary purpose of a referral is to inform those responsible that a student is experiencing difficulties that affect his or her educational progress and that these difficulties do not seem to be alleviated by a variety of instructional adjustments attempted by the student's teacher. The action part of the referral process is usually a simple and straightforward affair. The teacher who identifies that a problem exists fills in a referral form and submits it to the individual in his or her school responsible for such referrals (usually the person in charge of special education issues). This form is accompanied by the following supporting documentation:

- a variety of student products depicting the actual problem that the student experiences, usually in the form of assignments, work done in class, and/or tests
- grades accumulated to that point, especially if they indicate a dramatic change in performance
- details of the types of instructional adjustments attempted by the teacher and the outcomes of those attempts
- any other relevant information that the teacher was able to garner from either the student, the parents or other individuals that the teacher may have contacted about the problem (such as guidance counselors or previous teachers)

A comprehensive referral such as this usually ends up being presented to the *school-based team*. While this team is described by different titles throughout North America, its composition and function are basically the same. As the name implies, this team is based within a school and it is usually comprised of the individual responsible for special education, the referring teacher (after all, they are most familiar with the situation), other teachers who work with the particular student, a school administrator, and often the guidance counselor in the case of junior and senior high schools. Depending on the jurisdiction and the nature of the student's difficulty, the parents of the child may be part of the team (although this differs across the country). Parents are almost always included when their child's needs are very high since they usually have a great deal of relevant information to contribute. In instances where the child's specific difficulty is not a high need and/or has not yet been identified, many school-based teams notify parents if further assessment has been recommended and then invite the parents to participate as a team member when the results are to be presented and discussed. Depending on the child's age and their ability to contribute information to the team's decision-making process, school-based teams are encouraged to include the affected child as much as possible in their deliberations. In our experience, children with exceptionalities have much to offer, especially when it comes to insights about how they learn well and/or what it is that seems to prevent them from learning effectively.

Teachers and support personnel form a team to make decisions about a student's education program.

The function of the school-based team is to analyze the referral information and any other applicable information that may be in school files or can be gleaned from other relevant sources (such as doctors, coaches, adult siblings, etc.). Once they have analyzed all the data, they suggest a course of action that usually falls under one of the following options:

- the use of additional or alternative teaching strategies that have not already been implemented (these are usually implemented for a trial period and with a precise date for re-evaluation)
- the completion of further **informal assessment** measures (usually conducted by the referring teacher or special education personnel), or
- the completion of a **formal assessment** (usually conducted by a psychologist or a qualified special education teacher, but may also involve other professionals depending on the nature of the child's area of difficulty)

In the case of students with emotional and/or behavioural problems, the process is exactly the same except the options are slightly different. It must be kept in mind that "behavioural problems" does not only mean behaviours that cause problems between people, it also means behaviours that interfere with learning such as not paying attention, an inability to focus, and/or an inability to work in groups. Therefore, the team's referral options for behavioural issues are:

- the completion of a **functional behavioural analysis** (FBA) (some straightforward analyses can be performed by teachers but a full analysis is usually

informal assessment
A variety of data gathering processes that allows variation in administrative procedures and more subjective interpretations of results.

formal assessment
Testing that has standardized administration procedures, is usually scored on norm-referenced criteria, and uses a formal interpretive procedure to provide reliable and valid assessment data.

functional behavioural analysis
A process of determining why a student engages in problematic behaviour and how that behaviour relates to his or her environment.

conducted by special education personnel) and the implementation of alternative behavioural interventions as derived from the FBA, or

● the referral of the child to a psychologist or otherwise qualified professional for counselling and/or the design of a detailed behavioural intervention program

Most of the students who receive special education services are those who are ultimately referred by the school-based team to psychologists or other assessment experts for a psycho-educational assessment. These assessments are carried out by a variety of experts in consultation with school personnel and this process usually results in education programs developed specifically for each student who is under consideration.

From the Psychologist's Notebook...

The psycho-educational assessment is mostly a confirmatory process to determine whether problems exist that compromise a student's educational (learning) or social (behaviour) performance. The ultimate goal is to identify a student's strengths and needs so that suitable educational interventions can be designed. The focus of the assessment is usually determined by the comprehensive descriptive information contained in the school's referral to the psychologist. These details usually form the starting point for the examiner's testing procedure. For example, if the referral indicates that the grade nine student in question demonstrates problems with learning algebra but has no reading problems or related behavioural issues, then the examiner's investigation may only involve testing for math and math related issues.

A psycho-educational assessment is predominantly a series of tests, most of which are standardized *and* norm-referenced*. The results from these tests inform educators how a student performs certain tasks compared to his or her same-age peers. The student's specific performance on these tasks provides the basis for educational interventions. For example, in the scenario above the examiner may find that the student's difficulty with algebra is due to an overall deficit in abstract reasoning, but the student's calculatory abilities are fine. Depending on the severity of this deficit, the educational solutions can range from the teacher simply providing more concrete ways to learn algebra, to providing the student with specific assistance in a resource setting, to the more dramatic step of replacing algebra with another math course that is not dominated by abstract reasoning. Any and all of these solutions, individually or combined, are decided upon once the psycho-educational report is reviewed by the school-based team.*

See Salvia & Ysseldyke (2004) for more complete details of the tests most commonly used in psycho-educational assessments and the rules governing who can administer them.

standardized tests
Tests prepared by experts, administered under exactly the same conditions, and used primarily to compare students' performances.

norm-referenced
A test that dictates a student's performance based on how the student's score compares with the scores of other similar students.

It is not uncommon for students who are referred for a psycho-educational assessment to wait months to receive this service. The question is, "What do teachers do in the meantime?" This is a sensitive issue because it would be inappropriate for a student's schooling to come to a complete halt until the assessment is finished, but, at the same time, teachers should not attempt dramatically different educational interventions. Remember, at this point the teacher(s) and the school-based team have already exhausted all the typical educational interventions that they could think of, to no avail. Using dramatically different interventions without a valid assessment-based rationale will most likely prove ineffective and will more than likely negatively affect a student's self-efficacy for school work and his or her overall self-esteem. If many changes are repeatedly tried and proven ineffective, the student may feel like they are completely incompetent.

As a first course of action, it is highly recommended that the student continue to participate in as much schooling as possible as long as there is a reasonable expectation of successful learning or improved behavior. Educators do not want to give the student the impression that they "don't have to do anything" just because they are waiting for their psycho-educational assessment. In the majority of cases of students who have high-incidence exceptionalities, their difficulties are not so pervasive that all areas of schooling are equally negatively affected. We do not want to give you the impression that during this time teachers are to stop trying to find ways to help the student because they may in fact happen upon something that helps the situation. However, it is more likely that the teacher's solution(s) will need to be augmented by the psychologist's recommendations.

At the same time, we suggest that the school-based team ask the consulting psychologist for an expedited analysis of the student's file and to suggest some assessment tools that can be administered and interpreted by the school's special education teacher (not all tests used in psycho-educational assessments have to be administered by a psychologist). After a brief consultation with the psychologist regarding their findings (usually by phone), the special education teacher and the classroom teacher(s) can then map out a new series of educational interventions. The school then documents the details of this procedure and provides documentation to the psychologist so that he or she can include it in the full-scale assessment.

Despite all of the above, there are instances in which it is obvious to all concerned that the student is in a course or class that is clearly beyond his/her abilities. This mostly happens at the junior high and high school levels. It may be preferable in these cases to assign the student to another comparable, but not-so-demanding, course/class pending the results of the assessment, rather than let them languish in the original course/class.

self-efficacy
Beliefs about one's capability to produce certain levels of performance in order to influence events that affect one's life.

self-esteem
Our subconscious beliefs about how worthy, lovable, valuable, and capable we are.

Phase Four: Assessment/IEP

Once a psycho-educational assessment has been completed, the results are presented in a comprehensive report usually prepared by a psychologist. The report may also contain results and interpretations from a variety of other professionals, such as **speech language pathologists**, **physical** and **occupational therapists**, other psychologists or psychiatrists, and **social workers**. This confidential document usually includes an interpretation of all test results after they have been weighed and considered in light of all the other evidence gathered by educators about the student. In the latter part of the report, the psychologist usually includes suggestions for instructional interventions, curricular adjustments, behavioural intervention plans, and/or placement recommendations, depending on the student's particular situation and the educational environment in which he or she functions. These suggestions are often made after some preliminary consultations with school personnel to make sure that the suggestions are feasible within the student's school. The completed comprehensive report is then formally presented to the school-based team. If the assessment results reveal that the student has learning and/or behavioural skill sets that fall too far outside the norm to be dealt with by typical classroom adjustments or interventions, that student is said to have exceptional educational needs.

A description of how the student's special needs are going to be met is then formally and collaboratively laid out by the school-based team and the parents (and the student where appropriate) in a document called the IEP or *individualized education program*. The value and importance of this education program cannot be overstated because the essence of special education is individualization. The IEP is designed as a very detailed and specific blueprint for one student's personalized instructional program for one school year and it typically includes the following:

- the student's current level of functioning (learning and behaviour)
- the measurable annual learning and behavioural goals for the student (in the case of students with pervasive or moderate developmental disabilities, post-school goals are also considered)
- the measurable short-term objectives that will be used as benchmarks of the student's progress, broken down by subject or behavioural environment
- the demonstrable special education and related services that the student requires (such as instructional adjustments, curricular modifications, pull-out resource support, or speech therapy, etc.)
- where necessary, the environment in which these services will be provided (the regular classroom is usually the first option but the regular classroom might not necessarily be appropriate)
- the schedule of periodic checks that will be conducted to measure, evaluate and report on the student's progress

We hope it is now absolutely clear why we emphasized the importance of the assessment and data-gathering process in the earlier parts of this chapter. How else could

---

speech language pathologist
A certified specialist who evaluates and treats communication disorders.

physical therapist
A certified specialist who evaluates and treats physical ailments using physical therapy programs.

occupational therapist
A certified specialist who evaluates and treats muscle and joint disorders to determine their impact on daily living activities.

social worker
A certified specialist trained in psychotherapy who helps individuals deal with mental health and daily living problems in an effort to improve overall functioning.

educators and parents collaborate on the development of this very specific blueprint for a student's special type of education if they did not have the right kind of information to base their decisions on? Without proper assessment there can be no IEPs, without IEPs we do not have an individualization of the learning process, and without individualization we lose the very essence of special education.

While it is necessary that specialized and individualized programs be provided for students with exceptionalities, this does not mean that the regular curriculum will be irrelevant. In fact, this process ensures that all elements of the regular curriculum will have to be *deemed* appropriate for each individual student based on the assessment and decision-making processes described above. For example, the IEP of a student who has a specific learning disability defined as an expressive oral language disability would clearly state that the student is required to fulfill all the learning expectations of grade ten social studies except for those involving expressive oral language (e.g., public speaking, project presentations, or other oral demonstrations of learning such as class plays or group discussions). However, the IEP of another student in the same class who also has a learning disability, but not the same learning disability, would clearly state that different learning expectations must be excluded, depending on the exceptional difficulties the student experiences. The purpose behind omitting or altering regular curriculum learning expectations is to allow students with exceptionalities to participate in the regular classroom as much as possible without requiring them to learn or demonstrate their learning by using modes or skills that they cannot use very well.

Despite the vital role that the IEP plays in special education and the benefits it provides for students, there is considerable evidence that the IEP also causes problems. Teachers clearly lack information about the development and use of IEPs (Werts, Mamlin & Pogoloff, 2002) and it has been frequently reported that IEPs demand so much time and excessive paperwork that it is one of the major reasons that special educators are leaving the profession (Edgar & Pair, 2005; Whitaker, 2003). We contend that a large part of this problem is due to the often overly complicated IEP forms used in various jurisdictions. Most IEPs are four or five pages long and some are even as long as eight pages. These documents take onerous amounts of time to develop and complete, and when added to the already significant administrative load of teachers, IEPs can be burdensome to revise. In the best interests of students with exceptionalities, it would be ideal if their IEP was changed whenever substantial changes occurred to their learning ability, their curriculum progress, and/or their behavioural interactions. If the IEP is to be an accurate representation of a student's current state of functioning and act as the student's educational roadmap for the school year, this amount of change is logical, but probably too time-consuming given their length. Therefore, most Canadian jurisdictions require an evaluation (and possible revision) of an IEP every twelve months, as a minimum. It should be noted that although the educational regulations governing IEPs differ across Canada, it is usually the case that the IEP is considered a legal document and the person primarily responsible for its creation, implementation, and management is the principal of the school.

To solve the various problems that contribute to IEPs being perceived as onerous, we have condensed the Ontario government's outline of what an IEP is, and is not, into a one-page form that we feel contains all the relevant and necessary information that would go into an IEP developed for students with *mild disabilities* (see page 49). The vast majority (89%) of Canadian students with exceptionalities have mildly disabling conditions ("Prevalence…," 1995) which fall under the high-incidence categories outlined in Chapter 1. In our experience, the vast majority of IEPs for these students will easily fit into our one-page design. Obviously, students with moderate disabilities (8%) and students with severely disabling conditions (3%) or those who require multiple services from numerous professionals will require longer IEPs to properly document their unique situations. However, IEPs of this sort will only be required for a very few students.

Our description of what should and should not be part of a student's IEP is a condensed version of the details provided in *The Individualized Education Plan (IEP): A Resource Guide* (Ontario Ministry of Education, 2004):

> An IEP is a working written document that outlines, based on appropriate assessment, a specialized educational program for a particular child's learning and/or behavioural strengths and needs. It details the accommodations or modifications required to achieve his/her prescribed learning expectations and outlines how their achievement will be evaluated and reported. An IEP is not a description of everything to be taught, of all teaching strategies to be used, of non-altered learning expectations, nor is it a daily lesson plan.

The reason that most IEPs are so large and onerous is that they contain many unnecessary duplications of information that is contained in reports that were interpreted or consulted in order to construct the IEP in the first place. This type of information is redundant because these reports are readily available in students' files.

The one-page IEP in Figure 3.2 is a condensed version of the actual six-page IEP designed for Karl whom we portray in Chapter 5 (an excerpt of his six-page IEP is presented on page 93). Our revised version of Karl's IEP provides a demonstration of how a one-page document can contain the critical information necessary to a teacher's understanding of a student's learning needs. This IEP provides the answers to the following twelve questions about the student's situation:

1. *Who is the student and how old are they?*

2. *What grade are they in, what school year is it, and who are the teachers who will implement this plan?*

3. *Why was the student referred in the first place?*
   This provides an indication of similar behaviours for which the teachers should be on the alert.

FIGURE 3.2
Karl's IEP (Condensed Version)

Individualized Education Program

Student Name: **Karl Hildebrandt**   Date of Birth: **June 28, 1995**   Age: **11**
Date/Grade/Teacher(s): **September 1, 2006/Grade 5/Jill McCarthy**
Reason for Referral: **Dramatic reduction in academic performance, not reading at grade level**

Current Levels of Achievement by Relevant Subject*: Reading–Level 3 in grade 4 expectations; Writing–Level 2 in grade 4 expectations.

Student Strengths and Needs Derived from Assessment: Positive attitude toward learning, above average cognitive abilities, hard worker, verbally expressive, good general knowledge, creative. Difficulty with reading, spelling and mathematics, can be hyperactive and impulsive, is not well organized.

Short-term Learning Expectations*:

Reading–   Term 1   Level 4 in grade 4 expectations
                      Term 2   Level 1 in grade 5 expectations
                      Term 3   Level 2 in grade 5 expectations

Writing–Make appropriate progress within each reporting period as Karl moves from Level 2 to Level 3 in grade 4 expectations.

Long-term Learning Goals*: Reading–Level 2 in grade 5 expectations; Writing–Level 3 in grade 4 expectations.

Successfully Implemented Teacher Interventions: Reminders for following instructions and turn-taking; reading aloud improved with practice; written work improved with revision and editing; reminders to remember math symbols have improved achievement.

Learning Expectations Omitted/Added/Modified: Karl is expected to fulfill all the grade 5 learning expectations except for those noted above for reading and writing.

Required Accommodations/Adaptations/Modifications: Cueing from educational assistant or teacher; use of manipulatives in math; teacher provides written notes where appropriate; allowed a scribe and extra time for independent tasks and tests; use of quiet work area.

Special Considerations: Candidate for use of assistive technology.

Description of Progress Indicators: Evaluations according to grade 4 and 5 expectations.

Schedule of Progress Indicators: Reported according to grade 5 assessment periods.

Principal's Signature: _____ **Date:** _____

Parent/Guardian _____ **Date:** _____

Signatures: _____ **Date:** _____

Student Signature: _____ **Date:** _____

---

*In the province of Ontario, four levels of achievement are identified for each learning expectation (Level 1 — *limited* achievement, Level 2 — *some* achievement, Level 3 — *considerable* achievement, and Level 4 — *a high degree* of achievement).

4. *How is the student currently doing in his or her courses/subjects?*
   Barely mastering something is different from struggling with it, which is different from failing it.

5. *What does the student do well, struggle with, and/or not do at all?*

6. *What do we want the student to accomplish over the term/school year?*

7. *What have teachers done before that has proven successful?*
   This provides insights as to the continued use of particular interventions or how to make minor modifications.

8. *Based on the student's strengths and needs, what curricular learning outcomes have to be omitted, added (in the case of students who are gifted), or modified?*
   These are often called short-term objectives but we feel that it is better if they are more precisely expressed as learning expectations.

9. *What accommodations, adaptations, or modifications are needed to allow the student to successfully attain his or her learning expectations?*

10. *Are there any unique circumstances that need to be considered, such as whether the student will participate in province-wide testing?*

11. *How and when will the student's progress be evaluated and reported?*

12. *Who has agreed that this document constitutes the student's plan for the year?*

Something To Think About...

Imagine you are a teacher in a regular classroom and you have a student who is going through the assessment/IEP process due to a possible learning disability. What types of assessment data might you provide to the school-based team and how would you collect it? What types of assessment data would you be unable to provide that must be collected by qualified professionals? What types of interpretations of assessment results would you need from qualified professionals in order to help your student to your fullest capacity?

Phase Five: Educational Intervention

Educational interventions are the actions that teachers and other educators take to provide students with exceptionalities with an appropriate education. Interventions can range from minor changes in teaching and curricula to the use of completely different teaching methods and curricula. The point is that these interventions are carefully and specifically designed and implemented to suit the individual educational requirements of each student based on the information gleaned from assessment data.

From the Psychologist's Notebook...

When it comes to designing educational programming for students with exceptionalities, it is important to understand that each child will have both inter-personal and intra-personal differences that have to be taken into account. Inter-personal differences are the ways in which the child's abilities are different from peers who are not exceptional, such as their inability to read at grade level. Intra-personal differences are the ways in which each of the child's abilities differs from one another (e.g., a child is proficient at math but is unable to read at grade level). The key concept here is that both types of differences are vital pieces of information when considering program design.

There are a variety of terms used to describe different types of educational interventions but the most common terms are *accommodation*, *adaptation*, and *modification* with accommodations meaning minor changes to what is normally done, adaptations being moderate changes, and modifications meaning major departures from typical teaching methods or curricula. We briefly define these terms below and provide details and examples of each of them.

An *accommodation* is something that is changed in the learning environment to eliminate or reduce minor learning or behavioural differences, such as changing seating arrangements to minimize peer interruptions that inhibit learning (and probably cause behaviour problems), installing extra-wide doors for students in wheelchairs, and using a Braille printer to produce notes or worksheets for students who are visually impaired. Accommodations are best thought of as alternate means of arranging the student's surroundings so they are not disadvantaged in any way.

An *adaptation* is a change to teaching methods, or teacher or student materials, that allows a student to learn or do something that they would not otherwise be able to easily accomplish. This can include notes being provided in cloze format for students who have difficulty with note-taking and the allowance of extra time on tests and exams for students who have expressive language processing deficits. However, the term adaptation most frequently refers to changes that teachers make to how they actually teach the regular curricula. For example, using manipulatives for secondary students who unlike their peers cannot master abstract reasoning, consciously and consistently using multi-modal teaching instead of just singular approaches, and/or allowing students options regarding the format that they use to present their in-class assignments or homework. Adaptations are best thought of as changes that are made so that students with exceptionalities can achieve the same academic outcomes as their classmates. In most cases, if these changes were not implemented by teachers, students with exceptionalities would fail.

Classroom environments can easily be arranged to meet the needs of students with exceptionalities. Note the availability of both individual work desks and small group work desks.

Finally, *modifications* refer to significant differences in the curricula being provided to a student because of their exceptional learning or behavioural strengths and needs. For example, the grade nine math curriculum may be used to teach a mathematically precocious student in grade seven, or a functional reading and writing curriculum may be taught to a grade six student with a mild developmental disability. Modifications are best thought of as changes that are required because the learning expectations of the prescribed curricula are not suitable for the particular student under consideration.

As you can tell from these three descriptions, knowing whether accommodations, adaptations, or modifications are required for any particular student necessitates a clear understanding of what the student is capable of accomplishing and what he or she cannot accomplish without some sort of intervention. It is noteworthy that all of the educational interventions suggested above, and those detailed in Chapters 5–10, are interventions that teachers either already use or can easily adapt to and master. They are simply examples of very good teaching done in a special way for very special reasons.

There are many students with exceptionalities who also require various types of therapy to enable them to properly function in their community school setting. These therapies are provided by expert professionals, usually during the school day, but some students may also have to receive therapy after school hours in clinics or hospitals.

Students with exceptionalities may require specialized therapy during the school day (i.e., speech language therapy.)

Therapeutic interventions can be a student's only special need, as in the case of occupational therapy for perceptual motor coordination, or they can be additional to a student's instructional needs, such as speech therapy to develop the language skills that support the minor adaptations the teacher makes in her teaching of language arts. Regardless of the form of therapy, these interventions also need to be identified and documented in the student's IEP.

Phase Six: Evaluation of Student Progress

Teachers working in inclusive classrooms frequently ask, "How do I evaluate the progress of students who have IEPs?" In the final section of this chapter, we will use the terms assessment and evaluation interchangeably as we refer to the process by which a student's progress is determined.

There are a variety of assessment tools or measures that are used to determine student academic performance. The most frequently used measures are standardized tests (e.g., provincial curricula tests) and in-class tests developed by teachers, often referred to as *curriculum-based assessment* (CBA). For students with exceptionalities, CBA is the preferred method of determining academic progress because, as the term implies, it is the teacher's assessment of a student's individual mastery of the curricula that he or she encounters in the classroom on a daily basis (McLoughlin & Lewis, 2005). Standardized tests of curricula are not preferred because they are primarily used to determine the overall performance of groups of students and essentially reveal nothing regarding the educational needs or abilities of students with exceptionalities (Gregory, 2000). If student-to-student performance comparisons are necessary, those derived from CBA results are fairer and more accurate because the student is being compared to their immediate classmates and peers. This is opposed to standardized assessment tools that are generically applied to a broad variety of curricular domains, such as board-wide or province-wide tests, and compare children indiscriminately.

CBA directly assesses mastery performance utilizing frequent but brief indicators of both the student's critical skills in core academic domains and the student's ability to execute them (Overton, 1996). For example, a teacher may design an assessment of a student's math skills in problem solving as well as an assessment of his or her organization of the steps to carry out those skills. These CBA indicators are typically derived from the annual and short-term goals outlined in the student's IEP as they relate to the overall expectations of the curricula to be delivered. This makes eminent sense because most students with high incidence exceptionalities will have IEPs and instructional interventions that are based on the regular curricula. Teachers are encouraged to design and use performance indicators whenever the student progresses from one curricular unit to another, and to systematically record and analyze the data that is collected. In addition to determining the student's curricular performance, these indicators can also be used to monitor the effectiveness of the instructional program in which the student participates. For example, a student may be unsuccessful at completing problem-solving questions, not because he or she cannot perform the calculatory functions of the problem, but rather because the process is misunderstood or they have a sequencing problem that confuses the steps in the process.

In a comprehensive study examining the effects of CBA on the mastery of IEP objectives and specific instructional objectives, Fuchs and Fuchs (1996) found that CBA was very effective in measuring progress toward the attainment of short-term goals. King-Sears, Burges, & Lawson (1999) provided an excellent description of the steps for effective CBA:

1. *Analyze the curriculum and select the critical skills to be examined based on the match between the student's IEP and the curriculum competencies or expectations.*

2. *Design assessment tools, sometimes called probes, for each of the skills being examined (for example, after a brief instructional period in math and an opportunity to practice, the students will answer five questions based on that lesson).*

3. *Administer the probes on several occasions across an instructional unit.*

4. *Assess the student's performance on each probe and chart the student's progress on a graph.*

5. *Analyze the student's progress within the instructional unit.*

There are four primary benefits to the CBA approach. First, each probe is specifically designed to meet a particular student's needs. Second, the probes are easy to design because they are extracted directly out of the daily lessons that teachers use for instruction. Third, these probes will be specific to the student with an exceptionality but they will not be dramatically different from the assessment items that the teacher will use for the rest of the students in the class. And, fourth, CBA is a formative assessment process that can provide earlier rather than later indications that things are not progressing as they should.

Based on the data gathered from the CBA process, teachers can easily record a student's progress (or lack thereof) at the end of an instructional unit or term and provide clear and precise reports to parents, school administrators, and the school-based team. Depending on the amount and type of progress made, the school-based team then decides with the teacher whether the IEP needs to be changed to reflect the student's next set of short-term curricular goals (or long-term goals if applicable). It is often the case that students with exceptionalities will progress more quickly in one subject than another, so it is probable that only some of the short-term learning expectations of the IEP will be changed while the others remain as they were. In this way, the IEP acts in concert with, and is impacted by, what happens in the classroom. We feel that this purposeful interactivity between the IEP and a student's documented academic progress will do much to bridge the disconnect that teachers often claim exists between the IEP and the classroom.

Summary

The identification, referral, assessment, and educational intervention process that we have outlined above forms the basis for exemplary special education services for students with exceptionalities. This process has proven effective around the world where special education is similarly defined and enacted. Everyday, children with exceptionalities demonstrate that they cannot cope with the typical expectations of the regular classroom. Without the above process, educators will not know how or why a student is different from their peers and they will not be able to proactively or effectively intervene on the student's behalf. The assessment process is not designed to label students nor is it designed to unnecessarily place students in special education programs. When properly carried out, the assessment process gathers and interprets multiple forms of data so that educators can make consistent, valid, and reliable education decisions that enhance the teaching and learning that occurs in classrooms.

Learning More About the Assessment and IEP Process

- Alberta Education – Working Through the IPP Process
  www.education.gov.ab.ca/k_12/specialneeds/ipp/ipp1b.pdf
  This document takes a comprehensive look at the IPP process and includes a sample IPP.

- Council for Exceptional Children – IEPs
  www.cec.sped.org/AM/Template.cfm?Section=IEPs&Template=/TaggedPage/ TaggedPageDisplay.cfm&TPLID=36&ContentID=5557
  CEC addresses many issues regarding IEPs, including how to reduce the paperwork connected with the IEP, strategies that will help with writing effective IEPs, and how to conduct positive IEP meetings.

- Manitoba Education – Sample IEPs
  www.edu.gov.mb.ca/k12/specedu/iep/samples.html
  This site provides examples of IEPs used in Manitoba for students with varying exceptionalities.

- Newfoundland and Labrador Department of Education – Individual Support Services Plan
  www.mcscy.nl.ca
  In their *Model for the Coordination of Services to Children and Youth*, the Newfoundland and Labrador Department of Education presents details regarding the development and use of the Individual Support Services Plan (ISSP).

- Ontario Ministry of Education – The Individual Education Plan
  www.edu.gov.on.ca/eng/general/elemsec/speced/guide/resource/index.html
  Ontario has produced a guide that is intended to help teachers and others working with students with special needs to develop, implement, and monitor high-quality IEPs. A five-step process is recommended. Suggestions and examples are provided.

- U.S. Department of Education – A Guide to the Individualized Education Program
  www.ed.gov/parents/needs/speced/iepguide/index.html
  This site provides a comprehensive look at the development of IEPs in the United States.

Please visit the Online Learning Centre for *Special Education in Canada* at **www.mcgrawhill.ca/olc/edmunds** for additional learning and study resources.

CHAPTER 4

Creating Exemplary
Learning Environments

Exemplary Learning Environments

The academic success of students with exceptionalities is dependent on the learning environment that they function in and the behaviours that take place in those environments. Within exemplary learning environments, educators facilitate the pursuit of academic excellence by carefully managing and controlling student behaviours and attitudes. The primary goal of classroom management is to provide all students with optimum opportunities for learning.

In the case of students with exceptionalities, exemplary learning environments are especially important because, by definition, most of these students have difficulty learning what schools present to them. Add to that the fact that many of them have co-occurring attentional, behavioural, and social adjustment problems and it is easy to see why learning environments that are well constructed and well managed are an absolute necessity. Just as Chapter 3 described how teaching students with exceptionalities is nothing more than good teaching, this chapter will outline how creating exemplary learning environments for students with exceptionalities is nothing more than good planning and good classroom management. To accomplish this, the teacher performs the same general management techniques for all students while paying close attention to the management elements that have to be implemented differently for students with special needs. There is no doubt that classroom management is a distinctly different function than other aspects of teaching, such as instruction and assessment. It must, however, operate as part of an overall teaching approach in order to be most effective.

Positive learning environments lead to academic success.

What We Know...

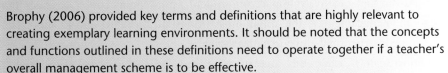

Key Terms and Definitions

Brophy (2006) provided key terms and definitions that are highly relevant to creating exemplary learning environments. It should be noted that the concepts and functions outlined in these definitions need to operate together if a teacher's overall management scheme is to be effective.

Classroom management refers to actions taken to create and maintain a learning environment conducive to successful instruction (arranging the physical environment, establishing rules and procedures, maintaining students' attention to lessons, and engagement to activities).

Student socialization refers to actions taken to influence personal or social (including moral and civic) attitudes, beliefs, or behaviours including the articulation of ideals, the communication of expectations, and the modeling, teaching, and reinforcing of desirable personal attributes and behaviours.

Disciplinary interventions are actions taken to elicit or compel improved behaviour from students who fail to conform to expectations, especially when their misbehaviour is salient or sustained enough to disrupt the classroom management system.

Source: Excerpted from Brophy (2006).

Classroom Behaviour

The Effects of Problematic Behaviour

Every teacher knows that problematic student behaviour can easily undermine well designed and creative lessons, and teachers quickly come to understand the emotional costs associated with constantly trying to remedy ongoing disruptions. Preparing lessons that go nowhere, falling behind a tight teaching schedule, and feeling emotionally drained at the end of most days is an overwhelming and daunting combination of factors that detracts significantly from the joy of teaching. Not only do educators feel an inherent professional responsibility to properly manage their classrooms, but they know from media reports that effective classroom management, or a lack thereof, is also viewed as a serious educational problem by the general public.

It is not difficult to understand why and how highly disruptive classrooms can negatively affect students' behaviours and their *attempts* to conduct themselves in appropriate ways (Woolfolk-Hoy & Weinstein, 2006). However, what does not seem so obvious to educators is the significantly negative effects that disruptive environments have on students' attempts to learn (Levin & Nolan, 2000). This is despite the fact that the research literature is replete with evidence that well managed and exemplary learning environments are conducive to excellent learning (Woolfolk-Hoy & Weinstein, 2006). In fact, Marzano and Marzano's (2003) meta-analysis of all the variables that positively impact on student achievement clearly suggests that classroom management is the single-most important variable, considerably outperforming instructional and curricular variables.

meta-analysis
A quantitative systematic analysis of the results of two or more studies that have examined the same issue in the same way.

Unfortunately, classroom management has become such a fundamental educational concern that it consumes as much as eighty percent of some teacher's instructional days (Sugai & Horner, 1999). Teachers consistently report that managing problematic behaviours is overwhelming (Martin, Linfoot, & Stephenson, 1999) and, according to Freidman (2006), classroom management issues are viewed as one of the primary causes of teacher burnout and job dissatisfaction. It is no wonder that classroom management consistently ranks as the most pressing concern of all teachers, whether they are novices or veterans (Jones, 2006).

Current Views

Why has classroom management become such a pressing issue? In our opinion, this serious educational situation has developed because teacher education programs, and the public to a degree, have embraced the postmodernist approach to education. This approach diminishes the importance of positivist concepts such as assessment and testing, direct instruction, and classroom and/or behaviour management and, as a result, student teachers are not properly trained in these areas.

postmodernist approach
An approach that negates the concept of scientific truth and supports the fragmentation of all academic subjects into a variety of perspectives – with no 'answers.'

The fundamental tenet of postmodern philosophy is that all forms of knowledge are exercises in power and those who construct knowledge have power, while those who do not construct knowledge, do not. Or, even worse, those who do not construct knowledge are under the power of those who do. To establish a philosophical foothold and gain power, postmodernists attempt to diminish the power they view as being held by those who use science to construct knowledge. They accomplish this by debasing scientific principles as a way of determining knowledge and by describing science as merely a social construction. The implication is that if science, and therefore knowledge, is socially constructed, then it can be constructed by anyone, not just scientists. Thus, postmodernism renders the findings of science as not objectively or universally true. The final outcome of the postmodernist position is that if the findings of science are not true, then postmodernists do not have to adhere to educational practices that are derived from them.

In a 2006 series of articles in one of special education's flagship journals, *Exceptionality*, Kauffman and Sasso (2006a; 2006b) make strong, reasoned, and irrefutable arguments about why and how postmodernism has undermined the guiding principles of special education. We have provided extracts from both articles to briefly, but accurately, outline this perspective:

…the consequences of postmodern philosophy for education in general and for special education in particular are severe and negative (2006b, p. 118).

… [it] lacks the intellectual resources to answer even the most basic questions regarding how to teach and help children with disabilities (2006b, p. 117).

The most damaging effect in special education, however, is that postmodern pessimism about finding truth or effective methods of intervention undermines efforts to see that teachers can contribute to a more equitable life for people with disabilities (Mostert, Kauffman, & Kavale, 2003, as cited in Kauffman & Sasso, 2006a, p. 67).

It is time for the field of special education to expel any vestiges of this form of posturing and move on with the business of helping our students to learn and adapt; to evidence measurably superior outcomes (2006a, p. 87).

Relative to classroom and behaviour management, then, postmodernists are not satisfied with how behavioural science systematically explains what it is, nor how it should be designed and implemented. They do not agree with the concept of student differences because of the science that determines those differences, and they loathe the notion that somebody would have the power to make decisions about who was different and to what degree. They argue that student behaviour is socially constructed, that there is no need for differential conceptions of student behaviour, thus, there is no need for different-than-normal ways of managing such behaviour. By extension, there are those within this movement that portray any systematized forms of management, and especially punishment (consequences), as being inflexible and rigid, and therefore unacceptable in teaching.

Somehow, education has totally embraced the notion that a child's behaviour is a direct result of the social context and that the problem with misbehaviour does not lie at all within the child. In adopting this position, education and educators have chosen not to confront and address the fact that a child with behavioural problems is a child that needs help, and a very special type of help. Therefore, the thrust of postmodernism postulates that if students' behaviours are not viewed as different enough to warrant being managed differently, there is no need for specialized courses on this topic in teacher education. The scope of this concern was best expressed by Landrum and Kauffman (2006):

A behavioural view of the management of behaviour in classrooms has been and continues to be a dominant and influential paradigm in both educational research and the preparation of teachers. To say that the behavioural view dominates current classroom practice, however, would be inaccurate . . . despite a rich history and extensive empirical underpinnings, the behavioural perspective on teaching and management is not highly regarded in the education community (p. 47).

At one time, the non-adherence to the behavioural view was a welcome and necessary philosophical difference amongst educators as there is evidence that this debate largely contributed to our ecological views of behaviour management (see Doyle, 2006 for a detailed explanation). However, when we look at how teachers are trained and what happens daily in classrooms, the following two facts warrant considerable attention: (1) a detailed examination of faculty of education Web sites across Canada and the United States (June-July, 2006) revealed that most teacher education programs do not have required courses in either behaviour management or classroom management, and (2) teachers consistently report that they do not have the training required to properly manage disruptive and challenging behaviour (Johnson & Edmunds, 2006).

Throughout our twenty years of university teaching experience, it has been consistently evident that coursework on classroom management, when it is provided, is far and away one of the most popular topics in preservice education courses and programs. Once aspiring teachers return from practicum placements and realize that there is much more to teaching than "knowing-and-saying," they anxiously develop a keen interest in the classroom management aspect of schooling. If, as a student, you have not already experienced this eye-opening phenomenon, you will. In addition, having delivered numerous professional development sessions to experienced teachers across Canada and the United States, it is also evident to us that classroom management is by far the most requested and most appreciated of all the professional development topics available to practicing teachers (for a detailed explanation see Jones, 2006). Whether they are novice or experienced educators, teachers have consistently told us that coming to understand the intricacies of establishing and managing an excellent learning environment has dramatically improved their teaching, and particularly their enjoyment of teaching. They report that with this knowledge their classrooms become busy but smooth operations that are home to engaged students who learn cooperatively and independently. These students act and behave responsibly because of their sense of community, rather than in an effort to avoid getting into trouble with the teacher.

In summary, we see the disruptive elements of schooling associated with classroom management as more a function of teachers' lack of knowledge and skills, and less a function of students' disruptive behaviours. While there is strong evidence that some of the disruptive behaviours (and outcomes from them) exhibited by students occur because they do not have the skills to cope, the vast majority of behavioural deficits stem from performance deficits (Maag, 2004). Performance deficits, according to Lane, Falk, and Wehby (2006, p. 439), "refer to those deficits in which students have the expected skill in their behavioural repertoire, yet they chose not to demonstrate a particular skill (e.g., managing conflict with peers or adults) due to a lack of motivation or reinforcement." The implication here is that if teachers can develop the knowledge and skills to properly motivate and reinforce students, the students are more likely to behave better.

The Tenets of Classroom Management

The fundamental premise guiding our approach to creating exemplary learning environments is that *teachers must have the mindset that the design and management of the learning environment is an integral part of their overall teaching process.* Classroom management cannot be seen as an *extra* part of the teaching process or as something that is separate from "real teaching". Nor should it be viewed as something that teachers just seem to acquire either by experience or by osmosis. Good learning environments and the proper management of all behaviours that occur in classrooms happens by design, not by accident. Teachers who leave the management of their environment to chance have little chance of good management. It is an accident that rarely happens.

The basic ideas that support our premise are excerpted from Johnson & Edmunds' (2006) book *From Chaos to Control: Understanding and Responding to the Behaviours of Students with Exceptionalities.* These basic ideas are as follows:

- nothing makes a classroom feel more chaotic and less psychologically secure than continually disruptive behaviours that are poorly managed
- not all disruptive behaviours occur for the same reason nor do they cause the same levels of disruption
- most problematic behaviours can be anticipated and prepared for, while many others can be prevented altogether

In keeping with these ideas, teachers need a two-phased approach: (1) they need to understand the causes of problematic behaviours, and (2) they need a comprehensive approach that establishes a psychologically secure environment within which they can effectively manage their classroom and encourage excellent student learning.

Phase 1–Understanding the Causes of Problematic Behaviours

Understanding why children exhibit disruptive behaviours is vital to the attitudes that teachers develop towards particular students. It prevents teachers from merely thinking of some children as "bad students" who choose to make teachers' lives miserable. Understanding the causes of misbehaviours also affects the types of interventions that teachers use to manage children. For example, let's look at two students who engage in the identical disruptive and annoying behaviour of calling out answers when they are supposed to raise their hand or wait their turn. The teacher will obviously react very differently to the student whom he knows is impulsive and cannot control blurting out her answers than he will to the student who has no such control problems and is merely trying to get attention. The way the teacher perceives and deals with each student will be different, but only because he has an understanding of the causes of the observed behaviour. Without this understanding, most teachers would suspect that both students were simply trying to be annoying and would deal with them in the same manner.

So what are the possible causes of behaviour problems that occur in classrooms and what do teachers need to know? Quite simply, if we understand why a behaviour occurs, we are in a better position to do something about it. More importantly, we are much less likely to do something to exacerbate the situation. As mentioned in Chapter 3, we are not concerned about the causes of *learning* problems because there is little that educators can do about them. There is, however, much to be learned from the causes of *behavioural* problems. In fact, as you will see later in this chapter, in the majority of cases, knowing the cause of a particular behaviour is usually the key to an effective behavioural intervention.

There are three main causes of problematic behaviour and these apply to students with and without exceptionalities: (1) psychological causes, (2) behaviours caused by learning difficulties, and (3) behaviours caused by the learning environment. Let's explore each of these in more depth.

Psychological Causes of Behaviour Problems

Why is it that some children seem to get along well with others and some do not, even when they may be from the same family background? Why is it that some students repeatedly engage in problematic and disruptive behaviours while others only do so occasionally, or not at all? Why is it that some children engage in the same problematic behaviours over and over again despite being constantly reprimanded for these behaviours? The most accepted and widely used explanation for all of the above was proposed by Dreikurs and Cassel (1992) in their landmark book, *Discipline Without Tears*. In it they state that all children have an inherent and powerful need to be liked and accepted by others but that some are under the illusion that they can gain this much-wanted acceptance by engaging in problematic behaviour to: (1) gain attention, (2) conceal inadequacy, (3) gain power or control over people or situations, and/or (4) exact retribution or revenge from real or perceived injuries or slights. Dreikers and Cassel suggested that teachers can improve the behaviours of such children by replacing their mistaken goals with goals that are more positive and appropriate for school settings.

Another perspective suggests that students are antagonistic towards adults (parents and teachers) because they have developed a strong mistrust of them and do not feel that adults have their best interests at heart (Canter & Canter, 1993). This partly explains why some children, when confronted about their behaviour, will not even comply with the smallest of demands from adults. Obviously, interventions to remedy these behaviours will have to re-establish the child's trust in the adults in their life.

Neurological factors also play a large role in the psychological causes of problematic and disruptive behaviours frequently demonstrated by students, most of which they cannot control without precise and specific interventions. The five most common neurological factors that cause behavioural problems in classrooms are:

1. Oppositional defiance (aggressive and purposefully bothers others, often loses temper, often argues with adults, often refuses to comply, often blames others for mistakes or misbehaviour).

2. Conduct disorder (same as oppositional defiance but the basic rights of others and/or society rules are constantly violated).

3. Inattentiveness (does not follow directions well, easily distracted, appears to not be listening, shifts from uncompleted task to uncompleted task).

4. Hyperactivity (fidgety, talkative, cannot sit still).

5. Impulsivity (acts instantaneously and does things without thinking of the consequences, some of which are dangerous).

The vast majority of students with oppositional defiance disorder and conduct disorder engage in so much disruptive behaviour that they usually receive their education in specialized classrooms, working with teachers and para-professionals who have specialized training in behaviour management and cognitive behavioural interventions. The last three factors are frequently associated with attention deficit hyperactivity disorder (ADHD) but often occur in many individuals who are not identified as having ADHD (a detailed description of ADHD is found in Chapter 6). The problem that teachers experience when they encounter behaviours resulting from inattentiveness, hyperactivity, and impulsiveness is that *everybody* engages in them from time-to-time. To be classified as having a behavioural problem, however, an individual has to: (1) exhibit these behaviours much more frequently, (2) display very intense emotions associated with the behaviour, (3) exhibit this emotional intensity for longer-than-normal durations, and (4) mostly engage in these behaviours in completely inappropriate situations. Here is an example of the differences.

Scenario I

A child gets up in the middle of the class to sharpen his pencil and stubs his toe on the leg of a chair. Despite an instinctive attempt to be quiet and suffer in silence, he yells out, gets angry, utters a few choice words under his breath, and maybe takes a swipe at the chair. All the while he is trying to do so quietly. Shortly, he gets himself under control and hobbles back to his desk, trying to be quiet and hoping he has not disturbed anyone.

This scenario portrays a fairly common and acceptable way of dealing with an uncomfortable situation, despite the fact that many of the behaviours the student exhibited could be construed as problematic.

Scenario II

Now, let's look at what typically happens to an individual with a behaviour disorder (or little self-control) who also stubs his toe. He yells out, but with little or no inhibition, and yells and curses loudly and frequently. He gets almost uncontrollably angry, topples the chair, and feels so angry for so long that he cannot get back to attending to his seat work. He intentionally disturbs everyone and has little or no consideration for their need for quiet. The remaining forty minutes of class time are a disaster and at the end of the class, he is still going to great lengths to tell everyone about his mishap.

This scenario points out the degrees of behaviours and reactions that differentiate students with behavioural problems from those who may engage in the same behaviours but who are not considered to have a behavioural problem.

The final contributor to psychological causes of problematic behaviour is *temperament*, a series of traits that account for the differences in the quality and intensity of individuals' emotional reactions (Berk, 1996; Thomas & Chess, 1977). Each of the following key traits operates on a continuum from low to high:

- *activity level* (the amount of time spent in active movement)
- *adaptability* (the ease with which one adapts to changes in the environment)
- *rythmicity* (the regularity of bodily functions such as eating, sleeping and eliminating)
- *distractibility* (how easily environmental stimulation changes one's behaviour)
- *attention span and persistence* (the length of time one is purposefully engaged in an activity)
- *approach/withdrawal* (the way in which one responds to new objects or people in their environment)
- *threshold of responsiveness* (the degree of stimulation required to get a response)
- *intensity of reaction* (the strength of one's reactions)
- *quality of mood* (the dominant attitude or feeling one demonstrates)

Unfortunately, temperament is often omitted as a cause or contributor to problematic behaviour when addressing educational remedies, even though it is commonly discussed in the literature on early childhood. It is also conspicuously absent from the factors that account for and describe the inter-individual variations that identify and classify students with exceptionalities. It may be that temperament is perceived as being too closely linked to personality and that both are considered out of line with the current thinking that embraces ecological models of special education. It may also be that three of the nine temperamental traits are identical to ADHD behaviours, therefore the overall concept of temperament gets lost in the discussion. Nonetheless, we think temperament is an important factor to consider when dealing with students who have behavioural problems because it is a factor that is not explained or accounted for elsewhere. More importantly, we feel that the emotional intensity described by temperament is what makes behaviours less controllable by the individual and more problematic for others to deal with. For example, in the two scenarios above, the first individual will probably be easily consoled by a teacher, parent or peer. The second individual will likely be inconsolable and this will make the person offering the comfort feel that they have nothing to offer. After several such rejections, the offer of empathy or comfort will stop. When a student consistently displays a number of these unflattering traits at the high end of the continuum, they are typically considered a difficult child (Turecki, 2000). Temperament tends to be universally established in childhood and it is fairly stable over time but there is evidence that temperament can be changed via the practices of adults (Berk, 1996).

Before we conclude this section, we want to make it clear that the psychological factors that contribute to misbehaviour are not evidence that children are inherently bad. However, it does mean that some children have conditions that need to be clearly understood and acted upon accordingly lest teachers perceive all children's misbehaviour as willful acts. Much of the difficulty lies in the fact that most of the above behaviours are *expected* to be positively-established parts of a child's behavioural repertoire by grade three or four. If the student exhibits those behaviours beyond the age of expectation, he or she is viewed as engaging in them willfully. Once teachers and parents think that a student's acts are willful, they are reluctant to look for reasonable explanations, reluctant to grant lenience, and reluctant to change their own behaviour to help the child.

How Learning Difficulties Cause Behaviour Problems

Efficient learning involves properly perceiving, processing, organizing, using, storing, and retrieving information through our visual, auditory, tactile, kinesthetic, and language modes. Minor or major problems with either the way information is processed or the mode through which it is processed results in a learning difficulty. The vast majority of students with exceptionalities who participate in inclusive classrooms have learning difficulties (see *What We Know* box on pages 68-69), even those students who are primarily classified by behavioural criteria (i.e., emotional/behaviour disorder, ADHD, autism). Students with exceptionalities often become frustrated because of how difficult it is for them to learn. They also develop anxieties about the teaching and learning process because it brings unwelcome attention to their deficits and further heightens their frustrations. Therefore, many students with exceptionalities exhibit problematic behaviours as a result of the emotions associated with their struggles to learn. Johnson & Edmunds (2006, p. 2) suggested that "since many of these students do not have the conceptual, verbal, or language skills required to express their feelings, these feelings are often acted out." It is not difficult to imagine how this continued cycle of failing to learn and getting into trouble for disruptive behaviours can negatively affect a student's self-concept and self-esteem and quickly set school up to be a very unpleasant place. To prevent this from happening, one of the primary functions of the

IEP process (see Chapter 3) is to have a professional assess the child's ability to learn, to describe any significant learning problems, and to suggest how teachers can alleviate or circumvent the problems so that the child can learn and perform better. This will not only affect learning but also help with disruptive behaviour.

What We Know...

Learning Difficulties

The most prevalent learning deficits and disorders in students with exceptionalities:

association reactions
involuntary body movements as reactions to the movement of other body parts

auditory association problems
difficulty understanding instructions/directions as stated

auditory awareness problems
difficulty responding properly to unexpected sounds especially when embedded in background noise

auditory discrimination problems
difficulty discriminating between similar sounds

auditory figure-ground problems
difficulty hearing sounds over background noise

auditory processing problems
difficulty understanding verbal information

auditory sequencing problems
difficulty hearing sounds in the right order

catastrophic response
a severe reaction to simultaneous sensory overload

cognitive discrimination problems
difficulty discriminating between similar concepts

cognitive sequencing problems
difficulty thinking or processing information in a logical or sequential manner

crossing the midline
difficulty executing tasks where body parts cross the center of the body

depth perception problems
difficulty determining how far away objects are

directional problems
difficulty distinguishing directions, or directions relative to each other

disinhibition
difficulty regulating one's actions despite knowing the difference

dyscalculia
difficulty with numerical functions and concepts

dysgraphia
difficulty expressing thoughts through writing or printing and/or writing and
  printing that is distorted/incorrect

dyslexia
difficulty reading words or sentences and/or comprehending what was read

dystaxia
difficulty speaking logically and using extended sequences of words

dystonia
difficulty finding the appropriate words to express thoughts

immature tactile abilities
disliking light touch and preferring heavy pressure touch

inter-sensory problems
difficulty using multiple senses or processes at the same time

perceptual motor problems
difficulty using sensory or perceptual skills in conjunction with motor skills

sequential processing problems
difficulty processing multiple pieces of information in the correct
  sequence

short-term memory problems
difficulty holding information for short periods and retrieving as necessary

simultaneous processing problems
difficulty processing multiple pieces of information at the same time

tactile defensiveness
avoiding touch usually due to immature system

tactile discrimination problems
difficulty discriminating between objects that feel similar

tactile pressure problems
difficulty determining how much pressure is appropriate

visual discrimination problems
difficulty seeing differences between similar objects

visual figure-ground problems
difficulty seeing objects against a background

visual orientation problems
difficulty determining objects that are dependent upon their orientation such
  as "b", "d", "p", and "q"

visual sequencing problems
difficulty seeing things in the correct order

Source: Johnson & Edmunds (2006).

Something To Think About...

Consider the common learning difficulties experienced by students with exceptionalities (see the *What We Know* box on pages 68–69) and how they might affect a student's behaviour. As you go through this list, try to imagine how difficult it would be to participate in school activities (e.g., learning how to read, taking a test, or learning a new sport) if you had one or more of these problems. Keep in mind that these problems do not usually operate as single on-off phenomena, they occur in varying degrees from very minor to severely problematic, and it is not uncommon for many students, especially those with learning disabilities, to have several of these problems concurrently.

Environmental Causes of Behaviour Problems

The psychological characteristics and learning difficulties of students with exceptionalities certainly have the potential on their own to cause persistent behaviour problems. However, a very important behavioural concept to understand and embrace as a teacher is that a child's behaviour does not happen in a vacuum. Behaviours mostly occur as the result of interactions between people and in nearly all instances at school, one of those people is a teacher. *Reciprocal determinism* is the key concept in Bandura's (1977; 1986) social cognitive theory that explains this behavioural phenomenon. In short, reciprocal determinism proposes that individuals are constantly engaged in mutual and reciprocal interactions in which their cognitive, personal, and behavioural factors operate as interacting determinants of each other. In the case of teachers, their "behaviour" also includes the physical, social, and attitudinal structures that they impose on the classroom environment within which each child interacts. What this really means is that student behaviour is influenced by teacher behaviour, and vice-versa, and that teachers cannot simply "blame" a student for bad behaviour, even though that student might be quite a handful. Instead, it means that teachers must look at how they are probably playing a role in facilitating or causing disruptive behaviours. Now, before we go any further, we want to make it clear that we are definitely not blaming teachers for student misbehaviour; that would be unfair and inaccurate. However, we are saying that the teacher is the one and only person in the room who can positively control nearly all the factors that contribute to problematic behaviour and non-efficient learning environments. By exerting positive control over how a classroom operates, teachers can focus the entire class on increasing good behaviours and attitudes while diminishing bad ones. A student may exhibit behaviours that cause teachers and other students lots of grief but that student's behaviour is not going to suddenly change unless the teacher does something more than simply saying, "I don't like that, please don't do it again."

In the pages that follow, we suggest a process for how you can go about creating an exemplary learning environment that is academically productive, well managed, and nearly devoid of common problematic behaviours. If you are a student-teacher, this process will be ideally implemented when you get your first teaching assignment during your first practicum placement. Then, like everything else in teaching, the more you experiment with it and refine it, the better you will be at classroom management when you get your first full-time teaching position.

Phase 2—Establishing a Psychologically Secure Classroom

The Invitation

The Invitation starts the moment you say hello and welcome your students to your classroom or course. Once you have finished with attendance issues, class lists, and the obligatory explanations of your course outline (in the case of higher grade levels) or the topics to be learned, your very first step is to set a positive, engaging, and determined tone that says in no uncertain terms that you intend that each and every student in the class will have a worthwhile and successful learning experience. Notice that the emphasis here is first and foremost on successful learning. The rest of the process is then naturally geared towards designing concepts, attitudes, and management tools that will encourage success to happen.

Teachers establish this overall tone by *The Invitation*, an approach to building optimal learning environments developed by Alan Edmunds as one of the cornerstones of *From Chaos to Control: Understanding and Responding to the Behaviours of Students with Exceptionalities* (Johnson & Edmunds, 2006). The basis of *The Invitation* is that it requires that teachers *explicitly* state and explain to students all of the elements that operationalize how the environment of the classroom will be set up and managed. As you will see, this approach applies to both what students will learn and how they, and the teacher, will conduct themselves. *The Invitation* was developed because one of the major causes of problematic behaviours between individuals is the misunderstandings they have of each other and/or their lack of a clear understanding of the distinct or overlapping boundaries within which each person functions, individually or collectively. Typically, these misunderstandings occur because someone has or develops expectations that do not get fulfilled, or because one of the parties *"thinks"* that the other person fully understands what was implicitly inferred. In both instances, problems are very likely to occur. The rationale behind emphasizing *The Invitation* as an explicit process is as follows:

- non-explicitness causes misunderstandings
- misunderstandings cause conflicting and problematic behaviours

- conflicting and problematic behaviours cause chaotic classrooms, and
- chaotic classrooms inhibit learning and cause more conflicting and problematic behaviours

The explicitness of *The Invitation* is multi-functional. It is designed to eliminate or minimize misunderstandings, to eliminate or minimize problematic behaviours, and to create an exemplary classroom environment that increases student learning and promotes positive student behaviours. You will see in the explanations that follow that this explicitness also has significant implications for how teachers will also operate in this environment. After all, teachers are a vital contributor to reciprocal determinism.

The steps of *The Invitation* appear in Figure 4.1, excerpted from Johnson & Edmunds (2006, pp. 58–59). Each of the teacher's spoken messages (in bold) is followed

FIGURE 4.1
The Invitation

1. ***Welcome to my classroom! Come along with me and we'll tackle this course together. I will do my very best to make your time in my classroom both productive and enjoyable.***

   Making this mostly implicit message *very explicit* has a significant impact on students because it spells out the teacher's genuine purpose and it establishes that the teacher will be accountable for good learning.

2. ***I really want all of you to be very successful in this course and I will help you accomplish that.***

   Expressing success in this way allows the teacher to set the stage for excellence and high standards. It also eliminates a common student perception that, 'My teacher wants me to struggle or fail,' or 'I will be made to feel stupid if I say I need help.'

3. ***However, in order for success to happen, we all have to agree on a set of rules or parameters that we will all operate within.***

   This establishes that there will be rules, that the rules will be out in the open, that the students have the *right* to help design those rules, and that the teacher also will live by the very same rules. It sets a tone of collaboration and cooperativeness, rather than having a dictatorial flavor.

4. ***First, let's agree on what my role is as the teacher and what your role is as the student. Finally, let's agree on what the rules of the classroom will be.***

   This element gives a very clear message that everyone will have a role to live up to and that these roles will be mutually agreed upon. This establishes that along with their *right* to have input into the rule-making process, students must also assume a *responsibility* for properly fulfilling their obligations.

5. ***Now that we have agreed on what our roles and rules will be, let's post the rules on the wall so that we can all refer to them if need be. Once we see how well they work, we can make changes if necessary.***

   This statement conveys three things: (1) that the rules will be obvious and explicit (as opposed to 'only in the teacher's head'), (2) that the rules will be used and referred to, especially if someone contravenes the rules (as opposed to rules that are susceptible to forgetfulness or manipulation), and (3) that the rules can be changed or modified (as opposed to being permanent).

   Source: Excerpted from Johnson & Edmunds (2006), pp. 58–59.

by an explanation of the implications the message has for the overall environment and atmosphere the teacher is trying to create. Again, we are not saying that teachers do not use or act upon the messages contained in *The Invitation*, we are just saying that doing so explicitly is much more effective. This no-nonsense process also establishes that the teacher is firm, fair, and flexible as opposed to harsh, unfair and rigid. We urge you to modify these five steps to suit the age/grade of your own students.

As you probably realize, these are messages that many teachers regularly use or subscribe to, but it is our experience that most teachers only convey them implicitly or they expect these concepts to be so well ingrained and understood by students that they do not convey them at all. It is fair to say that in the absence of clearly understood messages, students will often interpret messages or infer actions that directly contravene the teacher's intentions. This can happen accidentally and naively but it can also happen purposefully, particularly if students do not want to be involved in what the teacher wants them to do. Many times students will defend their disruptive or negative behaviours with variations on the following phrases: *"Well, I didn't know that's what you meant . . ."* or *"You never said that we couldn't . . ."* or *"How was I supposed to know . . ."* Unfortunately, without the teacher being explicit and clear about the rules of the classroom, these excuses can be seen as completely valid reasons for misbehaviour, especially when parents become involved in their children's actions at school. However, if teachers are explicit about establishing the behavioural parameters of their classroom, these phrases become indefensible excuses in light of the mutually agreed upon rules posted in the classroom.

The Invitation is conceptually consistent with current notions of classroom management and effective learning because it places the teacher in a proactive mode of purposefully managing education rather than in a disciplinary mode that reacts to educational occurrences (Paintal, 1999). Yes, this process will take some time and effort to implement at the beginning of a year or course or practicum period, but over the long term it will pay multiple dividends for teachers and students because it allows more class time to be spent on learning activities, it causes less time to be spent on non-goal-directed activities, and it prevents the day-to-day operation of the classroom from becoming a competition between the desires of the teacher and the non-complementary actions of students. *The Invitation* is an overview of how to set the stage for exemplary learning and good classroom management and it is designed to be easily implemented by all teachers, in all classrooms, and with all students. But, this approach cannot account for all the variables that teachers will encounter, so we encourage you to modify and adapt this approach to suit your own teaching style, personality, and school setting, and carefully consider the group(s) of students that comprise your class(es).

Students are encouraged to collaboratively design classroom rules with their teacher.

Designing the Class Rules

The simplest approach to establishing the rules of the classroom is for the teacher to announce that everyone in the room will participate in determining what the rules will be. We suggest doing this through small group discussions followed by an open

As you begin to understand and appreciate the benefits of *The Invitation*, imagine (or remember) the problems that arise in classrooms when teachers do not use this approach. Consider how these problems could be rectified using *The Invitation*.

forum facilitated by the teacher and one or two students. Within reason, every aspect of classroom functioning is open for discussion but it is best to allow the students a day or so to think about what they want included in the rules before asking them to decide on what they rules will be. This process is known as *participatory decision-making* (Lickona, 1987), a collective process amongst teachers and students that holds students accountable for decisions that influence the quality of classroom life. This means not only being part of the rule making, but also being genuinely involved in the welfare of the classroom and taking responsibility for the actions of all students. At this time it is also worth sharing with your students Weinstein's (1997) four principles for establishing classroom rules:

1. Rules should be reasonable and necessary.

2. Rules should be clear and comprehensible.

3. Rules should be consistent with instructional goals.

4. Classroom rules should be consistent with the school rules.

As well, during the initial discussions of the rule making process, the teacher should make the students acutely aware of the global rules that are not up for discussion. This enables the students to situate their own rules accordingly and in a complementary fashion. When explaining your global non-negotiable rules to the students, it is best to limit the number of rules that are black-or-white, or absolute, as these are often perceived as unreasonable/inflexible. However, you may find that some absolutes are necessary. We have provided four global rules that we suggest you incorporate as a package. They are all somewhat related but the last three are purposefully interconnected and thematic as this demonstrates a well thought-out and comprehensive approach.

Rule #1: No Disrespect

An excellent and mandatory classroom rule is that there will be zero tolerance for disrespectful statements and behaviours, even if they are meant or delivered in a teasing fashion. The two main reasons for this rule are simple: (1) disrespect in any form is the antithesis of the collective, collaborative, and cooperative intentions of The Invitation, and (2) there is no positive or constructive rationale for disrespectful behaviour.

Rule #2: Talking (Part A)

Another popular and effective global rule is designed to avoid the following common teacher expression, "Aargghh! They never listen to me!" which is usually heard after repeated instances of students talking or not paying attention to the teacher when the teacher has something to say. The rule goes something like this: "There are times when I will ask you to pay attention to me and I would like you to do so. Other than those times, you may pay attention to whatever you choose!" This is a reasonable rule, it is embedded with the concept of respect advocated in the previous rule and it indicates that students have options for their attention that they can select from. What it also says, however, is that there is a rationale as to why the teacher will ask for their attention.

If teachers are to introduce and adhere to the concept of student choice, however, they need to structure the available choices so that students do not feel that they can choose to do nothing. The next two rules satisfy that requirement.

Rule #3: Seatwork Choices

The "seatwork" rule is one that allows students to choose different tasks once they have completed their seatwork. Like all good rules, these options have to be reasonable and cannot contravene the policies of the school. It is best if students get to select something from their own list of options on one day and then select from the teacher's list of optional activities the next day, and so on. The teacher's list prevents the perception that these parts of the school day are completely unimportant and a waste of time while the students' lists allow them control and choices while acting responsibly.

There is no question that students like and need to talk to each other during class time. Rather than constantly fighting this guaranteed-to-occur phenomenon, we suggest you use the following structure that lets students talk, but under controlled conditions.

Rule #4: Talking (Part B)

If Talking (Part A) and Seatwork Choices are used, we suggest you also incorporate the Talking (Part B) rule, stated something like this: "I understand that you like and want to talk to each other and I think it is a good idea that you do. Therefore, let's agree that you are allowed to talk at a reasonable level whenever I am not teaching or giving directions or whenever somebody is doing their seatwork." You will have to specifically differentiate this from other class activities such as time allocated to project construction (secondary level) or learning centers (elementary level). This approach allows for a reasonable amount of quiet talking when appropriate, yet it restricts student-to-student discussions (disruptions) when the teacher is teaching or when students are engaged in seatwork.

Depending on your personality and the factors that affect your classroom, you will eventually come to clearly understand what rules you want to enforce to ensure that your classroom is an optimum learning environment. It is advisable that teachers also explain to their students that the entire set of class rules will be shared with the principal. Teachers do this to ensure that the rules are consistent with the overall operation of the school and to make sure that the students know that the principal knows how their classroom is supposed to function (the reason for this becomes evident when teachers have to enlist the aid of the principal to enforce the rules).

Designing Consequences and Rewards

It makes little sense for a teacher and a class of students to go through the effort of designing a set of rules for their classroom if they fail to decide upon the consequences that will occur if the rules are broken (or adhered to). Usually, the consequences are meted out by the teacher (or principal) as it is only through their authority and responsibility that consequences carry weight. Similarly, the group must also decide what the rewards will be for following the rules. The key here is to allow the students to assume responsibility for the process and its outcomes as the research has consistently shown that this increases students' commitment to schooling. The most straightforward way of determining both consequences and rewards is to do it during the open forum when the rules are selected and to do it by getting the group to complete the following phrases for each rule:

- *A reasonable and fair consequence for breaking this rule is . . .*
- *A reasonable and fair reward for adhering to this rule is . . .*

Both the consequences and the rewards have to be meaningful. To determine this, simply ask the students what they want, or do not want. By having a serious discussion with them about their preferences, you will quickly determine which rewards and consequences will be effective. If you are in doubt, make suggestions, maybe even outlandish suggestions or modifications to their suggestions. Your students will quickly let you know whether your suggestions are acceptable. Once you have collectively decided what they will be, make it clear that the rewards and consequences will be used for a set period and that they will be reviewed periodically, or at the request of either the students or teacher.

We strongly recommend that teachers do not in any way assign any form of school work or learning exercise as a consequence for misbehaviour. Practices such as assigning extra written work, handing out more, or longer, or more complex assignments or tests, and/or doling out academic penalties for social misbehaviours are inappropriate. These practices are unfairly punitive and they undermine the productive climate you are trying to create. It also gives your students the message that all their efforts to learn can be for naught if their behaviour is in question. If students have contravened the social contract of the group, they should encounter consequences that are suitable and appropriate. This does not mean, however, that students should not have to do for homework what they did not complete in class because they chose to chat and get off task. Rather, it means that they should not have to do extra homework because they broke one of the class rules, such as being disrespectful.

Enforcing the Class Rules

While it is preferred that the teacher engage students in collectively establishing the rules of the classroom, it always falls to the teacher to enforce the rules. As part of the collective rule-making process, teachers should explicitly state this fact and explain how they will immediately and consistently enforce the rules. When students are clear about what to expect, their psychological security is enhanced and their anxiety about being in a potentially problematic classroom is reduced.

By immediately and consistently enforcing the agreed upon rules of the classroom, you also send a message to your students that you are concerned for their overall welfare and you are willing to act upon your convictions. Let's take for example the zero tolerance rule for disrespectful behaviour mentioned above. If you use this rule, and we highly recommend that you do, you first have to recognize that if students were disrespectful before the rule was agreed upon, they will probably continue to be disrespectful after the rule is initially enacted, although hopefully less so. Take the time to point out and correct infractions as soon as they occur. It may take one or two days of immediate and consistent corrections by a teacher to get things under control and to establish an overall effect, but this approach will heighten students' awareness of disrespectful behaviours and therefore the behaviours are more likely to be extinguished. Because of the class-wide agreement that disrespectful behaviour will not be tolerated, all students will soon be vigilant about contravening behaviours and there is no better way to eliminate an obnoxious behaviour than through collective peer pressure supported by a teacher who acts immediately. Students quickly become accountable to each other and they realize that there is no refuge amongst their peers if they step out of line and disobey class rules.

Behaviour Problem-Solving

There are many different ways to deal with problematic behaviours in classrooms. We illustrate the six-step problem-solving model in Figure 4.2 because it is consistent with the proactive tenets of *The Invitation* and especially because it puts the onus on the student to acknowledge that there is a problem and that they will be part of the solution. This is a far better system than those systems that put the onus on the teacher to remind the student of the rules that were broken and to be the only one who has a vested interest in the solution. Each step is accompanied by its underlying message.

1. **STOP!! What is the problem 'we are having'?**

   Indicates that there is an inconsistency between what the teacher expects and what the student is doing.

2. **Which of our rules is being broken?**

   Forces the student to acknowledge that there are rules that everyone agreed upon and that he/she broke one of them.

3. **What did we agree would be the consequence(s) for breaking that rule?**

   Forces the student to acknowledge that the consequences were also collectively agreed to, and that the consequences are just and fair.

4. **What can *we* do about it?**

   Sends the message that the student will have to do something to pay for his or her actions but that the teacher is supportive and will not belittle him or her.

5. **Let's do what *we* have decided.**

   Sends the message that the consequence has been mutually decided on or agreed to and that there is a plan of action.

6. **Let's check in later and see how we did.**

   Indicates that there will be supportive follow-up.

FIGURE 4.2
Six Steps to Behaviour Problem-Solving

These problem-solving steps are effective at resolving most issues but there comes a time in every teacher's career when things get so out of hand in their classroom that their conventional approaches are not effective and they need support from their principal. Therefore, the final phase of proactively enforcing your rules is having a back-up plan. Like the rest of your overall approach, you should explicitly convey this plan to your students, rather than leaving it unsaid. The following is an example of how you might inform your students of your intentions:

> *There probably will come a time when I will have tried everything I can to resolve a behavioural problem, or it may be that too much time has been spent on a disciplinary issue, and we need to move along. In those instances, I will ask you to go see the principal. The principal and I have an understanding that when I send you to see him/her, it is because you will not agree to help me resolve the issue and that he/she will handle it from this point on.*

Obviously, you will have to have some discussions with your principal before explaining the plan to your students, but this also conveys to your students (and principal and your peers) that you are proactive in your approach to managing your classroom, as opposed to unprepared and reactive.

Regardless of what happens at the principal's office, teachers also often fail to properly plan for a student's return to the classroom. In Figure 4.3, we suggest a set of elements to be included in a plan to facilitate that transition.

FIGURE 4.3
Planning for Re-entry to Avoid Burnout

1. **The teacher and the principal will confer about what transpired.**

   This ensures that everyone involved knows what happened and what was done about it.

2. **The teacher indicates to the student that he/she is welcome back into the class.**

   This diminishes the student's feelings of isolation and rejection.

3. **The student has a private conversation with the teacher and they go over the six steps in the behaviour problem-solving model.**

   This refocuses the student's attention on the importance of the issue rather than the punishment (we suggest that teachers facilitate this by stating something similar to, "I really like you but I don't like what you did").

4. **The teacher indicates that he/she is confident that the student will govern themselves better from now on.**

   This reconfirms the student's sense that they can do it and reconfirms the teacher's expectation that it will be done.

5. **The teacher makes it clear that he/she will be keeping an eye on the student to see how *well* they are doing.**

   This re-establishes normal classroom operations but does not make the student feel picked on.

6. **A very short timeline is set (1–2 days maximum) to review how things are going.**

   This allows the student to prove themselves and be acknowledged by the teacher; it also provides another opportunity to review the class rules together.

Now that you understand *The Invitation* process, the next step is to consider how your actions will affect your classroom as a whole, and students with exceptionalities in particular.

How *The Invitation* Process Affects the Classroom Environment

While the parts of *The Invitation* and its overall intentions are fairly clear, we need to carefully examine the effects this approach has on actual classroom environments to fully appreciate its merits. The outcomes of *The Invitation* described below are consistent with the elements of productive learning environments detailed in one of the most comprehensive books available on the subject, the *Handbook of Classroom Management: Research, Practice and Contemporary Issues* (Evertson & Weinstein, 2006).

Nothing compromises teaching and learning more, and causes more behaviour problems, than classrooms that are unpredictable, unstructured, and/or without established routines. A lack of predictability, structure, and routine makes classrooms feel chaotic, seriously undermining the psychological security required for good learning. Worse still, students experiencing chaotic classrooms easily become agitated and frustrated and are very likely to engage in problematic behaviours, which, in turn, further contribute to the classroom's state of chaos. On the other hand, a teacher who explicitly spells out and demonstrates how his or her classroom will operate on a daily or class-by-class basis will leave no doubt about the logistical efficiency of the environment, especially if students participate in its planning and management. This systematic approach enhances the psychological security of all students. It also reduces the likelihood of problematic behaviours being exhibited by students who can easily become confused and/or over-stimulated by a frantic and chaotic environment. Furthermore, a greater sense of overall predictability allows students to easily adjust to, and cope with, minor changes to a classroom's structure. Psychological security also increases students' confidence about accomplishing learning activities and it increases their willingness to take on new learning risks. This is an important factor because many acting out behaviours are due to the anxieties that many students with exceptionalities experience when asked to engage in learning new material. They do not want to risk failing (again!) so they will do anything to avoid the task, even if they might be successful and even if avoidance gets them into trouble.

However, it is not enough that the organizational structure of the room be predictable, structured, and routine. It is also important that the presentation of the curricula have the same overall sense of structure, moving logically and systematically from general knowledge to more complex ideas, and from concrete examples to more conceptual and abstract portrayals. Just as the organizational function of each day supports good learning, so too does a step-wise progression of the curricula. A curriculum that is presented in a haphazard manner and is not thematic or interconnected in its design will only decrease psychological security, decrease learning efficiency, and increase problematic behaviours. This is true for all students but especially true for students with exceptionalities. However, when both the classroom and the curricula are managed together in a systematized way, teachers are said to have an integrative management approach to their classroom (George, 1991).

We hope that, by now, you have realized that the intent of *The Invitation* is to foster within students an ability to self-regulate their classroom behaviour. Nothing is more tiring or annoying for teachers than playing the role of "police officer;" it quickly becomes frustrating to have to constantly be on alert for disruptive behaviour and to constantly battle such behaviour. It is both good educational practice and good self-preservation to divest some of this responsibility to students through a self-regulated behavioural approach like *The Invitation*. *The Invitation* supports self-regulation because it promotes self-control and commitment, and it impedes impulsive behaviour.

What We Know...

Self-Regulation

According to McCaslin, Rabidue-Bozak, Napoleon, Thomas, Vasquez, Wayman & Zhang (2006), social cognitive theoretical perspective guides much of the research that is done on self-regulated learning and classroom management. They contend that effective behavioural strategies are acquired by methods that are applied to the self by the self. This includes self-monitoring, self-instruction, self-evaluation, self-correction, and self-reinforcement. Ultimately, the goal is to transfer teacher control of student behaviour to student control of their own behaviour. They also point out that what might be an ideal self-regulated learner from a teacher's perspective might not be optimal for students. Therefore, approaches that allow teachers and learners to negotiate the amount of self-regulation are preferred.

This negotiation can include, but is not limited to, the following practices:

1. Providing opportunities for students to make choices, reflect on those choices, and render personally meaningful the experiences and outcomes that accompany them.
2. Facilitating student processing of behavioural information that is mediated by mnemonics or cues or rules.
3. Providing a mixture of realistic learning opportunities—not all tasks are interesting and not all classmates are helpful—so that students can learn to persevere, see through and follow through on commitments.
4. Modelling and providing feedback and reinforcement so that students can learn the subprocesses of self-observation, self-judgment and self-reaction.
5. Providing multi-dimensional classrooms so that students can realize their identity and commensurate responsibility within the class.
6. Acknowledging that students will not change their behavioural approach without help to do so.
7. Initiating a process that explains the reasoning behind the teacher's expectations and goals and teaches students to do the same goes far in promoting the internalization and enactment of desired student behaviour and disposition.

Source: McCaslin et al. (2006).

How *The Invitation* Process Affects Students with Exceptionalities

In this chapter, we have purposefully not included specific interventions that teachers can use to remedy the particular behavioural problems that students with exceptionalities may display. This is because each child and their circumstance is unique, thus making it very difficult to explain and prescribe effective interventions for all the possibilities. Nonetheless, in this chapter we do provide several interventions that all teachers can use to manage the majority of student misbehaviours that happen in inclusive classrooms, including the behaviours of students with exceptionalities.

Regarding classroom management and students with exceptionalities, there are three very important issues that need to be addressed. The first concerns the ability or inability of students with exceptionalities to participate in *The Invitation* process. Based on the prevalence of students with exceptionalities in inclusive classrooms, the vast majority will have the cognitive and behavioural abilities to participate in this process. Those whose cognitive or behavioural conditions prohibit full participation can still do so to the best of their abilities and/or where appropriate. And, of course, they will still benefit from the overall structured and peaceful environment that is created in the classroom.

The second issue concerns the behavioural interventions that will be required for students with exceptionalities whose behaviours are beyond the control of the regular classroom teacher. Most of these students will not be in regular classrooms. For those who are in regular classrooms, they will likely have IEPs that clearly delineate their atypical behaviours and a specifically designed behavioural intervention plan (BIP) which suggests remedies for their particular behaviours (BIPs are described in the next section of this chapter). These students will also likely have educational assistants who are trained to manage them.

The last issue is that, unfortunately, students with exceptionalities will probably engage in more instances of disruptive behaviour than other students and they will probably be more disturbed by the disruptive behaviours of other students. Each of these situations will restrict or nullify their learning effectiveness, negatively affect their sense of well being, and, in the case of students who have behavioural and emotional problems, exacerbate their inabilities to manage their emotions and inherent misbehaviours. In this sense, these students are considerably *at risk*; "at risk" is a term used to describe students whose circumstances make them susceptible to developing a particular problem or disability. Whelan (1995) has suggested that if the external and internal stresses exerted on a person are great enough, they are at risk for developing extreme behaviours and/or an emotional disorder. While the primary objective of *The Invitation* is a productive learning environment for all students, there is no doubt that students with exceptionalities will benefit most from this approach.

Behaviour Analysis for Effective Intervention of Significant Behaviour Problems

There are times when *The Invitation* process will not be successful in eliminating behaviour problems. This is most often the case when behaviour problems have more significant underlying causes. Let's consider an example.

A student has been observed hitting a classmate on several occasions despite reminders of the class rules and having to suffer the consequences of breaking those rules. In order to stop this recurring behaviour, the teacher needs to know why the child is hitting his classmate so she can design a behaviour intervention plan (BIP). If she does not carefully examine what consistently happens before, during, and after the student's hitting behaviour, she is forced to guess about its cause. At best, she is likely to be ineffective in her choice of intervention; at worst she will exacerbate the situation.

What We Know...

Responding to Problematic Behaviour

When a student constantly and consistently engages in disruptive and problematic behaviours, educators need to respond appropriately. This is such a concern in the U.S. that they have laws (i.e., IDEA, 1977) that dictate that school professionals must use precise and systematic procedures to document and analyze behaviour in order to intervene. The two specific processes that are required are a functional behaviour assessment (FBA) and a behaviour intervention plan (BIP).

A *functional behaviour assessment* is a multi-faceted strategy used to determine the reasons why behaviours occur (their function) and within what situations (their context).

A *behaviour intervention plan* is a series of strategies that are used to change problematic behaviour.

FBAs and BIPs are processed slightly differently in different jurisdictions but the basic steps are as follows:

1. Identify and prioritize the problem behaviours and the settings in which they occur.
2. Directly observe and record data about the behaviours (this is often done using the *ABC* technique where *A* stands for the antecedents of the behaviour, *B* stands for the behaviour, and *C* stands for the consequences that result from the behaviour).
3. Collate all other relevant data and analyze the data to determine the function of the behaviour.
4. Design a behaviour intervention plan to deal with the behaviour and change it.
5. Set a trial period after which the intervention will be evaluated.

A BIP is a specialized and personalized plan for addressing and changing the behaviour of a particular student. It is conceptually beneficial to think of the BIP as a parallel document to the IEP. Both of these are student-specific intervention documents that result from a careful assessment of a child's situation; the functional behaviour assessment (FBA) and BIP process deals with the behavioural domain while the assessment and IEP process deals with learning issues.

By now you may be thinking that this is an awful lot to expect from an already busy teacher and many teachers have asked how they can conduct an FBA if they do not have the luxury of observers in their classes who can perform this task. The simplest method is to make a small and simple one-page chart that you keep close by when teaching the student in question. The chart lists, in point form: (a) the problematic behaviour, (b) any of your own ideas about what might be causing the behaviour, (c) a list of the different environments that the behaviour could possibly happen in, and (d) any of your own ideas as to why the student may be performing the behaviour. Unless you have some experience doing this, we strongly suggest that you focus on only one behaviour at a time, preferably on the one that is most problematic. When the behaviour occurs you simply and quickly place a check mark next to the conditions on your chart that were observable/present. After several instances of the behaviour (and this may only take minutes, or it could take days), you will have some hard data to help you figure out what is going on.

Let's look at how conducting a FBA resulted in a BIP that effectively resolved the scenario of the student who was constantly hitting a classmate, for no apparent reason. Prior to implementing the FBA/BIP process, the teacher had tried many disciplinary interventions with the student, all of which were unsuccessful, and made the teacher more frustrated. The student was truculent during many of these disciplinary exchanges and the victim was anxious, constantly felt threatened, and had complained to her parents who urged the principal and the teacher to do something about it.

By systematically documenting what happened before, during, and after the behaviour, the teacher quickly realized that the child only hit his classmate when he moved about the classroom and that he did it mostly for attention, both from the victim and from the teacher. Although the hitter did seem to enjoy having power over his victim (who did not retaliate or tell the teacher), gaining power was eliminated as a cause for the behaviour when the teacher noticed that the child only hit his peer when there was a likelihood that he would be caught, such as when both of the students were in the classroom and when the teacher's attention was only slightly diverted. The teacher also noted that the hitting behaviour did not occur outside the classroom, or within the classroom when the teacher was not present (information gathered from other students, teachers and a lunch-room monitor). Once the function of the behaviour was clear, it was simply a matter of using an appropriate intervention to address and change the behaviour. The teacher's BIP had four components that were implemented during a time when the student had not committed the behaviour. This was done to avoid the emotion and attention that an immediate action on the part of the teacher would cause for both parties. The four components of the BIP were:

1. The teacher outlined the problem behaviour and explained the rule it broke and required an acknowledgement of both from the student.

2. The teacher explained that the problematic behaviour was the reason why the child would now be seated immediately opposite the teacher's desk and that the teacher would be keeping an eye on him whenever he moved about the room.

3. The teacher made a point of quietly reminding the student to not engage in the hitting behaviour whenever he got up to move around.

4. The teacher commended the student for his appropriate behaviour.

Not surprisingly, because the student received the attention he wanted, and positive attention at that, it took only one forty-minute class before the behaviour stopped altogether. The student had replaced seeking negative attention from both the victim and the teacher with a positive behaviour—conducting himself appropriately so he could be affirmed by the teacher.

Summary

The purpose of this chapter was to provide you with a functional and practical method of setting up your classroom so it is conducive to exemplary learning. *The Invitation* involves being explicit about academic excellence and how you will systematically plan and manage behavioural variables so that academic excellence can be achieved. Consistent with the theme of this book, we used examples and stories where appropriate to explain student behaviour, collaborative rule-setting, and teacher's actions to support students, and/or intervene, as necessary. We are convinced that classrooms that *invite* students to participate in learning in this manner serve all students well, but we are even more convinced that they are especially productive environments for students with exceptionalities.

Learning More About Exemplary Learning Environments

- Center for Effective Collaboration and Practice – Functional Behavioural Assessment
  http://cecp.air.org/fba/default.asp
  This site is designed to provide teachers with the resources needed to understand the usefulness of functional behavioural assessments and behavioural intervention plans in addressing student problem behaviour.

- Council for Exceptional Children – Tips to Help New Teachers with Classroom Management
  www.cec.sped.org/AM/Template.cfm?Section=Search&template=/CM/HTMLDisplay.cfm&ContentID=6272
  Diane King provides tips to help new teachers manage their classrooms so that students can start learning on the very first day of school without interruption or interference from other students and before behaviour management is necessary.

- Dr. Mac's Amazing Behaviour Management Advice Site
  www.behavioradvisor.com
  This site offers thousands of tips on managing student behaviour, and provides step-by-step directions for implementing a great number of standard interventions. It also contains a bulletin board on which you can post your disciplinary concerns and receive suggestions from teachers around the world.

- Education World – Classroom Management
  www.educationworld.com/clsrm_mgmt/index.shtml
  Education World provides teachers with classroom management tips, information on how to create classroom rewards, and resources on bullying and teasing.

- National Dissemination Center for Children with Disabilities – Connections to Behaviour Assessment, Plans, and Positive Supports
  www.nichcy.org/resources/behavassess.asp
  NICHCY connects teachers with sources of information for helping children who have behaviour challenges.

- ProTeacher – Classroom Management
  www.proteacher.com/030001.shtml
  ProTeacher is a site where teachers from across the world go to share and discuss ideas on a wide range of topics. There is a special section on classroom management which includes an archive of thousands of strategies used by teachers.

Please visit the Online Learning Centre for *Special Education in Canada* at **www.mcgrawhill.ca/olc/edmunds** for additional learning and study resources.

CHAPTER 5

Students with Learning Disabilities

Name: Karl Hildebrandt
Current Age: 11
School: St. Paul's Elementary School
Grade: 5

Karl is a well-spoken student who has a flair for the arts. He is especially interested in drama and takes part in theatrical productions both in school and in the community. Upon first meeting Karl, you might not suspect that he has learning difficulties. He is highly social and is quite comfortable when conversing with others, especially adults. However, if you were to observe him in the classroom, you would quickly recognize that he has problems with reading, spelling, and mathematics. He is certainly like many other students who have learning disabilities in that he has a complex pattern of cognitive strengths and weaknesses. Karl's early experiences in the regular classroom provide an example of how early elementary teachers can be somewhat hesitant to identify a child as possibly having a learning disability. It is only when the child enters the middle elementary grades, a time when reading and writing expertise is required in all subject areas, that teachers become more concerned with increasingly obvious deficits.

Formal Assessment Results

Age at Time of Assessment: 9 years

Test	Percentile
Wechsler Intelligence Scale for Children – 4th edition	
Full Scale I.Q.	82nd
Verbal Comprehension Index	82nd
Perceptual Reasoning Index	79th
Object Assembly	63rd
Working Memory Index	68th
Processing Speed	66th
Woodcock-Johnson III Tests of Achievement	
Broad Reading Cluster	17th
Basic Reading Skills	22nd
Math Calculation Skills	20th
Applied Problems	53rd
Writing Samples	92nd
Writing Fluency	69th
Spelling	8th
Academic Knowledge	72nd
Comprehensive Test of Phonological Processing	
Phonological Awareness	73rd
Phonological Memory	84th
Rapid Naming	89th
Wide Range Assessment of Memory and Learning	
Story Memory	98th
Picture Memory	75th
Design Memory	84th
Verbal Learning	25th
The Beery-Buktenica Developmental Test of Visual-Motor Integration	
Visual-Motor Integration	39th
Visual Perception	34th
Motor Coordination	47th

The results of Karl's psycho-educational assessment present a complex pattern of cognitive strengths and weaknesses. First and most importantly, Karl is a student with above average cognitive abilities. In addition to his strong intellect, he is also a hard working, motivated student who has a very positive attitude toward learning. Most of the cognitive skills measured were equally strong such as phonological processing, learning sound-symbol associations, and many different types of memory (visual, verbal, working or short term, phonological). Academic strengths were noted in his general academic knowledge and his ability to write detailed, meaningful sentences when errors in punctuation, spelling and grammar were not penalized. Karl's visual/motor integration skills were in the average range with visual perception and motor coordination also in the average range.

Karl has some difficulties within the areas of academic skills assessed. Reading skills for decoding, fluency, and comprehension were in the low-average range. Spelling was well below average and basic math facts or calculation skills were low-average. When math problems were read aloud to him, Karl was able to solve math problems at an age appropriate level. Karl does better when he is given a richer context for information to be embedded in. For example, his memory of stories was stronger than his memory for a list of numbers. The context of math problems seemed to help him arrive at correct answers more easily than when he was asked to simply complete rote calculation questions.

Karl seems to have attention-related difficulties as noted in the information collected from his parents and teachers. Given Karl's learning difficulties, it is likely that these attention-related behaviours are secondary to his learning.

There is a significant discrepancy between Karl's full scale I.Q. and his academic achievement in reading, spelling, and math (1.7 to 2.4 standard deviations). What is not clear is what is causing this discrepancy. At this time, it would appear that perceptual skills, such as his visual/motor integration skills, are affecting his reading and spelling, and to a lesser extent, mathematics. These difficulties are consistent with a diagnosis of a Learning Disability or Learning Disorder.

Summary of Karl's Strengths and Challenges

Strengths	**Challenges**
positive attitude toward learning	difficulty with reading
above average cognitive abilities	difficulty with spelling
hard worker	difficulty with mathematics
verbally expressive	can be hyperactive and impulsive
good general knowledge	not well organized
creative	
artistic	

Karl Hildebrandt

Teachers' Reports

Ms. Yoon (Kindergarten)

Karl has made excellent progress in learning to read. He knows all the letters of the alphabet in and out of sequence, he is able to read familiar personal words, he can identify words with the same beginning sound and he attempts to spell words using knowledge of beginning, middle, and final consonants. Karl is also doing well in the area of mathematics. He can count beyond 30, solve addition and subtraction problems greater than five, identify patterns, and complete seatwork with no difficulties. Karl does need some reminders to follow instructions and to stay focused on activities. He also needs to develop his listening skills and learn when it is appropriate to express his opinions.

Mr. King (Grade 3)

Karl's marks have dropped somewhat from the marks he received in grade two. He is now receiving mostly Cs in English and mathematics. His written work tends to be short with few complex ideas and details. However, his reading aloud has improved and he demonstrates good qualities in oral presentations (e.g., eye contact, voice quality). In mathematics, he may perform better if he re-read problems to ensure comprehension. He also needs to review his basic facts, concepts, and skills. I am concerned about his inattentiveness and lack of cooperation. He needs to wait his turn to speak.

Mrs. McCarthy (Grade 5)

Karl has gained some confidence in his reading and writing skills this term. He shows a general understanding of the reading material presented and connects ideas that he includes in written responses. He should continue to read every night with an adult to improve fluency and comprehension. I am encouraging Karl to continue to revise and edit his written work carefully using available technology and his spelling wordbook. Karl is also doing well in mathematics. His solutions to problems are usually accurate with minor errors and omissions. He should remember to include appropriate symbols, labels, or units in all calculations. Karl continues to excel in music, visual arts, and drama.

Karl usually works and plays cooperatively with others and usually listens to, acknowledges, and considers differing opinions. He demonstrates a positive attitude toward learning and persists with tasks. Karl worked hard this term and showed improvement in homework completion.

Excerpt from Karl's IEP

Student:	Karl Hildebrandt
Current Grade:	5
Subject Area:	English Language

Current Level of Achievement*:	
Reading Writing	level 3 within the expectations for grade 4 level 2 within the expectations for grade 4

Annual Program Goal*:	
Reading Writing	level 2 within the expectations for grade 5 level 3 within the expectations for grade 4

TERM 1:

Learning Expectations	Teaching Strategies	Methods for Assessments
Writing		
Spell words correctly	Encourage Karl to use personal word lists of difficult words and book for Everyday Writers.	Note frequency of spelling errors in daily work. Spelling tests.
Reduce letter reversals	Ensure Karl has easy access to an alphabet for referral. Always correct letter reversals.	Informally monitor printing in daily work.
Use the correct conventions for grade level	Cue Karl to slow down when writing. Review basic grammar rules. Provide a proofreading partner (EA, teacher).	Compare Karl's written work over time. Evaluate by Provincial Standard for grade.
Reading		
Read independently	Review additional decoding strategies, looking at root words, sounding out, etc… Encourage the use of context cues.	Listen to Karl read for fluency and retell for accuracy.

* In the province of Ontario, four levels of achievement are identified for each learning expectation (Level 1 — *limited* achievement, Level 2 — *some* achievement, Level 3 — *considerable* achievement, and Level 4 — a *high degree* of achievement).

Karl Hildebrandt

Samples of Karl's Writing

Age 8–Grade 3

TO Day is tus June 29 2004
To Day is my firstful
DAy of Being ait cool to
be 9. I got brasis the caler
are mGoldand mGreh.
at person camp I mad a
mak out of clay it was
cool for lonch we had pizza.
Ice-crem ahd orig Jouce it was
goodg we olsow startid to
cat ont saps for our mobieis
the saps wer mad out of clay.
We cam home ahd went
for a swim the tampa cheer
was 24% it was can of cowld.
for biner we had hah
be ger and veges it was yomeg
We went for ahoter swimh
it had vorm d yp a bit
put not to much it was 25%
we bib a skit for the
parihts it ws caid parints
Pantug

Today is Tuesday June 29, 2004.
Today is my first day of being 9. It cool to be 9. I got braces the colour are medium gold and medium green. At Pearson Camp I made a mask out of clay it was cool for lunch we had pizza, ice cream and orange juice it was good! We also started to cut out shapes for our mobiles the shapes were made out of clay. We came home and went for a swim the temperature was 24C. It was kind of cold. For dinner we had hamburgers and veggies it was yummy! We went for another swim it had warmed up a bit but not too much it was 25C. We did a skit for the parents. It was called parents party!

Age 11–Grade 5

Hurricanes

One summer day there lived a happy orange was walking down the street of New Orleans with his friend apple. They had lived in New Orleans since they were just seeds But one fateful day what they would never forget when Hurricane Brussel Sprout came to town wow what was it oh yes on the day orange said what's that oh it's just a hurricane coming to destroy the town of New Orleans and in two seconds they turned into apple juice/orange juice

Karl Hildebrandt

Sample of Karl's Artwork

Karl – Age 11

Why is Karl Considered to have a Learning Disability?

Definition of Learning Disabilities

According to the Council for Exceptional Children (2006), the largest international professional organization dedicated to improving educational outcomes for individuals with special needs, individuals with learning disabilities generally have average or above average intelligence yet they often do not achieve at the same academic levels as their peers. While Karl seemed to progress well in the early elementary grades, his parents became concerned during his grade three year when he began having several difficulties that involved spelling, mathematics, and reading.

What We Know...

Problems with Reading, Writing, and Math

According to Willows (1998), students who experience great difficulty in their written language acquisition, irrespective of whether they manifest any sign of processing difficulties in their aural/oral language (indeed, some may have superior oral language abilities), often show the following characteristic set of problems as they are learning to read and write:

In reading:
- difficulty learning to recognize letters and numbers
- confusion between similar-looking letters and words
- great difficulty recognizing words "by sight"
- over reliance on context for word recognition
- failure to analyze the internal structure of words
- slow word-by-word reading

In writing:
- difficulty learning how to form letters
- confusion between similar-looking letters
- mirror-image printing of letters and numbers
- difficulty in remembering "how words look" to spell them
- phonetic spelling, based on the sounds in words

According to Garnett (1998), the most common math learning disabilities include:
- difficulty remembering basic math facts
- difficulty performing math calculations despite understanding the concepts
- confusion about the conventions of written math notation
- confusion about math terminology
- difficulty understanding math concepts
- poor number sense

Source: Excerpted from Willows (1998) and Garnett (1998).

Karl's difficulties persisted despite significant support at home. Worrying that Karl may fall further behind in the basic skills required to do well in various subjects and failing to be reassured by teachers' statements that Karl was a bright student, his parents took him to an independent psychologist for a complete psycho-educational assessment.

What We Know...

Definition of Learning Disabilities

Adopted by the Learning Disabilities Association of Canada (January 30, 2002)

"Learning Disabilities" refer to a number of disorders which may affect the acquisition, organization, retention, understanding or use of verbal or nonverbal information. These disorders affect learning in individuals who otherwise demonstrate at least average abilities essential for thinking and/or reasoning. As such, learning disabilities are distinct from global intellectual deficiency.

Learning disabilities result from impairments in one or more processes related to perceiving, thinking, remembering or learning. These include, but are not limited to: language processing, phonological processing, visual spatial processing, processing speed, memory and attention, and executive functions (e.g., monitoring, planning, and decision-making).

Learning disabilities range in severity and may interfere with the acquisition and use of one or more of the following: oral language (e.g., listening, speaking, and understanding), reading (e.g., decoding, phonetic knowledge, word recognition, comprehension), written language (e.g., spelling and written expression), and mathematics (e.g., computation, problem-solving).

Learning disabilities may also involve difficulties with organizational skills, social perception, social interaction and perspective taking.

Source: Excerpted from Learning Disabilities Association of Canada, www.ldac-taac.ca. Please note that this box represents only a part of the official definition of learning disabilities adopted by the Learning Disabilities Association of Canada in 2002. To access the full definition, please visit www.ldac-tacc.ca.

Something To Think About...

There is no one definition of learning disabilities that is universally adhered to by education systems across Canada. Rather, each province and territory has developed their own definition of LD. Even within the provinces and territories, you may find that the conceptual definitions produced by ministries or departments of education are different from the operational definitions used by psychologists. What can you find out about the definitions used in your home province or territory?

Assessing Learning Disabilities

Karl was assessed at the end of his grade three year, just before his ninth birthday. The psychologist met with him on three separate days. She reported that Karl was extremely friendly and cooperative. He talked about school and indicated that his teacher was very nice and he really liked working in groups and doing school projects.

During the assessment, Karl worked hard despite being somewhat fidgety. The psychologist noted that it was evident that Karl tired easily while doing many of the tasks so she allowed several breaks. She also reported that he responded well to praise and encouragement and this type of reinforcement was necessary to facilitate his best performance. He completed most verbal tasks with ease but became discouraged when faced with difficult nonverbal tasks. However, in general, Karl showed good motivation and effort leading the psychologist to conclude that her assessment was a fair and accurate estimate of Karl's ability.

The assessment included a battery of standardized tests (see Formal Assessment Results on page 90). The *Wechsler Intelligence Scale for Children Fourth Edition* (WISC-IV) contains four indices: Verbal Comprehension, Perceptual Reasoning, Working Memory, and Processing Speed. Karl performed consistently well on this test of cognitive ability resulting in a Full Scale I.Q. at the eighty-second percentile which indicates high-average intelligence. *The Woodcock-Johnson III Tests of Achievement* (WJ-III) allows assessment of reading skills, written language, mathematics skills, oral language, and academic knowledge. This test revealed that Karl has good academic knowledge and a highly developed ability to write meaningful sentences when surface errors were overlooked. However, the WJ-III also revealed that Karl has significant difficulties in the areas of reading, math calculation, and spelling. A further test of reading-related skills was administered to assess Karl's **phonological awareness**, **phonological memory**, and his ability to name numbers and letters rapidly. This *Comprehensive Test of Phonological Processing* (CTOPP) showed that Karl is competent with this type of processing. In an effort to determine why Karl might be having the difficulties that were evident from the WJ-III, the psychologist administered two other standardized tests. On the *Wide Range Assessment of Memory and Learning* (WRAML), Karl's weakness was verbal learning, which means he has trouble understanding information that is presented through written and spoken words. The *Beery-Buktenica Developmental Test of Visual-Motor Integration* (VMI), a test designed to detect deficits in **visual perception**, fine motor skills, and hand-eye coordination, identified further difficulties experienced by Karl when he attempts to complete tasks that require an integration of his visual and motor abilities. He scored below average on all three subtests. It was these test results that the psychologist used to explain the discrepancy between Karl's cognitive ability and his academic achievement in reading, spelling, and math. She proposed that it is Karl's impaired perceptual skills that are

phonological awareness
The awareness that language is composed of sounds and these sounds (syllables) are related to letters.

phonological memory
The coding of information according to its sounds for temporary storage in working or short-term memory.

visual perception
The ability to see and to interpret what is seen.

affecting his ability to succeed in school. Because of these findings, she diagnosed Karl as having a learning disability.

From The Psychologist's Notebook...

When considering performance on standardized tests, results are interpreted in terms of norm referenced age equivalency, standard scores, and percentiles. Age equivalencies indicate the age at which typical children obtain the reported score. Standard scores reflect performance in comparison with a standardized sample of same age peers. On a test with a mean of 100 and a standard deviation of 15, as is the case with most standardized tests, a score between 85 and 115 would be considered to fall within average limits. Percentiles indicate placement out of 100 people taking the test, with the first percentile representing the low end of performance and the 99th percentile reflecting the highest. A percentile between 16 and 84 would be considered to fall within the range of average limits. Standardized scores provide useful information; however, standardized test results are limited in the scope of skills they measure and limited in the length of time they are considered valid, as an individual's skills and abilities may change with time.

Upon receiving the psychologist's report, Karl's parents approached the Identification, Placement, and Review Committee (IPRC) at his school to share the information they had learned from the independent assessment. Early in the fall of Karl's grade four year, the IPRC officially identified him as having an exceptionality and designated his exceptionality as a "learning disability." Their "Statement of Decision" indicated that Karl would be placed in a regular classroom with resource assistance as outlined by his individualized education program (see page 93 for *Excerpts from Karl's IEP*).

The process that led to Karl's designation as a student who is exceptional is fairly typical of how Canadian students who have learning disabilities are identified within the various education systems. While there is no uniform identification process across the provinces and territories, most students who are identified as having a learning disability have exhibited a discrepancy between their cognitive ability and their academic achievement. This discrepancy is usually noted by parents and/or teachers in the middle to upper elementary grades when the curricula focuses more intensively on reading, writing and mathematical skills. As in the case of Karl, a psycho-educational assessment confirms a difficulty with one or more of the processes related to perceiving, thinking, remembering, or learning.

From The Psychologist's Notebook...

There have been some changes in the U.S. identification process for determining whether or not a student has a learning disability. It is important to consider these changes as special education in Canada is highly influenced by practices across the border. In 2004, the Individuals with Disabilities Education Improvement Act (IDEA; P.L. 108-446, 2004) presented changes that permit educators to use responsiveness-to-intervention (RTI) as a substitute for, or as a supplement to, the I.Q.-Achievement discrepancy model of identifying students with learning disabilities (Fuchs and Fuchs, 2005). The primary objective of the changes was to encourage educators to intervene earlier in identifying students who exhibit learning problems and to decrease the number of children who are identified as having a learning disability when, in fact, their poor achievement is due to poor instruction. According to Cortiella (2006):

> *There is currently no formal definition of RTI, nor is there an RTI model that is well established and widely endorsed by researchers and educators. However, the following could serve as a description of the essential elements: RTI is an individualized, comprehensive assessment and intervention process, utilizing a problem-solving framework to identify and address student academic difficulties using effective, efficient, research-based instruction (www.schwablearning.org/articles.aspx?r=840).*

A similar description, but with a slightly different emphasis, was provided by the National Joint Committee on Learning Disabilities (NJCLD)(2005):

> *Core concepts of an RTI approach are the systematic: (1) application of scientific, research-based interventions in general education, (2) measurement of a student's response to these interventions, and (3) use of the RTI data to inform instruction (p. 2).*

In the NJCLD model, students who experience difficulties are provided with a series of ever increasing intensive and specific curricular interventions that are designed and delivered by teachers in cooperation with special educators and/or psychologists. The interventions are based on proven research and their effectiveness is continuously monitored. Students who do not "respond" to these interventions are deemed to be in need of specialized educational services in order to prosper. From my perspective, the RTI process is not much different than the Diagnostic Instruction Phase of the Assessment and IEP Process described in Chapter 3 of this text. The fundamental difference is that RTI interventions are purposefully and gradually intensified and monitored under the guidance of special educators and psychologists. I would only endorse this approach if, and only if, these collaborative and research-based supports are omnipresent. RTI should not be used by teachers without these mechanisms in place. Thus far, the main criticisms educators have of RTI are not of its approach or of its intent. Some educators are fearful that RTI will be used to replace the more formal and costly assessment and IEP processes as a way of identifying students with learning disabilities. In my estimation, RTI is not sufficient to identify a specific learning disability and should therefore only be used in conjunction with the LD discrepancy criteria and other precise indices of specific learning disabilities. Another particular, and often voiced concern, is:

> *… whether RTI is prone to systematic errors in identifying students with LD. For example, the underachievement criterion may exclude some high-ability students with LD from special education. These students, by compensating with their intellectual strengths and making good use of support services, often manage to achieve within the normal range and, therefore, are unlikely to receive the early individualized instruction that would enable them to make academic progress consistent with their abilities (National Joint Committee on Learning Disabilities, 2005; p. 7).*

RTI has considerable implications for teachers in regular classrooms who provide instruction to students with exceptionalities. Educators will have to remain vigilant and carefully examine whether studies on the efficacy of RTI empirically demonstrate improved academic achievement for students with learning disabilities.

What Factors Contributed to Karl's Learning Disabilities?

The causes of learning disabilities are diverse and complex, and still not clearly understood by researchers today. It is apparent, however, that Karl's brain functioning is atypical in that he does not learn as most children do. The factors that have lead to Karl's learning differences can only be considered in terms of the information received from his parents. He has not had any medical tests that have examined the physical aspects of his brain function.

Heredity

Karl's parents both have post-secondary degrees and hold professional jobs in their areas of expertise. Neither parent has experienced any learning difficulties. However, Karl has two uncles who struggle with various aspects of learning. His father's brother has a reading disability that was very apparent during his school years. Despite this difficulty with reading, he excelled in math and went on to become an engineer. Karl's mother also has a brother who struggled in school. He never learned to spell and his writing skills have always been poor. While he was never diagnosed as having a learning disability, his parents were continually trying to understand why their son failed to attain these basic skills despite being of average intelligence.

According to Bender (1998), learning disabilities do tend to run in families, so some learning disabilities may be inherited. However, Bender emphasized that because many of the research studies described in the literature did not take the participants' environment into account, environmental factors cannot be ruled out as the cause of multiple cases of learning disabilities within a family. In Karl's case, he has a family history of learning disabilities on both sides—maternal and paternal. If genetics does play a role, he certainly had a significant chance of having learning difficulties. Karl does have a sister who does not have any learning disabilities; however, this does not rule out the possibility that Karl inherited his disorder, because more males than females are diagnosed with learning disabilities. In fact, Karl has no female relatives who have had learning difficulties.

What We Know...

The Causes of Learning Disabilities

Learning Disabilities are due to genetic and/or neurobiological factors or injury that alter(s) brain functioning in a manner which affects one or more processes related to learning. These disorders are not due primarily to hearing and/or vision problems, socio-economic factors, cultural or linguistic differences, lack of motivation or ineffective teaching, although these factors may further complicate the challenges faced by individuals with learning disabilities. Learning disabilities may co-exist with various conditions including attentional, behavioural and emotional disorders, sensory impairments or other medical conditions.

Source: Excerpted from Learning Disabilities Association of Canada, www.ldac-taac.ca. Please note that this box represents only a part of the official definition of learning disabilities adopted by the Learning Disabilities Association of Canada in 2002. To access the full definition, please visit www.ldac-tacc.ca.

Environment

Bender (1998) noted that **teratogens** have been mentioned in the literature as potential prenatal causes of learning disabilities. Karl's mother confirmed that she had a completely normal and healthy pregnancy. She did not drink alcohol nor did she smoke cigarettes or take drugs of any kind. Karl was born full-term and there were no difficulties with the birthing process. Karl's development from birth onwards has been normal in terms of milestones achieved. He has not experienced any serious injuries nor has he had any medical problems that required medical

teratogens
Agents classed as radiation, maternal infections, chemicals, and/or drugs that disturb the development of an embryo or fetus.

intervention. He has never been prescribed drugs of any kind. He does not have any vision or hearing problems.

Something To Think About...

Liam was a high achieving student until at the age of ten a car accident left him with an acquired brain injury (see www.nichcy.org/pubs/factshe/fs18txt.htm to learn how children are affected by a traumatic brain injury). Now Liam has various difficulties with learning and socialization. How might Liam be similar to other students who have been identified as having learning disabilities? How might his situation be different?

How Have Karl's Learning Disabilities Affected His Development?

Cognitive Development

According to Karl's parents, there were no early indicators that he may have learning difficulties. In fact, Karl appeared to be a very bright child right from the start. He spoke single words at ten months and was combining words by seventeen months. He loved books and when his parents read to him, he would eagerly chime in with the appropriate rhyming word. His mother remembers thinking at the time that Karl would obviously have no problems with reading when he entered school. Her prediction seemed to be correct as Karl successfully completed kindergarten and grade one. His teachers were very pleased with his progress, both in the areas of reading and mathematics (see *Teachers' Reports* on page 92).

It was when Karl was in the second grade that his mother first thought that "things just weren't quite right." Despite assurances by Karl's second grade teacher that he was an "amazing student," his mother noticed that his reading and spelling skills were not progressing. He was able to read but he seemed very dependent on his excellent memory skills. He also had some difficulties learning how to spell simple words. However, since his teacher was a very experienced educator, Karl's mother did not pursue the issue any further. She was just thankful that Karl had such a dedicated teacher who emphasized all of his strengths.

Things really began to unravel in grade three when the first report card came home. For the first time, Karl's marks were no longer all As and Bs. He received Cs in reading, writing, and mathematics. His parents went to the teacher conference with real concerns. They asked his teacher if she thought he may have a learning disability and her reply was, "I don't know much about that." She was a relatively new teacher who had limited experience with children at the grade three level. Unfortunately, this inexperience resulted in no action on her part to determine whether or not Karl did indeed have a learning disability. His parents were left with no answers and decided to wait and see how Karl did during the remainder of the school year. However, before his grade three year ended, Karl's frustrations with learning were becoming more apparent so his mother, convinced there was a significant problem, spoke to a psychologist in the community about Karl's difficulties. The psychologist recommended a complete psycho-educational assessment and that assessment was completed at the end of Karl's grade three year (see *Assessing Learning Disabilities* on page 99).

Karl – Age 11

Social and Emotional Development

Karl is described as a pleasant child by all who know him. He is always enthusiastic and excited about participating in both school and extracurricular activities. However, his mother describes his negative emotions as being just as intense. She said that while he can sometimes get quite despondent over things that do not go well for him, he generally handles negative situations well. When he is having trouble with a task, he sometimes comments to his parents, "Oh well, that's just my learning disability."

Karl has been aware of his learning disabilities since the time of his diagnosis. His parents have been quite open with him right from the start. Prior to the sessions with the psychologist, they talked with him about the assessment process and why it was necessary. They emphasized that the assessment was being done because it would provide information that "would help him learn better." They were careful not to make him feel like he was stupid or unable to do the tasks necessary to be successful in school.

This does not mean that Karl never has moments of frustration when he claims that he just cannot do something. On rare occasions, he attributes his inability to complete school work, especially homework, to being "stupid." However, his parents do not let him use this mechanism to get out of his assigned work. Homework is done at the kitchen table where both parents are available to help him. They will often suggest strategies that he can employ to make tasks easier. While Karl is sometimes overwhelmed by the thought of having to do a particular task, he usually responds well once his parents help him break the task down into smaller steps. His negative feelings usually give way to feelings of accomplishment.

Karl's awareness of his learning disabilities is reflected in his desire to be good at something. He will often ask his parents, "Do you think I am good at this?" Karl is obviously keen to determine what he does well. His parents have been diligent about exposing him to activities that he excels at, especially activities that involve drama since it is one of his passions. However, it is not always possible to completely avoid having his learning difficulties affect his participation in these activities. For example, Karl would have liked to attend a public school for the arts starting in grade five. The comprehensive audition for entry into the school required him to complete academic-based tests. He was subsequently not accepted.

When asked about other behaviours that reflect Karl's emotional development, his parents commented that he can be somewhat "fidgety." While they do not believe he is hyperactive, they do feel that he has always exhibited some impulsivity. He often "gets wound up," and acts before he thinks. For example, one of his birthday parties was held at a local children's restaurant where an employee organized activities for Karl and his guests. One of the planned activities was to have Karl dip his hands in some paint and then place his hands on a special wall that marked the birthdays of restaurant guests. Karl was already overly excited from the party atmosphere when it was time for him to participate. Upon dipping his hands in the paint, he immediately placed his hands on the employee's shirt. Right away his face showed his emotions; he knew he had done something wrong and he felt very remorseful. He had acted spontaneously without giving the consequences of his actions any thought. It is not uncommon for students with learning disabilities to exhibit *attention deficit hyperactivity disorder* (ADHD) type behaviours, including inattention, impulsivity, and hyperactivity.

From The Psychologist's Notebook...

I had Karl's mother and his teacher complete the Behaviour Rating Inventory of Executive Functioning (BRIEF). It is a questionnaire for parents and teachers that professionals use to assess eight aspects of executive functioning: Inhibit, Shift, Emotional Control, Initiate, Working Memory, Plan/Organize, Organization of Materials, and Monitor. The only significant finding in regards to Karl was that he was rated as slightly elevated on measures of emotional control. Therefore, he may need some extra time and consideration when he gets excited. Both his parents and his teachers should realize that when entering situations where the emotional tone is elevated, Karl may become more excited than others and later need the time and opportunity to calm down. He may also benefit from relaxation techniques and strategies (e.g., visualization, deep breathing).

Motor Development

Karl walked earlier than most toddlers. He has been an active boy throughout his childhood. His parents describe him as coordinated in terms of large muscle movement. However, they say he is not fast moving and more like "a bull in a china shop" in some situations. In other words, he lacks fluidity and grace. While he has no problems riding his bike or climbing trees, he has had some difficulties learning to skate and learning to swim different strokes. Karl feels that he is not good at sports. While he loves volleyball, he has had negative experiences related to his participation in this sport at school. The other children have called him hurtful names that have referred to his physique and they have also commented on his lack of athletic skills.

Poor motor abilities are a common characteristic of children with learning disabilities. While Karl does exhibit some awkwardness in terms of gross motor abilities, he is certainly not lacking in general coordination. He may not be a star athlete but he is quite capable physically. Karl is also able to complete fine motor tasks with ease. He enjoys doing craft activities and he has a real flair for drawing as demonstrated in the samples of his artwork that appear throughout this chapter.

What We Know...

Common Learning and Behavioural Characteristics of Children with Learning Disabilities

Characteristic	Description
Disorders of attention	Does not focus when a lesson is presented; short attention span, easily distracted, poor concentration; may display hyperactivity.
Poor motor abilities	Difficulty with gross motor abilities and fine motor coordination (exhibits general awkwardness and clumsiness).
Psychological processing deficits	Problems in processing auditory or visual information (difficulty interpreting visual and auditory stimuli).
Lack of phonological awareness	Poor at recognizing sounds of language (cannot identify phoneme sounds in spoken language).
Poor cognitive strategies	Does not know how to go about the task of learning and studying; lacks organizational skills; passive learning style (does not direct own learning).
Oral language difficulties	Underlying language disorders (problems in language development, listening, speaking, and vocabulary).
Reading difficulties	About 80 percent of students with learning disabilities have disabilities in reading (problems in learning to decode words, basic word-recognition skills, or reading comprehension).
Writing difficulties	Poor in tasks requiring written expression, spelling, and handwriting.
Mathematics	Difficulty with quantitative thinking, arithmetic, time, space, and calculation facts.
Social skills	Does not know how to act and talk in social situations; difficulty with establishing satisfying social relationships and friendships.

Source: Excerpted from Lerner & Kline (2006).

What is School Like for Karl?

Karl is quite articulate and able to clearly describe his learning experiences. In the following passage, Karl shares what school is like for him:

I have trouble reading and writing and I don't learn as quick as other people do in these two subjects. With writing, my problem is mostly spelling. I have great ideas but it is hard for me to get them on paper. I am better at telling people. With reading, I have trouble with the bigger words. I have some trouble with math too. It takes me longer than other people to do the problems and sometimes I need someone to explain the problem to me. But I do some things better than other people in my class, like drawing and playing card games. I am pretty good at playing the piano and I like acting too. Right now I am rehearsing to be the Wolf in "Little Red Riding Hood" in French class. I am good at French. Sometimes I help other people in my class with translation from French to English.

I use a computer at school. It is at the back of the classroom. I am the only kid in the class who uses it right now because the school is just testing it out. Other kids who have problems go to the Resource Room just like I did last year. But I prefer staying in my classroom because my friend sometimes helps me. If he is walking by and he sees that I am having trouble with something, he will help me with it.

When I am writing, I use WordQ. It will say the word that I wrote and if it is wrong, it will show me a little prediction box and I get to choose the word I meant to write. For reading, I use something called Kurzweil. I scan whatever I am reading into the computer and it will read it back to me. I only use Kurzweil if I have to read a long piece because I still need to practice reading on my own. My teacher usually tells me when I should use the computer. If she doesn't say anything, I know she wants me to try it on my own.

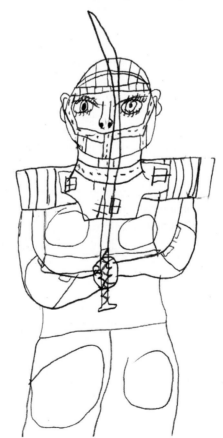

Karl – Age 11

What We Know...

Assistive Technology

According to the Learning Disabilities Association of Canada (2005), assistive technology (AT) means any item, piece of equipment, product or system, whether acquired commercially off the shelf, modified, or customized that can be used to directly assist, maintain, or improve functional capabilities of individuals with learning disabilities. AT provides alternative approaches that work around an individual's deficits while capitalizing on their strengths. The key to effective AT is finding the right match between the AT tool, the learning disability, and the task at hand.

Marino, Marino, & Shaw (2006) emphasized the importance of collecting preliminary data prior to AT implementation in order to establish the viability and efficacy of a particular AT intervention. They suggested that those who are involved in developing IEPs for students should consider the following questions as a starting point:

- What are the student's needs and abilities?
- What materials are available to support the student?
- Is the physical arrangement of the learning environment conducive to student success?
- How will the environment need to change for the student to be successful?
- What activities must the student complete as an active member of the learning community?
- How do these activities relate to the curricular goals?
- Would assistive technology improve the student's ability to participate in the general education curriculum?
- What types of technology should be considered?

Marino and his colleagues recommended that once an AT device is identified for an intervention, training for the teacher and student should be followed by a documentation of progress.

Source: Learning Disabilities Association of Canada (2005) and Marino, Marino, & Shaw (2006).

Sometimes school is frustrating. I feel that way when I just want to get something done and I can't get it done as fast as I would like to. But sometimes I like it because I can get extra help. In grade one, two, and three, before I was told that I had learning disabilities, it was more frustrating because I didn't have any extra help.

My Mom got someone to test me for learning disabilities. After we got the whole thing sorted out, I started doing better in school. I don't make a big deal out of having learning disabilities. I am just a bit different from other people. First when I found out though it made me sad. Then I found out that I was going to get some help so it sort of made me happy. In that way, the whole thing made me both happy and sad.

I don't really talk about my learning disabilities to other people. Sometimes I just explain that I have trouble with spelling and reading. My friends don't make a big deal of it. I don't tell some people in my class about my learning disabilities because I think they would call me names. They already tease me about how I do in sports.

The most difficult thing for me to do in school is writing. If I could just use a pencil to write, it would be easier but then I know I would make a lot of mistakes. So I have to use the computer and that takes more time. I have to find the right keys. I am getting better at keyboarding, so that should help. I just wish I could write with a pencil and not worry about making mistakes. Then I would really enjoy writing.

The easiest subjects for me at school are Religion and Social Studies. I really like historical things. Ever since grade one, I have been waiting to do Medieval times. We finally did it this year and it was so cool. Now we are on to Ancient Civilization. I am going to do my project on Greece. My grandmother has travelled there so she is going to help me. I have a book that shows the outfits and types of helmets they wore during that time. I will write a report and probably draw some pictures to go with it.

I like school. The only thing that really bothers me is how some other kids tease me and my friends. They take things from us and won't give them back. It's the only thing about school that I really don't like.

What We Know...

Loneliness and Students with Exceptionalities

According to Nowicki (2006), children with special needs are at a greater risk for social rejection, isolation, and bullying. Pavri and Monda-Amaya (2000) noted that school-related loneliness stems from several factors including boredom, a lack of companionship and friendship, and skill deficits experienced by the child. They emphasized the important role that school personnel play in helping students with exceptionalities feel socially comfortable and accepted at school. Pavri and Monda-Amaya stated that "teachers play an important role, both as leaders of the academic environment and as facilitators of social relationships among students with and without disabilities…teachers can create a classroom environment in which they assist students to learn the skills and strategies needed for social problem solving and conflict resolution, for the development of friendships, for learning to work cooperatively with others, and for the enhancement of their self-esteem" (p.30).

Source: Excerpted from Nowicki (2006) and Pavri and Monda-Amaya (2000).

What Educational Approach is Best for Karl?

When Karl was first designated as "learning disabled" by the school system, an IEP was developed by his classroom teacher, the educational assistant, and the student services support teacher. Based on the psychologist's assessment report, this group of educators decided the learning expectations and type of accommodations and adaptations that would be most appropriate for Karl. Their goal was to design a program that best facilitated his learning across all subject areas. The resulting IEP reflected the following recommendations made by the psychologist:

- decrease the amount of written work he has to complete
- allow alternatives to written presentations (e.g., oral presentations)
- allow him to take tests orally or have him write his tests with his peers and later review his answers with him orally
- verbally explain instructions that are given in written form
- give him extra time to complete written assignments
- allow him to use dictionaries, spelling lists, or other aids when doing his work
- allow him access to written notes from peers or the teacher
- tape a copy of the alphabet to his desk
- correct his letter reversals but do not penalize him for them
- provide support with study skills, proofreading, editing, and the mechanics of writing
- encourage him to use computer-assisted technology (e.g., spell checkers, text-to-voice software, voice-to-text software, reading fluency software)
- provide small group or individual assistance with reading

mnemonics
Simple mental aids such as abbreviations, rhymes, or images that help people remember more complex material.

- encourage him to use **mnemonics** to help him memorize facts
- allow him to use multiplication tables or calculators for math tasks
- show him examples of completed work to help him visualize what he has to do
- break down tasks into individual steps

In terms of Karl's *attention-related difficulties*, the psychologist recommended the following:

- decrease the distractions around him when he is working
- have him clear his desk of everything other than what he is working on
- decrease or mask the noises around him (e.g., use of headphones or earplugs)
- chunk his work into shorter bits and change the work frequently so he does not get bored
- cue him when giving instructions
- tell him ahead of time the question you will ask him in the group discussion so he is less likely to interrupt others
- approach him in a low key manner so he does not get over excited

In terms of his *organizational difficulties*, the psychologist recommended that his teachers:

- help him with strategies such as underlining, outlining a passage, and summarizing
- consider the use of coloured folders or binders to help him organize each subject
- help him organize his work with checklists and homework books
- encourage him to use date books and calendars
- check with him to be sure he has all the materials in his backpack that he needs to complete his homework
- try to keep things as simple as possible

Not all of these recommended strategies were incorporated into Karl's IEP, but they are available to his teacher via his school file. They are also available to his parents as they have a copy of the psychologist's report. Karl's father indicated that these recommendations have been very helpful at home, especially in terms of helping Karl with his homework.

What We Know...

Teaching Strategies for the Inclusive Classroom

Not all students with learning disabilities have exactly the same problems. However, there are some teaching strategies that have proven effective for most students with learning problems. Lerner and Kline (2006) presented a variety of these strategies for the teaching of math, reading, and writing. They are as follows:

Mathematics
- Determine the students' basic computational skills in addition, subtraction, multiplication, and division.
- Have students use manipulatives to help them understand a concept.
- Teach the students mathematics vocabulary.
- Use visuals and graphics to illustrate concepts to the students.
- Have students make up their own word story problems.
- Teach students how to use a calculator.
- Teach money concepts by using either real money or play money.
- Teach time by using manipulative clocks.
- Provide many opportunities for practice and review.

Reading
General Modifications
- Increase the amount of repetition and review.
- Allot more time for completing work.

- Provide more examples and activities.
- Introduce the work more slowly.

Phonics
- Play word and rhyming games.
- Analyze the phoneme elements that make up a word.
- Build word families.

Fluency
- Help students recognize sight words.
- Find opportunities for students to reread passages aloud.
- Use predictable books.
- Use read-along methods.
- Use the language experience method to let the children read their own language.

Vocabulary
- Teach content vocabulary before reading a chapter in a science or social studies text.
- Find words in the students' areas of interest and use the words for study.
- Use word webs to study vocabulary words.

Reading Comprehension
- Provide students with background knowledge about a story or content-area reading.
- Use the K-W-L strategy (Ogle, 1986) to improve comprehension (see p. 117).
- Have students predict what will happen next in a story.
- Use graphic organizers to visualize the reading passage.
- Show movies or videos about a book to enhance interest.
- Have students act out passages in a story.

Writing

Written Expression
- Allocate sufficient time for writing (at least four times a week).
- Encourage students in the primary grades to use invented spelling.
- Use brainstorming to create ideas about writing topics.
- Give students a range of writing tasks, both creative and functional.
- Teach students the stages of the writing process.
- Use a graphic organizer, such as Inspiration, to plan a story.
- Use a presentation program, such as PowerPoint, to develop a story.
- Use the Internet to conduct research on a topic.

Spelling
- Limit the number of spelling words to be learned at one time.
- Analyze the phonemes of new words.
- Point out the syllables in multi-syllabic words.
- Teach word families.
- Provide periodic retesting and review.

- Use multi-sensory strategies (e.g., see it, say it, write it in the air, see it in your mind, write it on paper, and compare it to the model).

Handwriting
- Begin with manuscript writing and explain that it consists of lines and circles.
- The teacher says the name of the letter to be written.
- Have the students trace the letter with their finger.
- Use dotted lines for a letter and have the students trace the dots with a pencil.
- The teacher gives stroke directions to the students (e.g., first go down).
- Have the students copy a letter (or word) on paper while looking at a model.
- The students write the letter from memory while saying the name of the letter.

Source: Excerpted from Lerner & Kline (2006).

Accommodations and Adaptations

The specific accommodations and adaptations that are in place for Karl during his current school year include access to a computer that has software designed to help with reading (Kurzweil) and writing (WordQ). He also has access to concrete materials and number lines for math and he is allowed extra time to complete written assignments. He is encouraged to ask for help reading math problems. In terms of evaluation, he is sometimes required to complete a limited number of questions on tests and he is asked at times to demonstrate his knowledge orally rather than in written form. These accommodations and adaptations have enabled Karl to improve his performance across all subject areas. In fact, in math he now works at grade level.

Assistive technology is key to Karl's success in the classroom.

Many children who have learning disabilities benefit from the use of assistive technology. For example, Andrea is a seventh grader who has great difficulty with writing and spelling. While her IEP states that she should have access to computer software that will aid her with this learning disability, her parents are very hesitant to go along with this recommendation. Their concern is that by allowing Andrea to use AT she will never develop the skills necessary to become a good writer. They consider AT "the easy way out." If you were Andrea's teacher, how would you respond to her parents' concerns?

Learning Strategies

meta-cognitive ability
The ability to understand and monitor one's own cognitive systems and their functioning.

Karl, like many students with learning disabilities, tends to have a limited repertoire of learning strategies and he does not readily devise new strategies, particularly for novel problems or situations. He also seems to lack the **meta-cognitive ability** to recognize when the strategy he is using is not producing efficient learning. This presented a perplexing problem for Mrs. McCarthy, his grade five teacher. If she did not teach Karl any learning strategies, he would not learn efficiently. On the other hand, even if she did teach Karl appropriate learning strategies, he still might not use those strategies in the most expeditious manner and he still might not recognize when to stop using an inefficient strategy. Another dilemma for Mrs. McCarthy was that in order for the teaching of learning strategies to be most effective, she would have to monitor and revise Karl's implementation of strategies on an ongoing basis. Karl was already becoming somewhat dependent upon her for help with his schoolwork.

Efforts to overcome this complex set of problems lead Mrs. McCarthy to explore the use of the Cognitive Credit Card (CCC) (Edmunds & Blair, 1999). The CCC is a credit card sized laminated set of cognitive and/or meta-cognitive cues designed to elicit student thinking about their thinking as they attempt to learn or problem solve. The design of the CCC allows a student to carry their CCCs in a wallet or attached to their binder thus giving the student some privacy and control in regards to their learning.

The process of developing a CCC begins when a teacher or student recognizes that the student does not use a particular strategy in trying to learn a particular school topic. In Karl's case, he felt that there were "just too many things to keep in my head at the same time" when trying to do subtraction in math class. Together with Mrs. McCarthy, he came up with a set of cues that helped him think about what he needed to do when subtracting (see Figure 5.1). They revised these cues a number of times until they were exactly what he needed at this period in his skill development. Mrs. McCarthy made sure that the cues were cognitive prompts and that they provided little or no curricular content and little or no content-specific procedural information. The

CCC then became a cognitive organizer for Karl. It focused on how he learns rather than on what he is to learn.

FIGURE 5.1
Karl's CCC for Subtraction

Math — Subtraction

- Is the question written in the right form?
- Do I have to borrow?
- Are my numbers in the right places?
- Are my numbers easy to read?
- Are there any symbols I need to include?
- Did I check my answer?
- Does my answer make sense?

Karl and his teacher also developed a CCC to assist with homework (see Figure 5.2).

FIGURE 5.2
Karl's CCC for Homework

Homework

- What does my notebook say I need to do?
- What materials do I need before I start?
- How do I keep track of what I have completed?
- Did I finish all of my homework?
- Has my Mom or Dad checked my work?
- Is my work ready to take back to school?

Both of these CCCs have resulted in positive learning experiences for Karl. He likes the feeling of being able to pull out his "credit cards" when he needs them and he is proud of the work he accomplishes on his own while using them.

Karl has a similar strategy that he has just begun to use for helping with reading comprehension (see Figure 5.3). The K-W-L strategy (Ogle, 1986) stands for what I *Know*, what I *Want* to learn, and what I did *Learn*.

FIGURE 5.3
Karl's Reading Organizer

My Reading Organizer

What do I **KNOW** about this already?	What do I **WANT** to know about this?	What did I **LEARN** about this?

When Karl has a reading assignment, Mrs. McCarthy starts the "Know" step by discussing with Karl what he already knows about the topic at hand. She encourages him to brainstorm about where and how he acquired this knowledge and together they organize the brainstormed ideas into general categories. Then they move on to the "Want" step where Karl is asked to determine what he wants to learn from reading the assigned article. Mrs. McCarthy has him write down the specific questions in which he is most interested. After Karl has read the article, the final "Learn" step requires him to write down what he learned from the reading and compare this acquired knowledge with what he identified as "Want to Learn" in the previous step. According to Karl, he is not keen on having to write all these things down but he is surprised about how much he does learn from reading.

What We Know...

Learning Strategies Instruction

Students with learning disabilities benefit from knowing how to use learning strategies because without these tactics they tend to be inefficient learners. Learning strategies are the tools and techniques we all use to: (1) help ourselves understand and learn new material or skills, (2) integrate new information with what we already know in a way that makes sense, and (3) recall the information or skill later, even in a different situation or place. Our strategies include what we think about (e.g., planning before writing, realizing when we are not understanding something we are reading, remembering what we have learned previously on the topic under study) and what we physically do (e.g., taking notes, re-reading to clear up confusion, making a chart, table, or story map to capture the most important information). Research has shown that using knowledge about learning strategies, including which strategies to use in different situations, can help make students more effective, purposeful, and independent learners.

Source: Excerpted from National Dissemination Center for Children with Disabilities (1997).

Evaluation of Progress

Karl is currently evaluated similarly to the other students in his class, except in the areas of reading and writing. Based on classroom observations and his performance on assigned work, Karl's teacher assigns a grade for each subject area and comments on his strengths and areas of difficulty. While he completes the same class work as his peers in reading and writing, his teacher evaluates his progress based on the appropriate expectations outlined in his IEP.

As mentioned in Chapter 3, the IEP is a key component in the evaluation of a student's progress since it includes the student's short- and long-term learning goals. An evaluation determines whether or not these goals have been met and what goals need to be modified and/or added to the IEP. As we stated earlier, the IEP is not intended to be a static document; it should be a continually evolving description of the student's education program.

Unfortunately, in Karl's case, the modification of his IEP has been given little attention, especially in terms of successfully noting implemented teacher interventions and the types of accommodations and adaptations that have been put in place. Karl's mother indicated that within Karl's school there is no active school-based team. She feels very fortunate that Karl currently has an experienced teacher who understands Karl's needs. As noted in Chapter 2, according to the policies and guidelines that generally govern the implementation of IEPs in Canada (and the United States), there is usually a mandatory requirement that a student's IEP be reviewed and updated (if necessary) at least every twelve months. In Karl's case, his teacher seems to be well in tune with his educational needs so the educational programming he is receiving is appropriate at this time. However, Karl's parents are justifiably concerned about what will happen when Karl moves on to grade six and a different teacher is responsible for his learning program.

Karl – Age 11

How is Karl Different from Other Students who have Learning Disabilities?

Despite his above average cognitive abilities, Karl has difficulties with reading, math, and writing. He also has some minor problems with emotional control. Many children with learning disabilities face similar challenges. Like Karl, their poor academic performance is not consistent with their average or above-average performance on tests of general cognitive ability. Like Karl, they have problems in reading; in fact, many students with learning disabilities encounter difficulties that affect their ability to comprehend written language. Like Karl, they also have difficulties with writing; it is understandable that a difficulty with one form of language (e.g., reading) often appears in another form of language (e.g., writing). And like Karl, they have difficulties with math; reading difficulties as well as information-processing deficits can affect an individual's ability to complete math tasks.

However, this is where the similarities with Karl end. Each of these children most likely differs from Karl in the combination of problems that they have, the severity of each of their problems, and the instructional accommodations that are needed to facilitate their learning. In other words, children with learning disabilities are a heterogeneous group; each child must be considered as unique and different from other children with learning disabilities. The following examples highlight just some of these differences:

- *ADHD and Learning Disabilities.* Hoshi is a sixteen-year-old high school student who has very few close friends. His classmates describe him as "weird" and a "social misfit." They say he just does not know how to act around other people and he embarrasses them constantly by his odd behaviours. To compound his social problems, he is not doing well in school and displays a negative attitude toward learning. Hoshi's parents say that he was a difficult child right from birth. He was an "overactive" preschooler and once he entered school, his short attention span combined with his severe difficulties with reading lead to a comprehensive psycho-educational assessment. Hoshi was diagnosed with both attention deficit hyperactivity disorder (ADHD) and learning disabilities. For a short period, he was given the stimulant medication Ritalin. While it helped him focus in school, he had trouble sleeping and the drug was discontinued. Hoshi has failed to learn to read beyond the elementary level. Consequently, he has had many negative school experiences that have lead to poor self-esteem and a desire to avoid learning altogether. Now that he is a teenager, his problems with social relations further exacerbate his feelings of failure. He has been thinking of dropping out of school and finding a job.

What We Know...

Children with ADHD and Learning Disabilities

ADHD is a common co-occurring condition for children with learning disabilities. It is a chronic neurological condition characterized by three classes of symptoms: (1) inattention, (2) impulsivity, and (3) hyperactivity. An example of an inattention symptom is that the individual has difficulty competing tasks or doesn't seem to listen. Impulsivity symptoms describe instances of acting without thinking (blurting out answers or having difficulty taking turns)...hyperactivity symptoms contain descriptions of restless or fidgety behaviours such as squirming while seated, or repeatedly getting up from a chair for no reason (p. 75).

Although it is quite common for LD and ADHD to co-occur in the same individual, there is considerable evidence that the two conditions are not causally related. The strongest evidence against a causal relationship stems from neurological evidence that different brain regions seem to be involved in each of the two conditions (p. 98).

Source: Excerpted from Conte (1998).

- *Nonverbal Learning Disorders.* Gabrielle is an eight-year-old child who began talking at a very early age. In fact, her parents said that she sounded like a little adult when she was only a preschooler. Her love of books resulted in an ability to read simple stories before she started kindergarten and she has excelled in oral reading and spelling throughout her first few years of school. Gabrielle has also quickly mastered her math facts and seems to have an excellent memory for recalling factual information. Despite these considerable strengths, Gabrielle has some significant difficulties that affect her in all aspects of her life. She is not well coordinated and finds it frustrating to participate in physical activities such as her neighbourhood soccer league and gym classes at school. Her participation in neighbourhood play and school sports are made even more difficult due to her poor social skills and her inability to adjust to new situations. Her mother says that Gabrielle just does not know how to make friends with other children and when she is placed in a new situation she is simply frozen in fear. These difficulties with social interaction have become more and more pronounced of late and they are now affecting Gabrielle's performance in school. Her mother and her teacher have decided that Gabrielle should be assessed by a psychologist.

What We Know...

Children with Nonverbal Learning Disorders (NLD)

NLD is a neurological disorder which originates in the right hemisphere of the brain. Reception of nonverbal or performance-based information governed by this hemisphere is impaired in varying degrees, causing problems with visual-spatial, intuitive, organizational, evaluative, and holistic processing functions. NLD is a syndrome of assets and deficits. In each individual with NLD, the assets and deficits manifest in different combinations and different intensities. Most people with the diagnosis, however, share the basic configuration of relative impairment in social perception, visual-spatial abilities, and mechanical arithmetic, with well developed verbal skills and rote memory.

Source: Excerpted from Nonverbal Learning Disorders Association, www.nlda.org.

Common Characteristics of Children with NLD:

- performance I.Q. significantly lower than verbal I.Q.
- early speech and vocabulary development
- remarkable rote memory skill
- attention to detail
- early reading skills development and excellent spelling skills
- expresses himself/herself eloquently
- lack of coordination
- severe balance problems
- difficulties with fine motor skills
- lack of image, poor visual recall
- faulty spatial relations
- lack of ability to comprehend nonverbal communication
- difficulties adjusting to transitions and new situations
- significant deficits in social judgement and interaction

Source: Excerpted from NLDline, www.nldline.com.

● *Dyslexia.* Pamela is a fourteen-year-old high school student who excels in the visual arts and music. Pamela attends a public school for the fine arts where she is able to take many classes in these two subjects. However, school is not a completely positive experience for her. After years of individualized instruction at school and tutoring at home, she still struggles to read at the grade four level. It is an embarrassment to her that she cannot read as fluently as her peers. She knows she is dyslexic but that does not remove the fear she feels when confronted with reading tasks. She would love to be involved in the drama club but the thought of having to read a script aloud in front of her classmates is just too intimidating. Pamela's parents are very supportive of her situation. They have tried to emphasize her strengths by providing her with the opportunity to increase her skill level in art and music. As well, they have brought to her attention people like Jay Leno, Bruce Jenner, and Tom Cruise who have excelled despite being dyslexic. While they had hopes early after Pamela's diagnosis that she might be able to overcome her disability, they realize now that dyslexia is something that will affect her throughout her life. They plan to get her some counselling as she faces the difficulties of going through adolescence with a learning disability.

What We Know...

Children with Dyslexia

Dyslexia is a specific learning disability that is neurological in origin. It is characterized by difficulties with accurate and/or fluent word recognition and by poor spelling and decoding abilities. These difficulties typically result from a deficit in the phonological component of language that is often unexpected in relation to other cognitive abilities and the provision of effective classroom instruction. Secondary consequences may include problems in reading comprehension and reduced reading experience that can impede growth of vocabulary and background knowledge.

Source: Excerpted from The International Dyslexia Association, www.interdys.org.

From The Psychologist's Notebook...

Karl's set of circumstances are a classic description of a student with a learning disability. However, he is different than a lot of children with LD in that he is in grade five and he still has a fairly positive outlook about school and life in general. Unfortunately, many students with LD do not experience a lot of success in school due to their lack of cognitive strategies which are the thinking engines that drive effective learning. Their lack of success often leads to a poor perception of themselves and thus leads to low self-esteem and low self-efficacy.

Compare Karl's story to the story of Alan, a high school student I have just recently met. Alan's school history reveals how cognitive strategy deficits contribute to negative attributions in individuals with LD. It is why we often see high school students with LD who are just no longer interested in school or motivated to even try to do well.

Alan's First School Years

Alan was a happy and enthusiastic little guy as he bounded through the doorway of his kindergarten classroom. He knew all his numbers up to 83, all the letters of the alphabet, all the colors in his box of 15 crayons, he could read a few words like "stop," "McDonald's" and "Toronto," and he could write his name and a few other words. His chatty and exuberant behaviour continued through the first few years of school as he really enjoyed the basic academic tasks in those early grades. Like all the other students in his class, his basic cognitive strategies were strong for the tasks presented and learning happened fairly easily. From these encounters, Alan realized that he *had the ability to do what was required and that his **effort** determined his academic results – good or not-so-good.*

Alan's Middle School Years

In November of Alan's grade three year, his teacher sent home a note remarking that Alan seemed to be struggling compared to the rest of the students, particularly in reading and writing. As grade three became grade four and then grade five, the complexity and sophistication of most academic tasks, especially reading and writing, pushed Alan's basic strategies to their maximum. Even the newer/better strategies he had learned since coming to school were only good for some tasks, but not for all tasks. Alan's perspective changed slightly: "I still have the ability (I successfully accomplish a lot of tasks) but my efforts do not 'always' pay off." His attribution becomes one of, *"I might not have all the cognitive abilities required for what my teacher asks me to do, therefore, I have to try harder to be as successful as my classmates."*

From grade five onward, Alan really struggled with school work because at this point, *all tasks* required complex and sophisticated cognitive strategies. Alan didn't have them and, unfortunately, without very specific and individualized help, he had no way of developing them. His cognitive strategy deficits were particularly evident because of: (1) curricular shifts from "learning-to-read" to a reliance on "reading-to-learn," and (2) curricular emphases away from oral communication and manipulatives to a predominance of print formats.

Alan's High School Years

Now, in the shadow of senior high, Alan looks around and readily notices that his classmates are doing OK and, because of society's emphasis on doing well in school, *"they are OK."* Alan's perspective has changed demonstrably: *"I don't have the ability and now my efforts, which were sometimes successful in the past, **never** pay off. Therefore, trying harder is useless. Another good reason to not 'try harder' is that I will not continually show people that I'm stupid!"*

Closing Karl's File

Karl will not outgrow his disabilities. Undoubtedly, learning will be a continual challenge for him as he progresses through upper elementary school and high school. High school will be particularly demanding as it is focuses on mastery of content across all subject areas. These more complex, extensive, and sophisticated curricula will be presented by a number of teachers whose teaching methods will differ and may not be suited to Karl's learning strengths. To make matters worse for Karl, acquiring information through reading will be emphasized and information will presented at a fast pace. While these characteristics of high school appear daunting in the context of Karl's learning disabilities, he will be better able to handle these challenges as he acquires more and more effective learning strategies. As well, he will benefit from appropriate accommodations and adaptations that are implemented to facilitate his learning. Karl is fortunate to have parents who will continue to advocate for him to ensure that these accommodations and adaptations are put in place. His parents' efforts to make him aware of his learning disabilities will also empower him to advocate for himself. As Reiff (2004) pointed out, understanding one's learning disabilities offers a number of benefits: "knowing about one's learning disabilities seems to be related to higher levels of self-esteem…such self-awareness provides a greater sense of autonomy…such knowledge provides practical advantages, particularly in the areas of self-advocacy and obtaining reasonable accommodations" (p. 187).

When asked about his future, Karl's parents responded with enthusiasm. They expect that with their ongoing support Karl will graduate from high school and enter a post-secondary institution. They do not foresee any major problems in his completion of a degree in whatever field he chooses. His mother said, "He may not get all As but he will achieve his goals." Right now Karl's goal is to become a computer animator, a police officer, or a priest.

From The Psychologist's Notebook…

My advice to Karl's parents is to continue their strong advocacy role. Parents are sometimes better educational advocates than professionals in the field due to their extensive knowledge of the child's complete history, their unparalleled concern and responsibility for the child's well-being, and their ability to speak freely without placing themselves in a conflict of interest with the education system. Unfortunately, many parents do not take on the role of educational advocate due to a number of factors, such as cultural and language difficulties, logistical barriers that restrict participation, a lack of knowledge about special education procedures, negative professional attitudes towards parents, parental burnout, and feelings of alienation from schools (Fiedler, Simpson, & Clark, 2007). Educators should be aware of these barriers and actively encourage parents of children with special needs to participate in the decision-making process that surrounds the education of their child.

In terms of Karl's situation, I also advise both his parents and his future teachers to continue to focus on his strengths. Encourage him to be involved in activities he enjoys and in which he excels. Provide him with opportunities to demonstrate his skills. He has an excellent attitude toward learning and remains motivated to do his best despite the difficulties he encounters on a daily basis. It is important that he continue to receive as much encouragement and positive reinforcement as possible for his efforts and achievements.

What We Know...

Success Attributes of Persons with Learning Disabilities

According to Goldberg et al. (2003), longitudinal research of individuals with learning disabilities has shown that *successful* individuals demonstrated an enhanced self-awareness and the ability to compartmentalize their LD allowing them to acknowledge strengths as well as weaknesses. "They were engaged in the world financially as well as socially, often rising to leadership roles in the family, at work, and in the community. They were decisive, often consulting others for information or advice, and they took responsibility for outcomes. They showed persistence in their pursuits, yet they could be flexible in altering the path by which they skirted obstacles. Successful individuals set realistic goals for themselves and demonstrated an awareness of the steps that would be required for their attainment. They made use of social support available to them in reaching these goals and sought help when needed. In adulthood, they demonstrated the ability to reciprocate and provide care and support for others. Finally, they developed strong and intimate peer and family relationships that assisted them in many ways to cope with stressful times and maintain emotional stability" (p. 230).

Source: Excerpted from Goldberg et al. (2003).

Learning More About Students with Learning Disabilities

Academic Journals

Exceptional Children

Journal of Learning Disabilities

Journal of Special Education

Learning Disability Quarterly

Learning Disabilities Research & Practice

Books

Bender, W. N. (2003). *Learning disabilities: Characteristics, identification, and teaching strategies.* Boston: Allyn and Bacon.

Lerner, J.W. and Kline, F. (2006). *Learning disabilities and related disorders.* Boston: Houghton Mifflin Company.

Wong, B. (ed.), (2004). *Learning about learning disabilities.* 3rd ed. San Diego: Academic Press.

Web Links

● LD OnLine

www.ldonline.org

LD OnLine offers information for parents and teachers about learning disabilities and ADHD. There is a "Questions + Answers" link that provides advice and answers to frequently asked questions. Under "LD in Depth," there are links to many "expert reviewed" articles. Visitors to the Web site can post questions to experts in the field.

● Learning Disabilities Association of Ontario

www.ldao.ca

Besides providing information about types of learning disabilities and common signs of learning disabilities, this site includes a section devoted to how to help students with learning disabilities in different environments, such as at school and at home.

● Learning Disabilities Association of Quebec

www.aqeta.qc.ca/english/general.htm

General information on learning disabilities is provided on this site as well as a list of relevant publications and archived copies of the association's newsletter.

● National Center for Learning Disabilities

www.ncld.org

Included on this comprehensive site is the LD InfoZone which provides links to major reports, research-based interventions, and other effective teaching practices.

- Nonverbal Learning Disorders Association
  www.nlda.org
  This NLDA site provides information about nonverbal learning disorders, including an outline of diagnostic criteria and a list of positive interventions. A support forum allows interested individuals to discuss topics relevant to NLD.

- The Learning Disabilities Association of Canada
  www.ldac-taac.ca/index-e.asp
  This LDAC site presents comprehensive information on learning disabilities for parents, teachers, and adults who have learning disabilities. The section for teachers provides a number of resources to help teachers better deal with the issues they face in the classroom when they have a student with a learning disability.

Please visit the Online Learning Centre for *Special Education in Canada* at **www.mcgrawhill.ca/olc/edmunds** for additional learning and study resources.

Taking It Into Your Classroom...

Including Students Who Have Learning Disabilities

When a student who has a learning disability is first placed in my classroom, I will:

- review what I know about learning disabilities and locate resource materials
- read the student's file
- consult with the student's previous teachers
- consult with the student's parents
- meet with the school-based team to discuss the student's current school year

Other: _____

_____

When I suspect a student in my classroom has a learning disability, I will:

- review what I know about learning disabilities and locate resource materials
- collect information about the student through classroom interventions
- consult with other school personnel who are familiar with the student
- consult with the student's parents
- meet with the school-based team to present the information I have collected

Other: _____

_____

Key points to remember in my daily interactions with a student who has a learning disability:

- the student may have low self-esteem and low self-concept
- the student may exhibit a discrepancy between ability and performance
- the student may be impulsive and speak without thinking
- the student may not be able to interpret body language and tone of voice
- the student may have difficulty understanding spoken language
- the student may not react well to change

Other: _____

_____

Key points regarding curriculum differentiation for a student who has a learning disability:

- change, modify, or adapt the curriculum according to the student's IEP
- use visual aids to supplement oral and written information
- include hands-on activities rather than just having the student listen and observe
- use learning aids such as assistive technology to motivate the student
- implement any additional accommodations recommended in the student's IEP

Other: _____

_____

Key points regarding evaluation of the progress made by a student who has a learning disability:

- follow the evaluation plan outlined in the student's IEP
- consider the student's current learning expectations to determine his or her progress
- observe how the student's behaviour affects his or her learning
- recognize the student's strengths
- modify existing learning expectations or develop new ones as needed
- implement new accommodations and/or adaptations as needed

Other: _____

_____

CHAPTER 6

Students with Behavioural Disorders

Name: Lindsey Woods
Current Age: 12
School: M.H. Landon School
Grade: 7

Lindsey is a highly creative individual who is considering a career as a visual artist. Fortunately, her parents support her artistic talents by providing her with private art lessons outside of the school setting. These lessons are a welcome departure from the frustrations Lindsey faces in school. As a child with both attention deficit hyperactivity disorder and a learning disability, school is not always pleasant for Lindsey. Like other students with behaviour problems, she has difficulty attending to academic tasks and struggles with the social aspects of school despite her desire to establish friendships with her peers. Lindsey's story allows educators to consider the need for educational placements other than the inclusive classroom for some periods during a particular student's schooling.

Excerpts from Lindsey's
Psycho-Educational Assessment

Lindsey's age at time of assessment: 10 years, 9 months

This psycho-educational assessment was requested by Lindsey's parents in an effort to update information on her intellectual and academic functioning. Previous assessments identified Lindsey as having ADHD as well as significant language-based learning difficulties.

Intellectual/Cognitive Functioning

Wide variability in Lindsey's performance on the *WISC-IV* rendered the reporting of a Full Scale I.Q. meaningless. Results included:

Skill	Percentile	Range
Auditory-Verbal Skills	8th	Borderline
Verbal Reasoning	16th	Low Average
Perceptual Reasoning	32nd	Average
Working Memory	3rd	Borderline
Processing Speed	84th	Above Average

Executive Functioning

Lindsey's mother completed the *Behaviour Rating Inventory of Executive Functioning* to assess Lindsey's behaviour in the home environment. An elevated score was obtained on the *Working Memory Scale* which means that Lindsey has difficulty holding information in memory that is needed to complete a task and, therefore, she also has difficulty sticking to a task. She has a short attention span and is easily distracted. Lindsey also received an elevated score on the *Inhibit Scale* which means she has difficulty resisting the urge to act on her impulses.

Memory Functioning

On the *Wide Range Assessment of Memory and Learning* (2nd edition), Lindsey's performance was low average on the *Verbal Memory Index* (19th percentile) and average on the *Visual Memory Index* (34th percentile).

Academic Functioning

The *Woodcock-Johnson Tests of Achievement* were administered to assess Lindsey's current level of functioning in reading, mathematics, and writing skills. Results indicated:

Reading	Lindsey's overall reading skills are in the low average range for her age, and fall around the early grade three level. Reading Fluency was a relative strength while she scored lowest on Reading Vocabulary.
Mathematics	Lindsey's math skills are well below average for her age, falling at the early grade two level. She had significant difficulties with all subtests.
Writing	Lindsey's scores on tests of writing skills are below average for her age, falling at the late grade two level. She scored well below average on all subtests.

Mother's Comments Regarding Lindsey's ADHD

My husband and I adopted Lindsey in Russia when she was just three days old. She has been with us since that time. We are not aware of her family or prenatal history. However, we were told that her birth was uncomplicated and no resuscitation was necessary. Her Apgar scores were nine and ten. When we first saw Lindsey, she was bright and alert. We did meet her birth mother but due to language difficulties we were unable to communicate. She looked to be about 19 or 20 years old and appeared to be healthy and well-nourished. Lindsey was examined by a paediatrician when she was five days old and we were told that she was a healthy baby. She was seen again at one month of age by a specialist and again we were told that she was healthy.

Lindsey was a cuddly, affectionate, and happy baby. She bonded very well to both of us. She bottle fed easily but was colicky during the first few months. We had difficulty switching her to solid foods and there were some concerns about her ability to swallow. Before she was one year of age, we were worried that she was not reaching developmental milestones at the appropriate age. She seemed to be floppy and had low muscle tone. She didn't walk until she was 16 months of age. Her speech was delayed as well. We arranged therapy to address her needs. She also had multiple ear infections during her early years and finally had her tonsils and adenoids removed at age five.

As a toddler, she had extremes in her moods. Most of the time, she was very friendly, affectionate, and happy. Her grandmother once commented that she sometimes seemed "too happy." However, on the other end of the scale, she would have temper tantrums. They were like black storms that would come in very suddenly. Lindsey would scream, cry and be very upset, and then 20 minutes later, she would be hugging and kissing me and everything would be fine.

She was diagnosed with ADHD early in her grade one year. Lindsey was displaying significant behavioural problems that the school didn't seem to know how to manage. She also had difficulty adapting to change and would easily get wound up. We were referred to a specialist who had both myself and her teacher complete the Conners' Rating Scales. The specialist put her on Ritalin (methylphenidate) at that time. She responded well and has been on medication ever since. She was switched to Concerta when it became available and that is what she currently takes now. A trial of Strattera resulted in a loss of appetite as well as withdrawn, uncommunicative behaviour. The medication was stopped after two weeks. Lindsey also takes Clonidine at bedtime for sleep as she has difficulty falling asleep without it. She used to take Clonidine in the mornings as well because of her physical tics but it is now being discontinued as the tics seem to have gone away. Her tics may have been a side effect of her medication.

Lindsey has always been a highly sensitive child. Even with medication, she still has problems adapting to new situations and she can get overly excited and/or overly emotional at times. She is easily distracted, easily frustrated, she does not always listen well, and she often forgets things. But with her medication and the strategies she has learned, her behaviour is definitely better controlled. She's more compliant and co-operative. She is better able to handle peer interactions. We have definitely seen an improvement.

Lindsey Woods

Parent's and Teacher's Assessment of Lindsey's Behaviour

Lindsey's age at time of assessment: 12 years

ADD-H Comprehensive Teacher/Parent Rating Scales (ACTeRS)

Behaviour		Teacher's Rating		Parent's Rating
Attention	----------	major deficit	----------	major deficit
Hyperactivity	----------	major deficit	----------	major deficit
Social Skills	----------	moderate problem	----------	moderate problem
Oppositional	----------	no problem	----------	moderate problem

Conners' Rating Scales

	T-Scores*	
	Parent	*School*
Oppositional	56	69
Cognitive Problems/Inattention	77	68
Hyperactivity	58	77
Anxious-Shy	58	74
Perfectionism	43	55
Social Problems	50	63
Conners' ADHD Index	79	79
Conners' Global Index: Restless-Impulsive	78	80
Conners' Global Index: Emotional Lability	60	61
Conners' Global Index: Total	74	76
DSM-IV Inattentive	79	70
DSM-IV Hyperactive-Impulsive	74	72
DSM-IV Total	80	74

*A T-score is a standardized score, based on a normal curve. A T-score of 50 is equal to the average score of some comparison or norm group. Approximately two-thirds of the scores in that norm group will fall between a T-score of 40 and a T-score of 60. This is the average range.

Lindsey's Behaviour Plan — Grade 7

Area of Concern – Impulse Control

Lindsey often speaks loudly and over what others are saying. This is particularly evident when she feels she "needs" to say what she is thinking and does not attempt to utilize cues from others to assist her in stopping. After she has completed what she wants to say, she will then accept cues from others.

Lindsey often interjects into conversations and/or speaks out of turn. She frequently misinterprets conversations and acts and speaks without thinking of the social consequences.

Lindsey is easily distracted when attempting to complete tasks. She will often follow peers to complete tasks. This is not always a beneficial strategy as her peers are often following their own agenda and not necessarily doing what is asked.

Current Goal

Lindsey will be observed listening to communications from others, pausing to assess whether she needs to respond, and responding positively if needed.

Interventions

- The school will provide individual counselling to assist Lindsey in understanding the impact of her impulsive comments on others during social interactions.
- School personnel will identify and label social interactions that are both positive and negative at the point of performance to assist Lindsey in recognizing and accepting how her responses affect her relationships with others.
- School personnel will assist Lindsey with her impulsivity during conversations by having her ask questions to clarify what she does not understand. She will be encouraged to respond to information in a positive manner. Lindsey will be given positive feedback upon completion.
- At the end of the day, school personnel will provide positive feedback to Lindsey by recounting situations where she has reacted positively, as well as situations where she has asked for clarification if needed.

Area of Concern – Social Interactions

Lindsey lacks an intuitive understanding of social boundaries. Her attempts to socially interact with peers are often out of context and not received well by others.

Lindsey lacks confidence in social interactions. In order to take part in an interaction, she will often repeat what is said by others in the form of a question; however, her attempts are often out of context and result in an end to the conversation.

Lindsey will often look to peers and follow their lead for direction regarding daily routines and social interactions. She has difficulty initiating both of these areas independently.

Current Goal

At the end of each day, Lindsey will identify to staff one instance when she shared something positive within a conversation.

Intervention
- During weekly social skills sessions, Lindsey's counsellor will focus on the skills needed to enter into a conversation and then participate in a conversation. Personal space will be discussed and demonstrated to assist Lindsey in learning this skill.
- School personnel will provide Lindsey with immediate feedback during social activities and encourage age-appropriate social language. Lindsey will be encouraged to observe peers and their behaviours during positive social interactions.
- The school will include Lindsey in social skills groups where topics such as self-acceptance, feelings, problem-solving, and "looking" like a positive learner are discussed.
- The school will provide Lindsey with individual counselling that focuses on having her recognize and accept her own positive and negative social behaviours and their effects on interactions.
- School personnel will encourage Lindsey to take risks during conversations by sharing her own experiences.

Area of Concern – Knowledge of Own ADHD and Learning Disabilities

Lindsey has difficulty discussing her strengths and needs and often will avoid conversations about her ADHD and her learning disabilities. She will often comment that she knows all about ADHD.

Lindsey will often make excuses for her behaviours by saying that she is ADHD or has learning disabilities. She has difficulty identifying behaviours that need change.

Lindsey will often respond with a negative tone of voice if she does not understand or misinterprets information. This often leads to a negative response from others and masks the true issue.

Current Goal
Lindsey will be observed during daily interactions as she asks questions to clarify information and then responds in a positive tone of voice.

Intervention
- A school staff member will meet with Lindsey on a daily basis to review positive aspects of her day. Lindsey will be encouraged to discuss and identify specific behaviours that are related to her ADHD and her learning disabilities.
- The school will include Lindsey in social skills groups where she has the opportunity to identify what type of learner she is. School personnel will assist Lindsey in utilizing this information so that she takes responsibility for her behaviours and makes changes where necessary.
- The school will provide Lindsey with individual counselling that assists her in identifying when and how her ADHD behaviours interfere with her learning and social interactions. Lindsey's counsellor will emphasize the importance of taking responsibility for changes in her behaviour.
- The school will provide Lindsey with individual counselling that assists her in identifying her feelings when she responds in a negative tone of voice. Lindsey's counsellor will assist her in taking responsibility for her feelings and help her acquire strategies that will lead to more appropriate responses.

Sample of Lindsey's Writing

Age 12 – Grade 7

Without you

It's impossible to breath because my heart is broken in two fracause and bleeding there's no beat there without you. I can't sleep at night so I don't have dreams to bring you back to me you are lost forever it seems without loveming you I can't go on I don't know how you are my life I told you that I meant it then, I mean it now My mind has become an echo chamber filled with your memories over and over they repeat there is no release Your shadow is all over me misty eyed tears fall I miss you I do I can't get over you at all I'm a lost soul floating alone in a vast universe and I don't ever in my life remember feeling worses Everything in my life all I ever knew suddenly becomes unreal a lie without you. That how it feels and no one can make it right friends try hard to comfort but they can't help me win this fight for all of your life wherever you go wherever you are I will always be in your heart your heart your distant, loving guiding star.

Sample of Lindsey's Artwork

Age 9 – Grade 4

Why is Lindsey Considered to have a Behavioural Disorder?

Definition of Behavioural Disorders

Although Lindsey's behavioural disorder was not diagnosed until she entered school, her family noticed that she engaged in troubling behaviours at an early age. While Lindsey was an affectionate and contented baby, she began to display significant mood swings during the toddler period. Her mother describes them as "black storms" (see *Mother's Comments* on page 133) that would end as abruptly as they began. They were marked by tantrum-like behaviours that contrasted vividly with the happy, bubbly toddler who loved to give hugs and kisses. Upon entry into kindergarten, more problems arose. Lindsey's teachers noted that she did not pay attention and her behaviour was disrupting classroom activities. She was also having difficulty establishing friendships with the other children. By grade one, it was apparent that Lindsey's behaviour needed to be addressed. A medical specialist was consulted and he confirmed the existence of a behaviour disorder.

What We Know...

Definition of Emotional Disturbance

Students with behavioural, mental, and emotional disorders are categorized as having an emotional disturbance. An emotional disturbance is defined as a condition exhibiting one or more of the following characteristics over a long period of time and to a marked degree that adversely affects educational performance:

1. An inability to learn that cannot be explained by intellectual, sensory, or health factors.
2. An inability to build or maintain satisfactory interpersonal relationships with peers and teachers.
3. Inappropriate types of behaviour or feelings under normal circumstances.
4. A general pervasive mood of unhappiness or depression, or
5. A tendency to develop physical symptoms or fears associated with personal or school problems.

Source: Excerpted from Individuals with Disabilities Education Act (IDEA) 1997 [Code of Federal Regulations, Title 34, Section 300.7(c)(4)(i)].

Attention Deficit Hyperactivity Disorder

Lindsey's behavioural disorder was more specifically diagnosed as attention deficit hyperactivity disorder (ADHD), a disorder believed to be caused by a deficiency, imbalance, or inefficiency in brain chemicals that affect certain brain regions (Rief, 2005). It should be noted that ADHD is a psychiatric diagnosis that should only be made by a **psychiatrist**, a clinical psychologist, a physician, or other qualified medical health professional using criteria outlined in the *Diagnostic and Statistical Manual of Mental Disorders IV* (American Psychiatric Association, 1994). There is no simple laboratory test or medical procedure that can lead to a quick and definitive identification of this condition. Rather, the diagnosis is based upon a careful history taken from parents (e.g., age of onset, type of symptoms, duration of symptoms, and degree of impairment), a physical examination, an interview with the child, and input from parents and teachers regarding the child's current behaviour. As is often the case, Lindsey's parents and teachers were asked to complete behaviour rating scales (i.e., Conners' Rating Scales) which use observer ratings to help assess ADHD and evaluate problem behaviour in children and adolescents. For example, in this type of assessment, teachers are presented with common behaviours that students display in school and they are then asked to rate how often a particular individual has exhibited each behaviour in the past month. The more frequently these problematic behaviours have occurred, the more likely it is that the student has experienced difficulties in the classroom. In Lindsey's case, her teachers indicated that the following behaviours occurred "*very frequently*" at school:

- forgets things she has already learned
- feelings are easily hurt
- excitable, impulsive
- emotional
- inattentive, easily distracted
- sensitive to criticism
- short attention span
- easily distracted by extraneous stimuli

While the above behaviours are problematic in and of themselves, they were even more of an issue because Lindsey also displayed the following co-occurring problematic behaviours, reported by her teachers as occurring "*often*":

- has difficulties engaging in tasks that require sustained mental effort
- has difficulty organizing tasks or activities
- has difficulty sustaining attention in tasks or play activities
- has difficulty waiting her turn
- blurts out answers to questions before the questions have been completed
- only pays attention to things she is really interested in

psychiatrist
A medical specialist who deals with the diagnosis, treatment, and prevention of mental and emotional disorders.

- mood changes quickly and drastically
- interrupts or intrudes on others

The results obtained from the administration of the *Conners' Parent Rating Scale* were similar. In other words, Lindsey's parents reported observing similar frequencies of the same behaviours at home and in other environments than school (e.g., extracurricular activities).

Since Lindsey's assessment uncovered a significant number of behaviours in all three areas, or types, of ADHD (i.e., inattention, impulsivity, and hyperactivity) and these had existed for a number of years and across a variety of settings, she was diagnosed as having "ADHD – Combined Type." ADHD is actually an umbrella term that describes three types of ADHD; the other two types are "Predominantly Inattentive Type" which describes individuals who do not exhibit hyperactivity and, "Predominantly Hyperactive/Impulsive Type" which refers to those who have few inattentive symptoms.

What We Know...

Definition of ADHD

(A) Either (1) or (2).

(1) six (or more) of the following symptoms of *inattention* have persisted for at least six months to a degree that is maladaptive and inconsistent with developmental level:

- often fails to give close attention to details or makes careless mistakes in schoolwork, work, or other activities
- often has difficulty sustaining attention in tasks or play activities
- often does not seem to listen when spoken to directly
- often does not follow through on instructions and fails to finish schoolwork, chores, or duties in the workplace (not due to oppositional behaviour or failure to understand instructions)
- often has difficulty organizing tasks and activities
- often avoids, dislikes, or is reluctant to engage in tasks that require sustained mental effort (such as schoolwork or homework)
- often loses things necessary for tasks or activities (e.g., toys, school assignments, pencils, books, or tools)
- is often easily distracted by extraneous stimuli
- is often forgetful in daily activities

(2) six (or more) of the following symptoms of *hyperactivity-impulsivity* have persisted for at least six months to a degree that is maladaptive and inconsistent with developmental level:

- often fidgets with hands or feet or squirms in seat
- often leaves seat in classroom or in other situations in which remaining seated is expected

- often runs about or climbs excessively in situations in which it is inappropriate (in adolescents or adults, may be limited to subjective feelings of restlessness)
- often has difficulty playing or engaging in leisure activities quietly
- is often "on the go" or often acts as if "driven by a motor"
- often talks excessively
- often blurts out answers before questions have been completed
- often has difficulty awaiting turn
- often interrupts or intrudes on others (e.g., butts into conversations or games)

(B) Some hyperactive-impulsive or inattentive symptoms that caused impairment were present before age seven.

(C) Some impairment from the symptoms is present in two or more settings (e.g., at school or work and at home).

(D) There must be clear evidence of clinically significant impairment in social, academic, or occupational functioning.

(E) The symptoms do not occur exclusively during the course of a Pervasive Developmental Disorder, Schizophrenia, or other Psychotic Disorder and are not better accounted for by another mental disorder (e.g., Mood Disorder, Anxiety Disorder, Dissociative Disorder, or Personality Disorder).

Source: Excerpted from American Psychiatric Association, *DSM-IV* (Washington, DC: American Psychiatric Association, 1994), pp. 83–84.

ADHD Medication

Upon diagnosis, Lindsey was immediately prescribed the stimulant Ritalin (methylphenidate). Although it appears odd that a stimulant medication would be prescribed for an already over-stimulated child, Ritalin fires up specific neurons in the brain that are not working as they should. These neurons tell us when to pay attention to certain activities and when to ignore other ones. According to ADHD Canada (www.adhdcanada.com/treatments.html), stimulant medications have shown to be the most effective treatment for individuals with ADHD. While they are not a cure, they can reduce the symptoms of the disorder. In Lindsey's case, her doctor monitors the effects of her medication and adjusts her dosage accordingly. Lindsey no longer takes Ritalin as it required frequent dosing (i.e., multiple pills a day); she is currently taking Concerta, a once-a-day pill that also contains methylphenidate. Concerta does have possible side effects, one of which is insomnia. Lindsey is prescribed Clonidine to help her sleep.

There is an alternative to stimulant medications. Straterra is a norepinephrine reuptake inhibitor that is used to treat ADHD. It is designed to increase the availability of norepinephrine which is thought to be essential to the brain's regulation of impulse control, organization, and attention. Lindsey was given a two-week trial of Straterra to see how she would respond. The medication resulted in a loss of appetite as well as withdrawn, uncommunicative behaviour and, therefore, it was stopped and she was placed back on Concerta which she currently takes today.

When recently asked how her medication affects her, Lindsey described a little "experiment" she conducted:

> *Whenever someone like my doctor asked me how my medication was working,*
> *I never really knew what to say because I have taken medication for as long as*
> *I can remember. I decided to find out how it affected me by not taking my pill*
> *one morning. I slid the pill under my tongue and then spit it out when no one*
> *was looking. At school that day, I couldn't stay still in my seat and I was off in*
> *la-la land much more than usual. I felt really weird and I just couldn't focus.*
> *The teacher even asked me if there was something wrong because I wasn't acting*
> *normally. So now I know that my medication does help me. I would never want*
> *to try that experiment again!*

Brain stimulants are among the most commonly prescribed drugs to Canadian children. Many parents and educators of students with ADHD have reported the positive effects these drugs have had on student behaviour. In 2006, Health Canada issued two public advisories regarding the drugs used to treat ADHD. The first advisory warned that ADHD drugs carry rare heart risks, including a risk of sudden death. The more recent advisory indicated that these drugs may cause psychotic reactions, including rare cases of hallucinations and agitation in children. If you had a child with ADHD, would you consider drug treatment? What information would you collect and assess before making your decision?

Something To Think About…

What Factors Contributed to Lindsey's Behavioural Disorder?

Given the lack of information regarding Lindsey's biological parents and the circumstances of her birth, it is impossible to point to any one factor that may have lead to her behavioural disorder. However, given the statistics evident in the literature, it is probable that a genetic factor may have contributed to Lindsey's ADHD. According to the National Institute of Mental Health (2006), attention disorders run in families. Studies indicate that 25 percent of close relatives of ADHD children also have ADHD, whereas the rate is about five percent in the general population (Biederman, Faraone, Keenan, Knee, & Tsuang, 1990). Many studies of twins have also shown that a strong genetic influence exists in the disorder (Faraone & Biederman, 1998).

There are also suspected environmental causes of ADHD. Jensen (2001) pointed out that trauma to the fetus may result in an injury or abnormal brain development that can lead to ADHD. This trauma can include: exposure to alcohol and/or cigarettes, exposure to high levels of lead, complications during pregnancy and birth (such as toxemia), and brain injury from disease or physical trauma. In Lindsey's case, because she was adopted and few details of her mother's pregnancy are available, it is impossible to know whether she experienced any of these insults.

There are also a small number of individuals who appear to acquire ADHD after birth through brain injury (LD Online, 2006). According to Lindsey's parents and medical reports, this was not the cause of Lindsey's ADHD. Other than ear infections, Lindsey has had a healthy childhood. She has not experienced any significant illnesses or physical injuries.

How Has Lindsey's Behavioural Disorder Affected Her Development?

Cognitive Development

Lindsey's cognitive abilities were not a concern when she was a young child. She seemed to be a bright, inquisitive child and her parents were really more focused on her behaviour problems and her delays in speech. It was not until she entered school that there were questions about her ability to learn. Even then, her disruptive behaviours captured the attention of her teachers much more than her ability to complete academic tasks. It was not until grade three that a psycho-educational assessment revealed that she has significant language-based learning difficulties. Several comprehensive assessments have been conducted since the initial diagnosis (see *Excerpts from Lindsey's Psycho-Educational Assessment* on page 132) and they have all confirmed that Lindsey has a severe, pervasive language-based learning disability (i.e., receptive, expressive, reasoning, written, social-pragmatic, memory) that has an impact on all aspects of her functioning, especially academic performance. The psychologist who assessed Lindsey over the past several years has been unable to assign a Full Scale I.Q. score because of the wide variability in Lindsey's performance on the *WISC-IV*.

What We Know...

ADHD and Learning Disabilities

According to the National Institute of Mental Health (2006), there are a number of other disorders that may occur with ADHD. These include learning disabilities, Tourette syndrome, oppositional defiant disorder, conduct disorder, anxiety and depression, and bipolar disorder. Barkley (1998) estimated that the prevalence of ADHD among children with LD ranges from 10 to 25 percent. More recently, this estimate was supported by Schnoes, Reid, Wagner, & Marder (2006) who examined data from a nationally representative study of students receiving special education in the United States. It should be noted, however, that despite the co-occurrence of ADHD and learning disabilities, numerous studies have confirmed that the two are independent conditions (Doyle, Faraone, DuPre, & Biederman, 2001). In other words, just because there are high rates of ADHD in children with learning disabilities and high rates of learning disabilities in children with ADHD, it does not mean that they are both symptoms of the same disorder. Each condition requires a separate and distinct clinical diagnosis and treatment. While ADHD is primarily marked by symptoms of inattention, impulsivity, and hyperactivity, learning disabilities are primarily characterized as discrepancies between academic performance and intellectual ability.

Lindsey – Age 12: Wood and Clay Sculpture.

Speech and Language Development

Lindsey's parents acted quickly when as a toddler she failed to reach expected language milestones. Speech-language therapy has been a part of Lindsey's life since then. While she does receive some therapy through the school system, Lindsey's mother commented that the 20 minutes a month offered by the school is of little value considering Lindsey's needs. Fortunately, Lindsey's parents are able to provide her with several hours of private therapy every week. Recently, the speech language pathologist summarized Lindsey's current status and outlined recommended classroom-based adaptations:

Lindsey is a delightful child who continues to demonstrate language impairments. These impairments impact significantly on her learning, literacy development, and academic performance. We are recommending that speech-language treatment continue with a focus on the following areas: listening comprehension and recall, auditory-verbal learning, oral and written discourse formulation, written spelling and editing, sight word recognition and word attack, conversational and social-pragmatic skills, and articulation of "l" (blends) and "th." Adaptations needed in the classroom include:

- *ensure that you have Lindsey's attention before giving important instructions*
- *provide oral directions in small steps, pausing between steps to allow extra processing time*
- *pair verbal commands with visuals (e.g., gestures, diagrams, written instructions on the blackboard)*
- *verify that important instructions and directions are understood (e.g., ask Lindsey to rephrase and review important information)*
- *provide word retrieval cues (e.g., first sound, word association) instead of saying words for Lindsey when she is struggling*
- *teach vocabulary from the curriculum deliberately and explicitly, and*
- *teach memory strategies explicitly and often*

What We Know...

ADHD and Speech-Language Difficulties

It is relatively common for children with ADHD to also experience problems understanding and expressing language. In fact, disorders of grammar, semantics, and pragmatics overlap significantly with childhood psychiatric disorders (Toppelberg & Shapiro, 2000). Furthermore, Cantwell (1999) reported that as many as 50 percent of individuals with ADHD have communication disorders. While the link between these two disorders is not fully understood, it may be that speech and language difficulties lead to attentional problems in some particular way or that they are both due to some common underlying factor, such as some type of central nervous system dysfunction.

Social and Emotional Development

Lindsey's social/emotional development has undoubtedly been affected by her difficulties with behaviour, learning, and communication. As her mother commented, Lindsey's tantrum-like behaviour began at the same time she was having problems with language acquisition. Then her behaviour became even more disruptive when she entered school where learning and communication were obvious problems. Ongoing difficulties within each of these domains are a source of great frustration for Lindsey. According to her parents, she has always been a child who wants to be socially involved and not being successful in this part of her life is very taxing on her emotionally. While she has an excellent relationship with family members who understand her disabilities, she has not always been a popular girl at school. It is easy to see why inattention (e.g., being easily distracted and not paying attention) and impulsivity (e.g., careless actions, blurting things out, and interrupting others) could lead to social rejection by peers. However, these rejections have not stopped Lindsey from seeking friendships. Her mother reported that she has more friends now that she has entered a provincial demonstration school for learning disabilities where her peer group is made up of students who also have ADHD and/or learning disabilities.

Lindsey – Age 12.

> Best friend
>
> To describe to me what you mean to me, A friend will just not do, Cause I have never had a friend I've loved as much as you By fate you come into my life to play a special part, And now it seems that you have got a place here in my heart. If I could only find a way to make my wish come true, I'd wish at times when you were sad I could be there with you. Cause I would do my very best to chase away your fears, And hold you Cradle in my arms and kiss away your tears And this is just a sample of how much you mean to me, But till they find a better word "Best Friends" we'll have to be.

From The Psychologist's Notebook...

It is important to realize that ADHD affects all parts of a child's life, not just school. Usually, children make many friendships outside of school, especially when they are taking part in extracurricular activities. This is not always the case for children with exceptionalities. Lindsey has been involved in many extracurricular activities; however, most of these experiences have been cut short due to her

behaviour. She has been enrolled in dance classes, a soccer program, skating lessons, and skiing lessons. Her instructors have commented on her inability to pay attention and her tendency to be easily distracted. Her father told me about an instance where she basically brought a soccer game to a stop when she was distracted by a butterfly. She also has had difficulty following instructions when they were directed at the group as a whole. Fortunately, Lindsey's parents now understand her needs and they have the financial ability to provide her with one-on-one or small group instruction. She currently takes horseback riding lessons where there are only four other students in the class. The instructor is aware of Lindsey's needs and talks to her before class about the technique they are going to be practising that day. The instructor also knows that Lindsey has difficulty discerning between left and right so besides using the words during class, she also points to the desired direction and lifts the hand that should be used for a particular manoeuvre. Lindsey also takes private art lessons from an experienced artist and art teacher. Lindsey has never exhibited any behavioural problems in these classes despite the fact that each class is two hours in length. In fact, the instructor has commented on Lindsey's high level of intensity and focus. It is interesting to note that Lindsey has a great passion for art and is quite talented in this area.

What is School Like for Lindsey?

According to Lindsey's mother, school has been a source of constant frustration for her child ever since kindergarten. Lindsey was enrolled in a bilingual junior and senior kindergarten. Her JK teacher reported that "Lindsey needs to listen and follow rules better." By the middle of SK, Lindsey's behavioural problems were causing significant disruptions in the classroom and her teacher was unable to manage the situation. Lindsey's parents decided to remove her from the school and they followed up on the principal's suggestion that a psycho-educational assessment should be conducted. The assessment was completed in June and Lindsey's parents followed the psychologist's recommendation to move Lindsey to a school where she would not have to attend a bilingual program. Unfortunately, her behaviour problems did not decrease upon enrolment in grade one at the new school. Another assessment at that time lead to the diagnosis of ADHD and a prescription of Ritalin. Lindsey's mother describes how school progressed from there:

> *The grade one teacher noted dramatic improvements once the medication was started. However, Lindsey continued to struggle academically. In hindsight, there were a lot of warning signs that these struggles were due to a learning disability.*
>
> *In grade two, the teacher seemed to have a lot of concerns but she did not recommend an IEP. The only academic support that Lindsey received that year was inclusion in a "Keys to Literacy" group that was comprised of about six students.*

By this time, Lindsey was doing over an hour of homework each night. It was a battle for us, usually with some screaming, weeping, and lots of frustration. Lindsey hated reading and would hide under her bed or throw books, even if I was going to read to her.

Grade three was the worst year for all of us. It was the year that Lindsey's stormy behaviour reached its peak. It was also the year that Lindsey talked about wishing to be dead which was very upsetting for us. Her teacher was really gunning for good results in the grade three testing and it seemed obvious to us that Lindsey represented a big failure. The teacher was not prepared to deal with Lindsey's learning difficulties and interpreted everything that was going on as behaviour problems. A good example of this was when Lindsey was caught stuffing her homework notes in the mesh fence in the schoolyard. Rather than seeing this as Lindsey's way of coping (since she was clearly unable to do the homework), the teacher saw it only as defiant behaviour. It was obvious that there was no empathy for Lindsey. The teacher actually told me that Lindsey did not have any learning problems and was just pulling the wool over everyone's eyes. To me, this was a perfect example of a teacher not understanding learning disabilities. I do admit, however, that it must have been very difficult to have Lindsey in a large class where there was a lot of material to plough through, especially when the majority of the class was capable of keeping up with the fast pace.

It was also during her grade three year that Lindsey began picking at her skin and making it bleed. This was frustrating for us because of all the different problems she was having that year. The school brought in a behavioural specialist to address the picking and they began to count the number of times she was picking in an hour. In my mind, the picking was clearly anxiety-driven as she would pick at her earlobe and make it bleed or pick at her fingers rather than address what her needs were and why she was so anxious. They told me that the purpose of counting the times she picked was to determine a baseline for a behaviour modification program. However, that program was never implemented. By the end of the school year, we were offered a spot for her in an LD class at another school.

We were asked to go see this new school and meet the teacher. I remember that day so clearly. We met with the teacher and saw her classroom. She had ten students, all of whom appeared very happy and friendly. The teacher told us that they all had ADHD and learning disabilities. We spoke for close to an hour and I remember coming out of the school, getting into my car, and crying. I was so happy and overwhelmed that Lindsey would be going into that classroom. I knew right away that it was the right class for her. The program was individualized and while all the kids had ADHD, the room was reasonably quiet, but not suppressed. The teacher was friendly but clearly the boss and in control. The kids obviously loved her and respected her.

Lindsey entered the new school for her grade four year even though the school was a 45 minute bus ride from our house. We quickly decided to move closer to the school when this long bus ride caused us concern. At this time there was no long-acting medication for Lindsey and the extended school day was making it difficult for us to get her medication right without having it wear off too soon or giving her too much. This is just an example of the kind of things parents of children with ADHD have to do to help their children.

In her grade four year, Lindsey finally made some friends. The kids were amazingly accepting of each other and her, even though she was a year younger than the other students. Lindsey stayed with the same teacher in that LD class for grades five and six. During that time, she never had a suspension, although she did have to go to the principal's office a few times for being rough on the playground. Her teacher also noticed that because of her impulsivity she would follow behind other kids and not use her own good judgement. I really see her making some good gains with this over the past year. We do worry though about high school and her tendency not to think before she acts. In terms of her overall behaviour, she now has fewer stormy periods and seems much more cooperative in general. The worst behaviour we ever saw was during the grade three year and things got progressively better after that.

Grade seven has brought Lindsey to another new school as the LD class she attended for grades four to six does not extend into grade seven. We decided to have her assessed for entry into a provincial demonstration school for learning disabilities and we were successful in having her placed there. We didn't feel she was ready for the regular classroom quite yet as she has just begun to develop some needed self-confidence within the small class setting. This new school offers a one-year program that not only addresses academic difficulties but also deals with ADHD behaviours.

From The Psychologist's Notebook...

It is clear that Lindsey's parents are not only strong advocates for her in terms of her educational needs but they also take part in her education, especially in terms of homework. While this can be quite frustrating for parents of a child like Lindsey, it is critical to her progress (both in the learning domain and in the behavioural domain) that she experience consistent messages at home and at school. Lindsey's father spoke to me about how they try very hard to provide Lindsey with a calm home environment. When she was in the early grades, it was necessary for her mother or father to sit with her throughout the whole homework period. They could not even get up from the table where she was working without distracting her.

These homework sessions were often quite emotional for both parents and child. Eventually, Lindsey's parents cleared a space in their family room, furnished it with a table and two chairs, and designated it her "work area." Now the television is always off during homework time and an effort is made to provide a very quiet atmosphere where Lindsey can focus on the tasks at hand. Her parents make them-selves available when needed, whether it is to provide motivation or to actually help with the homework tasks. They have learned to use strategies that are consistent with those used at school. With time, these homework periods have become less emotional and more productive. This is in part due to the willingness of Lindsey's parents to learn how they can best assist their child with the challenges she faces.

What Educational Approach is Best for Lindsey?

Placement Options

As mentioned earlier, Lindsey currently attends a provincial demonstration school for learning disabilities. Demonstration schools were established in Ontario to provide special education programs for students who need intensive help with academics and social skills. The goal is to have these students return to regular programs operated by local school boards within one or two years. Before entering the demonstration school, Lindsey's school experiences included time in both an inclusive classroom (kindergarten to grade three) and a self-contained classroom for students with learn-ing disabilities (grades four to six). The inclusive classroom was a not a good fit for Lindsey at the time because her behaviour and learning difficulties were just being assessed, her teachers were unable to meet her needs, and she had not learned any effective coping strategies. She was very disruptive in the classroom and her frustra-tions with learning were causing her great anxiety. Her move to the self-contained classroom was definitely a positive one. By this time, her specific needs were estab-lished and an experienced teacher of students with ADHD and learning disabilities took responsibility for her education. This teacher was able to provide an environ-ment where Lindsey felt accepted and ready to learn strategies that would assist her with both academics and social skills. According to Lindsey's mother:

> *Lindsey made her most significant gains so far in the LD classroom (grades four to six). The teacher emphasized organization and routines. She had a very strict requirement that students must constantly refer to a planner where they would record the work that needed to be done and the deadlines that had to be met. This planner had to be signed by her on a regular basis. She also demanded that students keep their notes organized. This teacher just seemed to know how to implement good strategies for teaching students like Lindsey.*

What We Know...

Assisting Students with ADHD in the Classroom

Classroom strategies that may assist the student with ADHD:

- Develop a model of behaviour management which is compatible with both the home and classroom environment, and which is clear in its expectations. Students with ADHD can be trained to monitor their own behaviours.

- Recognize the issue of compliance versus comprehension and be able to discriminate between these two types of behaviour.

- Set predictable intervals of "no-work" periods which the child may earn as a reward for effort. This helps increase attention span and impulse control through a gradual training process.

- Plan for success. Break tasks into manageable sequential steps the student can handle with frequent breaks which can be seen as rewards for appropriate behaviour. Provide a sequential checklist for longer assignments and projects.

- Help the student get started with individual tasks.

- Supplement oral instructions with visual reinforcement, such that the student can frequently check that s/he is following instructions (e.g., write the assignment on the board, photocopy printed instructions, use of an overhead, or have matched instructions on tape).

- Encourage the use of a homework journal so that the student has a record of assignments completed and those yet to be done.

- If the student has difficulty taking notes, supply a copy of the notes from another student or from the teacher's notes.

- Frequent breaks can be created by allowing the student with ADHD to compare responses with a strong student on assignments that require drill and practice such as math questions.

- Modify tests if necessary (e.g., provide extra time or divide the test into two parts to be completed at different times during the day).

- Modify assignments, if necessary (e.g., assign fewer questions in math, use contracts for longer assignments).

- Consider where the student with ADHD is seated. A quiet seat in close proximity to the teacher may assist the student in staying on task.

- Offer a screened corner to your class as an earned privilege during scheduled times rather than a punishment. This avoids segregating the child who may need the screened corner to reduce distractions.

- Try a variety of teaching strategies including: assigning a peer tutor, class-wide peer tutoring, development of class meetings, and life-space interviewing.

- Give responsibilities that can be successfully carried out to help the student feel needed and worthwhile.

- Work with the student to develop social interaction skills (e.g., interpreting non-verbal communication cues). Modeling and role playing along with reinforcement of appropriate skills tend to be most effective.

- When transitions or unusual events are to occur, try to prepare the child for what is to come by explaining the situation and describing appropriate behaviour in advance.

- Offer the student training in study skills, time management, organizational skills, communication skills and test taking.

Source: Excerpted from BC Ministry of Education, www.bced.gov.bc.ca/specialed/awareness/24.htm.

It was during this time, in grades four to six, that homework became a less frustrating experience for our family. Lindsey's teacher seemed to have a better understanding of the purpose of homework and how it can be quite a challenge for a student with ADHD. She did things at her end that made it much easier for Lindsey. Homework time at our house became shorter and much more productive. We appreciated this because it made our evenings with Lindsey more enjoyable and not all about her learning difficulties.

What We Know...

Homework Tips for Teachers of Students with ADHD

Just as homework was an extremely frustrating activity for Lindsey, it is often a source of stress for many students with ADHD. Rief (2005; pp. 219-222) outlined valuable tips for teachers when considering homework assignments for these students:

- Be responsive to parents reporting great frustration surrounding homework. Be willing to make adjustments so that students with ADHD spend a reasonable, but not excessive, amount of time doing their homework.
- Realize that students with ADHD who receive medication during the school day (to help them focus and stay on-task) often do not receive medication in the evening. Students with ADHD are in class during their optimal production times, yet will not manage to complete their assigned work. It is an unreasonable expectation that parents will be able to get their child to produce at home what you were not able to get them to produce all day at school.
- When assigning homework, realize how critical it is for students with ADHD to participate in extracurricular activities. They need every opportunity to develop areas of strength. Also, remember that these students may work with other professionals or participate in academic training programs outside of school hours.

- Many teachers have a practice of sending home unfinished class work. Avoid doing so with ADHD students. Instead, provide the necessary modifications and supports so that in-school work is in-school work, and homework is homework.
- Remember that homework should be a time for reviewing and practicing what students have been taught in class. Don't give assignments involving new information that parents are expected to teach their children.
- Homework should not be "busy work." Make the homework relevant and purposeful so that time isn't spent on obscure assignments that are not helping to reinforce skills or concepts learned in class.
- Never add on homework as a punishment or consequence for misbehaviour at school.
- Make sure you have explained the homework and clarified any questions.
- Supervise students with ADHD before they walk out the door at the end of the day. Make sure they have materials, books, and recorded assignments in their backpacks.
- Assign a student buddy (or two) to your students with ADHD. They should have one or two classmates, who are willing to answer questions, to call on if necessary in the evenings.
- One of the most important things you can do to help all students (and their parents) keep on top of homework, tests, and long-term projects is to require the use of an assignment calendar. With some students, require that parents initial the assignment calendar daily. This is a good way for you to communicate with parents. You may write a few comments or notes to the parents on the assignment sheet and vice versa.
- Modify the homework for students with special needs. Ask yourself: What is the goal? What do I want the students to learn from the assignment? Can they get the concepts without having to do all the writing? Can they practise the skills in an easier, more motivating format? Can they do fewer practise questions and still accomplish what I want them to?
- Communicate with other teachers who have your students in their classes. Students may be assigned a number of tests, large projects, and reading assignments at the same time from a number of different teachers. Be sensitive to this by staggering due dates.
- Always collect homework and give feedback. It is very frustrating for students to spend a lot of time on assignments that the teacher never bothers to collect.
- Some teachers find it helpful to have their students graph their own homework completion and return rates. Improved performance can result in some kind of reinforcement.
- Provide incentives for turning in homework.

Lindsey stayed in this special segregated class for three years, the maximum time allowed. As stated earlier, rather than place her back in the regular classroom for grade seven, her parents, with the support of her teacher and her psychologist, sought a placement in the demonstration school. They all agreed that Lindsey was not ready to re-enter the inclusive classroom. An extensive application process was completed and Lindsey was accepted to the school.

Lindsey's mother wrote the following letter to the principal of the new school so he would better understand his new student:

> *Lindsey's strength is her artistic ability. She is confident in her skill as an artist and has begun to formulate a life goal of becoming a visual artist. Not surprisingly, her preferred mode of learning is visual. She finds pictures and visual clues very helpful for following instructions, telling a story and remembering details. However, even with these types of aids, she must deal every day with the frustration of learning something like addition tables, spelling words, or new vocabulary, only to find the next day that her memory has failed her. She has spent numerous years learning the same material over and over (e.g., the grade four math book has been done three times over three different school years) but each time it seems like it's the first time she has ever experienced the tasks being presented to her. Reading remains a great source of frustration and continues to be the area we have the most struggle with at home. This includes even a dislike of being read to. It is also a source of embarrassment in situations outside of school when she is with a group of her peers and reading is a part of the activity that they are participating in (e.g., camp, church).*

Lindsey – Age 10.

We think that it is important that Lindsey be able to read at a level sufficient to allow her to move forward in other areas that require reading. We would like her to be able to read, or to use technology to read, material that interests her as well as material that is required to complete her other academic courses. In the past, she has enjoyed novel studies where the teacher has read the chapters out loud and a large part of the course work involved discussing ideas in class. She would completely have missed out on this experience if she had been left to read the novel by herself.

In terms of basic numeracy, she has already made some gains in this area. We have noted that she is making an effort to tell time and she has begun to understand fractions of the hour. She still does not have the concept of money. She can do some math by rote (e.g., adding with carrying) but we are not sure she fully understands the concepts behind what she is doing.

Lindsey's ADHD affects all parts of life. Her behaviour both at home and at school can affect how others view her and how she views herself. She can be impulsive, blurting out comments before she thinks about what she is saying and interrupting others. She has trouble paying attention and staying focused on tasks. She can become quite anxious at times. Occasionally, she will act silly and out of control and then has trouble calming herself down. She has difficulty with social interactions because of these behaviours.

We have some goals for Lindsey. In the short-term, we would like her to become more adventurous and daring in her learning, to not be so anxious about what she does not know or what she thinks she cannot do. We hope she learns not to shy away from a book on art or horses simply because she is afraid she cannot read it. In the long-term, we hope that Lindsey will be able to graduate from high school and perhaps pursue further training in art if that is her choice. We would like her to be able to understand and manage her behaviour so that she can have meaningful, positive interactions with others.

There were some immediate changes to Lindsey's overall education plan when she entered the demonstration school. While she has had an IEP since grade four, she now also has a "Behaviour Plan" (see *Lindsey's Behaviour Plan* on pages 135–136) that specifically addresses her behavioural needs. This plan describes her current behavioural areas of concern, states the goals that are expected to be met in the short-term, and outlines how school staff will intervene to help Lindsey meet these goals. The plan is an ever evolving one. Lindsey's teacher has already provided the following report, one month into Lindsey's first semester at the school:

Lindsey is a positive participant in her new school. She participates in all group activities and is always willing to try her best. Learning the rules and routines of the school has been the focus during the first half of this semester. As noted in her goal areas, Lindsey often follows the lead of her peers to maintain her focus within the program. This has been a successful strategy for her to this point; however, as the program progresses she will be required to maintain more independent programming.

Lindsey has had a difficult time identifying behaviours that have a negative impact on her interactions with others; therefore, internalizing strategies and using these independently are a challenge for her. She has difficulty discussing situations with staff at the point of performance and will often avoid these interactions.

Assisting Lindsey to identify personal strengths and areas to concentrate change will be the focus of the remainder of the semester. Lindsey will continue to be encouraged to take risks to develop new behaviour patterns and to move forward in a positive direction.

Based on this report, Lindsey's current Behaviour Plan identifies three areas of concern (see pages 135–136). They are impulse control, social interactions, and knowledge of how her ADHD and learning disabilities affect her life. These concerns, the new program goals, and the planned interventions are clearly outlined in the updated plan and they are familiar to all staff members who work with Lindsey.

From The Psychologist's Notebook...

It is clear from Lindsey's story that, so far, she has done much better when not in an inclusive classroom. This does not mean that she should never return to such an environment, it simply means that both Lindsey and her teachers will have to be precisely aware of her specific conditions and fully understand the strategies they both will employ to overcome her behavioural and learning difficulties. Lindsey's grade three teacher certainly did not have the knowledge or the skills to help her. Lindsey was probably engaging in exactly the same school work avoidance behaviours displayed by non-ADHD students. And, this is often a teacher's dilemma: how do they know if a child is behaving inappropriately on purpose (non-ADHD) or if the child's behaviour is something they do not have full control over (ADHD)? It is in these instances that a teacher's awareness and knowledge can prevent problematic situations from becoming worse. Even if the teacher does not know what to do to correct the child's behaviour, their understanding of the condition can keep them from exacerbating the problem.

Evaluation of Progress

Just as Lindsey's academic progress is measured by the attainment of learning objectives, her behavioural progress is currently measured by the attainment of behavioural goals that are outlined in her Behaviour Plan. Input from her parents, her teachers, and the clinicians who work with her allow decisions to be made regarding future behaviour goals. These individuals use their observational skills to note any increases in desirable behaviours and any decreases in undesirable behaviours. In addition to these observational reports, Lindsey is directly involved in evaluating her behaviour. She is asked for her own assessment on how she is doing and she is actively involved in evaluating past behaviour and formulating new behavioural goals that will help her both inside and outside the classroom. This is a critical component of behaviour management because it will enhance Lindsey's self-regulatory abilities as we described in Chapter 4. This will, in turn, make the overarching process of classroom management easier for her teachers.

Something To Think About…

You find yourself teaching in a regular classroom where two of the students have been diagnosed with ADHD. Both are easily distracted and their hyperactivity is often disruptive to classroom activities. In an attempt to help these students improve their behaviour, you implement behaviour therapy techniques, including positive reinforcement, time-outs, and response costs. One of the students responds particularly well. Her parents notice the difference in her behaviour and begin using the same techniques more consistently at home. The other student shows signs of responding positively to your approach but seems to need "re-training" after weekends and holidays. You talk with his parents regarding your concerns. They indicate that while they would like to help their child, nothing seems to work. Their attempts at discipline all seem to end in yelling and tears. What advice do you give these parents to help them change the situation at home?

How is Lindsey Different from Other Students who have Behavioural Disorders?

Behavioural disorders cover a wide spectrum of behaviours, including attention disorders, conduct disorders, and anxiety disorders. Within each of these groupings, there are obviously many unique combinations of behavioural characteristics. For example, even within ADHD there are three identified subtypes (i.e., Combined Type, Predominantly Inattentive Type, Predominantly Hyperactive/Impulsive Type) and within these three subtypes two individuals with exactly the same diagnosis can have very different behavioural profiles. As well, someone who has been diagnosed with one type of behavioural disorder may exhibit some of the behaviours common in other disorders. This is true in Lindsey's case as she experiences anxiety in addition to her attention disorder. To complicate matters even further, individuals can be considered exceptional in other areas thus making their situations even more unique. For example, Lindsey has *both* a learning disability and speech difficulties, and while she has never been identified as gifted, she exhibits remarkable artistic talents. However, despite all of these possible differences, students with behavioural disorders do have one thing in common. Like Lindsey, they are all having difficulty meeting societal expectations for acceptable behaviour, especially within the education system. This is apparent in the following two cases, each of which outlines a different behavioural disorder:

- *Conduct Disorder.* Ryan is a troubled thirteen-year-old who comes from a **dysfunctional environment**. His mother has had an ongoing problem with drug addiction and Ryan does not even remember his father who left when he was just a toddler. Ryan's chaotic home environment has most likely contributed to his conduct disorder. His school file is full of negative reports regarding his behaviour. He is outspoken, rude, and has no respect for others or their possessions. He has been caught stealing, lying, and using alcohol. Ryan is not well-liked by his peers and, in fact, he is considered a bully. Most students in his school are afraid of him. The school principal and Ryan's teachers are finding it more and more difficult to manage him. He is usually very disruptive in the classroom and is beginning to show signs of physical aggressiveness. School suspensions have not been effective. Ryan actually seems to enjoy confrontation and, according to him, not having to go to school is a bonus. Ryan is slipping further and further behind in his schoolwork. The school team, along with his social worker, is considering that he be placed temporarily in a special educational facility where he can receive behavioural management and support.

dysfunctional environment
Surroundings that contain or perpetuate a persistent series of high stress incidents that threaten one's sense of psychological security.

What We Know...

Conduct Disorder

According to Hannell (2006), conduct disorder is marked by "...a major disturbance in the student's behaviour and relationship with others" (p. 65). Students with this disorder often exhibit socially inappropriate behaviour, destructive behaviour, disrespect for authority, physical aggressiveness or cruelty, and deceitful and dishonest behaviour. Drug and alcohol abuse is common. Hannell reported that research studies support both a genetic and environmental basis for conduct disorder. In terms of environmental factors, family dysfunction may disturb normal emotional and social development.

cognitive behavioural therapy
An action-oriented form of therapy used to alter distorted attitudes and resulting problem behaviours by identifying and replacing negative and/or inaccurate thoughts with more positive ones.

● *Anxiety Disorder.* Ellen has always been an anxious, shy child. Even though she is now thirteen years old, she still does not like to be away from her parents. She has rarely been away from home overnight and she worries constantly when one of her parents has to be away for any length of time. Unable to cope with the anxiety of taking the school bus, her mother drives her to school and picks her up each day. If her mother is just a few minutes late, Ellen panics and fears something horrible has happened to her. Panic attacks are all too familiar to Ellen. She has them frequently, whether it is because she is faced with a new experience (e.g., start of a new school year) or because of social anxiety (e.g., having to give a presentation in front of the class). Unfortunately, there are very few situations that do not cause anxiety for Ellen. The only time she can begin to relax is when she is at home with her parents. Even then she is constantly worrying about what "dangers" she has to face in the coming hours and/or days: a dentist's appointment, a math test, a neighbourhood picnic. There is nothing in Ellen's life that does not provoke feelings of fear. Ellen's anxiety disorder has become so debilitating that her success in school is being seriously jeopardized. In the early grades, her behaviour was explained away by shyness but now the behaviour is obviously affecting her more severely. She loves to learn and has an above average I.Q. She completes her homework assignments with ease. However, the demands placed upon her in the classroom are just too overwhelming and she is failing to complete assigned classroom tasks successfully. A psychologist has recently become involved. Ellen has just begun **cognitive behavioural therapy** and her parents and her teachers are learning how to best support her.

What We Know...

Anxiety Disorders

According to Hannell (2006), all anxiety conditions are marked by feelings of fearfulness and apprehension. They may involve physical symptoms, obsessive-compulsive symptoms, and/or specific phobias. Anxiety disorders often run in families and a child's tendency to be anxious can be exacerbated by inappropriate treatment by adults. Anxious children are often perfectionists. Treatment for anxiety disorders includes cognitive behaviour therapy, building up resilience to anxiety triggers, and relaxation training. Teachers can assist students with anxiety disorders by:

- providing a predictable, secure and nurturing environment
- recognizing situations that the student finds fearful and not forcing participation
- providing relaxed opportunities for the student to be near their anxiety triggers, and
- providing reassurance and remaining calm during a student's anxiety attack

Closing Lindsey's File

Lindsey has faced many hurdles in her school life and, to her credit, she still remains motivated and positive about learning. While academic tasks can be very frustrating for her, she now finds herself in a supportive school environment where she is becoming more aware of how her behavioural disorder and her learning disability affect her on a daily basis. She is acquiring more and more strategies that allow her to have both successful social interactions and positive learning experiences. For now, it appears that the provincial demonstration school for learning disabilities is the desired placement for Lindsey. She is making friends and she is motivated to try her best at academic tasks. Lindsey described the changes in her school life as follows:

> *When I was first in school, like in grade two, I felt completely ignored. The teacher thought I couldn't do anything so she never called on me in class. I just sat there all day. I only had one friend in that whole school. Then I went to a special class in a different school where all the kids in the class were like me. Our teacher was really nice and seemed to understand us. She could get inside our brain and know why we acted the way we did. Now in my new school I am in an even smaller class with more kids like me. There are only six of us. It feels like a family. We don't have to feel embarrassed. You can put up your hand and the teacher will listen to what you have to say. I will be sad when I have to leave this school and go back to a regular school. Maybe I will just hide in a box and not go.*

Lindsey's mother echoed her daughter's obvious satisfaction with her new school. She and her husband have noticed the following positive changes in Lindsey's behaviour:

> *Lindsey definitely has more confidence now. While she always had confidence in her artistic abilities, she is now talking about her abilities in other areas like in science and sports. She seems to actually enjoy learning and sharing what she has learned with us. Most surprising is the fact that she is writing poetry and taking an interest in books. Just the other night I found her in her bed using a thesaurus to write a poem. Not that long ago she was doing anything she could to avoid having to read. It is remarkable to see this change in her. She really seems to enjoy school and has made very good friends. In fact, she loves to chat on MSN with her schoolmates when she is at home. Of course, she still has difficulties with learning and behaviour so we are trying to extend her time at the demonstration school for one more year. She is the youngest student there now and I think one more year will help her mature even more and prepare her for her high school years. We know it will be difficult for her to go back to the regular classroom where her differences will again be more apparent.*

Lindsey – Age 10.

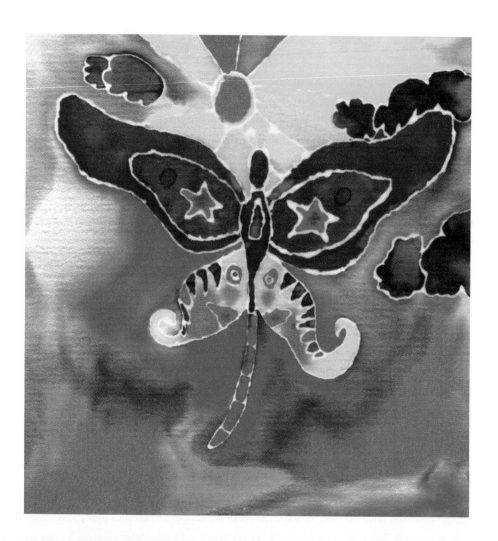

From The Psychologist's Notebook...

It will be important that Lindsey's parents and her teachers continue to pro-
vide her with significant support as she enters her teen years. Recent research by
Hinshaw, Owens, Nilofar, and Fargeon (2006) indicates that adolescent girls with
ADHD are at a greater risk than their peers for substance abuse, eating disorders,
depression, and anxiety disorders. Given that individuals with ADHD are usually
impulsive, it is not hard to see why they may quickly give in to peer pressure and
try things like drugs and alcohol. They may also be motivated to partake in inap-
propriate activities just because they so desperately want to "fit in" and be accepted
by their peers. Paradoxically, it is this very problem — lack of social relationships
— that can also lead to feelings of depression and anxiety.

Lindsey is certainly at risk as she enters her teen years. She is a sensitive and somewhat anxious child who desires to be an active member of her peer group. Yet, she is impulsive and has difficulty interacting with others. The adolescent years will clearly be a challenging time for her. Not only will she continue to experience difficulties with academics, but peer relationships and self-esteem issues will become even more of a challenge. Her parents can support her through this period by staying aware of her friendships and her activities, by encouraging open communication within the home, and by developing mutually agreed upon rules and consequences for behaviour.

Suppose you are a secondary teacher who has a student like Lindsey in your class. How might you help support this student as he or she tries to "fit in" with his or her classmates? What actions can you take inside the classroom to influence how your students interact outside the classroom?

Something To Think About...

Learning More About Students with Behavioural Disorders

Academic Journals

Behavioural Disorders

Journal of Attention Disorders

Journal of Emotional and Behavioural Disorders

Journal of the American Academy of Child and Adolescent Psychiatry

Books

Brown, M. (2002). *The ADHD companion: Attention deficit hyperactivity disorder.* East Moline, IL: LinguiSystems, Inc.

Rief, S. (2005). *How to reach and teach children with ADD/ADHD: Practical techniques, strategies, and interventions* (2nd edition). San Francisco: Jossey-Bass.

Web Links

- *ADHD Canada*

  www.adhdcanada.com/index.html

  ADHD Canada designed this Web site with the intent of supporting individuals with ADHD, and their parents, caregivers, and teachers, by increasing understanding.

- *Attention Deficit Hyperactivity Disorder (National Institute of Mental Health)*

  www.nimh.nih.gov/publicat/adhd.cfm

  On this Web site, the NIMH presents a detailed booklet on ADHD that describes symptoms, causes, and treatments, and provides information on coping.

- *Canadian Attention Deficit Hyperactivity Disorder Resource Alliance*

  www.caddra.ca

  The CADDRA site presents the voice of doctors who support patients who suffer from ADHD.

- *Childhood Anxiety Disorders*

  www.cfpc.ca/cfp/2004/Mar/vol50-mar-cme-1.asp

  The Canadian Family Physician site presents a peer-reviewed article by Katharina Manassis which addresses childhood anxiety disorders and approaches to interventions.

- *Children and Adults with Attention-Deficit/Hyperactivity Disorder*

  www.chadd.org

  The CHADD organization provides education, advocacy and support for individuals with ADHD. Their Web site provides access to the National Resource Center on ADHD (NRC), a clearinghouse for the latest evidence-based information on ADHD.

- *Conduct Disorder in Children and Adolescents*
  www.kidsmentalhealth.ca/get_help/conduct.php
  Children's Mental Health Ontario presents an overview of conduct disorder and provides links to other resources on the topic.

- *Council for Children with Behavioural Disorders*
  www.ccbd.net
  The CCBD, a division of the Council for Exceptional Children, is committed to promoting and facilitating the education and general welfare of children and youth with emotional or behavioural disorders. On their Web site, there are position papers on relevant issues and a useful "Links" section.

Please visit the Online Learning Centre for *Special Education in Canada* at **www.mcgrawhill.ca/olc/edmunds** for additional learning and study resources.

Taking It Into Your Classroom...

Including Students who have Behavioural Disorders

When a student who has a behavioural disorder is first placed in my classroom, I will:

- review what I know about behavioural disorders and locate resource materials
- read the student's file
- consult with the student's previous teachers
- consult with the student's parents
- meet with the school-based team to discuss the student's current school year

Other: _____

_____

When I suspect a student in my classroom has a behavioural disorder, I will:

- collect information about the student through classroom interventions
- observe and document behaviours across various times and settings
- consult with other school personnel who are familiar with the student
- consult with the student's parents
- meet with the school-based team to present the information I have collected

Other: _____

_____

Key points to remember in my daily interactions with a student who has a behavioural disorder:

- the student may have difficulty remembering and following directions
- the student may have difficulty staying focused
- the student may have trouble staying still
- the student may talk excessively and interrupt others
- the student may act before thinking
- there is a neurobiological reason for the student's behaviour and performance

Other: _____

_____

Key points regarding programming for a student who has a behavioural disorder:

- behavioural expectations should be clearly stated and reinforced
- the student should be allowed many opportunities to show his or her strengths
- the student should have options as to where and how they work
- the student may need modified assignments with reduced written work
- the student may need help with organizational and study skills
- the student may need more time to complete assigned work

Other: _____

_____

Key points regarding evaluation of the progress made by a student who has a behavioural disorder:

- evaluation should be based on stated behaviour goals
- evaluation should include input from those who spend time with the student
- evaluation should include observation of the student in different settings
- evaluation should identify any increase in desirable behaviours
- evaluation should identify any reduction in undesired behaviours
- evaluation should include the student's own assessment of their behaviour

Other: _____

_____

CHAPTER 7

Students who are Gifted and Talented

Name: Geoffrey MacInnis
Current Age: 9
School: Jackson Elementary Public School for the Gifted
Grade: 4

Geoffrey is a student who excels in language-related tasks. He is a precocious writer and an avid reader of complex material, particularly books that address scientific and philosophical issues. While he may be described by some as the stereotypical gifted student, his story is real and highlights many of the challenges faced by students with exceptional abilities. Geoffrey's experiences in the regular classroom as well as in a classroom for the gifted provide a consideration of how teachers, not classrooms, make a difference in students' lives. While some may deem the classroom for the gifted the ideal situation, it is important to note that best practices are teacher-driven and can occur in any setting.

Assessment Results

Age at Time of Assessment: 7 years

Informal Assessment

Geoffrey began reading at age three and writing prolifically at age five. He continues to produce numerous literary works, all of which can be considered far more advanced than the writings of his peers. His precocity is not limited to writing; he has advanced skills in science, reading, music, art, and some areas of mathematics.

Strengths:
- highly creative
- musical
- able to focus intently on tasks of interest
- excellent memory
- inquisitive
- keen sense of humour
- sensitive of social issues
- wide range of abilities

Challenges:
- picking up on social cues
- leaving a task of interest to participate in scheduled classroom activities
- managing stress and anxiety

Formal Assessment

WISC-III (Full-Scale I.Q.)	139
Raven Standard Progressive Matrices	>99 percentile

Note: An IEP was never developed for Geoffrey. Now that he attends a public school for the gifted, school personnel feel that an IEP is not necessary.

Teachers' Notes

November 2003   Mr. Campbell (Grade 2)

Geoffrey is a talkative child who finds it difficult to follow instructions. He seems immature and asks endless questions that interrupt most classroom activities. Geoffrey's parents have spoken to me several times about the possibility that Geoffrey is bored. They think he is gifted and they try to prove this by bringing me samples of his writing. The writing is impressive but probably a joint effort by Geoffrey and his parents. He has never produced similar work at school.

I do not think that Geoffrey is bored. However, he does have a problem focusing on what we are doing in class. Yesterday, we were doing a mathematics activity and half way through Geoffrey stood up and went to look at a book in our library corner. When I asked what he was doing, he said he wanted to finish reading the book on wolves that I had started to read to the class earlier that day. I insisted that he return to his seat immediately and with that he began to cry. I think that Geoffrey has been allowed to do whatever he wants at home. He cannot seem to handle being told what to do. I think that the best approach is to insist that he focus on his work and refrain from speaking out or leaving his seat during assigned work periods.

November 2005   Ms. Levesque (Grade 4)

Geoffrey is a caring and compassionate boy who excels in many areas, particularly writing. Last week, I asked the students to work in groups of two on a particular project, and no one would work with Steven because he often exhibits many negative behaviours. Geoffrey spoke in confidence with me, acknowledging Steven's behaviour and the fact that other students would not work with him. Geoffrey told me that he would be willing to have Steven as his partner. It was a very kind gesture and I told him that.

Geoffrey still has some behaviour issues that we are working on. I insist that he "follow the rules" and conform to the behavioural expectations of the classroom. For example, recently Geoffrey left the classroom without asking permission. When I realized that he was missing, I went to find him. He was walking in the hall upon his return from the washroom. I told him in a calm and sincere manner that I was concerned about his absence and the fact that he had not asked for permission to leave the room. Geoffrey asked me why this was important. I carefully explained why it was necessary to notify me of his needs and his whereabouts. I really feel it is necessary to give him an explanation that respects his sensitive nature and his desire to know and understand the reasoning behind a classroom rule.

Mother's Comments Regarding Geoffrey's Emotional Development

When he was very young, around age two, I can remember certain parts of stories really upsetting him, as well as loud noises, or Halloween costumes. Even now he is very sensitive to scary videos, television shows and cartoons. At age five, I remember him having to leave the room when a character fell in the river. It is the same with books, but it became more apparent when he moved out of physics and into fiction at about age seven. He becomes faint and nauseated at any description of graphic violence or injury, even in children's literature.

He is overly sensitive to anger or scolding as well. He has trouble sleeping if he is anxious. He is also very sensitive to the distress of others. He worries or gets upset if George [his brother] is angry at him, or if George is worried or has been scolded. He worries about things that might scare or bother George. I have never heard him tell George that he is stupid and he never presents himself as superior in any way. In fact, when George does a good drawing or writes something, Geoffrey is genuinely enthusiastic and encouraging.

Of course there is a great sensitivity to beauty as well. He likes walks in nature, likes to look at and do paintings, enjoys watching the beauty in sports, and his love of language is remarkable. There is also a strange, sometimes amazing sensitivity around certain holidays. He gets very excited before the event and a great deal of effort is put into writing stories that relate to the holidays, planning activities and making decorations. For our wedding anniversary, he concocted an elaborate ceremony called the "glorification of the heart" complete with handmade confetti, a confetti dispenser and a ritual circle dance during which he improvised a song and orchestrated what we would do. At Christmas, he planned the Christmas morning festivities himself, sneaking his violin into his room and leading a musical procession with his brother into our bedroom to wake us up. Along with this celebration of the holidays, comes a great sadness when the day is actually over.

Tears are probably more frequent than in other kids, not tantrums or manipulative tears but genuine sadness at things that probably do not upset most other children. He frequently says that he just cannot help it.

Aggressive and competitive boy talk seems completely foreign to him. His sensitivity is noticed by other kids — his literary, artistic, musical, non-athletic and non-aggressive demeanour as well as his physical appearance (small in stature) result in him being called names by many of the boys at school. He also has trouble with any kind of physically rough play. He worries that someone may get hurt.

I think Geoffrey's sensitivity presents more of a challenge at school than at home. There is no doubt that it is more difficult to manage at school although this year his teachers are doing a great job, mostly by just acknowledging it and giving him time to decompress if he needs to and not making a big deal of it. This is unlike a previous school year that was devastating for Geoffrey. Since he picks up non-verbal signals very well, he knew that his teacher did not like him and thought he was weird. He internalized this and spent the next two years talking about how he was weird. None of this negative self-talk is evident this year. His current teachers seem to strike a good balance between praise and criticism.

Samples of Geoffrey's Writing
(presented exactly as Geoffrey wrote them in terms of spelling and grammar)

Age 5 (written in response to his readings about the universe)

George solved one large irreversibility problem with a theory called Mary Poppins Time. It was a theory of quantum gravity. It istated that whenever tesserarts have their antiantiquarks joined, they merge to form a giant antitesserart (we will discuss antitesserarts in the part The particles of time) called a Megairreversitron, which makes time irreversible. And this is happening everywhere in the universe. Why did he call it Mary Poppins Time? Because he was imaginative. He knew that it was made of sugar, those Megairreversitrons. And he imagined that they were irreversible medicine to cure the universe's reversibility disease. And if you make the sentence "Sugar helping medicine" into a bigger sentence, you end up with "Just a spoon full of sugar helps the medicine go down.

Age 6 (written in response to a newspaper article on Afghanistan)

More terrorists, new government, more attacks, holiday worries, etc. I accept the idea to put a new government in afghanastan, but there is one problem. That means the religious government may become self-supporting terrorists, along with Bin Laden and his gang, which must undergo the same supporting change to keep terrorizing. But if this happens, the war will become longer and more difficult, even with a new government. I wonder if we can send in better peacekeeping forces in Afghanastan and U.S.A? This also may affect holiday season since the terrorists might not even want worldwide Christmas, which is a totally different religion. Who knows? They may even kill Santa. People could maybe use grinch protection.

Age 7 (written in response to his readings about philosophy and religion)

QUESTIONIS PHILOSOPHICUS

How can we tell right from wrong? Can religions tell us right from wrong?

If you believe in that certain religion, it can for you. But they do not necessarily vet the basic human moral code. Then what is, or tells us, the basic moral code? I can only tell you the moral code that i believe should be the basic human moral code. I believe humans should not kill, steal, or hate and they should help, care for, and love each other.

What am I?

What's so philosophical about this question? It's really more about the meaning of life, and how you think about yourself, and how other people think about you and how they blend.

Geoffrey MacInnis

So what is the meaning of life?

Now that's a tricky one. It's one of the great philosophica questions of all time. Let's start with animals. Okay. Some people in the old days thought that pigs only lived so that they could be sacrificed. But I think that one isn't true. Wait a minute. I have an idea. Let's skip a bit. What's your idea? Maybe people live so that they can make their unique contribution to the world. What about people who don't? O, Quit simplifying around! Everyone makes contributions to the world.

Age 9 (written in response to a school assignment about the changing seasons)

SPRING

I
Spring opens its eyes
A lonely white crocus
A snowdrop for Blodeuwedd
Across her sea
A young green goddess
Crowned in blue sky
Beats a rhythm on the snowclouds.

He, the crocus
Has known the meltwater
Below the snow.
Where she, spring, is, we know
There soon shall be more green
And soon shall be more snow.
There I sing of spring
Beneath an invisible pussywillow.

II
The pussywillow has flowered
Beneath the willow
Where wanders pussy
In a home of spring
It's something near 10°,
An early, pussywillow-mattressed
Spring?
She, young green spring,
Adorns the wood with pussywillow
buds,
Detesting the stubborn snow-clouds,
Preferring the young pussy.

(Mated animals
Have their young.)
Showers fall, hope of bright colours
(Blue and then green).
There is an egg, lying in a green
Grass patch, painted.
A single rabbit hops through
The last patch of dirty snow.
The ducks wander from the pond
(Gloria!)
A perfect Easter overcast
Ducks in the rain.

He, the crocus, in summer-like bloom,
She, spring, calls for the spring-cleaning
broom,
Little pussywillow, their young.

III
Now summer starts,
Or so the old folks say,
For now 'tis May Day.
The forest now is art,
April showers have what they must.
The pussywillow now crowns
The willow in her season,
The flower-crowned, May queen,
Spring goddess of the green.

Geoffrey MacInnis

Why is Geoffrey Considered to be Gifted?

Definition of Giftedness

While there is no one universally agreed upon definition of "giftedness," Feldhausen and Jarwan (2000) point out that "technically a 'gifted' child is one who scores high on an intelligence test or an academic achievement test…giftedness is basically genetic endowment that paves the way to the development of specific abilities, aptitudes, and talents" (p. 273–274). While Geoffrey's giftedness was certainly identified by his parents before he even entered school, it was indeed the administration of an intelligence test (a formal assessment tool) by a school psychologist that lead to Geoffrey's "gifted" designation within the school system. School personnel also considered Geoffrey's behaviour both at home and in school (part of an informal assessment) to determine his areas of strengths and needs.

What We Know…

Definition of Giftedness

The following definition of giftedness, first constructed by Former U.S. Commissioner of Education Sidney Marland in his report to Congress in the early 1970s, continues to be one of the most widely used both in Canada and the United States:

> Gifted and talented children are those identified by professionally qualified persons who by virtue of outstanding abilities are capable of high performance. These are children who require differentiated educational programs and/or services beyond those normally provided by the regular school program in order to realize their contribution to self and society. Children capable of high performance include those with demonstrated achievement and/or potential ability in any of the following areas, singly or in combination: general intellectual ability; specific academic aptitude; creative or productive thinking; leadership ability; and, visual and performing arts.

Source: Marland (1972), p.10.

Across the provinces and territories of Canada, educators use a variety of definitions or descriptions of giftedness. Consider the following descriptions that are used in British Columbia and in Newfoundland and Labrador:

British Columbia Ministry of Education

A student is considered gifted when she/he possesses demonstrated or potential abilities that give evidence of exceptionally high capability with respect to intellect, creativity, or the skills associated with specific disciplines. Students who are gifted often demonstrate outstanding abilities in more than one area. They may demonstrate extraordinary intensity of focus in their particular areas of talent or interest. However, they may also have accompanying disabilities and should not be expected to have strengths in all areas of intellectual functioning.

Newfoundland and Labrador Department of Education

Students with an exceptional ability demonstrate or have the potential to demonstrate: an exceptional ability to learn well above average cognitive ability (specific abilities or overall general cognitive ability); and/or high levels of task commitment (perseverance, endurance, determination, dedication and practice); and/or exceptional characteristics, talents and aptitudes in non-academic areas (e.g., exceptional creativity, leadership, psychomotor ability or other talents which society may consider important). Exceptional ability may co-exist with a learning disability. Therefore the child/youth may not be performing at a level of academic achievement commensurate with indicators of high ability. Exceptional ability is dynamic, thus it may not be readily observable. It may only become evident when the child is exposed to an experience that evokes his/her potential.

How are these descriptions of giftedness similar? How are they different? How might these descriptions affect the services provided to students who are gifted and talented? If you live in a region of Canada other than the two mentioned here, determine how giftedness is defined in your province or territory.

Sources: www.bced.gov.bc.ca/specialed/ppandg/planning_4.htm and www.ed.gov.nl.ca/edu/dept/exceptionalities.htm#Exceptional%20Ability.

Other Definitions of Giftedness

There are a variety of terms that are used to describe extremely capable children such as *gifted*, *prodigy*, *precocious*, *expert*, *creative*, and *genius*. Many of these terms are used interchangeably because they are accepted common or colloquial descriptors in everyday vernacular. However, when using the categorical model of special education (see Chapter 2), it is always best to be as specific as possible when identifying a child's abilities so that the most effective programs can be implemented. In the case of giftedness, there are precise and discrete definitions of each of the above terms. Gardner (2000) and others (Edmunds & Noel, 2003; Robinson, 2000) have provided an excellent differentiation of their criteria and use.

What We Know...

Definition of Terms

Gifted	"at promise" in any domain recognized as involving intelligence
Prodigy	extreme promise in any domain recognized as involving intelligence; distinguished by performance that is not only promising but also impressive by adult standards
Precocious	earlier-than-expected, domain-specific development that ranges from mildly advanced to astonishing; distinguished by performance within an age group and not measured against adult standards
Expert	has achieved a high level of competence in a domain, irrespective of whether the approach is novel or experimental
Creative	regularly solves problems or fashions products in a domain in a way that is initially seen as novel but that ultimately is recognized as appropriate
Genius	produces work that is expertly executed and creative, and has a profound effect on the domain

Geoffrey is correctly referred to in the educational system as a child who is gifted. However, to be more accurate, Geoffrey is a precocious child in that he is a child writer who has demonstrated a prolific literary output (more than 8,000 pages of writing by age nine) and a complex and sophisticated writing style. This means that Geoffrey's achievements/creations: (1) are not measured against adult standards, (2) are precocious when measured against age-relative standards, and (3) focus on the specific tasks of writing.

Assessing Giftedness

Geoffrey was assessed shortly after entering school on the urging of his parents. They were very concerned about his unhappiness with school and his apparent boredom with classroom activities. The assessment process began with the collection of information through an informal assessment. Members of the school-based team were interested in Geoffrey's behaviour both at home and in school. Teachers and support staff were asked to comment on how Geoffrey responded to assigned tasks, how he interacted with other children as well as adults, and how he performed in different subject areas. Examples of his in-class work were examined. As well, Geoffrey's parents were interviewed to determine their perspective on his strengths and challenges. They were asked to share examples of the work he completed at home, particularly his writing. The information collected through this informal assessment was compiled and summarized (see *Assessment Results* on page 170). It served as the impetus for the formal assessment conducted by a school psychologist. In other words, those involved in Geoffrey's education provided enough evidence to warrant further examination of his intellectual abilities.

Geoffrey's formal assessment required him to complete two standardized tests of cognitive ability. *The Wechsler Intelligence Scale for Children-III* (WISC-III) is a test of general intelligence that is administered individually. It is organized into subtests allowing for an examination of verbal and nonverbal abilities. The test results include three I.Q. scores: a Verbal I.Q., a Performance I.Q., and a Full-Scale I.Q. In Geoffrey's case, he performed very well across all subtests and was assigned a Full-Scale I.Q. of 139 putting him in the superior range of general intelligence. The second test that Geoffrey completed during his formal assessment was the *Raven's Progressive Matrices* (RPM) which is a nonverbal test of figural reasoning. The RPM includes 60 items, each one containing a figure with a missing piece. Below each figure are alternative pieces to complete the figure, only one of which is correct. On this test, Geoffrey scored better than 99 percent of the same-aged children in the test norming group, confirming Geoffrey's superior ability to understand visual-perceptual relations and to reason by analogy independent of language and formal schooling.

The assessment process that lead to Geoffrey's designation of "gifted" was typical of how precocious Canadian students are identified within the education system. Their outstanding academic performance in a particular domain combined with evidence of superior ability on an I.Q. test allows for a relatively easy decision regarding the necessity of special education programming.

The identification of students who are gifted, but not necessarily precocious, may be somewhat more challenging as these students may not have such visible "gifts." For example, they may simply have above average abilities across a range of academic subjects or they may be highly creative and these creative abilities may not be apparent in certain classrooms or situations. While there is no uniform identification process across the provinces and territories to identify children who are gifted and talented, the assessment and identification process should be comprehensive and the "gifted" designation should only rarely be based on one test alone, regardless if it is an I.Q. test. The preferred process is to use a battery of assessment tools in conjunction with an I.Q. test. This allows for the full scope of the child's abilities and needs to be examined so that proper educational programming can be provided. Some of the complementary assessment tools that are often used to reach these conclusions are teacher/parent nominations, samples of the student's work, tests of creativity, academic achievement tests, tests of **visual-spatial abilities**, and assessments of social adjustment.

It should be noted that, to date, an IEP has never been developed for Geoffrey. While he is recognized as being gifted, it has been left to his teachers to design appropriate curricula for him. As you read about Geoffrey and his school experiences, consider how a well-developed IEP may have made a difference in his school life.

visual-spatial abilities
The ability to efficiently visualize and manipulate objects in space.

> Across Canada, there is considerable variation in the services provided for students who are gifted. You may find yourself teaching in a school board that offers limited services for these students. Some educators feel that students who are gifted will excel despite this situation. Do you think it is even necessary to identify students who are gifted as exceptional? Do they really have special needs?

Something To Think About...

What Factors Contributed to Geoffrey's Giftedness?

Typically, the first question one asks after coming to grips with the reality of Geoffrey's abilities is, "What are the conditions under which he has developed and flourished?"

Heredity

Geoffrey's parents are highly successful individuals. Both his mother and father have graduate degrees that have lead them to academic careers in areas that require high degrees of creativity. His mother recalls her frustration with school while growing up. She felt that her elementary and secondary schooling failed to provide her with the challenging type of education she needed.

Researchers have long been studying the genetics of intelligence. There is considerable evidence that differences in intelligence are significantly influenced by genetic factors (Plomin, 1997). This does not mean that intelligence is due entirely to genetics, but rather that both genetic and environmental influences play a role in determining general cognitive ability. As Simonton (2005) stated, giftedness has an "…elementary connection with biological inheritance" and the environment "…plays an important role in the realization of that genetic potential" (p. 278). Given the genetic basis of giftedness, it is not surprising that Geoffrey's parents have two children who are high functioning and exceptionally creative.

Environment

Contrary to the early beginnings of many children who are gifted, Geoffrey has thrived without early exposure/practice/repetition and without any urging or pushing from his parents. Even when his verbal precocity and writing talents became obvious, his parents purposefully did not tell him to write but they did pay attention to his work and they gently celebrated what he wrote by reading his stories with him and asking questions about characters, pictures, and storylines. This parental approach has continued; Geoffrey's parents just let his prolific writing happen and, within reason, they try to not get in his way. Like any parents, they are enthused by his desire to write and the enjoyment he derives from writing, but they "are not about to let his writing become him." They provide the raw materials such as a multitude of markers and pencils and lots of blank paper. Geoffrey's room is dominated by two pieces of furniture: his adult-sized single bed and an equally large rectangular work table with legs cut down to suit the height of his child's chair.

There is no doubt that Geoffrey's **conceptual information** comes mostly from what he reads. His parents encourage him to read whatever he is interested in and while his room and home are filled with numerous books, there are no more books available to him than in other homes where parents value reading and make use of libraries. The major difference is that Geoffrey reads many more books designed for adults. He does this of his own volition with no expectations from his parents. Most importantly, perhaps, his parents do not allow his descriptions or discussions about what he reads to be superficial. They ask him meaningful questions and seek detailed explanations. As his mother explains, "it is like taking the lid off a bottle of pop" because Geoffrey has the wherewithal and verbal precocity to handle their inquiries and they often get more than they bargain for. However, these exchanges are not only of the serious and/or purposeful variety. There are made-up words and silly repetitive expressions, and moments of fun and hilarity for both Geoffrey and his parents. Thus, there do not appear to be any boundaries confining Geoffrey's explorations.

conceptual information
Mental representations of the knowledge one has about concrete (dog) or abstract (love) objects.

Parents play an important role in fostering children's interest in language.

Perhaps the most striking characteristic of Geoffrey's environment is that his time for writing, within the family's schedule, is never questioned. Like clockwork, he goes to his desk and writes, completely unsupervised, and only rarely is he interrupted. This is not to say that the family's life revolves around Geoffrey's writing time, rather, it is to point out that his parents recognize his need for this time and deliberately make the necessary accommodations. Lastly, there is no doubt that this highly favourable element of his environment is as much due to Geoffrey's abilities and motivation as it is due to the "space" his parents give him. The point being that one should not conclude that all children would/could thrive as prolific writers under such favourable conditions.

Geoffrey's environment is similar to that of many gifted children; it contains a richness of resources and stimulation. However, except for not allowing Geoffrey to get away with frivolous or illogical descriptions/discussions, his world is without the parental demands for performance frequently presented elsewhere. The conduct of his parents is akin to Fowler's (1981) description of a responsive and incidental parenting style.

From The Psychologist's Notebook...

Intelligence, or intellectual ability, is best defined as goal-directed adaptive behaviours (Newman & Just, 2005) that are predominated by problem-solving abilities (Wenke, Frensch, & Funke, 2005). There is a growing consensus amongst intelligence researchers and theorists that heredity appears to set the limits of one's intellectual ability and that our environment determines how much of that limit is realized (Greenough, 2000). A good way of thinking about the heredity/ environment interactive contribution to the development of intellectual ability is to think of one's intelligence as a bookcase with moveable shelves. Our genetic code (heredity) determines roughly how big the bookcase is in terms of width, height and depth and the number of shelves it contains. The intellectual stimulation that our environment provides then determines how many different types and sizes of books, magazines, pictures, videos, etc., that fill up the various shelves. And, to a limited degree, this overall intellectual influence (called learning) can slightly expand the bookcase or parts of it. Therefore, the more stimulating one's environment, the more complete one's bookcase becomes; the less stimulating one's environment, the less full the bookcase will be. This does not mean, however, that an enriched environ-ment can make a child more intelligent than the capacity provided by their genetic code. There is obviously a limit to the number of books an individual's bookcase can hold. It also does not mean that those who may have a larger than normal bookcase do not have to do anything to fill it up. Without proper environmental stimulation, those bookcases will be barren. In summary, children's environments (especially school) should be as rich as possible so that they can attain their maxi-mum intellectual potential.

How Has Geoffrey's Giftedness Affected His Development?

Cognitive Development

Geoffrey was read to from a very early age, a task that his parents enjoyed and per-formed quite often. He spoke a few words and phrases at around eight or nine months of age and then, for reasons unknown, he stopped speaking altogether. However, this does not mean that he did not utter a word, it just meant that he did not "speak" in the usual sense. Instead, he transformed the lyrics of songs that he knew into new versions about his family's activities and/or daily occurrences and sang them joyfully and repeatedly. Similarly, he would recite, verbatim, complete paragraphs from books that his parents had read to him. His parents realized that he was of speaking age and of speaking capacity, so they were considerably frustrated that he did not speak. When he did talk, a late bloomer at two and a half years of age, it was in complete sentences: (to his Mom) "I hear a sound out there but I don't know what it is," and (to his Dad) "I'm not really sure that George understands the difference between a car and a truck." Since that time, the spoken word has literally and figuratively poured out of Geoffrey and, for the most part, his has been purposeful speaking, almost without the meaningless, but playful, banter in which most children engage.

So, what is it that allows Geoffrey to easily and rapidly absorb and digest what he wants to learn and then to recreate it and express it through complex and sophisticated writing? He has extraordinary abilities in a variety of language-related areas, including verbal precocity, reading comprehension, and written expression. Underlying these abilities are a series of cognitive and motivational characteristics that are typically found in gifted children (see *What We Know* on page 184).

When writing, Geoffrey often demonstrates extraordinary immediate and long-term memory as well as highly developed meta-cognitive abilities for organizing and monitoring his work and for supervising his thinking. These traits are repeatedly evidenced during discussions of his stories, some created years ago, some just underway. Perhaps the best insights into Geoffrey's precocity can be gleaned from his very highly developed and sophisticated language abilities, as these have an overarching influence on all that he does. Externally, this is evident in his spoken and written expressiveness while internal manifestations are evident in his logical arguments, book conceptualizations, and the overall planning and execution of writing tasks. His language/thinking has all the adolescent qualities of what Vygotsky (1978a) termed "the logicalization of thought" in which words become the principal tool for abstraction and generalization. As Noel and Edmunds (2007) pointed out, Geoffrey uses writing to examine, in a very intentional manner, his own thinking.

Perhaps Geoffrey's most striking characteristic is a dogged persistence to satisfy his need to fully understand what he encounters and to then express what he knows through writing. He possesses a crystal clear determination of purpose and this is accompanied by his passionate affection for the nuances of language. Therefore, writing fulfills not only his need to express his knowledge, but it also acts as a further consolidation process for what he knows. While his parents provide the milieu, Geoffrey facilitates his own learning trajectory by asking for books on particular topics, making trips to the library for even more books, and engaging whomever he can in spirited conversations about his current topic of interest. His intense involvement and commitment to his domain and his obvious desire to direct this involvement and commitment are the hallmark indicators of precocious children (Goldsmith, 2000). But, Geoffrey's modus operandi is more than motivation, it is what Snow (1994) referred to as an intrinsic "unrest" of the organism, a conscious tendency to act, and a conscious striving by which mental processes or behaviours tend to develop into something else.

Geoffrey also has an extensive attention span and he regularly works for hours without pause. His work sessions are not flurries of activity; they are more the mark of a quiet purposefulness guided only by his penchant for knowing, and then writing and drawing from his knowledge. He shows an intense interest in the details of what he writes and draws but these are only measured against his own understandings. Toward the end of his first year of writing, he did ask a variety of individuals if they liked his writing/stories, but those questions seemed more a courtesy than attempts to establish a measure of his work.

What We Know...

Characteristics of Students who are Gifted

Learning Characteristics
- has unusually advanced vocabulary for age or grade level
- possesses a storehouse of information about a variety of topics
- has quick mastery and recall of factual information
- has rapid insight into cause-effect relationships; wants to know what makes things (or people) "tick"
- has a ready grasp of underlying principles and can quickly make valid generalizations about events, people, or things
- is a keen and alert observer; usually "sees more" or "gets more" out of a story, film, and so forth, than others
- reads a great deal on his or her own; usually prefers adult-level books
- tries to understand complicated material by separating it into its respective parts
- reasons things out for him or herself; sees logical and common sense answers

Motivational Characteristics
- becomes absorbed and truly involved in certain topics or problems; is persistent in seeking task completion
- is easily bored with routine tasks
- needs little external motivation to follow through in work that initially excites him or her
- strives toward perfection; is self-critical
- prefers to work independently; requires little direction from the teacher

- is interested in many "adult" problems such as religion and politics — more than usual for age level

- often is self-assertive; stubborn in his or her beliefs

- likes to organize and bring structure to things, people, and situations

- is quite concerned with right and wrong

Creativity Characteristics

- displays a great deal of curiosity about many things; is constantly asking questions about anything and everything

- generates a large number of ideas on problems; often offers unusual, clever responses

- is uninhibited in expressions of opinion; is sometimes radical and spirited in disagreement

- is a high risk taker; is adventurous and speculates

- displays a good deal of intellectual playfulness; fantasizes; imagines; is often concerned with adapting, improving and modifying institutions, objects, and systems

- displays a keen sense of humour and sees humour in situations that may not appear to be humorous to others

- is unusually aware of his or her impulses and is more open to the irrational in him or herself (freer expression of feminine interest for boys, greater than usual amount of independence for girls); shows emotional sensitivity

- is sensitive to beauty

- is nonconforming

- criticizes constructively; is unwilling to accept authoritarian pronouncements without critical examination

Leadership Characteristics

- carries responsibility well

- is self-confident with children his or her own age, as well as adults

- seems to be well liked by his classmates

- is cooperative with teacher and classmates

- can express him or herself well, has good verbal facility, and is usually well-understood

- adapts readily to new situations

- seems to enjoy being around other people; generally directs the activity in which he or she is involved

- participates in most social activities connected with the school

- excels in athletic activities; is well coordinated and enjoys all sorts of athletic games

Source: Coleman & Cross (2001) pp. 35–36, as adapted from Renzulli, Hartman, & Callahan (1971).

Social and Emotional Development

When Geoffrey was six years of age, he was fascinated by the study of the universe, particularly the concept of black holes. It led him to read about Steven Hawking. He was drawn to this famous scientist and, on his own accord, sent Professor Hawking a Valentine's card. It was with great delight Geoffrey received a letter from the scientist, thanking him for the first Valentine he had received in many years.

During his grade four year, Valentine's Day proved to be more difficult for Geoffrey. As usual, he looked forward to this special occasion, an opportunity to let those you care for know that they are loved. Geoffrey sent cards to all the girls and boys in his class. Not surprisingly, at this preadolescent stage of development, this was not an act that the other boys appreciated. Unfortunately, this type of behaviour on Geoffrey's part, a genuine caring for others and an outward expression of sensitivity, has already resulted in some school children calling him names.

What We Know...

Sensitivity and Students who are Gifted

The literature on giftedness is abundant with references to *sensitivity*. While the definition of giftedness is continually debated and modified due to the heterogeneity of the population, the existence of a sensitivity factor amongst individuals who are gifted appears to be widely accepted. Many compilations of giftedness characteristics, particularly those focusing on the affective domain, include phrases such as *morally sensitive, emotionally sensitive, personally sensitive,* and/or *extremely compassionate*. The dictionary defines "sensitive" as being "highly responsive or susceptible" and when referring to a sensitive person, being "delicately aware of the attitudes and feelings of others" and "being easily hurt emotionally" (Merriam-Webster's Collegiate Dictionary, 2003). Shavinina (1999) included vulnerability, fragility, empathy, and social responsiveness as manifestations of this sensitivity.

One would think that the sensitivity exhibited by many intellectually gifted children would result in an ability to fit in and get along with others. After all, if an individual is sensitive to others' feelings and perceptions, it would be reasonable to predict that he or she is quite socially competent. Porath (2000) suggested that this may not be the case. She proposed that when a child who is gifted exhibits a depth of understanding in the social domain, this may not transfer to actual behaviours. In her research, Porath found that a child who is gifted may experience great sensitivity towards others yet receive low teacher ratings of social acceptance and behavioural conduct. Mendaglio (1995) presented a similar scenario when proposing a definition of sensitivity based on the gifted literature and his counselling experience. His definition, which includes the use of four psychological concepts — self-awareness, perspective taking, emotional experience, and empathy — also emphasizes that "a person's experience of sensitivity is not necessarily expressed directly to others" (p. 171). This lack of expression obviously has implications for the social acceptance of the gifted individual.

Acceptance, however, does not always occur with overt expression of this sensitivity. As Silverman (1993) pointed out, we live in a culture that does not view heightened emotionality in a very positive way. Outward demonstrations of sensitivity are discouraged, especially in males. Perhaps the most critical period for this negative feedback is during pre-adolescence and adolescence. Being gifted already sets children of this age apart from their peers, but adding the sensitivity factor can make life very difficult, or even unbearable. If these children are to benefit from their emotional intensity, which according to Dabrowski (1972) may be the very trait that acts as the catalyst for their intellectual/ creative achievements, then researchers, educators, and parents should perhaps focus more attention on their "sensitivities" rather than on their "talents." As Dabrowski and Piechowski (1977) emphasized, there is a strong positive correlation between intellectual level and emotional intensity.

Source: Edmunds & Edmunds (2005) p. 69.

What is School Like for Geoffrey?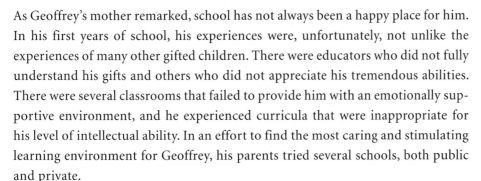

As Geoffrey's mother remarked, school has not always been a happy place for him. In his first years of school, his experiences were, unfortunately, not unlike the experiences of many other gifted children. There were educators who did not fully understand his gifts and others who did not appreciate his tremendous abilities. There were several classrooms that failed to provide him with an emotionally supportive environment, and he experienced curricula that were inappropriate for his level of intellectual ability. In an effort to find the most caring and stimulating learning environment for Geoffrey, his parents tried several schools, both public and private.

Geoffrey started primary school at the appropriate age but he was very bored. In grade two, his teacher ignored his abilities and thought he was a problem child (see

Teachers' Notes on page 171). School was particularly difficult for Geoffrey during this time. The curricula were not appropriate and the atmosphere was less than ideal. When asked by Mr. Campbell to write about what he would do if he were in charge of the school, Geoffrey started by saying "I don't know," and then proceeded to repeatedly write the word "don't" for a page and a half. This was his direct response to previously being told by Mr. Campbell to copy lines and letters as punishment. Geoffrey ended the piece by emphasizing again that he did not know what he would do if he were in charge of the school. He advised the reader to "Ask the future or my angel." In a postscript he stated:

> *I know one thing I would love everyone, be friendly to everyone, not allow punishments bigger than time-outs. I would be nicer to the kids. And I would let them have daily desserts, have a stand for free sweets, only payed for in play money. I would teach them all subjects required.*

This was undoubtedly an expression of both his own reaction to his school environment and his understanding of the needs of himself and his peers.

His current school situation is the most successful to date. He attends a public school for children who are gifted. The setting is intellectually stimulating, but perhaps most critical to Geoffrey's well being, his teachers provide a very emotionally supportive environment (see *Teachers' Notes* on page 171). When he first entered the school, his new teachers took the time to learn about Geoffrey both through observation and meetings with his parents and his psychologist. Their efforts to recognize their new student's strengths and weaknesses have resulted in the implementation of teaching strategies that appropriately address Geoffrey's needs.

Despite the positive classroom environment created by Geoffrey's teachers (see *What We Know* on page 189), he still faces the reality of being a nine-year-old boy who is different from many of his schoolmates, even though they too have been identified as gifted. Geoffrey's precocity includes an intellectual level and an emotional intensity that surpasses many of his peers. His pre-adolescent schoolmates are not always tolerant of his abilities and they are especially not always tolerant of his sensitivities. It is undoubtedly difficult for them to understand some of Geoffrey's behaviours. This in turn makes school a continuing challenge for Geoffrey, a challenge that must be recognized and addressed if he is to reach his potential.

What We Know...

Characteristics of Successful Teachers of Students who are Gifted

Personal Characteristics

- understands, accepts, respects, trusts, and likes self: has outstanding ego strength

- is sensitive to others, less concerned with self; supports, respects, trusts others

- is above average intellectually; exhibits an intellectual style of conceptualizing, generalizing, creating, initiating, relating, organizing, imagining

- is flexible, open to new ideas

- has intellectual interests, literary and cultural

- desires to learn, increase knowledge; has high achievement needs

- is enthusiastic

- is intuitive, perceptive

- is committed to excellence

- feels responsible for own behaviour and consequences

Personal-Professional Predispositions

- to guide, rather than coerce or pressure

- to be democratic, rather than autocratic

- to focus on process, as well as product

- to be innovative and experimental, rather than conforming

- to use problem-solving procedures, rather than jumping to unfounded conclusions

- to seek involvement of others in discovery, rather than giving out answers

Teaching Behaviours

- develops a flexible, individualized program

- creates a warm, safe, and permissive atmosphere

- provides feedback

- uses varied strategies

- respects personal self-images and enhances positive ones; respects personal values

- respects creativity and imagination
- stimulates higher order mental processes
- respects individuality and personal integrity

Source: Lindsey (1980), as cited in Coleman & Cross (2001), p. 321.

Something To Think About...

Geoffrey's feelings about school improved when he was transferred to a public school for gifted students. His new teachers took the time to learn about Geoffrey and they appear to have the knowledge and expertise required to provide him with positive learning experiences. Do you think these positive learning experiences could take place in a regular classroom? How would you feel about having a student like Geoffrey in your classroom? What concerns would you have?

What Educational Approach is Best for Geoffrey?

The Curricula

Geoffrey did not thrive in the early elementary grades when he was exposed to the regular curricula. He was obviously unhappy with his school experience. This unhappiness spilled over into all parts of his life, including a fixation on the fact that he was different or "weird." As VanTassel-Baska (1997) stated, "...an organized curriculum is a key ingredient in the complex blending of circumstances so central to the transformation of a gifted learner's initial capacity for intellectual activity into a mature competence for academic and professional accomplishment" (p. 126).

Geoffrey's parents were given two choices to consider after Geoffrey's assessment by the school psychologist. Should they allow their son to stay with his same-age classmates and experience an **enriched curriculum** or should they consider **grade acceleration**? They decided that an enriched curriculum was the best choice for Geoffrey as they had concerns about putting him at a maturational disadvantage in a classroom of older children. Thinking ahead to the higher grades, they feared that Geoffrey, who is small in stature, highly sensitive, and not athletic, would again have even more intense feelings of being different or "weird."

As a result of his parents' decision, Geoffrey's teachers were required to develop and provide a **differentiated curriculum** for him. As Renzulli and Reis (1997) described, modifications to the curriculum are designed to: "(1) adjust levels of required learning so that all students are challenged, (2) increase the number of in-depth learning

enriched curriculum
A program of study that is expanded beyond its typical depth and scope, usually involving independent study.

grade acceleration
Skipping a grade to participate in appropriate levels of curricula.

differentiated curriculum
A program of study that is altered in content or instructional method to suit the specific needs of a student who has an exceptionality.

experiences, and (3) introduce various types of enrichment into regular curricular experiences" (p. 145). However, as Geoffrey experienced, the success of the development and implementation of differentiated curricula depends very much on the skills and attitudes of the teachers involved. Geoffrey's school experiences did not improve significantly until he experienced an appropriate set of curricula delivered by knowledgeable and supportive teachers. In Geoffrey's case, this occurred when he transferred to his current school, a public school for the gifted.

Despite the fact that Geoffrey is now in a classroom where all the students have been identified as gifted, he still requires a differentiated curriculum due to his significantly superior skills in language and writing. For example, in the fall of his grade four year, his teacher taught a unit on the Medieval Period. She then asked students to write a report on a topic of interest that related to this period in history. Students were directed to either choose a topic from a suggested list, or self-select a topic that interested them. The only requirements were that the students must write a paper on their topic, produce artwork that visually displayed their topic, and present the content of their paper to the class. In a private conversation with Geoffrey, the teacher suggested that he self-select a topic of interest based upon his readings of a number of adult-level books on the Medieval Period. Once he focused in on the question, "Who was King Arthur?", his teacher then encouraged him to compare the ideas of various authors and come to some conclusions of his own. Geoffrey happily immersed himself in this project, reading 10 books before he produced his report on "King Arthur." This paper was divided into two parts: "Arthur of History: Romans, Celts and Saxons" and, "Arthur of Literature: Bards, Historians, and Romancers." For his visual display, Geoffrey presented a sketch of a "typical" Medieval castle. He had noted from his readings that some of the architecture depicted in this "typical" representation was not consistent with the architecture of the period. Therefore, he built a model of what he calculated an actual Medieval castle to look like. He then arranged his visual display so that you could view the "actual" model superimposed on his sketch of the "typical" castle, thus making the differences more obvious. Geoffrey concluded the project by presenting his ideas most succinctly to the teacher and his classmates.

As is evident from the "King Arthur" project, a number of teaching/learning strategies are employed to enhance Geoffrey's education. First, his differentiated curriculum is based on the regular curriculum, yet he is required to explore topics in more depth using higher level thinking skills such as analyzing, synthesizing, and evaluating. He has some control over the direction of his learning in that he self-selects topics that interest him and he is given the opportunity to work independently. As well, his teacher encourages interdisciplinary learning by allowing him to explore different subject areas within a topic of study. For example, while completing the "King Arthur" project, Geoffrey considered information that he gathered from the areas of literature, the visual arts, and architecture. It is apparent then, that through the completion of this one project, Geoffrey's teacher was able to incorporate many excellent learning experiences. These learning experiences are consistent with those highly recommended by researchers within gifted education (Renzulli & Reis, 1997; Sternberg & Grigorenko, 2003; VanTassel-Baska & Brown, 2001).

Other recommended teaching/learning strategies have also been a part of Geoffrey's recent education. He has been encouraged by his parents and his teachers to be creative through brainstorming, problem-solving, and role-playing. He has been encouraged to develop his research skills through exposure to researchers from various fields as well as opportunities to conduct and present his own research. He has been paired with adult mentors, individuals who share the same interests as Geoffrey (i.e., a physics professor and an English professor). He has been given socialization and leadership opportunities through small and large group work within the classroom, as well as through participation in extracurricular activities outside of school (e.g., violin and swimming lessons). All of these learning opportunities have facilitated Geoffrey's development and lead to the change in his feelings about school.

What We Know...

Curriculum for Students who are Gifted Learners

Key beliefs and assumptions that guide the development of curricula in gifted education:

- All learners should be provided curriculum opportunities that allow them to attain optimum levels of learning.

- Gifted learners have different learning needs compared with typical learners. Therefore, curriculum must be adapted or designed to accommodate these needs.

- The needs of gifted learners cut across cognitive, affective, social, and aesthetic areas of curriculum experiences.

- Gifted learners are best served by a confluent approach that allows for both accelerated and enriched learning.

- Curriculum experiences for gifted learners need to be carefully planned, written down, implemented, and evaluated in order to maximize potential effect.

Source: VanTassel-Baska (1997), p. 126.

Geoffrey's parents decided against grade acceleration for their son. How do you feel about moving a child to a higher learning level? What might be the advantages and disadvantages of this approach to educating children who are gifted? Can you suggest some criteria that may be used to help determine whether or not a student is a good candidate for grade acceleration?

Something To Think About...

What We Know...

The School-Wide Enrichment Model

Enrichment of the school curricula can obviously benefit students who are gifted and talented. However, Renzulli and Reis (1997) have demonstrated through their School-Wide Enrichment Model (SEM) that enrichment can enhance the learning experiences of all children. Based upon the notion that instruction must take into account the varying abilities, background interests, experiences, and learning styles of each student, the SEM promotes the formation of a talent pool within the school. The membership of the talent pool is not constant and includes students, who at a given point in time, are excited about a topic and demonstrate the ability and commitment to acquire further knowledge in the topic area. These students then complete the regular curriculum at a faster pace and engage in enrichment activities with clusters of similarly interested students from across several grade levels. Usually, these enrichment clusters are lead by a resource teacher who has experience in gifted education. After the students have participated in these small group sessions which focus on higher-order thinking skills and the creative and productive application of skills to real-world situations, they may take their learning experiences one step further by completing an independent study project.

Evaluation of Progress

Just as the curricula must be modified for the student who is gifted, so must the process of evaluation (see *What We Know* on page 194). For example, Geoffrey's teacher evaluated his knowledge of the Medieval Period by considering what she expected him to learn from her in-class presentation as well as what she expected him to learn by completing the assigned project. Earlier, when developing these activities and the accompanying learning expectations, she took into account both the provincial learning expectations for that unit and Geoffrey's individualized learning objectives. Her subsequent evaluation of Geoffrey's work was then based on her well-thought out expectations. The evaluation did not merely assess whether Geoffrey's work was better or worse than that of his classmates. In fact, Geoffrey's project was far more sophisticated than those of most of his classmates. This alone does not indicate that learning expectations have been met. Evaluation is only effective when it addresses a student's current strengths and needs and when it provides direction for ongoing instruction within the assigned curriculum. It should be noted that there must be a clear understanding that students who are gifted are not equally advanced in all areas. Otherwise, educators run the risk of not making the child's schooling appropriately challenging in the most suitable places.

What We Know...

Assessing the Work of Students who are Gifted and Talented

According to Stephens and Karnes (2001), students who are gifted should be involved in establishing the criteria for evaluation of their work. Ideally, a rubric is constructed so that both the teacher and the student are aware of the components of the assigned work as well as the exemplary characteristics of each component and their mark value.

Stephens and Karnes also stated that the "evaluation of student products should be multidimensional so students can receive helpful and extensive feedback from a wide array of sources" (p. 198). They suggested that while the teacher and the student can assess the student's work according to pre-selected criteria, the audience (e.g., classmates, school personnel, family members, topic experts) can also be asked to provide feedback. Once all of the evaluative data have been considered, the student should then be encouraged to reflect on the entire process and learn from both successes and failures.

How is Geoffrey Different from Other Students who are Gifted?

Geoffrey's set of abilities, or gifts, are unique, as are the gifts of all children. There may be children who score exactly as Geoffrey did on the *WISC* and the *RPM*, but they would likely be very different from him in many ways. In fact, while Geoffrey and these children may display common behaviours in their motivation to learn and how they learn, their superior cognitive abilities may be differentially displayed through a wide range of behaviours, such as academic proficiency, musicality, leadership, artistic ability, athletics, or like Geoffrey, the ability to write. Geoffrey may be gifted, but unlike many other children who are gifted, he is not athletic nor does he take leadership roles at school. It is critical then, to consider each child as being distinct and to refrain from stereotyping those who are highly capable in terms of intellect.

In Geoffrey's case, his gifts are most obvious to those who know him and to those who read his written productions. However, not all children who are gifted are quite so visible. The following are examples of children who are gifted, yet often overlooked:

- *The Gifted Underachiever.* Jean-Paul is a fifteen-year-old high school student who exhibits little interest in learning the grade 10 curricula. His primary interest outside of school is music as he has the ability to pick up any instrument and play it with little instruction. He scored very high on an I.Q. test in elementary school but this has never translated into high academic achievement. Despite little effort on his part, his grades have been consistently average. However, his grades are slipping below average in high school as he has developed very few study skills over the years. He displays no enthusiasm for any subject areas and claims that school is "too boring." He is in constant arguments with his parents regarding "not living up to his potential." On the other hand, he finds great comfort in the fact that he is just like all his friends. This is little solace to his parents who fear that he will lose interest in school and drop out.

What We Know...

Underachieving Children who are Gifted

Underachievement is seen as a discrepancy between assessed potential and actual performance. The discrepancy may be between two standardized measures (e.g., I.Q. and achievement tests), or between a standardized measure and classroom performance (e.g., teacher expectation and performance on daily assignments).

Highly intelligent students who are required to work at the same level and pace as their age-mates, when often they can grasp concepts years ahead, are at great risk of losing interest in school and falling short of their potential. In particular, one problematic area of underachievement is that of gifted children who feel acutely uncomfortable with the differences between themselves and the other children, and quickly adjust to conform to the social and behavioural norms of their age group.

Sources: Excerpted from Colangelo & Assouline (2000), p. 603; Bender (2006), p. 12.

How Teachers Can Motivate Students who are Gifted Underachievers

- explain the purpose for assignments and lessons

- help students set short- and long-term academic goals that are meaningful to them

- help students see beyond the present activity to the long-term benefits it produces

- integrate students' interests into your instruction

- offer students authentic choices about the ways in which they can learn and show mastery of the material in class

- utilize classroom activities that students can master, but not without effort and the use of appropriate strategies

- strive to build opportunities for immediate feedback into classroom activities

- treat students as if they already are enthusiastic learners

- encourage students to think seriously about how their performance in class can affect their future goals, as well as to explicitly articulate their reasons for choosing or failing to put forth effort

- discuss with students the obstacles they believe are keeping them from doing well and what options exist for them

- avoid letting students use their environment as an excuse

- help students set realistic expectations

Source: Excerpted from Siegle & McCoach (2005), pp. 23–26

- *The Gifted and Learning Disabled.* Bharati, an energetic, talkative nine-year-old, has great difficulty with reading and writing. However, when these difficulties lead to testing by the school psychologist, it was determined that while Bharati has learning disabilities in these two areas, she is of superior intelligence and she is remarkably advanced in her verbal abilities. Her parents were relieved when they learned of the assessment results as now they have an explanation for her poor performance at school. Her teachers were also relieved as they too received an explanation for why she performed so poorly on assigned tasks yet constantly demonstrated an ability to be highly creative and to think critically. Knowing Bharati's precise situation enables school personnel and her parents to make constructive decisions regarding her academic programming.

What We Know...

Children who are Gifted and Learning Disabled

Characteristics of giftedness include spontaneity, inquisitiveness, imagination, boundless enthusiasm, and emotionality; and these same traits are often observed in children with learning disabilities. Teachers can meet the unique needs of students whose strengths and talents lie outside the narrow view of knowledge by: helping students bypass their deficits as they access areas of strengths, modifying assignments and curricula for these students so that their true abilities may be demonstrated, and creating an environment that nurtures personal creativity and intellectual characteristics.

Source: Lerner & Kline (2006), p. 14.

Characteristics of Twice-Exceptional Learners

Areas of Giftedness

- specific talent or interest area often unrelated to school area
- superior vocabulary
- interested in the "big picture" rather than small details
- high level of problem-solving and reasoning
- penetrating insights into complex issues and topics
- advanced ideas and opinions that they are uninhibited in expressing
- highly creative in their approach to tasks, sometimes used as a technique to compensate for their disability
- unrelenting sense of curiosity
- unusual imagination
- advanced sense of humour that, at times, may appear bizarre
- capable of setting up situations to their own advantage as a means of compensating for their disability

Areas of Challenge

- inordinately frustrated by school
- deficient or extremely uneven academic skills resulting in lack of academic initiative and school-task avoidance
- low self-esteem often masked by inappropriate behaviours such as teasing, clowning, anger, withdrawal, apathy, denial of problems
- processing deficits may cause them to respond slowly, work slowly, and appear to think slowly
- difficulty with long-term and short-term memory
- frequently stubborn and inflexible
- gross- or fine-motor difficulties exhibited by clumsiness, poor handwriting, or problems completing paper-and-pencil tasks
- lack of organizational and study skills
- difficulty thinking linearly, resulting in an inability to understand cause and effect or to follow directions

- extremely impulsive
- highly distractible
- poor social skills sometimes demonstrated by antisocial behaviours

Source: Neilsen (2002), as cited in Neilsen & Higgins (2005), p. 9.

- *The Gifted and Physically Disabled.* Madison is a ten-year-old child who has cerebral palsy, a condition that affects her muscle control. She has great difficulty walking and performing fine motor tasks, such as writing. Her speech is sometimes hard to understand. However, she has a very rich vocabulary and she is a voracious reader, reading books far beyond her grade level. Madison is continually frustrated by her school's constant focus on her disabilities, rather than on her capabilities. Some teachers seem to have very low expectations in terms of what she can achieve, even on grade-level tasks. Madison has difficulty demonstrating that she is capable of much more in school because it takes her significantly longer than other students to complete written work. She has never been considered for the gifted program.

What We Know...

Children who are Gifted and Physically Disabled

Attention to the gifts of persons with disabilities has been sorely neglected. Identification procedures must consist of multiple measures, including informal observation…teachers must expand their knowledge of how children's abilities and disabilities affect learning. They must become proficient in disability-related instruction and technology, adaptive curricular strategies, communication, and collaborative teaming…Service provision must also include counselling to assist the student with disabilities in the development of a positive and realistic self-concept. The low self-esteem that often develops around the disability is combined with the often low and unrealistic expectations by others… Successful approaches are ones that accentuate a student's strengths and individual interests, as opposed to those that focus on remediating deficits.

Source: Johnson, Karnes, & Carr (1997), pp. 521–522.

How Teachers Can Assist the Child who is Gifted and Physically Disabled

- Encourage the use of technology to allow the child to be placed in the most "natural" and advantageous setting where academic self-esteem can be maintained.

- Teach to the child's strengths. Allow the child to use what they do well to compensate for, and to remediate, weaknesses (e.g., replace map-making skills with map-reading skills).

- Facilitate the development of independent learning and study skills to combat dependency habits and to assist the child in areas of weaknesses (e.g., time management).

- Explain the child's disability to fellow students to foster acceptance by classmates.

- Encourage the child to interact with others through cooperative learning opportunities.

- Expose the child to mentors and take the child on field trips in an effort to overcome possible experiential deprivation.

Source: Baldwin & Vialle (1999), pp. 192–194.

The Gifted Minority. Johnny, who is of Southern Tutchone heritage, lives in a major Canadian city. He is a grade four student who is exceptionally thoughtful and introspective. He has produced remarkable artwork and tells captivating and detailed stories based on what he gleans from his elders. His grade three teacher asked that he be assessed as she considered him to be gifted. Johnny did not score above average on the I.Q. test or the achievement tests that were administered and therefore was not deemed eligible for gifted programming. His current teacher does not encourage Johnny in the areas in which he is gifted. In fact, she discourages him from sketching during class time and she becomes impatient when he does not have immediate answers to her questions. As a result, Johnny is beginning to show a disinterest in school.

What We Know...

Minority Students who are Gifted

Minority students are underrepresented in gifted programs. They are less likely to be nominated by teachers as potential candidates for gifted programs and, if nominated, they are less likely to be selected for the program, particularly when such traditional measures as I.Q. and achievement tests are used for identification.

Source: Olszewski-Kubilius, Lee, Ngoi & Ngoi (2004), p. 129.

Identification Issues

Although there is consensus that gifted children can be found in every level of society and in every cultural and ethnic group, minority and economically disadvantaged students have not been found in gifted programs in proportionate numbers. The under-representation of minority student populations has been attributed to a variety of factors including test bias, selective referrals, and a reliance on deficit-based paradigms. Inequities in assessment need to be considered from a broad perspective that takes into account the multiple factors that affect the identification of gifted minority students (e.g., historical, philosophical, psychological, theoretical, procedural, social, and political). Suggested directions for future research include: addressing what constitutes giftedness and how it is manifested the same in all cultures and groups; designing and testing ways to improve the referral process and teachers' understanding of the different ways talent potential may be exhibited by students from different cultural, economic, and language groups; exploring the effective use of information about students from a variety of objective and subjective sources; and, developing effective programs and curricula that maximize the interactive relationships among assessment, curriculum, and instruction.

Source: Frasier, Garcia, & Passow (1995), pp. v–vi.

Geoffery – Age 8

UNITE

Sun and moon
Sun and moon
The moon shines
in the night,
letting fall the
radiance of her
silver face;
and calling to
the strong crashing
tides to come
in time
to her slower
rhythm or rhyme;
while she looks fair
upon the folded
flowers
whose faces be
curved innerwise
in sleep;
and calling to the
grey wolves
howling in the north
and west,
to the grand

tigers gazing in
the south and east,
to the strong
trees
tall though warped
in time,
and to creatures
lingering in the
captivity of
our minds;
She sings and
calls
sings and calls
sings and calls.

a tool of battle
in ancestral call,
as elemental as
time;
It warms softly
or heats in red fashion
as it plays with
power;
He is a star in space

but to us
he is a life-sustainer,
ever good,
he is the gold in
that life of ours
life of ours
life of ours.

Unite, O unite
thou pair of opposites
gold and silver
fire and water
golden fire and
silver water
dance together
in the more ancient
opposites' unity
that of space

and time;
In the moon's
dance around
the earth
and earth's
dance around
the sun,
become a crystal
of interaction
in the element
called
Eternity.

The sun is stronger
than all creatures
in combination,
a fire orb,
a cell,

Closing Geoffrey's File

As we close the file on Geoffrey, it is important to consider what his educational needs will be in the immediate future. His beginning school years were difficult and painful for both himself and his parents. However, his middle school years have been highly successful as he has been able to thrive both intellectually and emotionally. His parents and his current educators have put great effort into providing an intellectually stimulating environment within a caring and supportive milieu.

It is not hard to extrapolate to the school years ahead. As Geoffrey progresses through the upper elementary and junior high grades, his differences will likely be noticed even more by his peers. It is perhaps his sensitive nature that will set him apart the most. It would be a travesty if this gift of caring and compassion was stifled in his efforts to be accepted. Not only would his emotional well being be in jeopardy but it may dampen the outpouring of his highly creative and thoughtful prose, and also reduce his insatiable appetite for knowledge.

Given the emotional challenges Geoffrey will undoubtedly face as he enters the adolescent period, it will be necessary for those charged with his education to recognize and support his heightened sensitivity, or emotionality, rather than merely focusing on the curricula learned or the talents exhibited. He will need this support as he faces the pressures of conforming to societal expectations. As Roeper (1995) emphasized, children who are gifted and talented should be *educated for life* rather than *educated for success*. In other words, growth of the self and mastery of the environment are more important than the attainment and exhibition of a particular set of skills.

From The Psychologist's Notebook...

Geoffrey's happiness and academic success in recent school years has not been due to some special sort of program nor has it been due to a specialist teacher of students who are gifted. It can be best attributed to a sharing of information. Just a few years ago, Geoffrey's parents and I met with his teachers to talk about his abilities and needs. The teachers found this extremely helpful as evidenced by their many questions. Once they had a complete picture of Geoffrey's overall situation, they easily and readily designed and then successfully implemented a challenging but attainable educational program for him. Since these initial meetings, Geoffrey's teachers have continued the information sharing process with his next-grade teachers. The program that each of these teachers have implemented is not as extraordinarily different as many would expect. What his teachers are doing is nothing more than really good teaching. When Geoffrey's mother first called me for advice, she and his teachers were beside themselves as to what to do for him in school. I no longer get these types of phone calls.

Our ultimate educational goal for Geoffrey is for him to emerge from high school as a happy and fulfilled adolescent who happens to be an amazing writer. We think the right types of specific considerations have been made to accomplish that.

Learning More About Students who are Gifted and Talented

Academic Journals

Gifted and Talented International

Gifted Child Quarterly

Journal for the Education of the Gifted

Journal of the Gifted and Talented Education Council of The Alberta Teachers' Association (AGATE)

Journal of Secondary Gifted Education

Roeper Review

Books

Coleman, L.J. & Cross, T.L. (2001). *Being gifted in school.* Texas: Prufrock Press, Inc.

Karnes, F.A. & Bean, S.M. (Eds.) (2001). *Methods and materials for teaching the gifted.* Texas: Prufrock Press, Inc.

Heller, K.A., Monks F.J., Sternberg, R.J., & Subotnik, R.F. (Eds.) (2000). *International handbook of giftedness and talent* (2nd ed.). Oxford: Elsevier Science Ltd.

Web Links

- *Alberta Education, Planning For Students Who Are Gifted*
  www.education.gov.ab.ca/k_12/specialneeds
  This teacher resource addresses differentiated instruction, developmental concerns, metacognition, and career planning.

- *Centre for Gifted Education (University of Calgary)*
  www.gifted.ucalgary.ca/aboutus.html
  This site provides information for parents, teachers, and researchers. See the section titled "Information Services" for recommended readings as well as reports of research findings.

- *Council for Exceptional Children (Information Center on Disabilities and Gifted Education)*
  www.cec.sped.org
  The CEC offers answers to a long list of Frequently Asked Questions about gifted education. There is also a section devoted to ERIC EC digests on gifted education as well as a section that contains annotated readings on relevant topics.

- *Gifted Education: A Resource Book for Teachers (B.C. Ministry of Education)*
  www.bced.gov.bc.ca/specialed/gifted
  The Ministry of Education in British Columbia designed this site for teachers who may be seeking information on gifted education, including strategies for meeting the needs of the gifted learner in the regular classroom.

- *National Association for Gifted Children*
  www.nagc.org
  The NAGC Web site reflects the association's primary goals: they strive to train teachers, encourage parents, and educate administrators and policymakers in regards to the needs of children who are gifted.

- *The Association for Bright Children of Ontario*
  www.abcontario.ca/new/links.htm
  This site provides numerous links to a wide range of information on giftedness. The links are identified as those that may be of interest to teachers, parents, and/or students.

- *The Newfoundland and Labrador Association for Gifted Children*
  www.cdli.ca/nlagc/nlagc.html
  This NLAGC site provides resources for both teachers and parents. Included on the site are current articles of interest and a forum for parents where they can discuss issues regarding the education of their children.

Please visit the Online Learning Centre for *Special Education in Canada* at www.mcgrawhill.ca/olc/edmunds for additional learning and study resources.

Taking It Into Your Classroom...

Including Students who are Gifted

When a student who is gifted is first placed in my classroom, I will:

- review what I know about giftedness and locate resource materials
- read the student's file
- consult with the student's previous teachers
- consult with the student's parents
- meet with the school-based team to discuss the student's current school year

Other: _____

_____

When I suspect a student in my classroom is gifted, I will:

- review what I know about giftedness and locate resource materials
- collect information about the student through classroom interventions
- consult with other school personnel who are familiar with the student
- consult with the student's parents
- meet with the school-based team to present the information I have collected

Other: _____

_____

Key points to remember in my daily interactions with a student who is gifted:

- the student may be easily bored with routine tasks
- the student may be persistent about completing tasks of interest
- the student may be emotionally sensitive
- the student may be a perfectionist
- the student may have a keen sense of right and wrong

Other: _____

_____

Key points regarding curriculum differentiation for a student who is gifted:

- the student should be exposed to differentiation of the core curriculum
- the curriculum should emphasize depth and not just the learning of facts
- the student should be encouraged to develop higher level thinking skills
- the curriculum should emphasize interdisciplinary ideas
- the student should have the opportunity to work independently

Other: _____

_____

Key points regarding evaluation of the progress made by a student who is gifted:

- the student should have input into the development of an evaluation plan
- evaluation should be based on what the student is expected to know and understand
- there should be recognition that the student may not be equally advanced in all areas
- evaluation should include assessment of products and performance
- evaluation should include assessment of affective outcomes
- evaluation should identify strengths and weaknesses
- evaluation should lead to new instructional goals

Other: _____

_____

CHAPTER 8

Students with Intellectual Disabilities

Name: David Robertson
Current Age: 17
School: King Street High School
Grade: 11

David is a high school student who enjoys being active whether it is through participation in sports or playing a role in an in-class drama production. As a result of being born with Down syndrome, which is readily obvious through his physical characteristics, David has always had difficulty with academic tasks. His reading, writing, and mathematics abilities are significantly below those of his peers. Therefore, the focus of his high school program is on life skills and adapting to a workplace environment. David's story illustrates how the curricula in secondary school can accommodate students who need assistance as they move toward independent living.

Psycho-Educational Assessment

Age at Time of Assessment: 11 years, 1 month

Reason for Referral

David is currently placed in a grade five classroom and his program is significantly modified to meet his needs. He has Down syndrome and receives support from the resource program, an EA (four periods a day) and a volunteer placed in the classroom to assist all students. He is also receiving treatment from the school board speech language pathologist. He is able to count to 20 and can add and subtract with the use of manipulatives. He enjoys matching and sorting activities and is very athletic. A psycho-educational assessment was requested to determine David's strengths and weaknesses and to assist school personnel in designing his program.

Assessment Techniques

- review of student file
- consultations with classroom teacher, resource teacher, and parents
- Bender Visual-Motor Gestalt Test
- Wechsler Intelligence Scale for Children – 3rd edition – Canadian norms

Assessment Results

Behavioural Observations

David was accompanied to the testing session by an EA. She was able to interpret most of David's gestures and vocalizations. David was not pleased to attend the session and complained to the EA after every request and often indicated that he wanted to leave.

Cognitive Potential

David was unable to complete many of the testing items. On those subtests where he was able to give a response, he was below the six-year-old level. In a discussion with David's mother, she indicated that she believes that David is capable of more than these tests can measure. It was decided to put off assigning an I.Q. score at this time in the hopes that with maturity, David will be able to reliably complete more subtests in a future testing session.

Language Abilities

David's verbal comprehension skills are extremely limited. He appears to understand very little of what is said to him. His vocabulary, his general knowledge, and understanding of societal norms all fall below the six-year-old level. David also has speech difficulties and can be quite difficult to understand. Not surprisingly, he has considerable difficulty expressing his thoughts, reasoning abstractly, and forming verbal concepts.

Tests of Achievement

Age at Time of Assessment: 15 years, 6 months

Test Administered: Woodcock-Johnson III Tests of Achievement

Test Results:

Cluster/Test	Age Equivalent	Percentile Rank
Basic Reading Skills	6–9	<0.1
Academic Skills	6–8	<0.1
Academic Knowledge	4–2	<0.1

Additional Tests	Age Equivalent	Percentile Rank
Letter-Word Identification	6–8	<0.1
Calculation	7–1	<0.1
Spelling	6–2	<0.1
Word Attack	6–9	<0.1
Picture Vocabulary	3–8	<0.1

Test Observations:

David's conversational proficiency seemed very limited for his age level. He was cooperative, appeared at ease, and was attentive to tasks. David responded promptly, but carefully, to test questions. He gave up easily when attempting difficult tasks.

Test Summary:

When compared to others at his age level, David's academic knowledge and skills are both within the very low range. This includes his basic reading skills.

David Robertson

Teachers' Reports

Grade 9 – Semester 2

David has done some good work in Dramatic Arts this semester. He is a pleasure to teach and always open to new ideas and creative critique. Well done!

In literacy, David has improved in the areas of word matching (beginning, middle, and end), and visual word matching at level 1. The Academy of Reading has assisted David's development in these areas. His oral communication and social skills have been strengthened through journal presentations and role-playing.

In numeracy, David has developed his knowledge of one number addition and subtraction as well as improving in the areas of money identification and graphing. His biggest area of improvement has been his positive attitude in learning these concepts.

In terms of physical education, David participated on a regular basis and showed a positive attitude. His teamwork has improved as he is more aware of passing to his fellow team mates in scrimmage situations. I encourage him to remain active over the summer.

Grade 10 – Semester 2

David participated in meaningful activities during religion class this semester. The curriculum was modified to meet his learning needs, and to maximize his skills. His prayer service was well prepared, and he showed understanding of the idea of prayer.

In drama, David continued his good work. He is willing to take risks and invests all of his dramatic endeavours with energy and commitment.

In numeracy, David has enhanced his knowledge of addition and subtraction facts to 100, money identification, and graphing. His work habits have improved significantly. The ability to complete tasks independently has improved his self-esteem.

David is a pleasure to have in physical education class. He demonstrates a positive attitude and excellent effort. He almost always participates to the best of his ability.

Grade 11 – Semester 1

David demonstrated a moderate understanding of employer expectations during his work co-op placement. He has a limited understanding of job readiness skills and needs to improve on his communication skills and appropriate work habits.

In social skills class, David has shown enthusiasm. He participated well in all activities. He is a pleasure to have in class.

David continues to be a positive influence in drama classes. I would like to see him take more initiative in developing ideas and incorporating instructions.

David regularly participates actively in physical activities. He often shows positive encouragement for his classmates. He is encouraged to continue working towards attaining his fitness goals.

Excerpt from David's IEP

Grade:	11
Placement:	Regular Classroom with Withdrawal Assistance (David is working towards a Certificate of Accomplishment.)

Areas of Strengths:

- expressive skills (with EA support uses gestures, sign language, and computer software to express ideas)
- gross motor skills (enjoys sports and drama)
- peer interaction
- visual cues result in more appropriate responses
- good sense of humour

Areas of Need:

- communication skills (expressive and receptive language skills)
- fine motor skills
- functional academic skills
- life skills focusing on self-advocacy
- functional work-related skills

Instructional Accommodations:

- support verbal communication with natural gestures and facial expressions and non-verbal cues (e.g., pictures)
- make use of augmentative communication devices (e.g., communication boards, pictogram programs, electronic picture communication books, and pointing and typing aids)
- teach and model strategies that David can use to effectively communicate his strengths and needs
- focus on specific expectations that promote independence
- engage David's attention visually, verbally, and physically
- make use of alternative methods of sharing information (e.g., video, audiotapes)
- provide David with a computer

Assessment Accommodations:

David is a kinesthetic learner. Assessments need to include diversity. Assessing participation, collaborative group work, and completion of tasks will provide alternate, but meaningful assessments that reflect David's true abilities. Accommodations may include:

- adapting the assessment format (e.g., oral test, practical demonstration)
- allowing David to use assistive devices and technology resources (e.g., Kurzweil)
- providing prompts to return David's attention to the task, and
- reducing the number of tasks used to assess a concept or skill

David Robertson

Excerpt from David's IEP (continued)

Subject:	Food and Nutrition
Current Level of Achievement:	David is not working towards an academic credit. The course has been modified to meet David's social and academic strengths.
Program Goal:	To enhance knowledge of the factors that affect attitudes and decisions about food.

Learning Expectations	Teaching Strategies	Methods for Assessment
Demonstrate basic cooking and baking skills.	Provide modelling and repetition of basic cooking and basic skills.	- observation - self/peer assessments
Identify and demonstrate safe food-handling practices, including kitchen safety, sanitary methods, and proper food storage.	Use signs/pictures/symbols necessary in daily routines to determine appropriate response or course of action.	- daily work - observation
Identify, select, and effectively use appropriate kitchen tools to plan and prepare interesting and appealing meals in cooperation with others.	Provide opportunities for non-restrictive and creative endeavours.	- collaborative group work - daily work
Plan meals that address factors such as nutritional needs, likes and dislikes, special diets, and considerations related to time, money, and effort.	Allow for demonstration of this talent.	- observation

Excerpt from David's IEP (continued)

Subject:	Numeracy and Numbers
Current Level of Achievement:	David is not working towards an academic credit. Expectations are from the grade three math curriculum.
Program Goal:	To measure and compare the length, weight, mass, capacity, and temperature of objects, and demonstrate awareness of the passage of time.

Learning Expectations	Teaching Strategies	Methods for Assessment
Count by 1s, 2s, 5s, and 10s to 100 using multiples of 1, 2, and 5 as starting points.	Use visual aids (e.g., printable number line, computer programs).	- daily work - observation
Demonstrate an understanding of some standard units of measure for length and distance (centimetre, metre) and time (second, minute, hour, day).	Provide opportunities for system based enriching activities (e.g., being punctual for school functions).	- observation - individual/group presentation
Name and state the value of all coins and demonstrate an understanding of their value.	Use concrete materials to teach money identification, values, and counting.	- observation
Discuss the use of number and arrangement in the community (e.g., cans on a grocery store shelf, cost of a movie rental).	Use real life activities (e.g., counting money, grocery shopping).	- oral response - observation
Read digital and analog clocks, and tell and write time to the quarter-hour.	Use computer games, clocks, worksheets, schedules, etc…	- class discussion - observation

David Robertson

Excerpt from David's IEP (continued)

Subject:	Communication
Current Level of Achievement:	David is working at primary level in terms of reasoning skills and the ability to express his thoughts. His speech is affected by severe articulation difficulties.
Program Goal:	To increase David's oral and expressive language skills for the purpose of requests and social interaction (using signs and gestures to clarify).

Learning Expectations	Teaching Strategies	Methods for Assessment
Enhance positive communication skills needed for future independence.	Use drama, singing games, rhyming activities, etc. to enhance confidence and fluency.	- observation
Increase frequency/confidence in socialization/pragmatic skills.	Teach and rehearse responses to social situations.	- individual/group presentations
Improve articulation and individual sound production.	Involve in small group expressive language sessions.	- class discussion
Use five to six word phrases.	Use signs/pictures/symbols necessary in daily routines to determine appropriate response or course of action.	- daily work - self/peer assessments

Excerpt from David's IEP (continued)

Subject:	Social Skills
Current Level of Achievement:	With adult intervention and support, David interacts in an age appropriate manner with peers and adults.
Program Goal:	To improve social skills by maintaining appropriate behaviour in the classroom and improving peer interactions at school.

Learning Expectations	Teaching Strategies	Methods for Assessment
Follow class rules, routines, and behaviour expectations.	Modelling appropriate behaviour through role-play and collaborative group work.	- observation
Participate age-appropriately in conversations with peers and/or staff.	Provide opportunities for inclusionary activities to enhance David's verbal communication skills.	- observation - self/peer assessments
Respect personal space of self and others.	Empathetic prompting and cuing of appropriate personal space with peers and staff.	- daily work - class discussions
Learn social cues.	Modelling appropriate behaviour through role-play and collaborative group work in classroom.	- observation

David Robertson

Excerpt from David's IEP (continued)

Subject:	Healthy Active Living Education
Current Level of Achievement:	David is not working towards an academic credit. The course has been modified to meet David's social and academic strengths.
Program Goal:	To encourage David to use his knowledge of guidelines and strategies to enhance his participation in recreational and sports activities.

Learning Expectations	Teaching Strategies	Methods for Assessment
Encourage David to develop greater independence and leadership skills whenever possible.	Use inclusive language and facilitate group achievement.	Consistent communication with EA to assess David's effort and independent behaviour.
Increase David's understanding of what constitutes healthy active living (i.e., exercise and healthy eating).	Provide visual examples (e.g., overheads, pictures) to enhance comprehension.	Alternate forms of evaluation that address David's strength as a kinesthetic learner.
Maintain or improve fitness levels by participating in vigorous activities for sustained periods of time.	Provide consistent reinforcement to motivate David to complete activities.	Use charts and graphs to track David's success.
Experience the benefits of participation in different physical activities (e.g., social interaction, enjoyment, relaxation, self-esteem).	Recognize and praise effort and improvement as well as task completion. Use verbal and non-verbal feedback.	Use diverse assessment options, such as oral responses and role-playing.

Excerpt from David's IEP (continued)

Subject:	Computer and Information Science
Current Level of Achievement:	David is not working towards an academic credit. The course has been modified to meet David's social and academic strengths.
Program Goal:	To enable David to correctly create, name, copy, move, delete, and organize computer files. To increase David's understanding of how computers are used at home and at work.

Learning Expectations	Teaching Strategies	Methods for Assessment
Use file management techniques correctly to create, name, copy, move, delete, and organize files.	Teach and reinforce the use of key words, phrases, and terminology.	- daily work
Identify and explore computer programs pertaining to Microsoft Word, Corel Presentations, and All the Right Type.	Permit and encourage use of support tools (e.g., dictionary, word lists, and spell check).	- Corel presentation - oral response
Describe how computers change the ways in which people live, work, and communicate, and apply these theories to own life.	Provide real life examples. Encourage David to use the computer for a variety of tasks relevant to his life.	- oral response - role-playing - daily work

David Robertson

Why is David Considered to have an Intellectual Disability?

Down Syndrome

David was born with Down syndrome. His diagnosis was made shortly after birth. However, even before the medical staff confirmed Down syndrome through a blood test that detects chromosomal abnormalities, David's parents knew immediately what they were facing. They both quickly recognized the implications of their baby's physical features: slanting eyes, flat nose, and small head. He was most definitely going to have intellectual challenges that affected not only his education but also his ability to live a fully independent life. David's mother described this moment in their lives as one of great joy and great sadness. They had a new baby, a sibling for their two-year-old daughter, but their son was going to face many difficulties and perhaps never experience some of the dreams they had envisioned for him. In addition, they knew that Down syndrome is often accompanied by serious health concerns such as heart defects, gastrointestinal tract problems, low muscle tone, and/or difficulties with vision, hearing or speech. David's parents were well aware that the road ahead was going to be challenging for the whole family.

What We Know...

Down Syndrome

Down syndrome is the most common and readily identifiable chromosomal condition associated with intellectual disability. It is caused by a chromosomal abnormality: for some unexplained reason, an accident in cell development results in 47 instead of the usual 46 chromosomes. This extra chromosome changes the orderly development of the body and brain. In most cases, the diagnosis of Down syndrome is made according to results from a chromosome test administered shortly after birth.

There are over 50 clinical signs of Down syndrome, but it is rare to find all or even most of them in one person. Some common characteristics include:
- poor muscle tone
- slanting eyes with folds of skin at the inner corners (called epicanthal folds)
- hyperflexibility (excessive ability to extend the joints)
- short, broad hands with a single crease across the palm on one or both hands
- broad feet with short toes
- flat bridge of the nose

- short, low-set ears
- short neck
- small head
- small oral cavity
- short, high-pitched cries in infancy

Besides having a distinct physical appearance, children with Down syndrome frequently have specific health-related problems.

Source: National Dissemination Center for Children with Disabilities, www.nichcy.org/pubs/factshe/fs4txt.htm#orgs.

Canadian Statistics on Down Syndrome

In the period 1991 to 1999, the birth prevalence rate for infants with Down syndrome in Canada averaged 13.2 per 10,000 births. Within the same time period, cardiac anomalies were detected and reported in 49.2 percent of live born infants with Down syndrome. An average of 95.2 percent of infants born with Down syndrome survived the first year of life.

Source: Canadian Congenital Anomalies Surveillance Network, www.phac-aspc.gc.ca/ccasn-rcsac/ct2003/dsdata_e.html.

Definition of Intellectual Disability

Sixteen years ago, David's diagnosis of Down syndrome meant that he was labelled as mentally retarded — the appropriate term at the time. While the term "mentally retarded," or "mental retardation," has been used for almost 50 years and is still being used today, it is slowly being replaced by other terms such as the one used in this text: intellectual disability. The problem with the term "mental retardation" is not that it was initially intended to be derogatory but rather, over the years, it has become associated with a negative stereotype and many feel it is disrespectful to label a person with a term that demeans him or her in any way. It is important to note that respected organizations, such as the American Association on Mental Retardation (AAMR), continued to use the language that was established in the 1950s until very recently. However, in January of 2007, the AAMR officially became the American Association on Intellectual and Developmental Disabilities (AAID). Members of AAID decided it was time to move away from the term "mental retardation" so, like other similar organizations, they have officially replaced it with the term "intellectual disability."

What We Know...

Definition of Intellectual Disability

An intellectual disability is characterized by significant limitations both in intellectual functioning and in adaptive behaviour as expressed in conceptual, social, and practical adaptive skills. This disability originates before age 18. Five assumptions are essential to the application of the definition:

1. Limitations in present functioning must be considered within the context of community environments typical of the individual's age peers and culture.
2. Valid assessment considers cultural and linguistic diversity as well as differences in communication, sensory, motor, and behavioural factors.
3. Within an individual, limitations often coexist with strengths.
4. An important purpose of describing limitations is to develop a profile of needed supports.
5. With appropriate personalized supports over a sustained period, the life functioning of the person with intellectual disability generally will improve.

Source: American Association on Intellectual and Developmental Disabilities, www.aamr.org/Policies/faq_mental_retardation.shtml.

Something To Think About...

You will find that intellectual disabilities are classified in different ways by different groups. For example, sometimes intellectual disabilities are classified as mild, moderate, severe, or profound. You may also find that they are classified according to the amount of support an individual needs: intermittent, limited, extensive, or pervasive. How are intellectual disabilities classified in your home province or territory? Is there a difference in the classification systems used by different groups (i.e., the educational system versus advocacy groups)?

Diagnosing an Intellectual Disability

While David's intellectual disability was recognized from the time of his birth due to the physical characteristics of Down syndrome, the extent of his disability was not known until he was school age. At age 11, a psycho-educational assessment was conducted (see page 208) and David performed below the six-year-old level on all subtests to which he gave responses.

What We Know...

How is an Intellectual Disability Diagnosed?

An intellectual disability is diagnosed by considering: (1) an individual's I.Q. or intellectual functioning (i.e., ability to learn, think, solve problems, and make sense of the world), and (2) an individual's adaptive behaviour (i.e., whether or not he or she has the skills needed to live independently). In terms of intellectual functioning, an I.Q. below 70 to 75 indicates an intellectual disability. Adaptive behaviour is measured by comparing what a child can do in comparison to other children his or her age. Skills of interest are daily living skills (e.g., getting dressed, going to the bathroom), communication skills (e.g., understanding what is being said), and social skills (e.g., interacting with peers).

Source: National Dissemination Center for Children with Disabilities, www.nichcy.org/pubs/factshe/fs8txt.htm.

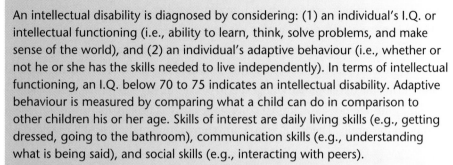

From The Psychologist's Notebook...

David was first presented to me as an eleven-year-old boy with Down syndrome who had difficulty adjusting to new situations and especially new people. At the time, he had been a student at the same school since kindergarten, moving with his peers from grade to grade. When I met him, he was in a grade five/six classroom where his classmates assisted him with daily tasks. Class routines and timetables were consistent and structured. He responded well to routines and motivations, such as free time. All forms of classroom assessment were completed by the classroom teacher or the EA. Therefore, these two individuals had a good understanding of David's abilities. Consequently, I considered my psycho-educational assessment of David to be a small part of his overall profile. His in-class work that was assessed regularly provided a more accurate reflection of his abilities, especially given David's reaction to my testing sessions.

What Factors Contributed to David's Intellectual Disability?

Because David's mother was young and healthy, and her pregnancy progressed as it should, there was no early warning that her baby would have an intellectual disability. In terms of Down syndrome, the exact cause of the chromosomal rearrangement is unknown. For example, David has Trisomy 21 which means there was abnormal cell division during the development of the sperm cell or the egg cell. Mistakes in cell division such as this are not an inherited condition. There is usually no history of Down syndrome in the family. There is also no known environmental cause of the syndrome.

What We Know...

Genetic Variations of Down Syndrome

There are three types of abnormal cell division that result in Down syndrome. They include:

- *Trisomy 21.* This most common type of Down syndrome is characterized by three copies of chromosome 21, rather than the usual two copies, across all cells in the body. Trisomy 21 is caused by abnormal cell division during the development of the sperm cell or the egg cell.
- *Mosaic Down syndrome.* This rare form of the condition, where only some cells in the body have an extra copy of chromosome 21, is caused by abnormal cell division during fertilization.
- *Translocation Down syndrome.* This uncommon form of Down syndrome occurs when part of chromosome 21 becomes attached onto another chromosome before or after conception.

Source: Mayo Clinic, www.mayoclinic.com/health/down-syndrome/DS00182/DSECTION=3.

chorionic villus sampling
A prenatal procedure in which samples of the placenta are used to determine genetic abnormalities in the fetus; usually done for women over 35.

amniocentesis
A prenatal procedure in which a small amount of amniotic fluid is extracted from the amnion surrounding the fetus to check for genetic abnormalities.

There is an increased risk of having an affected baby when the mother is older at the time of pregnancy, but this was not the case with David. However, if David's mother had been over the age of 35 at the time of pregnancy, she may have agreed to a screening test or a more definitive diagnostic test. These tests are offered to parents as an option, not a requirement, as parents must carefully think through the implications of knowing whether or not their baby has a condition such as Down syndrome. Screening tests are not invasive as they simply require a sample of the mother's blood to assess the likelihood that the fetus has the condition. On the other hand, diagnostic tests, like **chorionic villus sampling** and **amniocentesis**, can predict with almost 100 percent certainty whether Down syndrome is present. These tests are more invasive and do carry the risk of miscarriage.

From The Psychologist's Notebook...

While no one knows for sure why Down syndrome occurs, there are factors that are definitively known to cause other forms of intellectual disability. These factors are varied and can affect the child during the prenatal period (e.g., teratogens, infections, drug and alcohol abuse), during the birthing process (e.g., a lack of oxygen to the brain), and/or after birth (e.g., meningitis, physical abuse, neglect, accidental injury). Generally, the younger the child is when any of these insults occurs, the more seriously he or she is affected. Children with severe intellectual disabilities are usually recognized early simply due to their obvious delays in development. However, in many cases of mild to moderate impairment, the disability is not detected until the child enters school. Unfortunately, by this point, valuable time has been lost and the benefits of early intervention are not realized.

How Has David's Intellectual Disability Affected His Development?

Cognitive Development

Just like all individuals with Down syndrome, David has an intellectual disability. Because David's parents knew that intellectual disability was a characteristic of the syndrome, they were quite aware that their son would probably not meet early developmental milestones at the expected age. What they did not know was David's *degree* of intellectual disability. According to his mother, "it was good to know in advance that David would need help with his early development but it was difficult not to wonder just how severe his intellectual disability would be and how we might handle the different possible scenarios."

As an infant, David was a passive baby. He demanded little attention and his parents had to make purposeful attempts to pique his interest in his environment. His mother said that her nephew was born around the same time as David and she noticed that he was cooing, reaching for objects, and putting things in his mouth while David was content to sit quietly in his infant chair.

David did not begin talking during toddlerhood. He voiced few distinct sounds at the age when most young children are beginning to use several recognizable words. While he began to communicate his feelings through his body language and some vocalizations, he remained non-talkative until the age of four when he began to use words that were understandable to family members only.

He attended a preschool program for two years before entering kindergarten. He took part in all activities with the support of an EA. He showed little interest in colouring or using a pencil, and staying still long enough for a story to be read to him was challenging, to say the least, but he seemed to enjoy all activities that included large muscle movement. He especially liked to climb on the playground equipment and would cry when he had to come inside.

David entered school with few of the readiness skills identified as necessary for success in the kindergarten classroom. He also needed support with basic self-help skills (e.g., toileting and dressing himself). He was immediately assigned an EA who accompanied him throughout the school day. During the early elementary years, his IEP focused on math and reading readiness skills as well as self-help skills. His progress was slow but there were gains, especially in the areas of socialization. His mother commented on those gains:

> We tried to give David all the support and services he needed leading up to the time he started kindergarten but even then he was well behind the other kids. I think he really started to make some gains during those first few years at school. He finally started to talk more and he became more interested in what was happening around him. He seemed to enjoy playing with the other kids rather than just being on the outskirts of the group. While he still had trouble with new situations and being around strangers, he was fine around people he knew. I think most of this was due to him being a part of the regular classroom. It was the best decision we ever made.

What We Know...

The Cognitive Development of Children with Intellectual Disabilities: The Delay or Difference Debate

It has been long debated whether or not the cognitive development in children with intellectual disabilities is delayed (a slowed-down version of normal development) or different in fundamental ways from normal development (stages are missing, the order of stages is altered, and/or stages are incomplete). Wishart (1998) investigated the development of children with Down syndrome and suggested that there are significant differences in how development unfolds in this population, stemming at least partly from differences in the psychological environment in which these children grow and learn, as well as the biological disadvantages they exhibit from birth. Wishart pointed to the significant differences in the structure of the Down syndrome brain (e.g., reduced size of the cerebellum and the immaturity found in the frontal and temporal lobes) as supportive evidence for the "difference" viewpoint.

Social and Emotional Development

As David's mother indicated, his social development progressed well once he entered school and he was able to participate in activities with his same age peers. However, there was one significant challenge to his social emotional development. That first became evident when he was around three years old; David often became physically aggressive with others when his frustration rose to high levels. This aggressiveness was obviously a concern because he was a robust little boy and he could quite easily hurt another child. These problematic behaviours have fortunately diminished significantly during his school years. The professionals working with David identified the antecedents of his aggressive behaviour (e.g., extended seatwork involving pencil and paper tasks, an inability to communicate his wants and needs, and being in new situations where he did not know the routines) and changed his education program to address his frustrations. They also implemented behaviour management techniques that helped with both his aggressive behaviour and his learning behaviours.

Emotionally, David was very much affected by the death of his father which occurred unexpectedly when David was in grade five. He received a great deal of support during this time, especially from his mother and grandparents, but he still had much difficulty adjusting to life without his Dad. For a time, his aggressive behaviours returned and he became quite resistant to almost all activities at school. Eventually, however, he readjusted to the routine of school and his negative behaviours dissipated.

What We Know...

The Relationship Between Intellectual Disabilities and Behaviour Disorders

According to Taylor, Richards and Brady (2005), individuals with intellectual disabilities exhibit more behavioural problems than those without disabilities. Aggression is one of the most common of these behavioural problems. It is not known why this problematic behaviour occurs but it has been hypothesized that it may be due to difficulties in processing and retrieving information, frustration, and/or lack of opportunities for recreation and leisure. Silka and Hauser (1997) emphasized that aggression is not necessarily an indicator of psychiatric illness. They stated that "when verbal expression is impaired, distress resulting from many possible causes may be expressed through maladaptive behaviour such as aggression...Such behaviour may be seen as a final common pathway for various medical, psychiatric, interpersonal, and environmental circumstances" (www.psychiatry.com/mr/assessment.html).

Motor Development

David has always exhibited a love for large muscle activities. His mother said that for as long as she can remember, David has expressed great delight in running, climbing, and playing different sports. He engages in these athletic type movements with a sort of abandon, never faltering when he falls or hurts himself. While his gross motor movements have often lacked smoothness and fluency, there is no doubt that David is a willing and able participant in athletically-based activities. On the other hand, David has always had difficulty with fine motor skills and has never shown much interest in paper and pencil activities.

When David entered school, the *Movement Assessment Battery for Children*, a performance test that provides screening, assessment, and management for children with motor skill disabilities, was administered to assess his fine and gross motor skills. Not surprisingly, David's strengths were in the areas of ball skills (i.e., rolling a ball at a target) and dynamic balance skills (i.e., jumping over an object). However, he struggled with activities involving manual dexterity such as threading beads or using a pencil to trace a trail. These results have not really changed over his school years despite many more exposures to these types of skills and considerable maturation. His gross motor skills remain his greatest strength and he continues to struggle with fine motor skills.

What We Know...

Motor Development of Children with Intellectual Disabilities

Children with intellectual disabilities do not necessarily have difficulties with motor development. However, as reported by Harum (2006), it is not uncommon to find problems with fine motor control in this population. As well, Harum suggested that there may be subtle delays in gross motor acquisition recognized primarily as clumsiness.

In the case of children who have Down syndrome, the rate of gross motor development is affected by physical characteristics that commonly occur along with the intellectual disability. These children often have hypotonia, ligamentous laxity, decreased strength, and short arms and legs. As noted by Winders (2003), children with Down syndrome attempt to make up for these physical challenges by developing compensatory movement patterns that can develop into orthopedic and functional problems.

What is School Like for David?

David loves to go to school. In fact, even when he is obviously not feeling well, he insists that he cannot stay at home. It has become a very comfortable routine for him. His day begins with the task of getting his backpack ready and then setting out with a fellow student from his neighbourhood for the walk to school. He is greeted by many friends, both along the way and when he arrives at school, since most students in his small high school have known him since elementary school. He has always been a member of the regular classroom so he is quite familiar to his peers and they are well aware of his communication and learning challenges.

David's school day is filled with activities he likes. He currently takes a gym class, a cooking class, and he gets to participate in drama and role-playing activities in communication and social skills classes. He is less enthusiastic about the time he spends doing more academically-oriented activities. When he is required to do paper and pencil tasks or computer-related activities, his attention span is often quite short and he frequently begins displaying signs of frustration. When the frustration reaches a certain point, he will loudly voice his displeasure to his EA and often try to leave the room. According to his EA, "this is usually a sign that we have asked David to do too much and we need to re-look at whether or not we have moved along too quickly with our instruction or we have missed teaching David an important step that he needs to know in order to do the task at hand…David is getting much better though, and seems to be able to stick with these types of activities much longer than he used to."

David interacts well with his peers, both inside and outside of the regular classroom. He has a good sense of humour and enjoys being in the company of students who are being active and having a lot of fun. This is especially true when the students are engaged in sports activities. David is always willing to participate and his peers include him fully in whatever they are doing.

What We Know…

High School Inclusion of Adolescents with Intellectual Disabilities

Using a multiple case study approach, Dore, Dion, Wagner, and Brunet (2004) examined the inclusion of students with intellectual disabilities in the regular high school classroom. They concluded that "full-time inclusion in high school is pedagogically feasible, and to some extent, beneficial for adolescents with MR [mental retardation]" (p. 117). More specifically, they found that when students with intellectual disabilities moved from a self-contained classroom to a regular classroom:

1. They engaged more frequently in classroom activities.
2. They increased their social interactions with regular-class peers; however, social integration was not successful in the absence of specific strategies to enhance such an integration.
3. Teachers in the inclusive classroom were satisfied with the arrangement and stated that it resulted in very few modifications to their class routine (EAs were present in all situations).

It should also be noted that I.Q. level did not seem to be a factor in the ability of students with intellectual disabilities to benefit academically from the inclusive setting.

One of the most positive aspects of David's school day is the time he spends with Andrew, his classmate and assigned buddy. Andrew volunteered to help David with the tasks he is required to complete when he is in the regular classroom. While David has the support of an EA, it is Andrew who makes the attempt to fully involve him in the activities in which the rest of his classmates are participating. Andrew described his role as a buddy as follows:

> *I really like being David's buddy. It is my responsibility to help him in the classroom and usually that means making sure he is taking part in all of the stuff we do. Sometimes I do help him to learn new things, but mostly that is his EA's job. I am more of a friend for David. I make sure that he is in my group if we do small-group work and when we are given time to work on projects or free time to do whatever we want, I always check on David to see if he wants to be part of what I am doing. We have really become good friends. While it was hard at first to understand him when he spoke, I have gotten used to his speech. I pretty well know what he is trying to say most of the time. Once in a while he will get angry about something and I am not sure what is bothering him, but I am usually able to calm him down. The neat thing about being his buddy is the way he reacts when he sees me outside of class. He is always happy to see me and he loves to sit in the cafeteria with me at lunchtime. David is a real sports nut so we sometimes go to the gym together. Even if I am not in any of David's classes next year, I am sure we will still get together and do things like that.*

What We Know...

Peer Buddy Programs

Service learning has become a common focus of high school curricula. In other words, students are encouraged to take part in activities that address actual societal needs thus preparing them for an active and meaningful life in adult society. One type of service learning is participation in a buddy program. Students are given the opportunity to spend time with peers who have special education needs. According to a group of high school students who worked with peers who have severe disabilities (Hughes et al., 2001), their participation in a buddy program resulted in an increase in their interpersonal skills, personal growth, new friendships, an increased knowledge and awareness of people with disabilities, new strategies for interacting with students with disabilities, and an increased comfort level during these interactions. These same students suggested that their peer buddy experiences could have been even better if they had been provided with detailed information about their peer's disabilities, strategies for handling different situations that arose when spending time with their peers, and ongoing support through scheduled conferences with their classroom teachers.

It is estimated that nearly twice as many students with significant disabilities are included in regular elementary classrooms as compared to the number included in regular high school classrooms. Why do you think inclusive classrooms are less evident at the higher grade levels? How might this situation change as more inclusively educated students enter their high school years? To what extent would you support such a change?

Something To Think About...

What Educational Approach is Best for David?

High School Curricula

David spent his early school years in an inclusive classroom and when he entered high school, the goal was for him to stay with his peers as much as possible. However, given that David's secondary school program was going to focus a great deal on both independent and community living skills, it was decided that he would need to be in a resource room for part of his school day. His mother agreed with this decision since she was eager to have David learn these skills and she knew it would require explicit instruction that would be very difficult to deliver in the regular classroom. As well, she felt reassured that David would be just like other high school students, moving about the school attending different classes.

The decision to change the focus of David's program from the learning of academic skills to the learning of independent and community living skills was not a difficult one for the members of his school-based team. His mother had asked for this change with the stipulation that his reading, writing, and math skills not be ignored. The team agreed with her suggestions as they recognized that David was making very slow progress in the attainment of academic skills, despite many years of specialized instruction, and he needed to acquire skills that would prepare him for adult living. However, this did not mean that David's program would be devoid of academic instruction, rather, it meant his schooling would consist of functional academics tailored to foster independence.

What We Know...

Academic Instruction for Students with Intellectual Disabilities

There is ample evidence that students with intellectual disabilities can learn academic skills (Browder, Wakeman, Spooner, Ahlgrim-Delzell, & Algozzine, 2006). However, the learning of these skills can be quite challenging for many of these students and, therefore, instruction must be well thought out, carefully delivered, and evaluated to determine if it is of value to the student. It is especially important for educators to recognize the learning characteristics of students with intellectual disabilities (McLean, 2003). These students:

- learn at a slow pace and take a long time to complete tasks
- have a short attention span
- are easily distracted
- have short-term memory problems
- have conceptualization and abstraction difficulties
- have problems with generalization

Source: www.dsav.asn.au/global/articles/Common_Learning_Characteristics.pdf.

systematic prompting
An organized and predetermined series of prompts used to increase desired behaviors.

concrete referent
Something existing in reality or in real experience that is used to reinforce an abstract idea.

Browder et al. (2006) acknowledged these learning characteristics when examining reading instruction for students with significant cognitive difficulties. They stated that reading instruction should not be disregarded for these students as there is evidence that students with moderate or severe mental intellectual disabilities "can learn to identify and comprehend sight words using systematic prompting methods with concrete referents." They also emphasized that further research is required to determine the best possible instruction methods for teaching literacy skills to this special population. It is apparent then that in most cases of intellectual disability it is important to continue to address the attainment of academic skills.

Source: Bowder et al. (2006), p. 403.

David settled into the routine of high school with relative ease. He still benefits from the support of an EA as he did in elementary school. His EA has been the same individual for the past three years and that has eased his transitions from grade to grade. When David is in the regular classroom, his EA guides him through the activities set out by his teacher. His IEP (see pages 211–217) serves as the guide for curricular direction and it clearly outlines the learning expectations for each subject area. While David's program is modified significantly from that of his peers, it is still based on the general education curricular expectations whenever possible. For example, in Food and Nutrition class, David participates just as other students do in planning and cooking meals. However, David is not expected to design elaborate menus or prepare written reports on issues such as safe food handling-practices. Instead, with the help of his teacher and his EA, he is expected to verbally or pictorially describe a menu for a simple meal and he is taught such things as food handling techniques through a completely hands-on approach. While there are occasions when David experiences a far different curriculum than his peers (i.e., academically-oriented classes like math), every effort is made to have him follow the same class routines as his peers (e.g., similar amount of seatwork and free time).

The teaching approach used in David's case is one recommended for students with intellectual disabilities. It includes direct step-by-step instruction, lessons that are linked to the real world, increased opportunities for hands-on learning, the use of numerous examples, and the provision of considerable positive reinforcement. As one of David's teachers stated, "we work on learning things in very small steps making sure that David does the task successfully not only during that class but also the next day and even a week later…we make the task as relevant as we can to David's life and of course we celebrate every time he learns something new; especially when he uses his new skill without our prompting."

What We Know…

General Strategies for Teaching Students with Intellectual Disabilities

1. Provide instruction that is more explicit and is delivered at a slower pace than would normally be offered for students of that age.
2. Consider that students with intellectual disabilities learn less well through abstract teaching, but learn more successfully from a multi-sensory approach, in which they participate in the activity with hands-on learning.
3. Be as concrete as possible. Demonstrate what you mean rather than just giving verbal directions. Rather than just relating new information verbally, show a picture. And, rather than just showing a picture, provide the student with hands-on materials and experiences and the opportunity to try things out.
4. Break longer, new tasks into small steps. Demonstrate the steps. Have the student do the steps, one at a time. Provide assistance, as necessary.
5. Give the student immediate feedback.

Source: Adapted from Hannell (2006), and the National Dissemination Center for Children with Disabilities (2004).

David's high school education has also included the opportunity to take part in a work placement. This is considered a very important part of his schooling, especially by his mother who is worried about his transition from high school into the community. In grade 10, David was assigned a "job coach" at his school who helped him prepare for this new experience and accompanied him during his time on the job. His coach commented about how the work placement was organized and implemented:

David's work placement last term was at a local grocery store. In past years, students from our school have completed placements at the same store, so the manager and the staff were quite familiar with how our placements work. I went to the store ahead of time and talked with them about David, giving them an idea of what he is like and how he may respond to his new job in the community. Together we decided that collecting and breaking down boxes might be the best job for him since he likes to do physical tasks and he can sometimes become upset when placed in situations where his speech is not understood (e.g., communicating with customers or other workers).

I helped David get ready for the placement by teaching him how to do the <u>exact</u> same job at school. We began collecting boxes from the office and the photocopy room and breaking them down so they could be placed in the recycling bin. David caught on fairly quickly and actually let me know whenever he saw an empty box anywhere in the building. The next thing we did was to visit the store. We made a couple of visits so David could get used to the environment. He had a chance to see all the parts of the building and he met some of the staff. It was funny because he noticed all of the empty boxes before I even pointed them out to him.

When David first started working at the store, I was with him all the time. He didn't need much help with his job but he did need me there to keep him on task and to help him communicate with staff members and any customers who talked to him. Gradually, I stepped away a little and let him handle things on his own. I was always close by but David really could complete his work responsibilities fairly independently. He has made a few gains in his social interactions too, but that is definitely an area that needs to be worked on. He has trouble responding to people he doesn't know. These types of things need to be addressed at school and then again in his next work placement.

From The Psychologist's Notebook...

The coaching and support that David receives during his work placements are absolutely crucial to the quality of life he will lead once he gets out of school. The more independent he can become, the more fulfilling his day-to-day activities will be. Unfortunately, many teachers and parents are reluctant to change a student's curricular path away from academic subjects stating that this "seals their fate" and puts a glass ceiling on the student's learning. This reluctance is even stronger if a student's academic abilities are better than David's. However, the reality is that even if a student can continue to progress academically, it is unlikely that his or her life after school will revolve around the ability to perform academic type skills. Rather, the lives of students with intellectual disabilities are very probably going to revolve around their proficiency with skills that allow them to work and participate in society. Given that these students learn slowly and need lots of help when learning new things, the earlier their schooling focuses on life skills, work skills, social skills, and functional academics the better. In my experiences with the **Canadian Association for Community Living** *(CACL), students whose programs included learning these types of living skills in grades five or six have had many more successful work experiences as adults than students whose programs changed later (such as grade nine or ten).*

Canadian Association for Community Living
A Canada-wide association of family members and others working for the benefit of persons of all ages who have an intellectual disability.

You have a student with a moderate intellectual disability who is going to complete a work placement as part of their secondary education. A business owner has contacted you to discuss the possibility of having the student work at her florist shop. She is concerned that the student will cause her problems, such as slowing down the pace of work at her establishment and annoying customers. How would you respond to these concerns? How might you help the business owner prepare for this work placement?

Something To Think About…

Evaluation of Progress

David's IEP recommends that his progress be evaluated primarily through oral testing and practical demonstration (see pages 211–217). It is quite obvious that asking David to complete paper and pencil tasks to assess his learning is inappropriate. In fact, even relying solely on oral responses in David's case is inappropriate given his difficulty with communication. If David's teachers want to accurately evaluate his learning progress, they must depend mostly on their observation skills. And, it is apparent that this is currently the method of evaluation that is used most often by his teachers. For example, his drama teacher watches his class performances and looks for signs that his expressive skills are improving (e.g., whether or not he can understand and emote the feelings of his character), and in his social skills class, the teacher observes his interactions with his peers to see if he is communicating more often and more effectively. However, none of David's teachers describe using a systematic approach to conducting observational assessments. They appear to rely on their own judgement as to whether or not they are observing any gains in David's skill or knowledge. When asked how he determines and reports David's progress in communication class, his teacher replied, "I just know when he has learned something because I can see that he is doing it better in class and that's what I write about in my report." Further conversations with David's teachers indicated that many of them were unaware of other effective ways to evaluate David's progress.

A concern regarding the evaluation method currently being used for David is that it does not clearly identify if learning is occurring, if it is occurring efficiently, and if the provided instruction is impacting on David's learning. As Taylor, Richards, and Brady (2005) indicated, "inference or indirect measures of progress are not sensitive enough to measure learning in many students with mental retardation" (p. 311). They emphasized that observational assessment must be carried out in a much more systematic fashion if it is going to be the basis for instructional decision-making. This does not imply that teachers' general observations of student performance are of no value, but it does mean that these observations need to occur far more methodically in order to accurately identify what a student has learned and what instruction is necessary for the student to acquire the next step in his or her knowledge/skill development.

What We Know...

Conducting Observational Assessments

Taylor, Richards, and Brady (2005) recommended a four-step model of observation when monitoring the progress of student learning: (1) carefully and specifically identify the target behaviour/skill, (2) precisely measure the target behaviour/skill (e.g., compare number of times behaviour occurs in a specific time period with baseline data), (3) systematically introduce an intervention or teaching program, and (4) frequently evaluate the intervention/program effectiveness (p. 237).

Taylor et al. (2005) also presented three types of assessment (pp. 312–314) that can be made through observations in order to measure instructional effectiveness:

1. *Assess the percentage of accuracy or completeness.*
   Measure the total number of opportunities that the skill could have been given (e.g., peers provided 10 social initiations) and the number of times the target skill was actually given (e.g., the student responded to eight of these social initiations). Calculate the percentage of accuracy (e.g., 8 out of 10 indicates that the student responds to 80 percent of peers' social initiations).

2. *Assess the rate of progress.*
   Measure the number of times a skill occurs during a fixed period of time (e.g., number of correct keystrokes in one minute). Calculate the number of student responses (e.g., 68 correct keystrokes), divide by the time taken to perform all the behaviours (e.g., four minutes), and convert to number of responses per minute as this is the standard convention for teachers who use rate measures (e.g., 17 correct keystrokes per minute).

3. *Assess progress in time intervals.*
   Determine the presence of a skill during a predetermined interval of time (e.g., the display of positive social comments during recess). The total number of intervals of observation is the denominator (e.g., 20 intervals during recess) and the number of intervals in which the student displayed the skill is the numerator (e.g., positive social comments were made by the student during five of the intervals). Calculate the overall finding (e.g., the student's measure of positive social comments is 25 percent).

How is David Different from Other Students who have Intellectual Disabilities?

David is *similar* to other students who have intellectual disabilities in that he learns more slowly than students his age, he has limitations in his thinking skills, he has difficulties with attention and organizing information, and he has trouble seeing how things relate to each other. Given these challenges, David, like other students with intellectual disabilities, needs help with learning as well as assistance with attaining independent living skills.

Again, however, as we have mentioned in previous chapters, children with special needs that fall in the same category of exceptionality can never be considered to be identical. David is unique within the population of students who have intellectual disabilities, and he is also unique within the population of students who have Down syndrome. He is undoubtedly most similar to those students with Down syndrome but there are still many factors that set him apart and make it imperative that his education program be tailored to meet his specific needs (e.g., the severity of his intellectual disability, his specific difficulties with communication, his behaviour in social situations, and his desire to engage in large muscle activities).

To gain insight into the range of abilities and needs that are evident in students who have intellectual disabilities, consider the following two students. They have conditions other than Down syndrome so their differences from David are readily apparent.

- *Williams syndrome.* Maarika is a popular sixteen-year-old high school student who loves to play piano and sing. If it was up to her, she would spend her entire school day in the music room. Her peers recognize her talents and often encourage her to perform for them. Maarika responds willingly as she loves to immerse herself in music and she is always keen to please her classmates. She has a great memory for melodies and lyrics and can play and sing almost any song that they request. Unfortunately, Maarika is not as happy and relaxed in the classroom. She has significant difficulties with academics and even though she is now in a special program in high school, she still struggles with any tasks that involve math or spatial abilities. Surprisingly, she does not experience the same level of difficulty with reading, and her vocabulary is quite impressive. Maarika has Williams syndrome, a genetic disorder that is marked by missing genetic material on chromosome #7. This syndrome is the reason for her physical appearance (small in stature, upturned nose, wide mouth, small chin, and puffiness around the eyes) and her cognitive difficulties (mild intellectual disabilities). Williams syndrome is distinguished from Down syndrome, and most other forms of intellectual disability, by the presence of both strong and weak cognitive abilities as is evident in Maarika's case. It is expected that Maarika will master most self-help skills, complete her special program in high school, and live independently with some support.

What We Know...

Williams Syndrome

Williams syndrome is a rare neurobehavioural congenital disorder that impacts several areas of development including cognition, behaviour, and motor abilities. Due to the absence of the gene that produces the protein elastin, individuals with Williams syndrome have an elfin-like facial appearance: small upturned nose, curly hair, full lips, full cheeks, small teeth, a broad magnetic smile, and often especially bright eyes. Other common characteristics include: an outgoing social nature, a sense of the dramatic, overfriendliness, an affinity to music, low muscle tone and joint laxity, a short attention span, difficulty modulating emotions, anxiousness, and learning difficulties. In terms of intellectual ability, individuals with Williams syndrome often demonstrate strengths (e.g., speech, long term memory, and social skills) and weaknesses (e.g., fine motor and spatial relations).

Source: Williams Syndrome Association, www.williams-syndrome.org.

- *Fragile x syndrome.* Sasha, who has been diagnosed with fragile x syndrome, is a fourteen-year-old who looks and acts differently than his classmates. He has a large head, long face, prominent forehead, and large ears. His behaviour is described as "odd" by his peers. While he seems to want to be an active member of his peer group, he often stands at the periphery of the group and avoids eye contact. Sometimes he can be heard mumbling the same words over and over to himself, frequently mimicking the words of others. When he gets anxious, which is quite often, he begins biting his hands and "tuning out" even more than usual. This anxiety can be provoked by more than just social situations. It was apparent from the time he was a young child that he is hypersensitive to sounds, light, and touch. For example, Sasha becomes uncomfortable in environments that have bright lighting and he does not like to participate in school activities, like physical education, where he may be touched by others. Sasha also has problems with academics. His I.Q. of 65 indicates mild intellectual disability and this is most evident in his difficulty with higher level thinking and reasoning skills. His strengths are his memory and his relatively extensive vocabulary. When asked about his favourite TV show, "The Simpsons," he is able to talk in detail about the characters and what happened in specific episodes but he cannot describe the plots of the shows other than in simple terms. Sasha's parents report that he is quite calm and relaxed at home as they know the kind of environment that he requires. He is an active member of their household performing regular chores just like his siblings. He is also able to perform self-care tasks with relative ease. Sasha's parents feel his greatest challenge is socializing with others. He has no friends despite wanting to be part of his peer group. He spends most of his out-of-school time alone.

What We Know...

Fragile X Syndrome

Fragile x syndrome is the most common form of inherited mental impairment. It involves changes in the x chromosome that affect the FMR1 gene. Because males have only one x chromosome, the syndrome usually affects them more severely than it does females. While the syndrome can affect individuals in a variety of ways, the most common characteristics include: intellectual disability, hyperactivity, short attention span, tactile defensiveness, hand-flapping, hand-biting, poor eye contact, speech and language disorders, long face, large or prominent ears, large testicles, Simian crease or Sydney line, connective tissue problems, and a family history of intellectual disability.

Individuals with fragile x syndrome often display autistic-like behaviours. While the syndrome is a cause of autism (15–33 percent of individuals with fragile x have autism), many individuals with the syndrome do not have autism despite the manifestation of these behaviours. Because they are interested in social interactions, they do not meet the diagnostic criteria for autism.

Source: National Fragile X Foundation, www.fragilex.org/html/home.shtml.

Closing David's File

David's schooling to date has addressed all of the skill areas that need to be taught to students with intellectual disabilities (i.e., academic skills, communication skills, independent living skills, and community living skills). While he has not excelled in any of these areas, he has definitely benefited from the instruction provided by his many teachers. His early behaviour problems have diminished significantly, he has learned to communicate more effectively, and he has acquired skills that help him with independent living. It is noteworthy that his school placements have been predominantly in inclusive classrooms. He has undoubtedly enjoyed the company of his peers, and in return, he has been considered a valuable member of the regular classroom. A glance at the teacher's comments on any of his report cards and you can see what a "pleasure he is to have in the classroom."

David's education cannot be considered over as he gets ready to enter adulthood. Hopefully, he will benefit from further independent living instruction and additional community work placements in his final years of high school. To give their children the maximal opportunity to learn and develop, many parents of students like David opt to have their child stay in school until they are 21 years of age. This is the child's legal right. Once David graduates, he will require considerable assistance in the transition from school to the community. It is important to remember that adults with Down syndrome can, and do, continue to learn throughout their lives.

As a single parent, David's mother has great concern regarding what will happen to him once he finishes high school. She has many questions about what the future holds for her son. What kind of supports are there in our community to help him with employment? Are there social and recreational activities in which he can participate? How will I manage to juggle my work responsibilities with the time I will need to spend looking after David? Who will care for him should anything happen to me? It is these very questions that need to guide the curricular programming of students with intellectual disabilities. Every effort must be made to ensure that they have the opportunity to learn the skills necessary for a productive, fulfilling life.

With support, individuals with intellectual disabilities can be productive members of the community.

Learning More About Students with Intellectual Disabilities

Academic Journals

American Journal on Mental Retardation

Education and Training in Mental Retardation and Developmental Disabilities

Journal of Applied Research in Intellectual Disabilities

Journal of Intellectual Disabilities

Journal of Intellectual Disability Research

Journal on Developmental Disabilities

Mental Retardation

Research in Developmental Disabilities

Books

Taylor, R., Richards, S., & Brady, M. (2005). *Mental retardation.* Boston: Pearson Education, Inc.

B.C. Ministry of Education. (2001). *Students with intellectual disabilities: A resource guide for teachers.* www.bced.gov.bc.ca/specialed/sid.

Web Links

● *Canadian Association for Williams Syndrome*
http://caws.sasktelwebhosting.com/
CAWS was formed by a group of parents with the intent of raising awareness of Williams syndrome. Their Web site reflects their goal of supporting research that examines the educational, behavioural, social, and medical aspects of this syndrome.

● *Canadian Down Syndrome Society*
www.cdss.ca/en/main.htm#
The CDSS site is a resource linking parents and professionals through advocacy and education. The "Resources" link provides access to a library of the past CDSS newsletters (Canadian Down Syndrome Quarterly).

● *Learning About Intellectual Disabilities and Health*
www.intellectualdisability.info/home.htm
The main aim of this site is to provide up-to-date information about the health needs of people with intellectual disabilities. Articles address prevention, diagnosis, social care issues, and family issues.

● *Students with Intellectual Disabilities: A Resource Guide for Teachers*
www.bced.gov.bc.ca/specialed/sid/
This online resource guide was designed to address the common concerns teachers have regarding the education of students with intellectual disabilities. The section entitled "Tips for Teachers" covers a wide range of relevant topics.

- *The National Fragile X Association*
  www.fragilex.org/html/home.shtml
  This site provides comprehensive information regarding fragile x syndrome, including the discussion of educational issues and the presentation of current research findings.

Please visit the Online Learning Centre for *Special Education in Canada* at www.mcgrawhill.ca/olc/edmunds for additional learning and study resources.

Taking It Into Your Classroom...

Including Students who have Intellectual Disabilities

When a student who has an intellectual disability is first placed in my classroom, I will:

- review what I know about intellectual disabilities and locate resource materials
- read the student's file
- consult with the student's previous teachers
- consult with the student's parents
- meet with the school-based team to discuss the student's current school year

Other: _____

_____

When I suspect a student in my classroom has an intellectual disability, I will:

- review what I know about intellectual disabilities and locate resource materials
- collect information about the student through classroom interventions
- consult with other school personnel who are familiar with the student
- consult with the student's parents
- meet with the school-based team to present the information I have collected

Other: _____

_____

Key points to remember in my daily interactions with a student who has an intellectual disability:

- the student may have a short attention span
- the student may have both short-term and long-term memory problems
- the student may have a limited ability to express and understand language
- the student may need information delivered to them in short, simple chunks
- the student may have a decreased ability to generalize information across settings
- the student may exhibit behaviour problems, including aggression

Other: _____

_____

Key points regarding programming for a student who has an intellectual disability:

- the classroom environment should be structured and consistent
- pay particular attention to the student's learning style and what motivates him or her
- present information/tasks in a progressive step-by-step fashion
- give immediate feedback
- take advantage of teachable moments and recognize when the student needs a break
- include life skills in the curricula
- promote independence rather than dependence on adult support

Other: _____

_____

Key points regarding evaluation of the progress made by a student who has an intellectual disability:

- evaluation should focus on teacher observation of student learning
- evaluation should include oral response and practical demonstration
- evaluation should occur on a frequent basis (e.g., daily in some cases)
- evaluation should consider the measurement of target behaviours
- evaluation should provide data to assess instructional effectiveness (i.e., percentage of accuracy or completeness, rate of progress, and progress in time intervals)

Other: _____

_____

CHAPTER 9

Students with Autism

Name: Zachary Wong
Current Age: 6
School: Sandhill Elementary School
Grade: Kindergarten

Zachary is a cognitively capable young boy who has had difficulty interacting with his environment since around the time of his first birthday. Unfortunately, his sensitivity to sounds and touch made his early years very painful and frustrating for both himself and his family members. It was because of his parents' desperation to help him that he received a relatively early diagnosis of autism and subsequent treatments that addressed his autistic behaviours. Zachary's story highlights the importance of early intervention and the ongoing need for considerable support in the school environment for students who are autistic.

Assessment Results

Age at Time of Assessment: 3 years, 4 months

Developmental Paediatric Assessment

Pregnancy was normal with no significant maternal illness nor substance exposure known to potentially damage a developing fetus. Mother's pre-pregnancy health and blood tests were normal. Maternal emotional health during and after the pregnancy was normal. Birth occurred at full term. Breastfed until the age of two years. No significant illnesses or surgeries since birth. Developmental milestones achieved at expected rate except for language after 14 months and regression in social skills between 14 and 18 months. No dysfunctional family features recognized that might contribute to these problems. No significant relevant health problems in family history.

A limited physical examination (due to problems with cooperation) with an emphasis on the neurological system revealed no abnormality. No physical features to suggest a medical disease, syndrome, or substance exposure during pregnancy. Pattern of rocking and banging head was observed — appears to be a self-stimulating activity. Zach exhibited short concentration on chosen activities. Extensive jargon was evident with some understandable words. No immediate echolalia. Play activities were immature for age.

Conners' Rating Scales: scored in the very abnormal range for questions relating to anxious/shy behaviour, perfectionism and emotional ability (mood swings). *Stony Brook Inventory*: scored "often or very often" on questions associated with 7 of 12 autistic behaviours. *Childhood Autism Rating Scale* (marked by parents alone, physician alone, parents and physician together, and the psychologist): all indicated behaviours in the autistic range. When considering the *DSM-IV-TR* Criteria, Zach showed a profile consistent with the diagnosis of autism (autistic disorder).

Psychological Assessment

Bayley Scales of Infant Development – Second Edition
2 years, 5 months developmental age equivalent level

Vineland Adaptive Behaviour Scales – Interview Edition

Communication skills domain	9th percentile
Daily living skills domain	1st percentile
Socialization skills domain	3rd percentile
Motor skills domain	19th percentile

Developmental Test of Visual Motor Integration
2 years, 9 months age equivalent level

Zachary has an autistic spectrum disorder. There is no evidence of an associated medical disease or psychosocial cause for his challenges. He meets the criteria for the diagnosis of mild autism (autistic disorder). He appears to qualify for provincial government funding for a child less than six years with this diagnosis.

The cause of autistic spectrum disorders is unknown. They probably represent a number of different causes with similar clinical presentations. All children with autism are different. We are learning more and more as extensive research in this area continues. Zachary is a unique individual who will certainly progress in learning, social skill development, and communication. His progress will be best followed by a coordinated team who work together with his parents to optimize learning strategies.

Zachary exhibits many non-autistic behaviours which suggests that he will likely show very positive progress in an intensive multidisciplinary therapy environment with a strong emphasis on communication and social skills. It is recommended that he attend a highly structured preschool/daycare program several days per week where he can receive some one-to-one support in order to fully participate and benefit from the program. He will benefit from ongoing intensive speech language therapy and communication strategies shared with his preschool or daycare programs. Further, some support to reduce self-stimulatory behaviour and to encourage fine-motor skills is recommended.

The prognosis for Zachary in school and later years is impossible to assess at this time. He will require intensive multidisciplinary assistance in the school system. The present problems with program funding in the school system require strong, continuing parental advocacy to attain appropriate school programming. Often, supplementary privately paid therapists are needed for optimal management. Financial planning now may be wise.

Zachary will benefit from a review by professionals including a psychologist, developmental paediatrician, speech language pathologist, occupational therapist, and educator prior to kindergarten entry. This will assist in preparation for school entry, appropriate designation, school program planning, the preparation of an individualized education program, and monitoring of progress to date.

Zachary will benefit from a visual assessment, and hearing should be assessed annually. He should have a single blood test to screen for fragile x, blood lead level, and iron studies. Brain imaging studies such as CT and MRI scans are not recommended as they will not assist in management and rarely show significant findings. An EEG (electroencephalogram) is not recommended in the absence of symptoms that suggest seizures. Seizures are common in children with autism.

Zachary will benefit most if his mother and father seek to become experts in knowledge about autistic spectrum disorders. We can assist with references if desired. Reassessment is advised if regression rather than improvement occurs or if significant management problems develop.

Zachary Wong

Mother's Comments Regarding Zachary's Diagnosis

Zachary was our second born, and for the first year of his life all seemed normal. In fact, he was a quiet and mellow baby, compared to our first boy. He was born within a normal gestation period and he reached his developmental milestones of crawling, walking, and the beginnings of speech on time, albeit a bit later than our older child.

We started to notice subtle changes in Zach's behaviour after his first birthday and these changes became very apparent by 18 months. He had a vocabulary of around six words after his first birthday: "mama," "dada," "puppy," "bye," "car," and "hi." He stopped using these words altogether, and began to ignore us when we called his name. He went from being a happy and content baby to a toddler who appeared frustrated and inattentive. His constant smile seemed to evaporate and he would only seek affection from me. His brother and father were now on the sidelines. Zach began to constantly bang his head on his high chair, and gradually destroyed it. I knew a bit about autism but the term seemed too frightening and overwhelming to consider.

At first, we believed his behavioural changes were due to a hearing loss, since he stopped responding to his name. In addition, my husband's family had a history of hearing loss, so it seemed logical to start from there. We had no idea how exhausting the process would be. My first visit was to the local family doctor who could not even examine Zach due to his high pitched screams. The doctor actually asked if I needed anything! He referred Zach to a paediatrician who did not seem too concerned at first. He suggested that since Zach's older brother was slower to pick up words, this was probably the case for Zach as well. We were insistent that it was more than that. Zach had stopped speaking altogether. After a number of visits, the paediatrician put Zach on the waiting list for an autism assessment at the Children's Hospital in our region. We also began once a week visits with a private speech therapist.

I became consumed with reading everything I could find on autism. I spent hours researching the topic on the Internet. I also found some parents of autistic children and began to exchange e-mails with them. These resources helped me to detect other signs of Zach's autism. He did not point at things, he developed terrible sleep patterns, and he did not play with his toys in an age-appropriate manner. As well, he did not take any interest in visitors to the household, and was left out when kids came over to play. Noise and touch became overwhelming for him. Music could not be played at all. Washing, cutting, and brushing his hair were all out of the question. Despite sessions with the speech therapist, he was still not talking. The therapist said, "I would be very worried about this as a parent." It was a heartbreaking situation. Life was so difficult for our little guy.

One thing really nagged at me while I was doing my research on autism; I had read so much about the importance of therapy by the age of three years. We had been seeing doctors and speech therapists for close to a year, and the age of three was fast approaching. It would be another eight months before we would move up the waiting list and get our appointment at the Children's Hospital. We made the decision to see a developmental paediatrician who was in private practice. He had worked at the Children's Hospital, and had diagnosed a number of children on the autism spectrum. The parents I spoke with considered him to be an expert in this field of medicine. At this point, we needed to know for sure if Zach was autistic. After four visits, the doctor confirmed that Zach was a high functioning, autistic child.

Excerpt from Zachary's IEP

Communication Goals for Kindergarten

Communication Needs:
Zachary's expressive and receptive language skills are below age level. He is limited in his ability to respond to a communication partner, comment on what others are doing, maintain a conversation, and request information. He requires support to expand his play skills and engage in play activities with other children.

Communication Goals:
- Broaden conversations with adults.
- Initiate conversations with peers.
- Make comments on what others are doing.
- Give and take instructions.
- Increase understanding of language concepts (all/except, either/or, match, when, before, then, farthest, top/bottom, unless, first/second/third/last).
- Use appropriate questions in communication (how, why, who, where, when).
- Improve use of gender specific pronouns.
- Use of adjectives and adverbs.
- Use language to describe pictures and stories.
- Use an outline of his day.
- Use social stories for social interactions.

Staff Responsibilities:
- Speech language pathologist will provide consultation and training for school personnel to work with Zachary in the classroom and one-on-one.
- Education assistant will support Zachary in the classroom and use modelling techniques and reminders to improve language skills.
- Classroom teacher will use modelling techniques and reinforcement for language skills.
- Parents will provide information and support for language goals. They will use a back-and-forth book to communicate with school. This book will be kept at the front of Zachary's binder.

Measurement of Progress:
- Track communication skills in every day interactions.
- Formal and informal assessments by speech language pathologist.
- Record keeping by parents at home.

Zachary's Kindergarten Assessment — Term 1

Date of Assessment: October 2005

Literacy
Your child's score was 90 out of a possible 100.
The range of scores for kindergarten children in this school was 5 to 100.

Lower Case Letters
Your child's lower case letter recognition score was 26 out of a possible 26.
The range of scores for kindergarten children in this school was 0 to 26.

Upper Case Letters
Your child's upper case letter recognition score was 26 out of a possible 26.
The range of scores for kindergarten children in this school was 0 to 26.

Letter Sounds
Your child's letter sound recognition score was 24 out of a possible 26.
The range of scores for kindergarten children in this school was 0 to 26.

Math
Your child's score was 98 out of a possible 100.
The range of scores for kindergarten children in this school was 24 to 100.

Counting Aloud
Your child was able to count aloud to 79.
The range for kindergarten children in this school was 4 to 109.

Counting Objects One-to-One Correspondence (up to 20)
Your child's score was 20 out of a possible 20.
The range of scores for kindergarten children in this school was 2 to 20.

Numeral Recognition 1-20
Your child's score was 20 out of a possible 20.
The range of scores for kindergarten children in this school was 0 to 20.

Teacher's Comments:
Academically, Zachary scored very high on this assessment. He is in the grade one range for math and literacy. He reads at a grade two level.

Why is Zachary Considered to be Autistic?

Definition of Autism

Autism cannot yet be determined through genetic, neurological, or physical markers. Diagnosis is dependent on the observation of an individual's behaviour. As Wahlberg (2001) indicated, autism is a "very perplexing psychological disorder" that is usually diagnosed before the age of three years using the criteria contained in the *Diagnostic and Statistical Manual of Mental Disorders 4th Edition* (*DSM-IV*). According to the *DSM-IV* (American Psychiatric Association, 1994), *autistic disorder* is classified as a pervasive developmental disorder along with four other disorders: *Rett's syndrome, childhood disintegrative disorder, Asperger's disorder,* and *pervasive developmental disorder not otherwise specified* (PDD/NOS). These five disorders are often referred to as *autism spectrum disorders* (ASDs) because they cover a wide spectrum of similar symptoms. A diagnosis of autistic disorder (AD) means that the individual, usually a young child like Zachary, has met the following three distinct behavioural criteria: (1) qualitative impairment in social interaction, (2) qualitative impairments in communication, and (3) restricted, repetitive, and stereotyped patterns of behaviour, interests, and activities.

What We Know...

The Five Autism Spectrum Disorders

Autistic Disorder
Occurs four times more frequently in boys than girls and is characterized in some children by withdrawn behaviour or other unusual social behaviours, problems using language to communicate, repetitive patterns of behaviour, and the inability to engage in imaginative play. Usually the child begins with normal development and shows regression between 12 and 24 months of age.

Asperger's Disorder
Many experts view Asperger's disorder as high functioning autism. Children with Asperger's disorder have no significant delays in language skills or in cognitive development, self-help skills or adaptive behaviour. There is significant impairment in social functioning as well as stereotyped behaviours and repetitive mannerisms.

Rett's Syndrome
Only appears in girls to date. These children seem to develop normally until between 5 and 18 months of age, and then experience a deceleration of head growth, lose previously acquired language and hand skills, which are replaced by stereotypical behaviour (e.g., hand flapping). There is also a loss of social interaction, physical coordination, and impairment in receptive and expressive language. Recently a genetic marker for Rett's syndrome has been identified.

Assessing Autistic Disorder

It is not uncommon for a child's parents to be the first ones to suspect that their child is not developing normally. Since Zachary was their second child, Zachary's parents were even more aware of the behaviours that would be typical of a toddler his age. As his mother noted (see *Mother's Comments* on page 246), by the time Zachary reached 18 months of age, she and her husband had real concerns about the regression of his language skills, his withdrawal from social interactions, his sensitivity to noise and touch, and his repetitive head banging. Through their own research they knew that early intervention was critical if they were indeed dealing with an autism spectrum disorder; therefore, they decided to have Zachary assessed by highly qualified professionals who were in private practice rather than wait for an appointment at the Regional Hospital.

What We Know...

Early Identification of Autism

There is currently research being conducted in Canada that is examining the early identification of autism. The importance of early identification cannot be overstated as it can only lead to both a better understanding of the disorder and the development of more effective interventions. Zwaigenbaum, Bryson, Rogers, Roberts, Brian, & Szatmari (2005) reported that in their longitudinal study of high risk infants, preliminary results indicate that by twelve months of age, siblings who are later diagnosed with autism may be distinguished from other siblings and low-risk controls on the basis of: (1) several specific behavioral markers, including atypicalities in eye contact, visual tracking, disengagement of visual attention, orienting to name, imitation, social smiling, reactivity, social interest and affect, and sensory-oriented behaviors, (2) prolonged latency to disengage visual attention, (3) a characteristic pattern of early temperament, with marked passivity and decreased activity level at six months, followed by extreme distress reactions, a tendency to fixate on particular objects in the environment, and decreased expression of positive affect by twelve months, and (4) delayed expressive and receptive language (p. 149).

Zachary was subsequently assessed at age three years, four months by both a developmental paediatrician and a psychologist. The purpose of their assessments was to answer the following four questions:

1. Does Zachary have an autistic spectrum disorder?
2. Is there evidence of any other medical disorder or abnormality?
3. Can delays be explained by social or environmental causes?
4. What recommendations can be made regarding further investigation and management?

As is evident from the resulting assessment report (see *Assessment Results* on pages 244–245), Zachary was diagnosed with autistic disorder based on the *DSM-IV* autism criteria. The developmental paediatrician and the psychologist were able to determine through observation, standardized testing, and interviews with the parents that Zachary had significant difficulties with social interactions, verbal and nonverbal communication, age-appropriate play, and changes in routine. He also demonstrated repetitive patterns of behaviour. Neither the paediatrician nor the psychologist found any evidence of any other medical disorder or abnormality. Zachary's delays could not be explained by social or environmental causes. Therefore, the diagnosis of AD was made with certainty and recommendations were made regarding early intervention and preparation for entry into school.

What Factors Contributed to Zachary's Autism?

The cause of autism is not yet known. However, research is focusing on several areas of study including genetics, **neuropathology**, prenatal factors, and exposure to toxins. In Zachary's case, there were no obvious prenatal factors that may have altered his development. His mother's pregnancy was normal and there were no birth complications. As well, there was no obvious exposure to any type of toxin; however, some may question the fact that Zachary received his childhood vaccinations. There is some literature that suggests that exposure to mercury may be a factor in autism, and that some childhood vaccines contain thimerosal, which is 50 percent mercury; however, there is no clear evidence that vaccines or mercury are related to the incidence of autism (Autism Society Canada, 2005).

Given Zachary's non-eventful prenatal and early childhood history, one must consider other factors that may have caused his autism. According to Siegel (2003),

neuropathology
The study of diseases of nervous system tissue, most often using tissue from small surgical biopsies or examination of whole brains.

"the most important, and informative, likely cause of autism is genetics" (p. 18). The genetics of autism is thought to include both the possibility of a random one-time genetic mutation (which we cannot determine in Zachary's case) and the possibility that inherited abnormalities are passed to a child through their parents. According to Matson (1994), "…concordance for autism in monozygotic twins has been reported consistently in the literature" and research findings "…strongly suggest that autistic **genotypes** may aggregate in families" (p. 44). These links to genetics as a cause of autism are now being supported by Canadian scientists working on the Autism Genome Project (www.offordcentre.com/asd/study_genetics/genstudy_main.html). In their study of 1,600 families who have at least two members with ASD, they have identified areas of the genome that harbour genes linked to autism susceptibility (Abraham, 2007). This evidence of **genetic markers** for autism means that eventually DNA tests may ensure the early identification of autism.

In Zachary's case, there is no history of autism in his immediate or extended family. Both his parents have college diplomas; his father is an accountant and his mother was trained as a dental assistant but now stays home to care for her two sons. While Zachary's older brother was slow to speak, he is now a healthy eight-year-old boy who shows no signs of autism. However, having said that there is no evidence of autism in Zachary's family, Siegel (2003) noted that an inherited gene mutation may be passed through a family but it may not necessarily be expressed as autism, or it may cause a very mild case of autism that produces no notable problems.

Neuropathology is another factor identified by researchers as a possible cause of autism. While we do not know if Zachary has any abnormalities in his brain structure, we do know that "the interaction of intrinsic and extrinsic influences on neural development is considered a likely etiologic element in the autistic syndrome" (Matson, 1994, p. 45). Individuals with autism have been shown to have some structural and chemical differences in their brains that may interfere with the usual intricate connections that control and coordinate the areas of social interaction, sense perception, and communication (Autism Society Canada, 2005).

genotypes
The genetic makeup of a person.

genetic marker
A gene or DNA sequence that has a known location on a chromosome and is associated with a particular physical trait.

Something To Think About…

Zachary's parents have heard about a gluten-free/casein-free diet that has helped children with autism become more responsive to their environment. It is reported that positive outcomes are seen after one year of eliminating grains and milk. They have also heard about children who have improved significantly after taking supplements to reduce the amount of mercury in their bodies. If you had a child who was autistic, would you consider implementing a special diet or a supplement regime? What information would you need in order to make your decision?

How Has Zachary's Autism Affected His Development?

Cognitive Development

Zachary's parents were not concerned with his cognitive development during the first year of his life. In fact, he began to speak around the time of his first birthday, vocally identifying his "mama" and "dada" and a few familiar objects. However, not long after that, Zachary seemed to retreat from the outside world. He no longer spoke any words and seemed entirely uncomfortable with his environment. Much of his day was spent in distress as he struggled to cope with an extreme sensitivity to noise and touch, and a lack of sleep. It was not surprising, then, that he lacked an interest in exploration, and demonstrated an inability to play with toys in an age-appropriate manner, two activities that are critical to a child's early cognitive development. His parents were concerned that he would fail to develop intellectually.

What We Know...

Autism Spectrum Disorders and Intellectual Abilities

The research data consistently indicates that the majority of individuals with autism spectrum disorders perform within the subnormal range on standardized tests of intellectual abilities; it is the minority of this population who perform at normative levels. In fact, a large proportion of the autistic population meets the current diagnostic criteria for a dual diagnosis of autism and intellectual disability.

Source: Matson (1994).

During his psychological assessment at age three years and four months, Zachary's performance on *The Bayley Scales of Infant Development – Second Edition* indicated a significant delay. The behaviours and skills he demonstrated during testing placed him at approximately the two years, five months developmental age equivalent level, which is below the first percentile when compared to his same aged peers. It should be noted, however, that most standardized ability measures were designed for use with typical children and results must be interpreted with caution when used with children with sensory, language, or motor difficulties. It is likely that Zachary's performance on *The Bayley Scales of Infant Development* was affected by his autism-related behaviours.

Once Zachary was diagnosed with autistic disorder and began a series of different therapies, it became apparent that he was making advancements in a number of areas of development, including his intellectual development. As he progressed through preschool, his teachers noted that one of Zachary's strengths was his mental ability.

classification
The ability to recognize and construct relationships among objects, imagined objects, and classification systems themselves.

seriation
The ability to organize objects in a progressive sequence according to some measurable dimension (height, width, length, size, shape, etc.).

He learned to successfully complete tasks involving numbers, classification, seriation, and memory. These strengths were further confirmed when he entered kindergarten in 2006. His first Kindergarten Assessment (see page 248), conducted in the fall term, revealed a student who was doing very well academically. This progress has continued throughout the school year; Zachary is performing at grade level in math and he is a proficient reader whose literacy skills exceed those which are expected for a child his age. His academic success is further confirmation that standardized test results must be interpreted with caution when a child's behaviour affects the completion of tasks during the testing session.

It is important to note at this point that many high functioning children like Zachary are thought to have Asperger's disorder, or Asperger syndrome as it is often called. While Asperger syndrome does infer high cognitive functioning, it is also characterized by no significant delays in language skills, self-help skills, or adaptive behaviour. The individual's difficulties are limited to social functioning as well as stereotyped behaviours and repetitive mannerisms. Therefore, it is clear that Zachary has autistic disorder rather than Asperger syndrome.

Social and Emotional Development

It is not at all surprising that Zachary is significantly delayed in his socio-emotional development given that AD is characterized by impaired social interaction, problems with verbal and nonverbal communication, and unusual, repetitive, or severely limited activities and interests. Typical socio-emotional development during the first years of life includes the development of trust, security, and self-regulation, the development of play skills, and an increasing ability to understand and respond to the emotions of others. Zachary's behaviours during his preschool years obviously did not lend themselves to typical development in this area. He was a toddler who had great difficulty simply handling the environmental stimulation he faced on a daily basis. Playing with other children and relating to the emotions of others was given little attention as he and his family struggled to cope. While at age six Zachary is beginning to respond more to those around him, he is still very withdrawn and lacks the social skills necessary to independently take part in most play situations with his peers. It is likely he will have lifelong difficulties with social and emotional issues.

What We Know...

Autism and Social Development

From the start, typically developing infants are social beings. Early in life, they gaze at people, turn toward voices, grasp a finger, and even smile.

In contrast, most children with ASD seem to have tremendous difficulty learning to engage in the give-and-take of everyday human interaction. Even in the first few months of life, many do not interact and they avoid eye contact. They seem indifferent to other people, and often seem to prefer being alone. They may resist attention or passively accept hugs and cuddling. Later, they seldom seek comfort or respond to parents' displays of anger or affection in a typical way. Research has suggested that although children with ASD are attached to their parents, their expression of this attachment is unusual and difficult to "read." To parents, it may seem as if their child is not attached at all. Parents who looked forward to the joys of cuddling, teaching, and playing with their child may feel crushed by this lack of the expected and typical attachment behavior.

Children with ASD also are slower in learning to interpret what others are thinking and feeling. Subtle social cues — whether a smile, a wink, or a grimace — may have little meaning. To a child who misses these cues, "Come here" always means the same thing, whether the speaker is smiling and extending her arms for a hug or frowning and planting her fists on her hips. Without the ability to interpret gestures and facial expressions, the social world may seem bewildering. To compound the problem, people with ASD have difficulty seeing things from another person's perspective. Most five-year-olds understand that other people have different information, feelings, and goals than they have. A person with ASD may lack such understanding. This inability leaves them unable to predict or understand other people's actions.

Although not universal, it is common for people with ASD also to have difficulty regulating their emotions. This can take the form of "immature" behavior such as crying in class or verbal outbursts that seem inappropriate to those around them. The individual with ASD might also be disruptive and physically aggressive at times, making social relationships still more difficult. They have a tendency to "lose control," particularly when they are in a strange or overwhelming environment, or when angry and frustrated. They may at times break things, attack others, or hurt themselves. In their frustration, some bang their heads, pull their hair, or bite their arms.

Sources: Strock (2004) and www.nimh.nih.gov/publicat/autism.cfm.

Motor and Sensory Development

If you were to see Zachary's kindergarten class on the playground, at first glance you would probably have a difficult time identifying him. However, if you were to observe the children as they played, you would soon see a young boy who looks awkward when he runs and has difficulty balancing. Observation in the classroom would reveal further physical challenges. Zachary experiences problems with fine motor skills as well as gross motor skills. For example, he is not able to manipulate scissors like his peers and has some difficulties with printing using a pencil.

Zachary's low motor skills were noted when he was first diagnosed with autistic disorder. On standardized development tests, such as the *Vineland Adaptive Behaviour Scales – Interview Edition*, he scored at the 19th percentile on the motor skill domain. His mother was also reporting at this time that he was exhibiting odd physical behaviours, such as head-banging and an overwhelming response to noise and touch (see *Mother's Comments* on page 246). This normal looking young boy was obviously not reaching his motor milestones as one would expect and he was also responding differently than other children his age to basic sensations and perceptions.

What We Know...

Autism and Sensory Motor Difficulties

According to the U.S. National Research Council (2001), a review of the literature revealed that most children with autism exhibit sensory and motor difficulties at some time in their development. Some children exhibit these difficulties as early as the first year of life while others begin to manifest sensory difficulties during the toddler period, and motor delays and clumsiness when more complex skills are required in preschool and/or elementary school.

Ayres (1972) proposed that children with autism exhibit sensory and motor difficulties due to dysfunctional sensory systems involving the following three basic senses: tactile, vestibular, and proprioceptive. Hatch-Rasmussen (1995) summarized how difficulties with these senses may affect children with autism (www.autism.org/si.html):

The tactile system includes nerves under the skin's surface that send information to the brain. This information includes light touch, pain, temperature, and pressure. These play an important role in perceiving the environment as well as protective reactions for survival. Dysfunction in the tactile system can be seen in withdrawing when being touched, refusing to eat certain textured foods and/or to wear certain types of clothing, complaining about having one's hair or face washed, avoiding getting one's hands dirty (i.e., glue, sand, mud, finger-paint), and using one's finger tips rather than whole hands to manipulate objects. A dysfunctional tactile system may lead to a misperception of touch and/or pain (hyper- or hypo-sensitive) and may lead to self-imposed isolation, general irritability, distractibility, and hyperactivity.

The vestibular system refers to structures within the inner ear (the semi-circular canals) that detect movement and changes in the position of the head. For example, the vestibular system tells you when your head is upright or tilted (even with your eyes closed). Dysfunction within this system may manifest itself in two different ways. Some children may be hyper-sensitive to vestibular stimulation and have fearful reactions to ordinary movement activities (e.g., swings, slides, ramps, inclines). They may also have trouble learning to climb or descend stairs or hills, and they may be apprehensive walking or crawling on uneven or unstable surfaces. As a result, they seem fearful in space. In general, these children appear clumsy. On the other extreme, the child may actively seek very intense sensory experiences such as excessive body whirling, jumping, and/or spinning. This type of child demonstrates signs of a hypo-reactive vestibular system; that is, they are trying continuously to stimulate their vestibular systems.

The proprioceptive system refers to components of muscles, joints, and tendons that provide a person with a subconscious awareness of body position. When proprioception is functioning efficiently, an individual's body position is automatically adjusted in different situations; for example, the proprioceptive system is responsible for providing the body with the necessary signals to allow us to sit properly in a chair and to step off a curb smoothly. It also allows us to manipulate objects using fine motor movements, such as writing with a pencil, using a spoon to drink soup, and buttoning one's shirt. Some common signs of proprioceptive dysfunction are clumsiness, a tendency to fall, a lack of awareness of body position in space, odd body posturing, minimal crawling when young, difficulty manipulating small objects (buttons, snaps), eating in a sloppy manner, and resistance to new motor movement activities.

What Therapies did Zachary Experience Before Entering School?

Once Zachary was diagnosed at age three, his parents had to decide what therapies or programs would be best for him. They knew that early intervention was critical so they arranged for continuing speech therapy (private) and added occupational therapy to deal with Zachary's sensory difficulties (funded through Community Services). They also established a home-based Applied Behavioural Analysis (ABA) program. According to Zachary's mother, they chose this type of program for a number of reasons. First, they live in a small community where no centre-based programs are available. Second, they felt it was important to have Zachary learning from therapists who had experience working with autistic children and the ABA therapists met this criterion. Third, they wanted their child in a program that was reputable and had a history of success with children like Zachary. From their research, they concluded that ABA has the "longest and best-documented track record of any therapeutic intervention for children with autism." The ABA program requires therapists to use logically sequenced lessons to teach expressive, receptive, cognitive, fine motor, and gross motor skills, and the results of these lessons are carefully recorded. This meant that the data collected by Zachary's therapists would clearly indicate where he was excelling and where he needed extra help. Zachary's parents did consider other programs for him, such as auditory integration training and art therapy; however, these programs were not readily available in their region so implementation would be difficult. ABA seemed the perfect fit for their family and their situation.

What We Know...

Interventions for Children with Autism

There are a number of specialized interventions, or teaching methods, that are used to assist children with autism with their learning. According to Siegel (2003), there is no one method that is "best," rather there are methods that are "very good for some children some of the time" (p. 310).

ABA is one of these teaching methods. The Cambridge Centre for Behavioural Studies (www.behavior.org/autism) describes the key features of ABA as follows:

1. The person's behaviour is assessed through observations that focus on exactly what the person does, when the person does it, at what rate, and what happens before (antecedents) and what happens after behaviour (consequences). Strengths and weaknesses are specified in this way.
2. Skills that the person does not demonstrate are broken down into small steps.
3. To teach each step: (a) give a clear instruction, provide assistance in following the instruction (for example 'prompt' by demonstration or physical guidance) and use materials that are at the person's level, (b) get a correct response, and (c) give a positive reinforcer (a consequence that will lead the person to do the behaviour again in the future).
4. Many opportunities or trials are given repeatedly in structured teaching situations and in the course of everyday activities.
5. Instruction emphasizes teaching a person how to learn: to listen, to watch, to imitate.
6. As the person progresses, guidance is systematically reduced so that the person is responding independently; prompts are faded out.
7. As steps are acquired, the person is taught to combine them in more complex ways and to practice them in more situations.
8. Problem behaviour is not reinforced. The person is not allowed to escape from learning and is redirected to engage in appropriate behaviour.
9. The person's responses during every lesson are recorded. These data are used to determine if he or she is progressing at an acceptable rate. If not, that part of the program needs changing.

Jones (2002) identified the following strengths of ABA: (1) it is early intervention, (2) it involves individual teaching sessions, (3) it has structure and consistency, (4) the program involves and informs parents, and (5) parents are supported by trained therapists. On the other hand, Jones had several reservations about the ABA program. Do the children become prompt dependent? Which outcomes are chosen as measures of success? Which elements of the program lead to the outcomes observed? How are therapists recruited, trained and supervised?

Initially, Zachary's ABA program included four therapists who worked with him six days a week. Eventually, this was reduced to two therapists who visited the home three to four times a week. Zachary still receives ABA therapy, even though he has entered school. His therapist visits his home twice a week after school hours.

From The ABA Therapist's Notebook...

I first took the training necessary to become an ABA therapist from the consultant that the parents had chosen. I started working with Zachary when he was three years old and not talking. He only said a few words and was still in diapers. I worked three-hour shifts three days a week in the afternoons and another therapist worked the same amount of hours on three other days. We have been doing this for three years now and he has certainly come a long way. We teach Zachary the drills that the consultant writes up. We try to do this in as many different settings as possible and with many different types of materials. We keep doing the drill until he has mastered it five times with at least two or three different therapists.

Zachary has changed a lot since I first started working with him. He is much more social with his peers and people in general. He doesn't seem to have a problem talking to people he doesn't know very well. His memory for things has improved. He remembers the words to songs he has only heard once, can tell you about certain movies that he likes, and has become a fairly good reader. He is reading at a grade two level already. He loves to talk about, play with, or even read about airplanes, fire trucks, or big equipment. Zachary is doing great with his printing and has no problems spelling sight words out loud. He can do simple math questions, identify money, but has a hard time doing directive drawing. He loves the computer and has no difficulty playing games on it both at home or at school.

Zachary likes to go on outings with me to the beach, the park, McDonalds, and shopping. He never would go with anyone but his parents before. He is going to private swimming lessons and finally doesn't mind getting his hair wet. He also attends the "Friends" club once a week with other kids that have autism. Zachary is very eager to learn new things but at times needs some encouragement to keep going. We sometimes forget that he is a kid and needs to spend time doing things other than his ABA drills. He acts just like other kids do when it comes to interacting with his sibling. Sometimes they even get into trouble or have little arguments. Zachary is getting much better at not getting so mad when he doesn't get his own way.

If you were to meet Zachary, you would have no idea that he has autism. He looks and acts just like any ordinary child and that is the greatest compliment he could give us for all the hard work that we have put him through over the past three years.

Zachary's mother indicated that their only disappointment with the ABA program was that its intensive one-on-one approach did not help Zachary with his social development. They were aware of this quite early in Zachary's therapy program so they arranged for a specially trained child care worker to assist Zachary at daycare. Zachary attended daycare for two years prior to starting school.

Something To Think About...

ABA is only one of several specialized interventions used to help children who are autistic. Others that are commonly used include The Miller Method, Greenspan Method (Floortime), TEACCH (Treatment and Education of Autistic and Communication Handicapped Children), Pivotal Response Training (PRT), and Social Stories. If a parent asked you for information and recommendations regarding the use of one or several of these interventions for his or her child, how would you respond?

For information on specialized interventions for a child with autism, you can access the following Web sites and books:

- Autism Canada Foundation
  www.autismcanada.org/home.htm
- Autism Society Canada
  www.autismsocietycanada.ca/approaches_to_treatment/overview/index_e.html
- Autism Society of America
  www.autism-society.org/site/PageServer?pagename=about_treatment_home

Jones, G. (2002). *Educational provision for children with autism and Asperger Syndrome: Meeting their needs.* London: David Fulton Publishers.

Siegel, B. (2003). *Helping children with autism learn.* New York: Oxford University Press.

What was the Transition to School Like for Zachary?

School Readiness

Before Zachary entered kindergarten in 2006, he was assessed for *school readiness* by both daycare and school personnel. The daycare report reads as follows:

> *Zachary is a pleasant, happy boy who has been diagnosed with autism. He has attended daycare for two years and has acquired many skills during that time. Zachary appears to be comfortable in his daycare routine; he knows the daily routine and is usually able to make transitions smoothly as long as he is prepared ahead of time. Zachary is beginning to stand up for himself, for example he will say, "I sad" or "I frustrated."*
>
> *Zachary can often be found playing with Lego and prefers to play alone or parallel to others. He enjoys spending long periods of time in the sandbox using*

the diggers. He is beginning to ask children to join his play. He is also taking part in more group games. Zachary will usually watch the children playing and then physically move into the play. If there is a conflict, he does not appear to understand how to resolve it.

Children with autism will often engage in solitary play.

Zachary's fine and gross motor skills have improved. He has been showing more interest in using scissors. He appears awkward at times in his running and hopping on one foot and tends to avoid balancing games.

One of Zachary's strengths is his cognitive development, particularly in classification, seriation, numbers, and memory. He exhibits some difficulties with time, such as knowing what happened yesterday.

Zachary's spoken language is usually clear and he has no difficulty expressing what he does or does not want. He uses echolalia frequently, either repeating something he has just heard or something he has heard in the past. Often these statements or sounds are ones he has heard on television.

Areas of development that appear to be in need of strengthening are: prewriting and reading skills, art skills, and imaginary play. Zachary enjoys printing his name and will print some letters. He will draw basic shapes and has started to draw faces with eyes and mouths (no noses). Imaginary play is especially difficult for Zachary. He requires particular props to engage in pretend play and needs a lot of modelling before he will join in.

An area we have been focusing on with Zachary is respecting the personal space of others. He tends to get too close to his peers who in turn become upset. We have used booklets such as "A Tad Too Close" as well as role modelling to help

Zachary with this. His teachers and his peers have also learned to say "Too Close Zachary" in response to his behaviour.

We have seen Zachary grow in many areas of development over the past two years and have enjoyed being a part of his journey. We wish Zachary and his parents all the best!

Zachary was also assessed for school readiness by an early intervention specialist who works for the school district in which Zachary resides. Using the *Brigance Preschool Screen*, she had difficulty testing Zachary as he would not focus on task demands and required a great deal of prompting from both his mother and herself. Consequently, she stated that "the validity of the test results is questionable and must be viewed with caution." Zachary obtained a score of 41 percent. A score of less than 92 percent for a child Zachary's age indicates developmental delay. The early intervention specialist noted the following:

With prompting and one-on-one assistance where needed, Zachary was able to say his name and age, identify many body parts, build a tower with ten blocks, identify colours, and name pictures of objects. Zachary was unable to give acceptable descriptions for the use of common objects, print his name, draw a picture of himself, or demonstrate one-to-one correspondence.

It is recommended that Zachary have an individualized education program (IEP) in order to define the goals he will work towards in kindergarten. Zachary will require support in order to function within the school setting. The nature and extent of this support will be outlined in his IEP. Strong communication is recommended in order to provide coordinated support and to facilitate Zachary's transition into the kindergarten program.

Transition to School

Zachary's transition into school was carefully planned. A "Transition Meeting" was held in the spring before his fall entry into kindergarten. The teacher and support personnel who would work with Zachary in September met with his parents as well as all those individuals who had provided therapy services during his preschool years (i.e., ABA therapists, occupational therapist, and speech therapist). The meeting provided the opportunity for all these individuals to share information about Zachary and to take part in the decision-making regarding his upcoming entry into school. As a result of this collaboration, the following decisions and recommendations were made:

- the Support Services Teacher will write up an IEP for Zachary
- the IEP will be adjusted regularly
- Zachary will have a full-time educational assistant with him at school

- the school will provide all Zachary's current therapists with an outline of the school routine so that they can help Zachary become familiar with the routine before he enters school
- Zachary will experience some mock trials of fire drills before entering kindergarten
- Zachary will visit the current kindergarten classroom during the next month

As a consequence of this attention given to Zachary's transition to school, his entry into the classroom went as smoothly as could be expected. He had moments when he was overwhelmed by his new surroundings, but he soon settled relatively well into the routine of school life. His teacher and his EA quickly learned how Zachary would respond to the different classroom activities and, as a team, adjusted their behaviours accordingly. In particular, they became especially sensitive to when Zachary would need time away from the classroom to "de-stress."

What We Know...

Team Duties and Responsibilities of the Teacher and Educational Assistant

As in any team approach, it is critical that teachers and educational assistants work closely together to support the child with special needs. This requires a clear understanding of not only individual job responsibilities but also team duties and responsibilities. The Peterborough Victoria Northumberland and Clarington Catholic District School Board in Ontario provides their teacher-EA teams with the following direction:

The EA is assigned to meet the needs of specific students and/or program needs within the school; the EA is there because of a particular child, but is a support in order that all students' needs are met. The teacher is ultimately responsible for the education of all students in the class. Both the teacher and the EA are there for the benefit of the child.

Communication between the teacher and EA must be clear, concise, honest, and frequent to ensure the same goals for the students' needs are being met. There needs to be trust and respect, openness, acceptance, and active listening.

The teacher needs to keep the EA informed about day-to-day operations, changes in schedule, and special events (i.e., keep notes in a teacher/EA communication book so that issues can be discussed at an appropriate time).

Team meetings may be requested by either staff member.

Communication cannot be left to chance. Keep open lines of communication. At the beginning of the year and regularly throughout the year, the teacher and EA should meet and discuss the following:

- *duties required*
- *performance of EA — positive and corrective (teacher should be specific and find ways to tactfully correct and constructively criticize)*
- *written communication (teacher/EA communication book)*
- *lines of communication — parents should communicate with teacher*
- *educational plans, IEP lessons plans, teaching strategies, upcoming events, and conflicts*
- *what to do if a student is absent — the EA should report to the Supervisor to determine his/her duties*
- *keeping informed — the EA should inform the teacher of results of lessons, behaviours, etc…*
- *clarification of directions — the EA should ask questions to clarify anything that is unclear*
- *conflict resolution — implement problem solving approaches*

Source: Peterborough Victoria Northumberland and Clarington Catholic District School Board. *Educational Assistants Resource Guide.* Accessed at: www.pvnccdsb. on.ca/library/Special%20Education/EA%20resource%20guide.pdf.

What is School Like for Zachary?

The educational assistant who currently works full-time with Zachary in his kindergarten class keeps a journal of his school experiences. The following two journal entries are indicative of what a day at school is like for Zachary:

Journal Entry #1

> *First day after the holiday — Zachary's mother said he was reluctant to come to school. He was ten minutes late so we didn't have as much time as we usually do before recess. He was sad that we didn't do any ABA drills. We read two social stories and he was upset his name wasn't in the bus story while Jared's and Monica's were. He enjoyed playing "Memory." He was given a warm welcome by lots of his classmates at recess time. We went to the gym with about ten kids. Zachary had lots of fun but it was too noisy and he covered his ears a couple of times. He waited by the door at the end because of the noise. I will limit the group size to four or five from now on. We had a short music class because of an assembly. Zachary didn't want to go but when I said it would be just a short class, he agreed. He participated well but covered his ears again and bent over. I took him back to class and he played happily by himself until his classmates returned.*

Journal Entry #2

> *Excellent day! Zachary was happily on task when I arrived. He had no problems with seatwork except that Sasha had a disagreement with him over a crayon.*

Zachary got up in frustration and said he wasn't working anymore and he was a very bad boy. I told him that wasn't true. I tried to engage him in his work at a different table but he refused. He stood by himself for a few minutes and then returned to his chair and resumed his work. We had extra outside time in the morning. Zachary played on the swings. He and Cameron and Yannick had fun together pushing me on the swing. They thought this was hilarious. When we were eating lunch, Zachary suddenly announced that he didn't like everybody. I told him that sometimes we may feel that way for a while, but we shouldn't say it because it hurts people's feelings. Sasha agreed saying that his feelings were hurt. Zachary was fine after that and he and Sasha interacted well. At lunch playtime we played tag with Moira, Andrea, and Craig. Zachary played happily for at least 10-15 minutes but was tired then and lay down on the ground. As I was about to get him up, Moira lay down next to him and they began to play "naptime" so I let them be. Another child came and joined them. In gym class, Zachary started out playing "freeze-tag" but some kids were screaming and he became distressed and asked to leave. I said we'd leave for a few minutes and then try the gym class again. He led me to the library and chose a Pokemon book which he went through, telling me who all the characters were. He was very into this! Then he asked me to read him another Pokemon book. After this, we went back to the gym and had a great time playing "The Tide is Coming In." Later, at centre time, Zachary was cooperative and there were no significant problems.

It is important to encourage children with autism to socialize with their peers.

From The Psychologist's Notebook...

The EA's journal entries reveal how Zachary is typical of students with autism disorder. He perceives returning to school and the music class as slightly threatening new experiences (even though he knows what they are), so he is reluctant to go. His sadness over not doing his ABA drills speaks to the predictability, comfort, and personal reinforcement he gets from the daily routine of the ABA therapy. Conversely, the "Memory" game was enjoyed for the very same reasons. He wants his name to be in the story because of his strong egocentrism; a trait that makes the class's warm welcome that much more enjoyable, but also makes sharing the crayon that much more difficult. His emotional temperament makes recovering from the crayon exchange a longer-than-normal affair. His sudden announcement that he doesn't like everybody was probably due to a sense of social discomfort with Sasha (and maybe others) that had slowly built up. He needed a way of releasing or diminishing it. Finally, the separation time and the book in the library were his solace from the noisy gym (and perhaps social stimulation overload).

When reading these journal entries, we react to what Zachary does with understanding because we "know" that this is what he is all about. We are more tolerant of the patience that is regularly required to work with him and we realize that we will do some things that will not be successful. The success that the EA has with Zachary is directly attributable to these specific understandings.

What Educational Approach is Best for Zachary?

An Emphasis on Communication and Socialization

While Zachary is currently a full participant in his kindergarten class, he does have a very unique educational program that is clearly outlined in his comprehensive IEP. The learning expectations for his first school year were designed to specifically address his particular strengths and needs, and do not necessarily match the learning expectations designed for his peers. One of Zachary's major areas of need is improved communication skills (see his *Communication Goals for Kindergarten* on page 247). Other areas of need include improved social skills (sharing, waiting his turn, identification of emotions, playing games with peers), gross motor skills (jumping, hopping, balancing, and ball skills), fine motor skills (printing using a pencil), and behaviour (ability to deal with transitions and frustrations).

The following accommodations and adaptations were also identified for Zachary's kindergarten year and are currently being implemented by his teacher and the support staff:

- demonstrate/model communication
- demonstrate/model tasks
- teach at a slow pace
- teach key concepts and vocabulary
- reduce oral language expectations
- emphasize visual/tactile clues and support
- assign a class "buddy" for Zachary
- utilize a student planner/home-school book

Zachary is fortunate to live in a province that has a provincial outreach program dedicated to children with autism and related disorders. This program provides support to schools by offering workshops and training on autism. In addition, program professionals visit schools and consult with school-based teams regarding educational and behavioural programming. In other words, the school personnel involved in Zachary's education have access to resources, training, and expert consultation that enhances the services he already receives from the school-based team. Already, early in his kindergarten year, consultants from this outreach program have visited Zachary's school and observed him in the classroom. Based on their observations, and input from school personnel and Zachary's parents, they identified concerns/problems and proposed recommended strategies/interventions. For example, in terms of behaviour supports, the consultants' report stated:

> *Zachary is currently displaying some work avoidance behaviours. Zachary's educational assistant has implemented excellent supports. Consider implementing a visual timer (egg timer) to let Zachary know how long an activity or break lasts. Follow more difficult activities (journal, directed art) with a choice time. This would be a motivational strategy for Zachary ("first you do…. and then you can…"). Define one-to-three specific rules for Zachary to work on between now and June. Create a portable visual reminder of the rules to show Zachary the expectations. Implement a token economy and reinforce Zachary with stickers/check marks each time he displays the desired rule. Once Zachary has gained five stars, he can earn a highly desired reward. Coupled with this behaviour technique, try reading social stories to him (ones that target the specific skills you are working on). When social stories are read regularly, they provide an internal script for Zachary to follow so that he can meet social expectations.*

The consultants also observed that Zachary appeared to be an anxious child which is common in autistic spectrum disorders. They suggested the following:

> *when Zachary shows signs of anxiety, offer him a break. This break can be outside and timed. Give Zachary a tangible item (Koosh ball) to use during these break times. Once Zachary becomes familiar with this item, it will signal him to "calm down." It can then be used to keep Zachary calm when he is in class (e.g., squeezing Koosh ball during circle time). Read a social story on calming. Because there is*

a pattern to Zachary's avoidance behaviours, pre-empt these avoidance episodes by offering breaks and decreasing the amount of work to complete (e.g., spend less time at circle, offer a break from circle, implement a choice time).

It is apparent, then, that the current educational approach implemented for Zachary is one that clearly recognizes his special needs. Academics are emphasized, however, a great deal of attention is paid to helping Zachary with the communicative and social aspects of school. While his teacher is responsible for the delivery of curricula in the classroom, other professionals provide the additional support that is necessary to allow Zachary to function successfully in the school setting.

What We Know...

Teaching Students with Autism

Smith, Polloway, Patton and Dowdy (1998) identified the following three critical elements that affect the learning experiences of students with autism: (1) teacher attitude (how the teacher views the student and how the teacher feels about his or her ability to help that student learn), (2) teacher expectations (what the teacher expects that the student can learn), and (3) teacher competence (the teacher's knowledge and skill in teaching students with autism).

Given the increasing use of inclusion as an educational strategy, this does not imply that the onus is solely on the regular classroom teacher to take full responsibility for the success or failure of an autistic student's learning experiences. As the U.S. National Research Council (2001) noted, effective programming for children with autism and their families requires that the regular classroom teacher be a part of a support system team that works together to solve complex neurological, sociological, educational, and behavioural problems. In other words, regular classroom teachers do affect the learning of students with autism in a very significant way; however, they are not expected to do this alone. They should always have the support of other professionals who have specific skills in providing effective programming for this special population.

Strategies for Teaching Students with Autism

1. Use visual methods of teaching (i.e., objects, pictures, and graphic symbols). Visual aids can be examined for as long as needed to process information, while oral information is transient. It may be difficult for the student with autism to attend to orally presented information as they have to block out background noises. The use of visual supports enables the individual to focus on the message. Visual supports can be used for daily schedules, activity checklists, calendars, classroom rules, labeling, and social stories.

2. *Provide a structured, predictable classroom environment.*
Students should know where things belong, what is expected of them in a specific situation, and what will happen next.

3. *Provide a customized daily schedule.*
Vary tasks to prevent boredom, and alternate activities to reduce anxiety and possibly prevent some inappropriate behaviours. It may be helpful to alternate large group activities with opportunities for calming activities in a quiet environment. In addition, the incorporation of physical activity and exercise at points throughout the day is helpful.

4. *Know the individual.*
Maintain a list of the student's strengths and interests.

5. *Provide positive praise.*
Let the student know what he or she does right or well.

6. *Use meaningful reinforcements.*
The student with autism may not be motivated by common reinforcers. He/she might prefer some time spent alone, time to talk to a favourite staff member, a trip to the cafeteria, an exercise routine such as going for a walk, time to play with a favourite object, music, playing in water, getting to perform a favourite routine, items that provide specific sensory stimulation, or sitting at the window. It is important to know what is reinforcing for each child.

7. *Consider sensory factors.*
Are there distracters such as light, movement, reflection, or background patterns?
Are there fans, loud speakers, fire alarms, or several people talking at once?
What is the general sound level, and the predictability and repetitiveness of sounds?
Are there textures which seem to be aversive?
Are temperatures appropriate?
Does the student demonstrate a need to explore through touch and yet avoid being touched?
How does the student react to movement?
Does the student have taste preferences?

8. *Note tasks and activities which create frustration.*
Examine the environment for items, sounds, and activities that may result in sensory overload for the individual. Make available those sensory experiences that may be calming for the student. When feasible, decrease environmental distracters that interfere with learning or confuse, disorient, or upset the student.

9. *Have a relaxation area.*
Have a calm, quiet, designated area where the student can go to relax.

10. *Plan and present tasks at an appropriate level of difficulty.*

11. *Use age-appropriate materials.*

12. *Provide opportunities for choice.*

13. *Avoid long strings of verbal information.*
Break down instructions and use visual aids.

14. *Pay attention to processing and pacing issues.*
Give the student ample time to respond.

15. *Use concrete examples and hands-on activities.*

16. *Introduce unfamiliar tasks in a familiar environment.*
When this is not possible, prepare the individual for the new environment through the use of visual aids such as pictures, videotapes, and/or social stories.

17. *Use organizational aids.*

18. *Provide opportunities for meaningful contact with peers who demonstrate appropriate social behaviour.*
Involve the student in shared learning arrangements. Pair with buddies for walking down the hall, playing outside, and special school events. Vary peer buddies across time and activities to prevent dependence on one child. Peers may also be involved in providing individualized instruction.

19. *Encourage independent effort and incorporate proactive measures to reduce the likelihood of becoming dependent on prompts.*
Use visual aids to decrease the reliance on prompts from the teacher/EA. Be careful that the EA is not always closely positioned next to the student. Increase awareness of environmental cues. Teach in natural environments that contain the cues and reinforcement that prompt and maintain the behaviour.

20. *Plan for transitions and prepare the student for change.*
Social stories can be used to prepare the student for new situations.

21. *Direct and broaden fixations into useful activities.*

22. *Develop talent areas.*
If the child demonstrates a particular interest and strength in a specific area (i.e., music, drama, art, graphics, computer), provide opportunities to develop further expertise in the area.

Source: Adapted from Saskatchewan Education (1999), www.sasked.gov.sk.ca/branches/curr/special_ed/sepub.shtml.

Evaluation of Progress

Because of the complexity of Zachary's case, his progress in kindergarten is tracked by a number of people. First of all, his teacher evaluates how he is doing academically and how he is adjusting to the demands of school both inside and outside the classroom. Her guide for these evaluations is Zachary's IEP. The learning goals developed by the school-based team serve as the learning expectations designed specifically for him. Each goal is clearly stated and is followed by a description of how progress towards this goal should be measured. For example, one goal is for Zachary to improve his social skills by "sharing with others." His teacher is monitoring how well he is doing in this area by "observing and tracking appropriate behaviours on a monthly basis." In other words, she collects data each month (play time on Fridays), records how he is doing (the number of times he shares with others) and then compares the results across months. By following the recommendations in Zachary's IEP, such as how to monitor his progress, his teacher is able to provide valuable information to all members of the school-based team, including Zachary's parents.

Zachary is also evaluated regularly by his therapists (i.e., ABA therapists, speech therapist, and occupational therapist) and, as mentioned previously, the specialists from the provincial outreach program for autism. The advantage of having so many professionals involved in his education is that a comprehensive report of his progress is available to all of those involved. The teacher is certainly not left to manage Zachary's education on her own. As she stated, "I really feel like part of a team that has the best interests of Zachary as its goal. I am learning so much from the other professionals and I can depend on their feedback to guide me in determining Zachary's progress."

What We Know...

Evaluating the Progress of Students with Autism

Scott, Clark, and Brady (2000) addressed the issue of how teachers can tell whether or not their teaching is effective and the student with autism is learning efficiently. They emphasized that these students have learning difficulties that are serious and teachers cannot rely on guesswork to determine if learning is occurring as it should. Therefore, Scott et al. (2000) presented the following four principles for teachers to follow when evaluating their students:

1. Directly evaluate the skill being taught.
2. Measure the skill frequently.
3. Display the student's progress graphically.
4. Make instructional changes that reflect your findings.

How is Zachary Different from Other Students who are Autistic?

As mentioned earlier in this chapter, there are a range of similar symptoms that fall under the conditions collectively referred to as autism spectrum disorders. The fact that autism is referred to as a "spectrum" disorder correctly implies that individuals who are autistic can display varying abilities and disabilities. Knowing that a child has been diagnosed with ASD provides some insight into the areas of development that may be affected; however, it certainly does not provide a clear or precise picture of a child's level of functioning in each of these areas. As with other exceptionalities, each child who is autistic has a unique combination of strengths and needs.

Zachary has been diagnosed as having mild autistic disorder, which means that he has less severe symptoms than many other children who are autistic. Zachary is also very cognitively capable which means he is a high functioning autistic child and most likely to benefit from being in an inclusive classroom with his same age peers (Siegel, 2003). Zachary's cognitive abilities are also what set him apart from many other children who have AD. The following examples highlight these differences when you consider children with autism in terms of low, moderate, and high cognitive functioning:

- *The Low Functioning Child with Autism.* Daria is a six-year-old child who was diagnosed with AD when she was a toddler. It was not long after Daria's birth that her parents suspected something was wrong. She just never seemed to be like other babies her age. She slept a lot and seemed unresponsive to their attempts at playing with her. It did not seem to matter what environment she was in, nothing seemed to capture her attention. Instead, Daria responded to most new environments by crying, and despite their efforts to comfort her, her parents usually had to take her home in order to calm her down. Daria's troubling behaviours only increased as she entered the toddler period. She avoided cuddling and did not respond to any of her parents' attempts to connect with her. Most of the time she simply stared into space and rocked back and forth. She showed no signs of beginning to use language other than using a high pitched scream when agitated. She was diagnosed with AD and an intellectual disability at an early age. Despite great efforts by her parents and therapists, she has made few gains. As a six-year-old, she attends her neighbourhood school and has the full-time support of an educational assistant. She joins her same-age peers for some of their daily activities, such as music, gym, and outdoor activities; however, she works one-on-one with her EA outside the classroom for much of the school day as she becomes too distraught in the classroom setting.

What We Know...

Low Functioning Students with Autism

Over 75 percent of individuals with autism have I.Q.s below 70 (Alloy, Jacobson, & Acocella, 1999). This means that they are at the severely affected end of the autism spectrum. In other words, they may have little or no language and little awareness of others. They may also exhibit considerable unusual and repetitive behaviours, some of which may be self-injurious in nature.

Schooling for these children involves a focus on four critical skills: (1) mobility, (2) self-care, (3) communication, and (4) social interaction (Scott et al., 2000). Their intellectual disabilities limit the rate at which they learn and, in the most severe cases, typical interventions for autism are not successful (Siegel, 2003).

- *The Medium Functioning Child with Autism.* Nathaniel, is a six-year-old child who was diagnosed with AD at age four. Like Zachary, he seemed to be developing normally for the first year of his life. While he was a "fussy" baby, he seemed to be reaching the milestones that are expected of a child his age. Then, it was as if his development stopped abruptly: no more babbling, no more playing with his toys, and no more interest in the activities going on around him. His fussiness increased and he could not be consoled with cuddling and attention. His parents were very concerned but somewhat reassured when told by a medical professional that their child was fine. As Nathaniel grew and his behaviour seemed to differ more and more from other children his age, his parents became convinced that their child was developmentally delayed. They had little knowledge of autism and it was not until a routine check-up that a doctor recommended an assessment by a specialist. Nathaniel was four years old when he was finally diagnosed with AD and an intellectual disability. He had received no therapy to that point and because his parents were not financially able to pay for private therapists, Nathaniel's only treatment before entering school was speech therapy and attendance at a local preschool. He entered kindergarten with limited skills in the areas of language and social interaction. Nathaniel requires the full support of an EA and has been making the most gains in the areas of mobility and self-care.

What We Know...

Medium Functioning Students with Autism

According to Siegel (2003), most children with autism fall within the classification of "medium functioning" and those who do well are usually those who have "at least some capacity for spontaneous language use" (p. 461). However, in most cases, even those who do well continue to need support throughout their lives.

Medium functioning children with autism benefit from early intervention and may be successful in an inclusive setting for the early elementary grades but then benefit from special classes for at least a part of the school day.

- *The High Functioning Child with Autism.* Pierre, is a six-year-old kindergarten student who, like Zachary, is a high functioning child who has an autism spectrum disorder. However, Pierre differs from Zachary in that he was diagnosed with Asperger syndrome and not autistic disorder. Pierre has an above average I.Q. and excellent expressive language skills. In fact, before he entered preschool at age four, his parents thought their only child was exceptionally clever and without any learning difficulties. Pierre had an insatiable appetite for knowledge about electricity which his parents supported. Upon entry to preschool, concerns about Pierre rose immediately. He was having many problems interacting with his classmates, including an inability to take part in conversations and listen to others, an inability to understand nonverbal cues, and an inability to deal with others being in close proximity to what he perceived as his space. Preschool was extremely stressful for Pierre and the tension was causing him to have outbursts of hand flapping and crying. At first, his parents attributed his difficulties to the fact that he had spent his early years as an only child with little exposure to other children. After all, he seemed like a little adult in the way he talked. However, when Pierre failed to "settle in" to preschool, he was assessed by a clinical psychologist who determined that he has Asperger syndrome. Supports were immediately put in place to address Pierre's emotional, behavourial, and social skills.

What We Know...

High Functioning Students with Autism

According to Myles (2005), children with Asperger syndrome are often misunderstood as they have average to above-average intelligence as well as advanced verbal skills and good rote memory skills. However, despite the fact that they appear to be like their peers, they do have difficulties that affect their success in school. Myles describes the characteristics of those with Asperger syndrome as follows:

- unable to interact with others despite their desire for these interactions to occur (i.e., cannot share conversational topics, appear unwilling to listen to others, and engage in one-sided conversations)
- inability to understand nonverbal cues
- demonstrate concrete and literal thinking skills (e.g., difficulty comprehending abstract topics)
- become easily stressed and show this stress in unconventional ways (e.g., unusual behaviours)
- exhibit atypical sensory responses (e.g., exposure to loud noises may cause anxiety)
- often have poor motor skills along with coordination and balance problems

According to the Autism Canada Foundation (2004), Canada has an autism rate that equals that of the United States. A child born in Canada today has a 1 in 195 chance of being diagnosed with autistic spectrum disorder. Autism is by far the most rapidly advancing childhood disorder in North America. Because Canadian schools have adopted the inclusive approach to educating children with exceptionalities, children with autism are frequently placed in the regular classroom. Is the regular classroom the appropriate educational setting for all children (low, medium, and high functioning) who have autism?

Closing Zachary's File

The despair that Zachary's parents felt when their toddler began to retreat from the world is obvious from his mother's comments (see page 246). Fortunately, that despair has turned to pride as his parents look back on the past three years. While it has not been an easy journey, Zachary is a much happier child who is able to attend kindergarten with his same age peers. He has made great strides in his ability to communicate and in his ability to take part in daily activities both at home and in the classroom. These gains have been due, in large part, to the involvement of Zachary's parents in his therapy. According to Siegel (2003), "…research consistently points to parent involvement in a child's treatments as a critical factor in quality" (p. 444). Therapists and teachers can spend many hours working with a child who has autism but it is the parents who have the most opportune moments for teaching, reinforcing, and encouraging the child.

Zachary's parents have been exemplary in their efforts to help their son. They searched unwaveringly for answers when Zachary first showed signs of not developing normally. They researched autism and intervention options when they received the diagnosis of autistic disorder. They made sure that Zachary had the best therapists they could find. They took advantage of all the supports available to their family in the area in which they lived. They ensured that Zachary was prepared to enter kindergarten and now that he is in school, they continue to advocate for his special needs while supporting those who work with him. Zachary's parents believe strongly that the inclusive setting is where their son belongs.

Despite these efforts and successes, neither Zachary's parents nor his therapists or teachers are naive about the challenging road ahead. In terms of school, the early elementary years may be the easiest for Zachary. Once the emphasis in the classroom turns to independent learning primarily acquired through seatwork, Zachary may have difficulty coping with the learning environment. He probably will have difficulty learning non-rote material that requires him to understand the perspective of others, and many aspects of the curricula require this ability. Socializing with his peers will certainly be another challenge. In terms of life outside of school, he will need to further his communication and socialization skills in order to "fit in" and live an independent life. He will probably always be viewed as "different" but given his high intellectual functioning and the early interventions he has experienced, Zachary's future holds great promise.

From The Psychologist's Notebook...

When I first met Zachary's kindergarten teacher, she expressed concern about having a child with autism in her class. She was doubtful that she had the necessary skills to help Zachary learn. Her professional training had not included any course work in special education. We talked at length about Zachary, how he would be similar to other children in the class and how he might differ. We discussed his IEP and the role his educational assistant would play in helping him cope with the school environment. The more we talked, the more relaxed she became. I could see that it was her "not knowing" that was causing her anxiety. By the end of our conversation, she was the one making suggestions regarding teaching and classroom management strategies.

When Zachary's new teacher asked for one last word of advice, I told her to carefully foster the parent-teacher relationship because this is where she would get her greatest support. Once parents realize that a teacher truly cares and is trying his or her very best to help their child, a relationship of trust develops. The parents trust the teacher to be open about what is happening in the classroom and the teacher trusts the parent to support his or her efforts. This means that when things do not go as well as expected, the teacher and the parents can work together to make things better. On the other hand, when things do go well and the child experiences learning successes, the teacher and the parents can share in the joy of watching the child grow.

Learning More About Students with Autism

Academic Journals

Journal of Applied Behavior Analysis

Journal of Autism and Developmental Disorders

Journal of Child Psychology and Psychiatry

Journal of Communication Disorders

Journal of Developmental Psychology

Books

Myles, B. (2005). *Children and youth with Asperger syndrome.* Thousand Oaks, CA: Corwin Press.

National Research Council, Committee on Educational Interventions for Children with Autism, Division of Behavioral and Social Sciences and Education. (2001). *Educating children with autism.* Washington, DC: National Academy Press.

Scott, J., Clark, C., & Brady, M. (2000). *Students with autism.* San Diego, CA: Singular Publishing Company.

Web Links

- *Autism Canada Foundation*
  www.autismcanada.org
  This site was created to provide "uncensored" resources to parents and caregivers. It provides up-to-date news and opinions on research, treatments and other issues pertaining to autistic spectrum disorders.

- *Autism Society Canada*
  www.autismsocietycanada.ca/index_e.html
  ASC, a federation of Canada-wide provincial and territorial autism societies, promotes evidence-based services/treatment, best practices, and standards through its Web site. There is an informative section on approaches to treatment and education.

- *Autism Society of America*
  www.autism-society.org
  This ASA site provides comprehensive information about autism, including characteristics and causes, diagnosis, treatment, and educational issues.

- *Autism Spectrum Disorders (Pervasive Developmental Disorders)*
  www.nimh.nih.gov/publicat/autism.cfm
  The United States National Institute of Mental Health provides a detailed booklet on autism that describes symptoms, causes, and treatments, with information on getting help and coping.

- *Autism Spectrum Disorders Canadian-American Research Consortium*
  www.autismresearch.ca
  The ASD-CARC Web site includes interactive online questionnaires designed to uncover different information regarding individuals with an ASD, and their family members. It also provides links to important online resources and useful agencies.

- *Canadian Autism Intervention Research Network*
  www.cairn-site.com
  The CAIRN Web site provides up-to-date summaries of research from around the world as well as information for individuals and families living with ASD, educators, policymakers, and clinicians.

Please visit the Online Learning Centre for *Special Education in Canada* at www.mcgrawhill.ca/olc/edmunds for additional learning and study resources.

Taking It Into Your Classroom...

Including Students with Autism

When a student who has autism is first placed in my classroom, I will:

- review what I know about autism and locate resource materials
- read the student's file
- consult with the student's previous teachers
- consult with the student's parents
- meet with the school-based team to discuss the student's current school year

Other: _____

_____

When I suspect a student in my classroom has autism, I will:

- review what I know about autism and locate resource materials
- observe the student's behaviour in different classroom/school situations
- consult with other school personnel who are familiar with the student
- consult with the student's parents
- meet with the school-based team to present the information I have collected

Other: _____

_____

Key points to remember in my daily interactions with a student who has autism:

- the student may be unable to understand the social intentions of others
- the student may lack the ability to engage in appropriate social interactions
- the student may lack the ability to communicate through language
- the student may use echolalia
- the student may engage in repetitive activities

Other: _____

_____

Key points regarding programming for a student who has autism:

- the classroom environment should be structured
- classroom activities should be predictable and routine with attention to transitions
- curricula should address weaknesses (i.e., attending and language skills)
- curricula should address appropriate play and social interactions
- a functional approach to behaviour should be implemented

Other: _____

_____

Key points regarding evaluation of the progress made by a student who has autism:

- evaluation should be based on what the student is expected to know and understand
- evaluation should include careful observations of the student's behaviour
- evaluation should identify any reduction in behaviours that interfere with learning
- evaluation should include assessment of products as well as affective outcomes
- evaluation should identify strengths and weaknesses

Other: _____

_____

CHAPTER 10

Students with Multiple Disabilities

Name: Monique Levesque
Current Age: 14
School: C.M. Munroe Junior High School
Grade: 8

Monique is a good humoured teenager who loves to hum the melodies of her favourite songs. She also enjoys attending local sporting events and being around animals, especially horses and dogs. Due to her physical disabilities, Monique is dependent on a wheelchair for mobility. She also has severe communication problems that make conversing with others a significant challenge. It is apparent from Monique's story that it takes a great deal of support from a variety of professionals in order for some students to be accommodated in the regular classroom. However, it can be done if these professionals work together to provide an appropriate learning environment for the student. Regular classroom teachers certainly play a role in educating students with multiple disabilities but they must never be in a situation where they feel they are solely responsible for meeting the needs of these very special students.

Monique's Transition Into Kindergarten
Summary of Skills and Abilities

Age at Time of Transition: 4 years, 11 months

Monique is an engaging child who was born with multiple physical needs. She has decreased range and ease of movement in her joints. She may not have typical muscle groups and the muscles she has are weak. Monique has had surgery on her feet but has otherwise been healthy. Both hips are dislocated, but stable. Her right knee is unstable and causes some discomfort when bent, so she can not tolerate kneeling. Monique tends to tip her head back to look at things, however, vision is reported as normal.

Summary of Child's Current Functional Abilities

Mobility/Positioning

Monique uses a manual wheelchair to propel herself 10 to 15 feet on smooth, flat terrain. She requires assistance to negotiate corners and for longer distances. Monique can roll from her back to her side and can assist in sitting up. She lies down from sitting independently and tolerates lying on her stomach for five minutes. She sits independently in long-leg sitting but needs a pillow behind her as her balance reactions are slow. She can sit on a low bench with one person nearby, but needs full assistance to get on and off of it. Monique uses a standing frame for up to 40 minutes but needs full assistance to get in and out of it. She wears AFOs (ankle-foot-orthoses) daily.

Self Care

Monique can finger and spoon feed herself independently. She needs a raised edge on the plate/bowl to help her to scoop. Monique is slow in organizing and chewing food, may have decreased oral sensation, and tends to get distracted. In the past, Monique has had some coughing/choking episodes and therefore needs supervision while eating, especially for crunchy and chewy foods. She drinks from a regular cup. Monique needs maximal assistance for dressing, but should be encouraged to assist as much as she is able. She is not toilet trained. In school, she will require a change table and a supportive toilet seat with side/trunk support and a footrest.

Hand Skills

Monique needs to be well supported during fine motor activities. She can be seated in her wheelchair or in an adapted wooden chair but the table height must be no higher than her bellybutton for Monique to use her arms successfully. Monique has limited range of movement in her shoulders and arms and has difficulty in reaching above shoulder height, in turning her palms side up, and in bending her knuckles. She does best with movements with her hands close to her body and in midline. Monique can participate in crafts and activities with larger objects, however she has difficulty manipulating smaller objects. She uses loop scissors mounted on a wooden block for cutting. Activities using two hands together are challenging and she does better if she can stabilize objects against her body.

Communication/Symbol

Monique has a few words that she is able to say, "mom," "dad," and "yeah." Her vocalization typically consists of vowel sounds and "g" or "k" sounds. She tends to vocalize to indicate pleasure and has recently begun to vocalize the melody of songs. Monique has a small vocabulary of "signs" which have been modified in consideration of her limited hand and arm mobility. She tends to use her signs when prompted but not often spontaneously. At home, Monique typically communicates through signs, looking, pointing, and gesturing.

Monique also uses a laptop computer which is programmed for voice output. The computer is mounted on Monique's wheelchair by a metal post with a plastic key guard covering the keyboard. Monique can turn the computer on and off independently. She has six "pages" of pictures and she can move between the pages independently. The computer is set up with a touch-screen such that when Monique touches a picture on the screen her message is spoken aloud. Monique has been taking the computer to playschool since February 1997.

Monique attends playschool two afternoons a week. She uses the computer in the kitchen centre to interact with the other children and at circle time to take turns. Monique needs encouragement to use the computer to interact verbally with the other children. She wants to be close to the other children but tends to watch them or play parallel to them. Communication delays make cooperative play difficult. Monique uses paper picture boards at other centres in the classroom (playdough, craft, snack). The paper boards are taped to the table and the vocabulary is activity specific. Monique uses these boards if prompted.

Learning

Monique was seen by a psychometrist in June 1996 for an assessment of her developmental abilities to aid in therapy and learning goals. Monique demonstrated delayed performance in all areas with receptive comprehension of language and various terms and concepts being a relative strength for her.

Child's Support Needs

Monique requires assistance to move around on the floor and to get in and out of her wheelchair. She needs assistance with dressing/undressing and toileting, and should be supervised when eating. Monique needs prompting to use her computer, signs, picture boards, and words to interact with the other children and she needs support in helping the other children learn her ways of communicating.

Monique Levesque

Paediatric Review

Age at Time of Review: 6 years, 10 months

Monique is an only child. Monique's mother was 33 years old at the time of her pregnancy. Monique's father is a business owner who is in good health. There is a paternal cousin with mild cerebral palsy and developmental delay. He is ambulatory.

The pregnancy was complicated by pneumonia during the first month of gestation. The mother was treated with Erythromycin. An ultrasound done at 16 weeks gestation was normal. Movements were not very active throughout the pregnancy. Monique was born by spontaneous vaginal delivery at 39 weeks. Birth weight was 5 pounds 11 ounces. Resuscitation was required after birth. Monique was removed from the delivery room for a few minutes but then brought back to her parents. There was meconium stained amniotic fluid (may be aspirated during labour and delivery causing neonatal respiratory distress). Monique was noted to have multiple deformities of her limbs.

Monique is currently a 6 year, 10 month old girl with the following problems:

Arthrogryposis Multiplex Congenital
Monique has bilaterally dislocated hips, a subluxed right knee, and kyphosis. She has had extensive investigations including an MRI, muscle and skin biopsy, and EMG but no underlying diagnosis has been found. There is no current need for surgery.

Duane Syndrome
Monique recently had eye surgery. On examination, Monique has much less extension of her neck when fixating on items in front of her. Her posture is very functional and much improved over one year ago. There continues to be limited abduction and adduction of the eyes.

Expressive Language Disorder
Monique is using some PIC symbols and has these on her table. Monique has a small vocabulary of signs and seems eager to learn more. She uses some single words, however, she does not use them consistently. She has made excellent progress in early reading skills and recognizes letters of the alphabet. She attends well to conversation addressed to her and has comprehension skills that are well beyond her expressive skills.

Developmental Delay
Psychological testing done one year ago revealed a developmental delay. On the *Leiter International Performance Scale*, Monique's non-verbal abilities fell within the mild developmental handicap range. Completion of the *Peabody Picture Vocabulary Test* indicated a receptive vocabulary at approximately the three year level when her chronological age was five years, four months. On the *Boehm Test of Basic Concepts*, Monique's performance again indicated a mild developmental delay. Social adaptive functioning was at a similar level.

Speech and Language Progress Report

Age at Time of Review: 13 years, 9 months

Monique was seen for regular speech and language therapy throughout the school year. The following report assesses how she progressed towards the stated goals.

Answering questions
Monique enjoyed having stories read to her. During the reading of these stories, the therapist would ask simple comprehension questions related to characters, time/place, feelings, and events. Generally, it was observed that Monique would not typically want to respond using her Dynamite, instead she preferred to point to pictures and/or vocalize a response. When encouraged to use her Dynamite, Monique preferred responding with single words. Most often her responses were correct but limited in scope.

Monique participated fully in answering questions using her Dynamite when asked questions of a personal nature. She revealed many of her interest areas and activities both inside and outside of school.

Asking questions
Throughout the year, a question page on her Dynamite was being referred to more and more within her academic program. Monique was shown where her page was but appeared to have difficulty finding it efficiently. Practice and examples of asking questions related to her basic needs were demonstrated and attempts were made to encourage Monique to practice. However, Monique had not demonstrated the implementation of a single question word located on the Dynamite with the therapist. It was possible that since her routines have been established at school, perhaps the need for asking questions is limited to specific locations or people.

Building on early phonemic awareness training or early reading skills
Monique was asked to match an orally presented rhyming word with a key word located on a familiar page of her Dynamite. While several examples and practice opportunities were provided, Monique only showed a 50 percent success rate. It appeared that this activity did not hold her interest for very long and at times she would stop participating.

Monique was also encouraged to use her alphabet board to demonstrate initial letter and initial letter sound identification. The therapist would attempt to give either an isolated sound or an initial sound in a word and ask her to identify it on her key pad. Monique demonstrated some success; however, this task also had limited interest for Monique and typically she would stop participating after several turns.

Overall, Monique has a high interest in books and relaying personal information. These were areas in which she participated fully. As far as developing more functional and academic skills, she appeared less inclined to participate and thus actual progress was difficult to determine at this time. This may have been related to how the skill was presented, her ability to attend during the sessions, and her interest level.

Monique Levesque

Excerpt from Monique's IEP
Grade 8

Strengths:
- receptive language skills (comprehension)
- social skills
- interpersonal relations
- receptive language skills (listening)
- positive outlook
- rote memory skills
- visual awareness skills
- visual information skills

Needs:
- expressive language skills (speaking)
- expressive language skills (writing)
- fine motor skills
- gross motor abilities
- problem-solving skills
- receptive language skills (decoding)
- motor coordination skills
- perceptual reasoning skills
- phonological awareness skills
- visual tracking skills

Health Support Services:
- chokes very readily
- requires Occupational Therapy, Physiotherapy, and Speech and Language Pathology

Individualized Equipment:
- computer, monitor, and printer
- alternative keyboard producing software
- symbol-writing software
- talking word processor software
- augmentative communication device
- wheelchair
- change table and commode
- lift

General Accommodations:

Instructional

- assign one task at a time
- encourage use of assistive technology (symbol writing software, text-to-speech software, and word processing software)

- encourage use of augmentative communication system
- provide concrete/hands-on materials
- minimize distractions
- prioritize tasks for completion
- read all written instructions
- reduce new skills to small steps
- provide work samples on desk
- provide a scribe
- use a homework/communication book
- provide visual aids

Environmental

- provide alternative work space
- provide shelves for material storage
- provide a slant board, special chair, and special desk

Assessment

- allow use of assistive technology (talking word processor software and word processing software)
- extend time limits
- provide extra time for processing
- allow frequent breaks
- read questions on tests
- reduce the number of tasks used to assess a skill
- provide visual materials
- provide updated subject specific vocabulary as required
- allow use of augmentative communication system
- provide a scribe
- allow use of adaptive technology (touch screen)

Monique Levesque

Monique Levesque

Example of Teacher-Parent
Daily Communication Sheet

Date: September 20, 2006

Arrival: Happy — she told me she had a good time horse back riding
                    yesterday

Language: Grammar (appositives) — we did this together with Monique
                    using Dynamite

Mathematics: Patterning with beads — Monique used Dynamite to identify
                    patterns. I will get large beads to make manipulation easier for
                    Monique.

Science: Quiz — Monique did well!

Geography: Quiz — 12/12 well done!

French: Reviewed phrases on Dynamite.

Phys Ed: Practised for softball throw.

Special Events: Monique went to Skipping Class at recess and loved it.
                    Physiotherapist worked with Monique in the afternoon.

Comments: Monique wheeled down and got her own tickets today.
                    We are really trying to encourage independence.

Reminders: Monique should wear red and white or Canada shirt
                    tomorrow.

Homework: Geography — practise location of continents in atlas.
                    French — find pictures on computer for highlighted
                    vocabulary words.

What are Monique's Multiple Disabilities?

Physical Disability

Monique has been diagnosed with *arthrogryposis multiplex congenital* (AMC), a condition in which there are multiple joint contractures at birth. A contracture is a limitation in the range of motion of a joint. Unfortunately, Monique has a severe form of AMC resulting in contractures that affect many of her joints, including her hands, wrists, elbows, hips, feet, and jaw. She also has muscle weakness which further limits her movement. As a consequence, Monique is non-ambulatory and uses a wheelchair for mobility. She is dependent on caregivers for transfers in and out of her wheelchair, and for self-care activities such as dressing, bathing, and toileting. Her physical challenges are evident in most everything she does as she has difficulty with arm and hand movements and also lacks the ability to speak clearly. She also has difficulty swallowing.

What We Know...

Physical Disabilities

According to Heller and her colleagues (2000), physical disabilities that result in an inability to move well "can result in problems with most major systems of the body, including the musculoskeletal, integumentary (skin), sensory, respiratory, immune, and gastrointestinal systems, in addition to other body systems (e.g., renal, cardiovascular, and immune systems)" (p. 5). In other words, when an individual has a condition such as arthrogryposis multiplex congenital, the lack of normal muscle tone and movement can significantly impact his or her physical health. Therefore, a number of professionals (e.g., physiotherapists and occupational therapists) are usually involved in the individual's care. In order to maximize the health of the musculoskeletal system, attention is paid to muscle strength, range of joint motion, and bone strength and density.

Expressive Language Disability

Monique's physical disabilities have affected her ability to speak. Early in her development it was apparent that while she could comprehend language, she was unable to express language. This is not surprising given that speech relies on a complex system of sounds made by precise movements of the lips, tongue and palate (Parker, 1997). Just as Monique has difficulty swallowing, her AMC has affected her ability to complete the movements necessary to produce language. According to Parker, it is much more likely that it will be speech rather than language that will be affected by the structural problems encountered in AMC.

In order to allow her optimal opportunities to communicate, Monique was introduced to sign language and encouraged to use a picture board. By age two and a half, she was using some signs and had about 50 symbols on her board. By age four and a half, she was still using some signs but they were modified due to her limited hand and arm mobility. By this time, her picture board was now on computer and programmed for voice output (simply touching a picture on the screen results in a spoken message). At age six, there was still concern regarding Monique's limited ability to express herself. She tried to vocalize single words but these words were rarely understood. While she knew about 20 signs at this point, she usually pointed or used eye gaze to indicate what she wanted. She only used her picture symbols when encouraged to do so.

As a teenager, Monique still relies on vocalizations, facial expressions, and gestures to indicate her needs. She supplements these communication skills by utilizing her computer. While the computer is not usually her first choice of communication, she uses it more frequently and independently than she did in the past. According to Monique's speech language pathologist, vocabulary pages on Monique's computer are customized. Programming, typically completed by Monique's parents or her EA, allows vocabulary to be added as necessary (e.g., vocabulary highlighted in curricula). There are currently a large number of pages available to Monique and she is reported to be able to navigate through these pages to find required words and messages. She is noted to understand pop-up pages and can combine up to five words into a sentence, although the words are not always in correct sentence order. See the *Speech and Language Progress Report* on page 285 for more details on how Monique's limited communication skills affect her academic development.

What We Know...

Speech Disorders

Speech and language disorders refer to problems in communication and related areas such as oral motor function. These delays and disorders range from simple sound substitutions to the inability to understand or use language or use the oral-motor mechanism for functional speech and feeding.

Speech disorders refer to difficulties producing speech sounds or problems with voice quality. They might be characterized by an interruption in the flow or rhythm of speech, such as stuttering, which is called dysfluency. Speech disorders may be problems with the way sounds are formed, called articulation or phonological disorders, or they may be difficulties with the pitch, volume, or quality of the voice. There may be a combination of several problems. People with speech disorders have trouble using some speech sounds, which can also be a symptom of a delay. They may say "see" when they mean "ski" or they may have trouble using other sounds like "l" or "r." Listeners may have trouble understanding what someone with a speech disorder is trying to say. People with voice disorders may have trouble with the way their voices sound.

Because all communication disorders carry the potential to isolate individuals from their social and educational surroundings, it is essential to find appropriate and timely interventions. Because of the way the brain develops, it is easier to learn language and communication skills before the age of five. Technology can help children whose physical conditions make communication difficult. The use of electronic communication systems allow non-speaking people and people with severe physical disabilities to engage in the give and take of shared thought.

Source: National Dissemination Center for Children with Disabilities, www.nichcy.org/pubs/factshe/fs11txt.htm.

Visual Disability

Monique was also born with an eye movement disorder called Duane syndrome (DS). While she has good vision in terms of the ability to see, she has difficulty moving her eyes inward towards her nose (adduction) and outward toward her ears (abduction). Since Monique was trying to maintain ocular alignment by using poor head posture (chin up), it was decided that eye muscle surgery may be of benefit. When Monique was seven years old, she underwent a procedure designed to align her eyes and thereby reduce her abnormal head posture. Since the procedure, Monique's posture has significantly improved but she continues to have limited adduction and abduction. Because of her visual disability, Monique requires a larger than normal computer screen that is carefully positioned to allow optimal accessibility.

What We Know...

Visual Disabilities

The term *visual disabilities* refers to a broad spectrum of impairments. Individuals may be legally blind, have low vision, or have visual impairments that require special accommodations. According to Erin (2003), about one in 1,000 school-aged children has a visual impairment that significantly affects their ability to learn. Professionals with expertise in visual disabilities are required to help these students and their teachers with the necessary accommodations that are needed to facilitate learning. These accommodations may include: special lighting, optical devices for reading, enlarged print, materials written in Braille, auditory materials, and/or assistive technology.

Developmental Disability

When she was a preschooler, Monique was diagnosed as being "developmentally delayed." A developmental delay indicates a significant difference between a young child's current level of functioning (i.e., cognitive, motor, communicative, social, and adaptive) and his or her chronological age. In Monique's case, it was obvious that her motor development and her communicative abilities were delayed. However, Monique's cognitive abilities were unknown, especially given her inability to communicate effectively. Testing by a psychometrist at age four resulted in a report stating that Monique was "delayed in all areas" with a relative strength being her receptive language. On the *Leiter International Performance Scale*, a totally nonverbal test of intelligence and cognitive abilities, she scored in the mild developmental handicap range. Similar results were revealed when the *Boehm Test of Basic Concepts*, a test of basic positional concepts (e.g., size, direction in space, and quantity), was administered. Completion of the *Peabody Picture Vocabulary Test*, a measure of receptive vocabulary and a screening test of verbal ability, indicated a two year developmental delay. Despite these indicators of cognitive delay, there was, and still is, considerable concern on the part of both Monique's parents and the professionals testing her that these results may not be accurate. As stated by Monique's paediatrician, "It continues to be difficult to make an accurate assessment of Monique's underlying intellectual abilities based on standardized psychological tests due to Monique's physical limitations and her expressive language disorder."

What We Know...

Developmental Disabilities

"Developmental disabilities are a diverse group of severe chronic conditions that are due to mental and/or physical impairments. People with developmental disabilities have problems with major life activities such as language, mobility, learning, self-help, and independent living. Developmental disabilities begin anytime during development up to 22 years of age and usually last throughout a person's lifetime" (U.S. Dept. of Health and Human Services, www.cdc.gov/ncbddd/dd/dd1.htm).

"A developmental disability is a lifelong condition that means a person grows and develops differently and more slowly than others. Individuals with a developmental disability may have difficulty learning and processing information, understanding abstract concepts, or adapting to some of the demands of daily life. This disability varies greatly between individuals and may or may not be accompanied by other physical conditions" (British Columbia Association for Community Living, www.bcacl.org/bcacl_faqs/index.cfm).

Something To Think About...

It is clear that Monique requires considerable specialized attention from a wide variety of professionals and she needs very particular programming in order to derive benefit from her school experiences. Despite the current move towards more inclusive classrooms and schools, is it possible that Monique's educational needs exceed what can be reasonably expected from regular classroom teachers? What are the advantages and disadvantages of having Monique in an inclusive classroom versus a segregated classroom?

What Factors Contributed to Monique's Disabilities?

Monique's most significant challenge is her physical disability. According to medical professionals at *Avenues*, a support group for arthrogryposis multiplex congenital (www.avenuesforamc.com/index.htm), a genetic cause is found in only 30 percent of individuals diagnosed with AMC. Monique's case is similar to those of the majority of AMC cases; no genetic link can be found.

Furthermore, no definitive cause of Monique's AMC has been determined in terms of environmental causes either. However, there were some complications during pregnancy that must be considered as possible factors that lead to Monique's physical disabilities. Monique's mother developed pneumonia during the first month of gestation and was treated with an antibiotic drug. While an ultrasound done at 16 weeks gestation was normal, movements were not very active throughout the pregnancy.

What We Know...

The Causes of Arthrogryposis Multiplex Congenital

Research on animals has shown that anything which prevents normal joint movement before birth can result in joint contractures. The joint itself may be normal. However, when a joint is not moved for a period of time, extra connective tissue tends to grow around it, fixing it in position. Lack of joint movement also means that tendons connecting to the joint are not stretched to their normal length; short tendons, in turn, make normal joint movement difficult.

In general, there are four causes for limitation of joint movement before birth:
1. Muscles do not develop properly (atrophy). In most cases, the specific cause for muscular atrophy cannot be identified. Suspected causes include muscle diseases (for example, congenital muscular dystrophies), maternal fever during pregnancy, and viruses which may damage cells which transmit nerve impulses to the muscles.
2. There is not sufficient room in the uterus for normal movement. For example, the mother may lack normal amount of amniotic fluid, or have an abnormally shaped uterus.
3. Central nervous system and spinal cord are malformed. In these cases, arthrogryposis is usually accompanied by a wide range of other conditions.
4. Tendons, bones, joints or joint linings may develop abnormally. For example, tendons may not be connected to the proper place in a joint.

Source: Avenues, www.avenuesforamc.com/index.htm.

Monique's physical disability has further affected her ability to speak and her ability to swallow. Therefore, AMC is a direct cause of her expressive language disorder. The causes of developmental expressive language disorder in children who are not limited by a physical disability are still not known.

In terms of Monique's visual problems, Duane syndrome is a rare, congenital disorder that is more common in females. Unlike Monique, most individuals who have DS have no other disorders. The cause of DS is unknown; however, according to the National Human Genome Research Institute (www.genome.gov/11508984), many researchers believe that DS results from a disturbance (either by genetic or environmental factors) during embryonic development. Since the cranial nerves and ocular muscles are developing between the third and eighth week of pregnancy, this is most likely when the disturbance happens. It is interesting to note that this is the same period when Monique's mother was being treated for pneumonia.

The causes of intellectual disabilities are also varied. Again, genetic causes (e.g., Down syndrome) or environmental factors (e.g., complications during pregnancy) must be considered. Given that AMC does not usually affect intelligence, Monique's intellectual disability may be due to environmental factors. Resuscitation was required after birth so it is possible that Monique's brain was deprived of oxygen during that time.

How Have Monique's Disabilities Affected Her Development?

Monique's difficulties with movement and communication from the time of birth have undoubtedly affected her development. Her physical development has obviously been significantly delayed because of her severe case of AMC. Movement of both her upper and lower body is problematic, limiting her ability to care for herself and to interact fully with her environment. The fact that communication is also a problem for Monique impacts greatly on her cognitive development. Babies and young children use their mobility (e.g., reaching, crawling, and walking) and their development of language (e.g., babbling, talking, and questioning) to learn about the world around them. Theories of child development indicate that children are active learners who are influenced by adults and other children (Piaget, 1952; Vygotsky, 1978b). In other words, mobility and communication facilitate intellectual development. According to Forney and Heller (2004), when infants and young children are unable to experience sensory and motor experiences at critical periods in their development, many areas of development can be affected. This is also true of language disorders as they have the potential to isolate the child from their environment, thus reducing learning opportunities. Monique has been fortunate in that her parents have attempted to provide her with rich learning experiences that emphasize what she can feel, see, and hear. Despite their efforts, however, she has been challenged intellectually by her inability to actively seek out knowledge and extend what she knows by communicating with peers and adults.

Therapists assist young children with mobility difficulties in their efforts to explore the world.

From The Psychologist's Notebook...

When considering Monique's development, it is sometimes easy to get caught up in what she cannot do. However, there is lots of positive behaviour that we can talk about too. In terms of emotional development, Monique has always displayed a great deal of emotionality. She may not be able to communicate her feelings with words, but her body language and vocalizations exude a great deal of personal expression. Her smile can light up a room as it does so quite often. Monique is a very happy child; she experiences great delight in attending hockey games, playing with her two dogs, and being around horses. She has a great sense of humour and shares it with all those who she comes in contact with. She also loves music and while she has trouble speaking, she has no trouble humming along to her favourite melodies. Monique also uses her body language to express sadness, frustration, and pain. She is a wonderful child who has a great ability to make those around her see the joy in life.

What is School Like for Monique?

Monique's parents have always been very involved in her education. They believe strongly that she belongs in the regular classroom, and not just as a "token member of the class."

They continue to advocate for her full participation in classroom activities and they provide support to school personnel to make sure this happens. As they expressed, "We don't want Monique sitting at the back of the English class doing an unrelated activity and having that considered inclusion." They are in constant contact with Monique's teacher, her EA, and all of the professionals involved in providing services to their child. They realize that "the school system isn't perfect" so they have taken it upon themselves to ensure that all of these people work together in a unified effort. This means constantly monitoring, and participating in, their daughter's education. One way they do this is by attending school-based team meetings where they share information and make suggestions regarding Monique's current needs. This has not always been a positive experience for them. There have been school personnel who have not appreciated their high level of participation. As Monique's father stated, "It hasn't been easy when you see so many areas that could be improved in terms of how Monique is educated…as parents we have learned that we have to pick our battles and take some satisfaction in seeing small changes."

What We Know...

Family Involvement

Given the complicated learning needs of children with severe and multiple disabilities, it is critical that educators and families work together to provide the best educational experiences possible for these children. As Chen and Miles (2004) stated, teachers too often view parents who are very involved in their child's education as nuisances since they take up valuable time in the teacher's work day. Chen and Miles (2004; p. 32) suggested that teachers need to consider the following process of building effective family-professional relationships:

1. Analyze how the structure of educational programs affect family involvement.
2. Acknowledge that each family is a complex and unique system.
3. Understand the significant impact that a child with disabilities has on the family.
4. Implement family-friendly strategies that invite family participation and value family contributions.

Chen and Miles (2004; pp. 41–42) also presented the following tips that teachers can use when speaking with parents:

1. Pay attention to the parent's nonverbal expressions and listen carefully to what is said.
2. Monitor your own nonverbal behaviours and facial expressions.
3. Allow the parent sufficient time to express and describe his or her feelings.
4. Acknowledge and validate the parent's feelings and demonstrate that you understand him or her by reflecting the feelings that the parent has shared.

5. Respond to the parent's expression of difficult situations and emotional issues in a sensitive and caring way.
6. Do not ignore a parent's emotional statement about the child's disability by making superficial comments that ignore the parent's feelings and concerns.
7. Paraphrase what the parent says by restating the message. Paraphrasing helps to clarify the intended message.
8. Summarize what the parent has said to communicate that you understand and to check your perception.
9. Weigh what is being said, and do not make quick judgments. Resist the temptation to give advice or to make recommendations too quickly.

Due to the efforts of her parents and the dedicated professionals involved in her care, Monique is currently active and involved in all grade eight subject areas. Her EA describes a typical school day as follows:

> *Monique arrives by bus in the morning. While I am there to meet her, we always arrange for a peer to help her off the bus and into the schoolyard. Once the bell goes, Monique enters the school and I take off her coat and unpack her backpack. I have a look at her Home Communication Book (see example on page 288) to see if her parents have written anything that is important for me to know. Her parents are really involved in her education so that makes my job easier. Around this time in the school day, I also initiate communication with Monique by asking her things like what she did the previous night. Monique rarely initiates this type of communication but she does respond when I ask her questions. It is easy to tell if Monique isn't feeling well because she is usually smiling and very pleasant to work with.*

What We Know...

Encouraging Communication

Sometimes school personnel are too quick to meet the needs of the non-communicative student and, in doing so, they eliminate the student's need to communicate at all. Kaiser and Grim (2006; p. 464) suggested that those working with non-communicative students make use of the following strategies to increase the likelihood that these students will show an interest in their environment and, subsequently, make communicative attempts:

1. *Interesting materials.*
   Students are likely to communicate when things or activities interest them.
2. *Out of reach.*
   Students are likely to communicate when they want to gain access to something they cannot reach.

3. *Limited portions.*
   Students are likely to communicate when they do not have the necessary materials to carry out an instruction.
4. *Choice-making.*
   Students are likely to communicate when they are asked which of several options they would prefer.
5. *Assistance.*
   Students are likely to communicate when they need assistance in operating or manipulating materials.
6. *Unexpected situations.*
   Students are likely to communicate when something happens that they do not expect.

The school day starts with science. Monique is part of a small group so I usually stand back and let her fully participate with the other students. Her classmates are really good at helping her. For instance, when they have to look at things through the microscope, one of the students in her group will carry the microscope over to Monique so she can look through it. With prompting, Monique uses her Dynamite to take part in discussions.

What We Know...

Peer Relationships

Sometimes the physical and learning needs of a student with multiple disabilities are so great that their social needs are given much less attention. However, when discussing students with severe disabilities, Schwartz, Staub, Peck, and Gallucci (2006) noted that "the level of importance and value that teachers place on supporting and facilitating their students' relationships will influence greatly their successful development" (p. 400). Schwartz and her colleagues (2006; p. 384-386) offered the following intervention strategies that were designed to facilitate peer relationships in the inclusive classroom:

Small Group Membership (Teacher Developed)
Be sure there are opportunities for all students to make a substantial contribution to the group. This may mean making accommodations for students with disabilities. Encourage students within the small groups to suggest accommodations for their peers who are disabled.

Small Group Membership (Peer Developed)
Create unstructured situations for play and exploration. Plan ahead for peer support by conducting ability awareness training, setting up buddy systems, and having class discussions about ways in which peers with disabilities can be included in peer-directed activities.

Class Membership

Develop a strong sense of community in your classroom. Have regular class meetings that create opportunities for students to have a voice in decisions about how the class is conducted and the expectations for behaviour in the classroom community.

School Membership

Include students with disabilities in active roles at school (e.g., bringing the daily attendance sheet to the principal's office or taking tickets at a basketball game). Ensure that the necessary supports and accommodations are in place so that students with disabilities are included in school-wide rituals and celebrations (e.g., wearing a school sweatshirt, carrying a school bag, hanging out in a certain area during lunchtime, and attending graduation).

After science, it is recess time. Monique accompanies her peers to the playground. I don't go with her since an adult is always supervising the schoolyard. After recess, it is snack time. I open Monique's snack and then stay with her while she eats. We have to be careful because she sometimes has trouble with swallowing.

Then it is time for French class. Sometimes we miss this and/or other classes as Monique receives in-school speech, physio and occupational therapy on a regular basis. After French class, toileting is scheduled. Monique wheels herself to the specially equipped washroom. I get help from another EA to lift her into the sling and onto the commode. The whole process takes us about twenty minutes.

Next, the class has either history or art. I help Monique with art activities. She needs hand-over-hand support to do things like coloring. Then it is time for lunch. I set up her food and monitor her as she eats. Lunch is followed by math class and then geography class. Monique again takes part in the regular class activities. Her teachers modify the activities for her. I also take note of any new vocabulary that needs to be added to Monique's Dynamite. I usually send the list home to her parents and they enter it into the computer.

Physical education is the last class of the day. Monique really loves this class. A recreation therapist has provided Monique's gym teacher with adaptation ideas that allow Monique to fully participate in the class. For example:

- *Volleyball: Monique holds hands with a partner. A beach ball is placed on her hands/forearms. She moves her arms (guided by her partner) in a small up and down motion in order to bounce the ball without dropping it. She counts the number of successful bounces while trying to beat her personal best.*
- *Basketball: Monique throws a lightweight all-purpose ball to a target on the floor. She also practises passing the ball to a partner.*

- *Bowling: Bowling pins are set up approximately two feet from the gym wall. Using a ramp that rests on her lap, Monique rolls a medium sized ball down the ramp and knocks down as many pins as possible.*
- *Baseball: Using a baseball bat and a T-ball stand that Monique owns, she attempts to make contact with a ball placed on the T-ball stand.*

Monique's school day ends at 3:20. I dress her in her outdoor clothing, get her backpack ready, and strap her up for the bus ride home. Then I accompany her out to the bus.

From The Psychologist's Notebook...

It is obvious that Monique's Educational Assistant plays a greater minute-by-minute role in her educational life than any of her teachers. EAs typically help students like Monique with everything they do at school. Because they get to know the student so well, EAs often provide help with program development and implementation, the adaptation of teaching materials, and the fostering of student independence. EAs are usually assigned on a one-to-one basis for students like Monique but they can also be employed to help several different students in the run of a school day. It is also not uncommon that EAs are the main caregivers for students who may need assistance with feeding, toileting, taking medication, and/or participating in various therapeutic programs such as speech and language training or physical therapy. EAs also often help students participate in extra-curricular activities such as sports, plays, and school clubs and in some jurisdictions, they even assist with bus transportation.

Given all that goes on in a student's life, day-after-day, there is an obvious need for very close connections between students with exceptionalities and their EAs. In many cases, students have such great needs that they are wholly dependent upon their EA. It stands to reason, therefore, that teachers can also become dependent on a child's EA because of the EA's intimate knowledge. Nonetheless, it is important that teachers and EAs understand and respect their respective educational boundaries when it comes to helping the student in the classroom. Sometimes teachers allow EAs to take on more direct teaching responsibilities than they should. Therefore, it is worth noting that the role of an EA is to deliver specific services and programming to students with exceptionalities under the direction of the classroom teacher.

What Educational Approach is Best for Monique?

The Collaborative Model

Thus far, Monique's education can be best described as having been based on inclusive principles using a transdisciplinary model. In other words, her placement in the regular classroom has been planned and monitored by educators (i.e., teachers, special education specialists, and educational assistants), her parents, and professionals who provide her with specific therapies. While the therapists have developed their own therapy-related goals for Monique and provided direct services in the school setting, it has been primarily the teacher and the educational assistant who have been responsible for the delivery of Monique's education. They have received assistance from other members of the team, especially in terms of special education practices, physical positioning, and the use of assistive technology.

As is evident from Monique's current IEP (see excerpts on pages 286–287), the transdisciplinary team has gathered general information about Monique, including her strengths and needs. They have also summarized the special equipment she requires and the health services that are necessary. A large portion of her IEP is dedicated to the accommodations (i.e., instructional, environmental, and assessment) that are needed in the classroom in order for Monique meet her learning goals.

Is this the best educational approach for Monique? Monique's parents feel it is "a good start but there is room for improvement." They would like the transdisciplinary approach to be replaced by more of a collaborative approach. In other words, they would like the team members to work even more as a unit rather than as individuals who provide domain-specific services. "We would like the entire team to work together, learn from each other, and share the responsibility of the delivery of services."

What We Know...

Collaborative Educational Services

According to Cloninger (2004), "the collaborative model is the current exemplary practice in service delivery models for the education of students with severe and multiple disabilities" (p. 13). It involves forming a team of individuals (parents, educators, and those who provide related services) who are willing to share their knowledge and learn from other "experts" in the group. Together, these individuals collaborate on all aspects of the student's school program, including assessment, development of instructional goals, intervention, and evaluation. Cloninger (2004; p. 20) suggested that the collaborative model is composed of the following essential components:

- appropriate team membership
- a shared framework of assumptions, beliefs, and values
- distribution and parity of functions and resources
- processes for working together
- a set of shared goals agreed to by the team

Monique's parents also have concerns about the IEPs that have been developed for their daughter since she has been in school. While they are supportive of the IEP process, they are concerned that "…the IEP doesn't really have enough information, especially when it is for a child with multiple disabilities." For instance, they point out that the current IEP fails to detail how teachers make programming decisions within each subject area. "There seem to be general recommendations, but the IEP doesn't really give specifics about how Monique should be taught in a specific area — like what level she is at now, what the goals are for her in that subject and how these goals can be met by teaching her skills in a proper sequence." These concerns appear to be legitimate. When one of Monique's current teachers was asked how he decides the content of Monique's program, he was unable to explain how curricular decisions are made. Instead, he describes how Monique just does what the other children do but in a simplified form.

Something To Think About...

One of Monique's past teachers, who received limited support from resource personnel in the school, was vague when asked to describe how she modified the curricula to meet Monique's needs. She was unable to comment on the content of Monique's IEP. She indicated that while she did modify activities for Monique, her teaching was mostly guided by Monique's emotional expressions. She said her goal was to keep Monique happy so that school was an enjoyable experience for her. How do you feel about this teacher's goal? How would you react as a teacher if you received limited support in modifying curricula for a high needs child?

What We Know...

Developing Curriculum and Instruction

It is apparent that having an IEP for a student does not guarantee that the best educational practices are in place. IEPs can look very different depending on who has developed them and how they are intended to be used. In the case of students with multiple disabilities, the development of the IEP may require significant effort, yet the results ensure that everyone involved knows the student's program and how it will be implemented. Developing curriculum and instruction must be given considerable attention so that the student is not simply kept busy during the school day, but rather skills are learned in a sequence that leads to the attainment of stated learning goals.

Gee (2004; p. 97) pointed out that there should also be support plans for each curricular period of the student's day. These plans can be developed by answering the following questions:

1. What are the typical class activities and routines within this curricular unit?
2. What typical teaching strategies will be used?
3. What are the expectations for all students?

4. What are the expectations for the focus student?
5. How will the focus student receive information?
6. How will the focus student provide information?
7. What additional types of support are needed for the focus student?

Evaluation of Progress

Just as Monique takes part in the same learning opportunities as her classmates, she is also evaluated on the same schedule as her peers. According to her teachers, they simply modify the test that they are giving to the class (i.e., usually fewer questions) and they allow Monique to communicate her knowledge through the use of her computer. For example, the vocabulary that is used in a particular subject is programmed into her computer so that when she is asked a question, she can indicate the answer by touching the correct symbol on her screen.

When Monique's teachers were asked about how they decide the content of her test, they were again rather vague about their decision-making process. The IEP was not mentioned nor were any specific learning objectives.

What We Know...

Evaluating the Progress of Students with Multiple Disabilities

According to Kleinert and Kearns (2004), evaluating the learning outcomes of students with severe and multiple disabilities should be an integral component of a continuous process that revolves around the IEP. This process involves program planning (establishing appropriate learning objectives), instruction (providing opportunities for the student to meet the learning objectives), and outcomes assessment (monitoring and measuring student progress in order to facilitate ongoing program planning). Kleinert and Kearns emphasized that the IEP is not a static document, but rather an ever-evolving student plan that is based on the standards set for all students. In other words, the IEP is developed with the general curricula in mind. Just like their peers, students with severe and multiple disabilities work towards meeting the curricula demands. There should be no guesswork involved in what the student with disabilities should be doing in class and the evaluation of their progress is critical to ensuring that continuous learning occurs.

There are many evaluation or assessment formats that may be appropriate for students with severe and multiple disabilities (Kleinert & Kearns, 2004; Ysseldyke & Olsen, 1999). These include:

- structured interviews (reports of performance from parents and school personnel)
- checklists (using a list of targeted skills to assess performance)

- performance records (instructional data, graphs, anecdotal records)
- performance tests (observations of the student performing predetermined tasks)
- student portfolios (documents that provide a complete picture of overall performance)

It is important to use as many of these formats as is necessary to determine the student's progress. The continuous development of new learning objectives is only effective if the student has mastered the prerequisite skills that are required to move on to the next level of skill.

Something To Think About...

Monique's father was busy one weekend programming her *Dynamite* (a communication device with picture communication symbols) to include the symbols necessary for Monique to express her knowledge in a science test on Monday. The test was to be on the parts of a microscope and safety in the lab, topics that had already been covered in class the previous week. It was only after the material had been covered in class that the teacher had sent home the information that Monique's father needed to program her computer. Once the information was entered, he helped Monique prepare for the test. Do you think Monique was given the best opportunity to learn and to be evaluated? How could her communication technology be used more effectively?

How is Monique Different from Other Students who have Multiple Disabilities?

When multiple disabilities are involved, each child's situation is obviously unique. There are many possible combinations of cognitive, sensory, and physical disabilities and each disability can vary greatly in both its severity and how it impacts upon other existing disabilities. However, despite the uniqueness of each child's case, there are general similarities that can also be identified across persons with multiple disabilities. Like Monique, many children with multiple disabilities look different than other children. They are perhaps the group most readily identified as having special needs. They often have significant medical needs, difficulty communicating, difficulty with physical mobility that requires special equipment, and an inability to care for themselves. In other words, they require significant, ongoing support. In fact, many of these children are only seen in the company of an adult as they must have constant supervision for a variety of reasons. The children in the following examples typify the similarities that are often seen in persons with multiple disabilities but their individual circumstances also illustrate the uniqueness that one can expect to see in this special population:

- *Cognitive Delay, Visual Impairment, and Cerebral Palsy.* Caleb is a teenager who charms everyone he comes in contact with. He is sixteen-years-old and attends a high school where he spends one period per day in a special resource class and the rest of the day in the regular classroom. Due to his cognitive delay, he is working slightly below grade level in math and reading. His most significant disabilities, however, are a visual impairment and cerebral palsy. He was born prematurely and, as a result, he has retrolental fibroplasias, a condition where the development of retinal blood vessels is disrupted. Consequently, he has low vision that requires him to wear glasses and make use of low vision aids such as large print. In terms of his mobility, he is limited in both his poor vision and his cerebral palsy. Cerebral palsy is a group of neurological disorders that affect body movement and muscle coordination. Caleb has spastic cerebral palsy that is apparent in one leg. It causes stiffness and he has difficulty moving. Because Caleb basically drags the affected leg, he uses a rolling walker to get around the school. This is not always easy as his visual impairment sometimes prevents him from predicting what is in his path. Caleb takes it all in stride, however, and tries his best to keep up with his peers. He is very well liked by his classmates and is included in all school activities both inside and outside of the classroom.

What We Know...

Children who have Visual Impairments Along with Other Disabilities

According to Silberman, Bruce, and Nelson (2004), two of the most common visual impairments that affect children with multiple disabilities are cataracts and retinopathy of prematurity (ROP). Cataracts, caused by a number of circumstances, including the presence of certain syndromes, result in an opaqueness of the lens of the eye. Consequently, light rays do not pass through the natural lens as they should and vision is distorted. Surgery to remove the lens is required. Vision can be restored with intraocular lenses, glasses, or contact lenses. ROP is a condition related to prematurity and low birth weight. Blood vessel growth in the underdeveloped retina is incomplete. Scar tissue can develop, leading to retinal detachment and loss of vision.

- *Hearing Impairment, Microcephaly, and Intellectual Disability.* Tara is a fifteen-year-old high school student who lives with foster parents due to her parents' inability to deal with her disabilities. She has facial distortions and a small head. She is also short in stature. Her mother contracted rubella (German measles) during the first trimester of her pregnancy impacting Tara's development across a number of areas. Tara is hearing impaired and, even with the use of hearing aids, she is unable to hear normally. As a result, her speech is not easily understood. Tara also has an intellectual disability and performs well below the cognitive level of her same-age peers; she has microcephaly, a medical condition in which the circumference of the head is smaller than normal because the brain has not developed properly. Tara experienced inclusive education during elementary school but now that she is in secondary school, she spends limited time in the regular classroom. The emphasis of her high school curriculum is on the acquisition of life skills. She takes part in a special program designed to give students the opportunity to develop independent living abilities. Her progress has been slow but Tara continues to exhibit an eagerness to learn. She especially enjoys repetitive tasks that allow her to experience the satisfaction of working independently and following a task through to completion. Unfortunately, Tara has few friends but she does enjoy the company of her dog, Buddy. Her foster parents have encouraged her to be Buddy's primary caretaker and she takes this job very seriously.

What We Know...

Deafness and Hearing Loss

Deafness may be viewed as a condition that prevents an individual from receiving sound in all or most of its forms. In contrast, a child with a hearing loss can generally respond to auditory stimuli, including speech.

Sound is measured by its loudness or intensity (measured in units called decibels, *dB*) and its frequency or pitch (measured in units called hertz, *Hz*). Impairments in hearing can occur in either or both areas, and may exist in only one ear or in both ears. Hearing loss is generally described as slight, mild, moderate, severe, or profound, depending upon how well a person can hear the intensities or frequencies most greatly associated with speech.

Hearing loss or deafness does not affect a person's intellectual capacity or ability to learn. However, children who are either hard of hearing or deaf generally require some form of special education services in order to receive an adequate education. Such services include:

- regular speech, language, and auditory training from a specialist
- amplification systems
- services of an interpreter for those students who use sign language
- favourable seating in the class to facilitate lip reading
- captioned films/videos
- assistance of a notetaker, who takes notes for the student with a hearing loss, so that the student can fully attend to instruction

- instruction for the teacher and peers in alternate communication methods, such as sign language
- counselling

Source: National Dissemination Center for Children with Disabilities (2004), www.nichy.org/pubs/factshefs3txt.htm.

Closing Monique's File

As a result of concerted efforts by her parents and dedicated professionals within the education system, Monique will soon complete her middle school years and move on to secondary school. This transition evokes both pride and apprehension on the part of her parents. There is pride in the fact that Monique will complete middle school with her same age peers and in the fact that she has been a valued student of the regular classroom. As her father stated, "We worked very, very hard to make sure that Monique participated in all the same activities that the other children were doing…each year we had to work with new school personnel to make sure that everyone was aware of Monique's needs and it wasn't always easy but we were driven by the belief that Monique belonged with other kids her age." Now Monique's parents are expressing some apprehension about the new challenges Monique will face in secondary school. While they still want Monique to be a member of the regular classroom, they realize it will require significant adjustments on the part of all those involved. Their current focus is on the transition process itself; they are actively preparing a transition portfolio that will help them consolidate all of the information that will be of interest to the staff at Monique's new school. Their hope is that this portfolio will prevent them from having to "start all over again." Their comment was that "we and others have learned so much about Monique and how she learns that we just want to pass it along to help others who work with her…we know how daunting it can be to be responsible for the education of a child with multiple disabilities and this portfolio will only help reduce that anxiety."

What We Know...

Transition Portfolios

According to Demchak and Greenfield (2003; p. 2), a transition portfolio is a strategy that documents critical information about a student. It may be prepared by a teacher, support personnel, or parents. Demchak and Greenfield pointed out that transitions are likely to be more successful if relevant, student-specific information is provided in a non-technical manner. They recommended that transition portfolios contain the following components:

Personal information
    (history, strengths, and interests)
Medical information
    (medical issues and needs)
Education programming suggestions
    (educational focus and unique learning characteristics)
Ideas for adaptations and supports
    (modifications to environment/instruction and the use of technology)
Recommendations for physical impairments
    (adaptive positioning equipment and therapeutic handling techniques)
Expressive and receptive communication strategies
    (current methods of communication and instructional suggestions)
Reinforcement strategies and positive behavioural support plans
    (effective reinforcers and summary of behaviour assessment and behaviour plan)
Problem-solving techniques and team notes
    (past challenges and how they were resolved)

The idea is to present a whole picture of the child; one that allows teachers and support personnel to understand the strengths and needs of their new student without having to repeatedly sift through the many reports that may exist in the student's school file. The transition portfolio presents succinct yet comprehensive information written in an easy-to-read format.

From The Psychologist's Notebook...

From a schooling perspective, the greatest hurdle that Monique faces, and will continue to face, is her inability to easily and accurately convey to educators what she knows. It is clear from what her parents and teachers have reported that Monique often knows and understands much more than she is able to tell them. Therefore, it is very important that teachers make sure that they assess the full scope of Monique's learning with a variety of tests and assignments that provide her with the best opportunity to convey what she knows. This type of careful assessment and evaluation allows for a more precise determination of Monique's progress and also allows for the development of a more definitive set of future educational objectives. By encouraging Monique to demonstrate her learning more often, her computer may become her first choice of communication rather than her last.

Learning More About Students with Multiple Disabilities

Academic Journals

Augmentative and Alternative Communication

Journal of Developmental and Physical Disabilities

Journal of Special Education Technology

Journal of Speech, Language, and Hearing Research

Journal of the American Academy of Audiology

Journal of Visual Impairment and Blindness

Physical Disabilities: Education and Related Service

Research and Practice for Persons with Severe Disabilities

Special Education Technology Practice

Books

Demchak, M., & Greenfield, R. (2003). *Transition portfolios for students with disabilities.* Thousand Oaks, CA: Corwin Press, Inc.

Heller, K., Forney, P., Alberto, P., Schwartzman, M., & Goeckel, T. (2000). *Meeting physical and health needs of children with disabilities: Teaching student participation and management.* Toronto: Nelson Thomson Learning.

Orelove, F., Sobsey, D., & Silberman, K. (2004). *Educating children with multiple disabilities.* Balitmore, Maryland: Paul H. Brookes Publishing Company, Inc.

Snell, M., & Brown, F. (2006). *Instruction of students with severe disabilities* (6th edition). Upper Saddle River, NJ: Pearson Education, Inc.

Web Links

● *Council for Exceptional Children*

www.cec.sped.org/AM/Template.cfm?Section=Home&Template=/templates/ CECHomePage.cfm

The CEC site reflects the fact that the Council is the largest international professional organization dedicated to improving educational outcomes for individuals with exceptionalities, students with disabilities, and/or the gifted.

● *Disability in Canada*

www.sdc.gc.ca/asp/gateway.asp?hr=/en/hip/odi/documents/PALS/PALS004. shtml&hs=pyp

This government-produced site presents demographics and statistics related to Canadian children with disabilities.

- *National Dissemination Center for Children with Disabilities — Research*
  http://research.nichcy.org/default.asp
  On this site, NICHCY presents research-based information to guide teachers in
  their work with children with disabilities. NICHCY aims to connect individuals
  with the knowledge base that the field has accumulated over years of investigation
  and practice.

Please visit the Online Learning Centre for *Special Education in Canada* at
www.mcgrawhill.ca/olc/edmunds for additional learning and study resources.

Taking It Into Your Classroom...

Including Students with Multiple Disabilities

When a student with multiple disabilities is first placed in my classroom, I will:

- review what I know about the different disabilities and locate resource materials
- consider how the disabilities may impact upon each other
- read the student's file
- consult with the student's previous teachers
- consult with the student's parents
- meet with the school-based team to discuss the student's current school year

Other: _____

_____

Key points to remember in my daily interactions with a student who has multiple disabilities:

- the student may struggle to communicate both verbally and non-verbally
- the student's attempts to communicate may often go undetected
- the student may comprehend more than they are able to express
- the student may benefit from the use of multiple means of communication
- the student may need encouragement to use aided communication (i.e., technology)

Other: _____

_____

Key points regarding programming for a student with multiple disabilities:

- a collaborative approach to service delivery is considered ideal
- a carefully developed IEP should clearly outline the student's program
- the student should be actively involved in all relevant school activities
- skills should be taught in a logical sequence
- the student's school day should be carefully planned with supports in place

Other: _____

_____

Key points regarding evaluation of the progress made by a student with multiple disabilities:

- evaluation should measure the student's proximity to the standards set for all students
- evaluation should be based on the learning objectives stated in the IEP
- evaluation should include the most appropriate assessment formats for that student
- evaluation should include as many formats as is necessary to determine learning
- evaluation should provide the feedback necessary to develop new objectives
- evaluation should be ongoing

Other: _____

_____

CHAPTER 11

Creating Your Own Special Stories

Learning More

In this text, we have introduced you to several different categories of exceptionalities. We have presented a great deal of information on each of the categories but, as we stated in Chapter 1, it was not our intent to provide comprehensive information that would qualify you as an expert once you had read and discussed the material. However, we do hope that you have learned a great deal from each of the chapters, and you will now take the time to learn more about aspects of exceptionalities that are of particular interest to you.

At the end of each chapter, we have included some resources you can access. If you are mostly interested in research findings, you should explore the academic journals that are listed. General information, including teaching strategies, can usually be found in the books we have suggested. Obviously, both theoretical and practical information can be located through searches on the Internet.

Something To Think About...

There is a plethora of information available on the Internet about education, including information about students with exceptionalities. Sometimes this information is not complete or entirely accurate. How can you best use the Internet as a resource for your teaching needs? Are there any sites that you would recommend to your fellow students? What makes these sites better than others you have accessed?

Perhaps one of the most underused resources available to beginning, and less experienced, teachers is mentoring. While much can be learned from print material, there is often nothing more effective than learning from an expert in the area, someone who has a great deal of experience in carrying out the same tasks you will be expected to perform, and in the same setting with similar students. Appropriate mentors include experienced teachers, educational specialists, and school administrators who are willing to share their experiences and advice, and answer questions on a regular basis. Many of these individuals already perform a nearly identical task when mentoring prospective teachers during practicum placements. Therefore, they are quite comfortable with the mentoring process including having beginning, and less experienced, teachers observe them while working in classroom situations.

If your school does not have an established mentoring program, you may want to discuss with your principal the possibility of acquiring a mentor and/or starting a school-wide mentoring program. Or, you may choose to informally be mentored by a staff member with whom you seem to relate well. Either way, you will certainly benefit from having someone to talk with regarding your concerns and ideas.

What We Know...

Mentoring

According to the Mentoring and Leadership Resource Network (www.mentors.net), an international initiative designed to help educators with best practices, mentoring has a significant impact upon beginning teachers. Evaluations of mentoring programs have revealed that when experienced teachers engage in meaningful conversations with new teachers, and provide them with ongoing support, the mentored teachers are better able to confront the challenges in their classrooms. Feedback from teachers who have been part of mentoring programs indicates that having a mentor in their first year impacted upon their decision to stay in teaching. The participants emphasized that the emotional support the mentor provided, the non-judgmental feedback, and the opportunity to grow professionally were critical to their positive feelings about their chosen career.

The mentoring experience has also proven to be very positive for experienced teachers. Mentors have described four specific benefits of participating in mentoring programs: (1) improved reflective practices, (2) a higher level of professional responsibilities, (3) a broadened view of the profession, and (4) a renewed appreciation for the education field.

In a comprehensive analysis of ten studies of mentoring related to special education, Griffin, Winn, Otis-Wilborn, and Kilgore (2003) outlined the elements of mentoring that were associated with successful teaching experiences: (1) a culture of shared responsibility and support, (2) interactions between new and experienced teachers, (3) continuum of professional development, (4) de-emphasized evaluation, (5) clear goals and purposes, and (6) diversified content.

What are the characteristics that you would look for in a mentor? What kind of mentoring style would best suit your personality and your teaching needs? How might you approach a staff member about becoming your mentor?

Something To Think About...

Ongoing Professional Development in Special Education

As teachers, you are probably aware that you are expected to engage in **professional development** (PD) throughout your teaching career as another way to learn more about educational issues and best practices. This expectation is common, if not mandatory, for most teachers around the world and, if it is not, it should be. We encourage you to make this type of ongoing professional growth a personal mission rather than merely treating it as a professional obligation.

professional development
An ongoing commitment to ensure that one's skills and abilities to do one's job are always relevant and up to date.

Teachers benefit from ongoing learning opportunities.

Based on our years of experience in developing and delivering PD sessions for educators, we know that special education is always one of the most demanded topics. As you begin to experience the joys and challenges of teaching students with exceptionalities, you will quickly recognize areas of knowledge and training that you may want to augment. Professional development sessions addressing some of these areas may be provided by your school, school board, or teachers' union, but it is highly probable that your specific learning needs will not be addressed at the very time you require the new information and/or skills. In these instances, we recommend that you seek out professional development that provides you with exactly what you need. Think of this as your own form of special education.

One of the best sources for special education PD is the Council for Exceptional Children (CEC) and the Canadian Council for Exceptional Children (CCEC). As of January 2007, the Canadian CEC had chapters in all jurisdictions except New Brunswick, Nova Scotia, PEI, Quebec, and the three territories. By joining CEC you are automatically a member of CCEC (and the International CEC). Each of their Web sites lists the types of professional development currently available, usually listing the sessions and topics for the whole school year or more. The formats of the different types of PD varies from online coursework to Web seminars to the traditional sit down seminars that many educators attend. If you feel that you do not need a full-blown seminar but would like some specific information about a certain topic, CEC also provides professional development-related documents that can be downloaded.

Some examples of past sessions that were provided by the Canadian CEC include *Widening Circles: Literacy and Learning for All* (Manitoba CEC, October 2007) and

Sensory Assessment Tools for All (British Columbia, 2006). You can access their current PD listings at http://canadian.cec.sped.org/professionaldev.htm. Some examples of past sessions that were provided by CEC include: *Inclusive Assessment and Accountability: Effective Practices for Teachers and Students; From Chaos to Community: Building Effective Classroom Management Systems;* and *Accessing the General Education Curriculum: Universal Design and Technology.* The current PD listings offered by CEC can be found at www.cec.sped.org/AM/Template.cfm?Section=Professional_Development.

Finally, make a note to yourself to check out the Annual CEC Convention and Exposition. This annual convention is one of the most attended conferences on special education in North America, especially by teachers. Each year teachers, academics, researchers, and parents (and often students) gather to learn more about advances and changes in special education. There are a wide variety of sessions to suit whatever your requirements may be. It is also a great forum for networking with others who work with students with exceptionalities. This often leads to the informal sharing of excellent teaching ideas and the establishment of professional friends that you can call on as resources for teaching materials, instructional strategies, and moral support.

Something To Think About…

> If you are a beginning teacher, consider the coursework you will complete in your teacher education program. What professional development are you likely to need in your early years as a classroom teacher?
>
> If you are a more experienced teacher, consider both the coursework you have completed and the professional development experiences you have had to date. What professional development are you likely to need over the next five years?

Taking It Into Your Classroom

We know from experience that knowledge gained through participation in a college or university course does not always transfer readily into the classroom. In other words, it is sometimes difficult to remember and use information that you have been exposed to as a student. You may find yourself a little panicked as you stand in front of your class trying to recall exactly what you are supposed to do in a certain situation. While this is normal for a beginning or less experienced teacher, it is somewhat disconcerting and can sometimes be avoided with proper preparation. This was our intention when providing you with the *Taking It Into Your Classroom* summary at the end of each chapter. These summaries are meant to be used well after you have completed your coursework. Ideally, you will have copies of these summaries, with your own notes attached, in a binder or stored on a computer so that you can easily access them while working as a teacher. Then, when you are faced with a particular situation, you can quickly review your notes to see if you have the information that will help in your decision-making or in your choice of teaching strategies. Acting without thinking or being improperly informed is obviously not recommended in the classroom, especially in the case of a student with exceptionalities where many assumed norms do not apply.

As an example, suppose you have a student in your class who has an identified learning disability. During the first few weeks of school, the student is disruptive during reading and math classes and does not respond well to your stern looks or your prompts for him to focus and attend to his work. You wonder if you should implement more severe consequences for his disruptive behaviours. A quick scan of your notes on learning disabilities reminds you of the *key points to remember in your daily interactions with a student who has a learning disability:*

- *the student may have low self-esteem and low self-concept*
- *the student may exhibit a discrepancy between ability and performance*
- *the student may be impulsive and speak without thinking*
- *the student may not be able to interpret body language and tone of voice*
- *the student may have difficulty understanding spoken language*
- *the student may not react well to change*

In light of this information, you reflect on what your student is experiencing: a new classroom (i.e., a change in his routine and environment), a new teacher (i.e., may be difficult to understand the meaning of the teacher's body language and tone of voice), and exposure to the subjects he finds most difficult (i.e., reading and math). To complicate matters, the student is impulsive and blurts out comments without intending to disrupt the class. You now realize that implementing more severe consequences for his unwanted behaviours is not the ideal response at all. In fact, it will probably only result in lowering the student's self-esteem and self-concept, and increasing the very behaviours you are trying to eliminate. Instead, you decide to help the student settle into the routine of the classroom and speak with him about his unacceptable behaviours and how the two of you can work together to reduce those behaviours over time. You also decide to review his reading and math abilities with the special education expert in your school. This more thoughtful and informed response to your student was simply prompted by a quick review of your own notebook. We hope that this simple suggestion does not feel patronizing in any way. We presented it here as a reminder because in the reality of a very busy classroom, the specific details of working with students who have exceptionalities often get overlooked.

We hope that you recognize the value of having these notes available to you, even if they only contain brief summaries of information. You will be extremely busy as a teacher and most times you will have little time to research relevant issues by thumbing through a book or sifting through sites on the Internet. On many occasions, as in the example above, reviewing your notes will be enough to help you with a particular situation or at least get you started looking in the right direction. Other times, you will have to access more comprehensive resources and your existing notes will serve as an excellent guide in your search for the necessary information.

Because we believe in the importance of collecting informational summaries, we encourage you to add to your notebook whenever you come upon new information that may be useful at a later date. For instance, there may be a time when you have to research a new issue that relates to a student in your class (e.g., the first time you find yourself teaching a student who has a profound hearing impairment). Making notes to summarize this newly researched information will help you with your teaching throughout the school year and in any subsequent years when you have a student with a similar disability.

We are convinced that *Taking It Into Your Classroom* will be easier than you first thought and as you build upon your teaching experiences, you will not have to access your notes quite as often as you do during your first years in the classroom. Perhaps, when you have many years of teaching behind you, and you have the opportunity to mentor beginning and less experienced teachers, you can share your notes with them and encourage them to include the same practice in their school life.

Your Own Special Stories

If you already have experience as a teacher, you are certainly cognizant of the heterogeneity of students. If you are a beginning teacher, you will quickly become aware of the uniqueness of each and every one of the students who enters your classroom. Their varied strengths and needs may seem daunting to you at first, but you will soon come to appreciate what each student has to offer to the classroom as a whole.

Undoubtedly, some of your future students will have needs that are significant enough to require the input of a team of professionals. You will be one member of this team and will benefit from the support of team members who have expertise in delivering various special services. In other words, you should take advantage of the input offered by others and not be afraid to ask for advice and help in meeting the needs of a particular student. As we have mentioned previously, no regular classroom teacher is expected to be a specialist in the area of exceptionalities. However, you will most likely spend more time with the student than most other team members, so you should feel confident about sharing your observations regarding the student's experiences in the classroom. What may seem insignificant to you may be quite valuable to one of your colleagues who views the student from an entirely different perspective.

Being observant is an important characteristic of being an exemplary teacher. While this will not only assist you in your teaching of all students in the inclusive classroom (i.e., recognizing whether or not a particular student's needs are being met), it will also help you spot those students who may have unidentified disabilities. We recommend that you keep a notebook on your desk so that you can easily record any observations that you make during the school day. This notebook should have a designated section for each student in your class. Simply arrange the sections in alphabetical order (by last name) according to your class/attendance list and it will allow you to quickly make note of what you have observed. These observations may be random at first but you will probably notice a trend when a student is consistently having a particular difficulty. Once a trend is apparent, you can then make more specific observations, perhaps while trying some minor interventions that you feel may be of immediate help. If the student continues to have problems, you will have readily available documentation to bring to the appropriate special services personnel and the school-based team.

Over the school year, as you learn more and more about your students who have been identified as exceptional, you will begin to develop your own collection of special stories. You will undoubtedly build upon the information you first received in the student's file and, by the end of the school year, you will have a more detailed story to tell the teachers who will have that student in their classes the following year. So often, this information is lost as teachers fail to communicate with one another in this way across grade levels. However, you can certainly make a difference and set an example in your school. By being open to learning more about special education and actively playing a role on all your students' special services teams, you will be able to use what you have learned and what you have observed to enrich the stories that unfold in your classroom. By putting these stories into words, either verbally or in writing, you will allow future teachers of your students to have the insight you have had when reading the six stories in this text.

Something
To Think
About...

Imagine that at the beginning of the school year one of the six students presented in this textbook is actually assigned to your classroom. What affect would knowing the student's story have on your feelings about teaching a student with that particular exceptionality? How would the information you have learned about the student aid in your preparation for the school year? How would the student benefit from your extensive knowledge about his or her situation?

Closing Our File

Just as we have closed the file on the stories of each of the six students presented in this text, we now must close our file on the first edition of *Special Education in Canada*. Being an educator means always being open to learning and we have certainly learned a great deal as we wrote this book, both from the writing process and from the families we have met. We certainly hope that you have increased your knowledge as well and this knowledge will be reflected in your teaching of students who have special stories to tell.

Now that you are familiar with the stories of the six students presented in this text, how do you feel about teaching in an inclusive environment? Did any one particular story from this text have a significant impact on how you think and feel about special education? How will you use the information you have learned to better prepare for the inclusion of children with exceptionalities in your classroom?

References

Abraham, C. (2007). Canadian breakthrough offers hope on autism. *The Globe and Mail*, February 19, p. A1.

Alberta Education. (2006). *Individualized program planning.* Government of Alberta: Edmonton. www.education.gov.ab.ca/k_12/specialneeds/ipp.pdf.

Alloy, L.B., Jacobson, N.S., & Acocella, J. (1999). *Abnormal psychology: Current perspectives* (8ᵗʰ ed.). Boston: McGraw-Hill College.

American Psychiatric Association. (1994). *Diagnostic and statistical manual of mental disorders* (4ᵗʰ edition). Washington, DC.

Autism Canada Foundation. (2004). *Autism rate in Canada skyrockets – equal to U.S. rate.* Press release May 11, 2004. www.autismcanada.org/News/PRESS%20RELEASE-incidencerate.htm.

Autism Society Canada. (2005). *Research into causes.* www.autismsocietycanada.ca/asd_research/causes_of_autism/index_e.html.

Ayres, J. (1972). Improving academic scores through sensory integration. *Journal of Learning Disabilities, 5,* 338-343.

Baldwin, A.Y., & Vialle, W. (1999). *The many faces of giftedness: Lifting the masks.* Belmont, CA: Wadsworth Publishing Company.

Bandura, A. (1977). *Social learning theory.* Englewood Cliffs, NJ: Prentice-Hall.

Bandura, A. (1986). *Social foundations of thought and action.* Englewood Cliffs, NJ: Prentice-Hall.

Bedgell, J., & Molloy, A. (1995). Eleven-year-old Emily Eaton wins landmark charter victory. *Forum/Abilities, 23,* 52-54. www.enablelink.org/include/article.php?pid=&cid=&subid=&aid=133.

Bender, S.J. (2006). Struggles of gifted children in school: Possible negative outcomes. *Gifted Education Press Quarterly, 20*(2), 10-13.

Bender, W.N. (1998). *Learning disabilities: Characteristics, identification, and teaching strategies.* Boston: Allyn and Bacon.

Berk, L.E. (1996). *Infants and children: Prenatal through middle childhood.* Boston, MA: Allyn & Bacon.

Biederman, J., Faraone, S.V., Keenan, K., Knee, D., & Tsuang, M.F. (1990). Family-genetic and psychosocial risk factors in DSM-III attention deficit disorder. *Journal of the American Academy of Child and Adolescent Psychiatry, 29*(4), 526-533.

Bloom, B.S. (1964). *Stability and change in human characteristics.* New York: Wiley.

British Columbia Ministry of Education. (2006). *Students with special needs: How are we doing?* www.bced.gov.bc.ca/edinfo/index/#Special.

Brophy, J. (2006). History of research on classroom management. In C.M. Evertson & C. S. Weinstein (Eds.), *Handbook of classroom management: Research, practice and contemporary issues* (pp. 17-46). Mahwah, NJ: Lawrence Erlbaum Associates, Publishers.

Browder, D.M., Wakeman, S.Y., Spooner, F., Ahlgrim-Delzell, L., & Algozzine, B. (2006). Research on reading instruction for individuals with significant cognitive disabilities. *Exceptional Children, 72*(4), 392-408.

Bryson, S.E., Rogers, S.J., & Fombonne, E. (2003). Autism spectrum disorders: Early detection, intervention, education, and psychopharmacological management. *Canadian Journal of Psychiatry*, September. http://server03.cpa-apc.org:8080/Publications/Archives/CJP/2003/september/bryson.asp.

Bunch. G., Lupart, J., & Brown, M. (1997). *Resistance and acceptance: Educator attitudes to inclusion of students with disabilities.* North York: York University.

Canter, L., & Canter, M. (1993). *Succeeding with difficult students: New strategies for reaching your most challenging students.* Santa Monica, CA: Lee Canter & Associates.

Cantwell, D.P. (1999). *Comorbidity in ADHD and associated outcomes.* http://gradda.home.isp-direct.com/sp99como.html.

Chen, D., & Miles, C. (2004). Working with families. In F. Orelove, D. Sobsey, & R. Silberman (Eds.), *Educating children with multiple disabilities: A collaborative approach* (pp. 31-65). Baltimore, Maryland: Paul H. Brookes Publishing Company.

Cloninger, C.J. (2004). Designing collaborative educational services. In F. Orelove, D. Sobsey, & R. Silberman (Eds.), *Educating children with multiple disabilities: A collaborative approach* (pp. 1-30). Baltimore, Maryland: Paul H. Brookes Publishing Company.

Colangelo, N., & Assouline, S.G. (2000). Counseling gifted students. In K.A. Heller, F.J. Monks, R.J. Sternberg, & R.F. Subotnik (Eds.), *International handbook of giftedness and talent* (2ⁿᵈ ed.) (pp. 595-608). Oxford: Elsevier Science Ltd.

Coleman, L.J., & Cross, T.L. (2001). *Being gifted in school: An introduction to development, guidance, and teaching.* Texas: Prufrock Press Inc.

Conte, R. (1998). Attention disorders. In B. Wong (Ed.), *Learning about learning disabilities* (2nd ed.) (pp. 67-105). San Diego: Academic Press.

Cortiella, C. (2006). Responsiveness-to-intervention: An overview. In *A Parent's Guide to Helping Kids With Learning Difficulties.* SchwabLearning.org. www.schwablearning.org/articles.aspx?r=840.

Council for Exceptional Children. (2004). *Analysis for IDEA Conference: CEC recommendations H.R. 1350 and S. 1248.* Arlington, VA: Author.

Council for Exceptional Children. (2006). *Learning disabilities.* Arlington, VA: Author www.cec.sped.org/AM/Template.cfm?Section=Learning_Disabilities&Template=/TaggedPage/TaggedPageDisplay.cfm&TPLID=37&ContentID=5629.

Council for Exceptional Children. (2006). *New flexibility in testing students with disabilities a positive step.* CEC Position Document. Arlington, VA: Author. www.cec.sped.org/AM/Template.cfm?Section=Search&template=/CM/HTMLDisplay.cfm&ContentID=6247.

Dabrowski, K. (1972). *Psychoneurosis is not an illness.* London: Gryf Publications.

Dabrowski, K., & Piechowski, M.M. (1977). *Theory of levels of emotional development.* Oceanside, NY: Dabor Science.

Danforth, S. (1997). Postmodernism, narrative, and hope in special education. In J. Paul, M. Churton, H. Rosselli-Kostoryz, W.C. Morse, K. Marfo, C. Lavely, & D. Thomas (Eds.), *Foundations of special education: Basic knowledge informing research and practice in special education* (pp. 291-304). Albany, NY: Brooks/Cole.

Demchak, M., & Greenfield, R. (2003). *Transition portfolios for students with disabilities: How to help students, teachers, and families handle new settings.* Thousand Oaks, CA: Corwin Press, Inc.

Dore, R., Dion, E., Wagner, S., & Brunet, J. (2004). High school inclusion of adolescents with mental retardation: A multiple case study. *Education and Training in Mental Retardation and Developmental Disabilities, 37*(3), 253-261. Reprinted in R. Sandieson & V. Sharpe (Eds.) (2004), *Inclusion and employment in developmental disabilities* (pp. 110-118). Austin, TX: PRO-ED, Inc.

Doyle, A.E., Faraone, S.V., DuPre, E.P., & Biederman, J. (2001). Separating attention deficit hyperactivity dis-order and learning disabilities in girls: A familial risk analysis. *American Journal of Psychiatry, 158,* 1666-1672.

Doyle, W. (2006). Ecological approaches to classroom management. In C.M. Evertson & C.S. Weinstein (Eds.), *Handbook of classroom management: Research, practice and contemporary issues* (pp. 97-126). Mahwah, NJ: Lawrence Erlbaum Associates, Publishers.

Dreikurs, R., & Cassel, P. (1992). *Discipline without tears* (2nd ed.). New York, NY: Plume.

Dworet, D., & Bennett, S. (2002). A view from the North: Special education in Canada. *Teaching Exceptional Children, 34*(5), 22-27.

Eaton v. Brant County Board of Education. [1997] 1 S.C.R. 241.

Edgar, E., & Pair, A. (2005). Special education teacher attrition: It all depends on where you are standing. *Teacher Education & Special Education, 28*(3/4), 163-170.

Edmunds, A.L. (1999). Classroom teachers are not prepared for the inclusive classroom. *Exceptionality Education Canada, 8*(2), 27-40.

Edmunds, A.L. (2003). The inclusive classroom – Can teachers keep up? A comparison of Nova Scotia and Newfoundland & Labrador perspectives. *Exceptionality Education Canada, 13*(1), 29-48.

Edmunds, A.L., & Blair, K. (1999). Nova Scotia teachers' use of the Cognitive Credit Card. *ATEC Journal, 5*(1), 7-13.

Edmunds, A.L, & Edmunds, G.A. (2005). Sensitivity: A double-edged sword for the pre-adolescent and adolescent gifted child. *Roeper Review, 27*(2), 69-77.

Edmunds, A.L., Halsall, A., MacMillan, R.B., & Edmunds, G.A. (2000). The impact of government funding cuts on education: Report from a teacher survey. *Nova Scotia Teachers' Union,* Halifax, Nova Scotia.

Edmunds, A.L., & Noel, K. (2003). Literary precocity: An exceptional case among exceptional cases. *Roeper Review, 25*(4), 185-194.

Education, Culture and Employment. (2004). *Elementary and junior secondary school handbook 2004-2005.* Yellowknife, NWT: Government of the Northwest Territories. www.ece.gov.nt.ca/Divisions/kindergarten_g12/indexK12.htm.

Erin, J. (2003). *Educating students with visual impairments.* http://ericec.org/digests/e653.html.

Evertson, C.M., & Weinstein, C.S. (2006). Classroom management as a field of inquiry. In C.M. Evertson & C.S. Weinstein (Eds.), *Handbook of classroom management* (pp. 4-42). MahWah, NJ: Erlbaum.

Exceptionality Education Canada. (2003). *Preparing Canadian teachers for inclusion.* Volume 13(1).

Faraone, S.V., & Biederman, J. (1998). Neurobiology of attention-deficit hyperactivity disorder. *Biological Psychiatry, 44,* 951-958.

Feldhausen, J.F., & Jarwan, F.A. (2000). Identification of gifted and talented youth for educational programs. In K.A. Heller, F.J. Monks, R.J. Sternberg, & R.F. Subotnik (Eds.), *International handbook of giftedness and talent* (2nd ed.) (pp. 271-282). Oxford: Elsevier Science Ltd.

Fiedler, C.R., Simpson, R.L., & Clark, D.M. (2007). *Parents and families of children with disabilities: Effective school-based support services.* Upper Saddle River, NJ: Pearson Education, Inc.

Forney, P.E., & Heller, K. (2004). Sensorimotor development: Implications for the educational team. In F. Orelove, D. Sobsey, & R. Silberman (Eds.), *Educating children with multiple disabilities: A collaborative approach* (pp. 193-247). Baltimore, Maryland: Paul H. Brookes Publishing Company.

Fowler, W. (1981). Case studies of cognitive precocity: The role of exogenous and endogenous stimulation in early mental development. *Journal of Applied Psychology, 2*, 319-367.

Frasier, M.M., García, J.H., & Passow, A.H. (1995). *A review of assessment issues in gifted education and their implications for identifying gifted minority students* (RM95204). Storrs, CT: The National Research Center on the Gifted and Talented, University of Connecticut.

Friedman, I.A. (2006). Classroom management and teacher stress and burnout. In C.M. Evertson & C.S. Weinstein (Eds.), *Handbook of classroom management: Research, practice and contemporary issues* (pp. 925-944). Mahwah, NJ: Lawrence Erlbaum Associates, Publishers.

FSU Center for Prevention & Early Intervention Policy. (2002). *What is inclusion? Including school-age students with developmental disabilities in the regular education setting.* Tallahassee, FL: Florida State University. www.cpeip.fsu.edu/resourceFiles/resourceFile_18.pdf.

Fuchs, D. and Fuchs, L.S. (2005). Responsiveness-to-intervention: A blueprint for practitioners, policymakers, and parents. *Teaching Exceptional Children, 38*(1), 57-61.

Fuchs, L., & Fuchs, D. (1996). Linking assessment to instructional interventions: An overview. *School Psychology Review, 15*(3), 318-324.

Gardner, H. (2000). The giftedness matrix: A developmental perspective. In R.C. Friedman & B.M. Shore (Eds.), *Talents unfolding: Cognition & development* (pp. 77-88). Washington: American Psychological Association.

Garnett, K. (1998). *Math learning disabilities.* LD Online. www.ldonline.org/article/5896.

Garvar-Pinhas, A., & Schmelkin, L.P. (1989). Administrators' and teachers' attitudes toward mainstreaming. *Remedial and Special Education, 10*(4), 34-43.

Gee, K. (2004). Developing curriculum and instruction. In F. Orelove, D. Sobsey, & R. Silberman (Eds.), *Educating children with multiple disabilities: A collaborative approach* (pp. 67-114). Baltimore, Maryland: Paul H. Brookes Publishing Company.

George, H.V. (1991). Organization of one's classroom. *Guidelines, 13*, 95-99.

Gibson-Kierstead, A., & Hanvey, L. (2001). Special education in Canada. *Perception, 25*(2). www.ccsd.ca/perception/252/specialed.htm.

Goguen, L. (1993). Right to education for the gifted in Canada. In K.A. Keller, F.J. Monks, & A.H. Passow (Eds.), *International handbook of research and development of giftedness and talents* (pp. 771-777). New York: Pergamon Press.

Goldberg, R.J., Higgins, E.L., Rasking, M.H., & Herman, K.L. (2003). Predictors of success in individuals with learning disabilities: A qualitative analysis of a 20-year longitudinal study. *Learning Disabilities Research & Practice, 18*(4), 222-236.

Goldsmith, L.T. (2000). Tracking trajectories of talent: Child prodigies growing up. In R.C. Friedman & B.M. Shore (Eds.), *Talents unfolding: Cognition & development* (pp. 89-118). Washington: American Psychological Association.

Government of Yukon. (2002). *Education act: Revised statutes of the Yukon.* Whitehorse, YK: Author. www.gov.yk.ca/legislation/acts/education.pdf.

Greenough, W. (2000). Brain development. In A. Kazdin (Ed.), *Encyclopedia of psychology.* Washington, DC, & New York: American Psychological Association and Oxford University Press.

Gregory, R.J. (2000). *Psychological testing: History, principles, and applications* (3rd ed.). Toronto: Allyn and Bacon.

Griffin, C.C., Winn, J.A., Otis-Wilborn, A., & Kilgore, K.L. (2003). *New teacher induction is special education.* (COPSSE Document number RS-5). Gainesville, FL: University of Florida.

Hannell, G. (2006). *Identifying children with special needs: Checklists and action plans for teachers.* Thousand Oaks, CA: Corwin Press.

Harum, K.H. (2006). *Mental retardation.* eMedicine. www.emedicine.com/neuro/topic605.htm.

Hatch-Rasmussen, C. (1995). *Sensory integration.* Torrance, CA: Sensory Integration International. www.autism.org/si.html.

Heller, K.W., Forney, P.E., Alberto, P.A., Schwartzman, M.N., & Goeckel, T.M. (2000). *Meeting physical and health needs of children with disabilities: Teaching student participation and management.* Toronto: Nelson Thomson-Learning.

Hinshaw, S.P., Owens, E.B., Sami, N., & Fargeon, S. (2006). Prospective follow-up of girls with attention-deficit/hyperactivity disorder into adolescence: Evidence for continuing cross-domain impairment. *Journal of Consulting and Clinical Psychology, 74*(3), 489-499.

Houck, C.K., & Rogers, C.J. (1994). The special/general education integration initiative for students with specific learning disabilities: A "snapshot" of program change. *Journal of Learning Disabilities, 27*, 435-453.

Hughes, C., Copeland, C., Guth, C., Rung, L., Hwang, B., Kleeb, G., & Strong, M. (2001). General education students' perspectives on their involvement in a high school peer buddy program. *Education and Training in Mental Retardation and Developmental Disabilities, 36*(4), 343-356. Reprinted in R. Sandieson & V. Sharpe (Eds.) (2004). *Inclusion and employment in developmental disabilities* (pp. 175-188). Austin, TX: PRO-ED, Inc.

Hutchinson, N.L. (2002). *Inclusion of exceptional learners in Canadian classrooms: A practical handbook for teachers.* Toronto: Prentice Hall.

IDEA: P.L. 108-446 (2004). *Title I - Amendments to the Individuals with Disabilities Education Act.* Washington, DC: U.S. Government Printing Office.

Jay, J.K. (2004). Variations on the use of cases in social work and teacher education. *Journal of Curriculum Studies, 36*(1), 35-39.

Jensen, P.M. (2001). AD/HD: What's up? What's next? *CHADD: ATTENTION, 7*(6), 24-27.

Johnson, F.L., & Edmunds, A.L. (2006). *From chaos to control: Understanding and responding to the behaviours of students with exceptionalities.* London, ON: The Althouse Press.

Johnson, L.J., Karnes, M.B., & Carr, V.W. (1997). Providing services to children with gifts and disabilities: A critical need. In N. Colangelo & G.A. Davis (Eds.), *Handbook of gifted education* (pp. 516-527). Boston: Allyn and Bacon.

Jones, G. (2002). *Educational provision for children with autism and Asperger syndrome: Meeting their needs.* London: David Fulton Publishers.

Jones, V. (2006). How do teachers learn to be effective classroom managers? In C.M. Evertson & C.S. Weinstein (Eds.), *Handbook of classroom management: Research, practice and contemporary issues* (pp. 887-908). Mahwah, NJ: Lawrence Erlbaum Associates, Publishers.

Kaiser, A.P., & Grim, J.C. (2006). Teaching functional communication skills. In M. Snell & F. Brown (Eds.), *Instruction of students with severe disabilities* (pp. 447-488). Upper Saddle River, NJ: Pearson Education, Inc.

Kauffman, J.M., & Sasso, G.M. (2006a). Toward ending cultural and cognitive relativism in special education. *Exceptionality, 14*(2), 65-90.

Kauffman, J.M., & Sasso, G.M. (2006b). Certainty, doubt, and the reduction of uncertainty. *Exceptionality, 14*(2), 109-120.

King, A. (2000). Situated cognition. In A. Kazdin (Ed.), *Encyclopedia of psychology* (pp. 289-291). Washington, DC, and New York: American Psychological Association and Oxford University Press.

King, W., & Edmunds, A.L. (2001). Teachers' perceived needs to become more effective inclusion practitioners: A single school study. *Exceptionality Education Canada, 10*(3), 23-37.

King-Sears, M.E., Burges, M., & Lawson, T.L. (1999). Applying curriculum-based assessment in inclusive settings. *Teaching Exceptional Children, September/October*, 30-38.

Kleinert, H., & Kearns, J. (2004). Alternate assessments. In F. Orelove, D. Sobsey, & R. Silberman (Eds.), *Educating children with multiple disabilities: A collaborative approach* (pp. 115-149). Baltimore, Maryland: Paul H. Brookes Publishing Company.

Kuntz, S., & Hessler, A. (1998). *Bridging the gap between theory and practice: Fostering active learning through the case study method* (Report No. SPO37985). Washington, DC: Association of American Colleges and Universities. (ERIC Document Reproduction Services No. ED420626).

Landrum, T.J., & Kauffman, J.M. (2006). Behavioral approaches to classroom management and effective teaching. In C.M. Evertson & C.S. Weinstein (Eds.), *Handbook of classroom management: Research, practice and contemporary issues* (pp. 47-72). Mahwah, NJ: Lawrence Erlbaum Associates, Publishers.

Lane, K., Falk, K., & Wehby, J. (2006). Classroom management in special education classrooms and resource rooms. In C.M. Evertson & C.S. Weinstein (Eds.), *Handbook of classroom management: Research, practice and contemporary issues*, (pp. 439-460). Mahwah, NJ: Lawrence Erlbaum Associates, Publishers.

LD Online. (2006). *What causes ADHD?* www.ldonline.org/adhdbasics/causes.

Learning Disabilities Association of Canada. (2005). Brant County Board of Education v. Eaton [1997] 1 S.C.R. 241; (1996) 31 O.R. (3d) 574 (1996) 142 D.L.R. (4th) 385; 1997, Supreme Court of Canada. *LD and the law: Case summaries.* www.ldac-taac.ca/LDandtheLaw/casesBrant_Law-e.asp.

Learning Disabilities Association of Canada. (2005). *LD in depth: Assistive technology and learning disabilities.* www.ldac-taac.ca/InDepth/tech_ld-e.asp.

Lerner, J.W., & Kline, F. (2006). *Learning disabilities and related disorders.* Boston: Houghton Mifflin Company.

Lerner, J., Mardell-Czudnowski, C., & Goldenberg, D. (1981). *Special education for the early childhood years.* Englewood Cliffs, NJ: Prentice-Hall.

Levin, J., & Nolan, J.F. (2000). *Principles of classroom management: A professional decision-making model* (3rd ed.). Boston: Allyn & Bacon.

Lickona, T. (1987). Character development in the elementary school classroom. In K. Ryan & G.F. McLean (Eds.), *Character development in the schools and beyond.* New York, NY: Praeger. www.crvp.org/book/Series06/VI-3/chapter_vii.htm.

Lindsey, M. (1980). *Training teachers of the gifted and talented.* New York: Teachers College Press.

Lupart, J. (2000). *Students with exceptional learning needs: At-risk, utmost.* Paper presented at The Pan-Canadian Education Research Agenda Symposium. Ottawa, April 6-7.

Lupart, J., & Webber, C. (2002). Canadian schools in transition: Moving from dual education systems to inclusive schools. *Exceptionality Education Canada, 12*(2&3), 7-52.

Lupart, J., & Odishaw, J. (2003). Canadian children and youth at-risk. *Exceptionality Education Canada, 13*(2&3), 9-28.

Maag, J.W. (2004). *Behavior management: From theoretical implications to practical applications* (2nd ed.). Belmont, CA: Thompson Wadsworth.

MacKay, W.A. (1987). The Elwood case: Vindicating the educational rights of the disabled. *Canadian Journal of Special Education, 3*(2), 103-116.

MacLean, J. (2003). Common learning characteristics of children with an intellectual disability. Victoria, Australia: Down Syndrome Association of Victoria. www.dsav.asn.au/global/articles/Common_Learning_Characteristics.pdf.

Manitoba Education, Citizenship and Youth. (2006). *Appropriate educational programming in Manitoba: Standards for student services.* www.edu.gov.mb.ca/k12/specedu/aep/index.html.

Marino, M.T., Marino, E.C., & Shaw, S.F. (2006). Making informed assistive technology decisions for students with high incidence disabilities. *Teaching Exceptional Children, 38*(6), 18-25.

Marland, S.P., Jr. (1972). *Education of the gifted and talented: Report to the Congress of the United States by the U.S. Commissioner of Education and background papers submitted to the U.S. Office of Education,* 2 vols. Washington, DC: U.S. Government Printing Office. (Government Documents Y4.L 11/2:G36).

Martin, A.J., Linfoot, K., & Stephenson, J. (1999). How teachers respond to concerns about misbehaviour in their classroom. *Psychology in Schools, 36,* 347-358.

Marzano, R.J., & Marzano, J.S. (2003). The key to classroom management. *Educational Leadership, 61*(1), 6-13.

Matson, J.L. (1994). *Autism in children and adults: Etiology, assessment, and intervention.* Pacific Grove, CA: Brooks/Cole Publishing Company.

McCaslin, M., Rabidue-Bozack, A., Napoleon, L., Thomas, A., Vasquez, V., Wayman, V., & Zhang, J. (2006). Self-regulated learning and classroom management: Theory, research, and considerations for classroom practice. In C.M. Evertson & C.S. Weinstein (Eds.), *Handbook of classroom management: Research, practice and contemporary issues* (pp. 223-252). Mahwah, NJ: Lawrence Erlbaum Associates, Publishers.

McConaughy, S.H., Kay, P.J., & Fitzgerald, M. (2000). How long is long enough? *Exceptional Children, 67,* 21-34.

McKenzie, J. (2003). Gambling with children. *No Child Left, 1*(1). http://nochildleft.com/2003/jancov03.html#index.

McLoughlin, J.A. & Lewis, R.B. (2005). *Assessing students with special needs* (6th ed.). Columbus, OH: Pearson/Allyn Bacon.

Mendaglio, S. (1995). Sensitivity among gifted persons: A multi-faceted perspective. *Roeper Review, 17*(3), 169-172.

Merriam-Webster's Collegiate Dictionary (11th edition). (2003). Springfield, MA: Merriam-Webster, Inc.

Mostert, M.P., Kauffman, J.M., & Kavale, K.R. (2003). Truth and consequences. *Behavioral Disorders, 28,* 333–347.

Myles, B. (2005). *Children and youth with Asperger syndrome.* Thousand Oaks, CA: Corwin Press.

National Association of School Psychologists. (2002). *Rights without labels.* Position statement adopted by NASP Delegate Assembly, July 14, 2002. www.nasponline.org/information/pospaper_rwl.html.

National Dissemination Center for Children with Disabilities. (1997). *Learning strategies for students with learning disabilities.* www.nichcy.org/pubs/bibliog/bib14txt.htm.

National Dissemination Center for Children with Disabilities. (2004). *Deafness and hearing loss.* www.nichcy.org/pubs/factshe/fs3txt.htm.

National Institute of Mental Health. (2006). *Attention deficit hyperactivity disorder.* NIH Publication No. 3572. www.nimh.nih.gov/publicat/adhd.cfm.

National Joint Committee on Learning Disabilities. (2005). *Responsiveness to intervention and learning disabilities.* A report prepared by the National Joint Committee on Learning Disabilities representing eleven national and international organizations. Austin, TX: Author.

Newfoundland and Labrador Department of Education. (1997). *Model for the coordination of services to children and youth.* www.mcscy.nl.ca.

Newfoundland and Labrador Department of Education. (2005). *Pathways to programming and graduation.* St. John's, NL: Department of Education, Division of Student Support Services.

Newman, S.D., & Just, M.A. (2005). The neural bases of intelligence: A perspective based on functional neuroimaging. In R.J. Sternberg & J.E. Pretz (Eds.), *Cognition and intelligence: Identifying the mechanisms of the mind* (pp. 88-103). Cambridge, England: Cambridge University Press.

Nielsen, M.E. (2002). Gifted students with learning difficulties: Recommendations for identification and programming. *Exceptionality, 10,* 93-111.

Nielsen, M.E., & Higgins, L.D. (2005). The eye of the storm: Services and programs for twice-exceptional learners. *Teaching Exceptional Children, 38*(1), 8-15.

No Child Left Behind Act of 2001. 20 U.S.C.~6301 et. Seq. (2001).

Noel, K., & Edmunds, A.L. (2007). An analysis of highly precocious writing. *Roeper Review, 29*(2), 125-131.

Nowicki, E.A. (2006). A cross-sectional multivariate analysis of children's attitudes towards disabilities. *Journal of Intellectual Disability Research, 50,* 335-348.

Nova Scotia Department of Education and Culture. (1996). *Special education policy manual.* Government of Nova Scotia: Halifax.

Nunavut Department of Education. (2003). *Ilitaunnikuliriniq: Student assessment in Nunavut schools.* Iqaluit NU: Author.

Ogle, D. (1986). K-W-L: A teaching model that develops active reading of expository text. *The Reading Teacher, 38,* 564-570.

Olszewski-Kubilius, P., Lee, S., Ngoi, M., & Ngoi, D. (2004). Addressing the achievement gap between minority and nonminority children by increasing access to gifted programs. *Journal for the Education of the Gifted, 28*(2), 127-158.

Ontario Ministry of Education. (2004). *The individualized education plan (IEP): A resource guide.* Toronto, ON: Queen's Printer for Ontario.

Overton, T. (1996). *Assessment in special education: An applied process* (2nd ed.). Columbus, OH: Merrill.

Paintal, S. (1999). Banning corporal punishment of children. *Childhood Education, 76,* 36-40.

Palincsar, A.S. (1998). Social constructivist perspectives on teaching and learning. *Annual Review of Psychology, 49,* 345-375.

Parker, C. (1997). *Feeding and speech problems in AMC.* Paper presented at the Arthrogryposis Group Conference. www.tagonline.org.uk/articles/feeding_speech.txt.

Pavri, S., & Monda-Amaya, L. (2000). Loneliness and students with learning disabilities in inclusive classrooms: Self-perceptions, coping strategies, and preferred interventions. *Learning Disabilities Research & Practice, 15*(1), 22-33.

Piaget, J.P. (1952). *The origins of intelligence in children.* New York: International Universities Press.

Plomin, R. (1997). Genetics and intelligence. In N. Colangelo & G.A. Davis (Eds.), *Handbook of gifted education* (pp. 67-74). Boston: Allyn and Bacon.

Porath, M. (2000). Social giftedness in childhood: A developmental perspective. In R.C. Friedman & B.M. Shore (Eds.), *Talents unfolding* (pp. 195-215). Washington: American Psychological Association.

Prevalence of disability in Canada rises. (1995). *Disability Today* (Winter), p.7.

Pudlas, K.A. (2003). Inclusive educational practice: Perceptions of students and teachers. *Exceptionality Education Canada, 13*(1), 49-64.

Reiff, H.B. (2004). Reframing the learning disabilities experience redux. *Learning Disabilities Research & Practice, 19*(3), 185-198.

Renzulli, J.S., & Reis, S.M. (1997). The schoolwide enrichment model: New directions for developing high-end learning. In N. Colangelo & G.A. Davis (Eds.), *Handbook of gifted education* (pp. 136-154). Boston: Allyn and Bacon.

Renzulli, J.S., Hartman, R.H., & Callahan, C.M. (1971). Teacher identification of superior students. *Exceptional Children, 38,* 211-214, 243-248.

Rief, S.F. (2005). *How to reach and teach children with ADD/ADHD: Practical techniques, strategies, and interventions* (2nd ed.). San Francisco, CA: Jossey-Bass.

Robinson, N.M. (2000). Giftedness in very young children: How seriously should it be taken? In R.C. Friedman & B.M. Shore (Eds.), *Talents unfolding: Cognition & development* (pp. 7-26). Washington: American Psychological Association.

Roeper, A. (1995). Participatory vs. hierarchical models for administration: The Roeper School experience. In A. Roeper, *Annemarie Roeper: Selected writings and speeches* (pp. 109-123). Minneapolis, MN: Free Spirit.

Salvia, J., & Ysseldyke, J.E. (2004). *Assessment: In Special and Inclusive Education* (9th ed.). Boston, MA: Houghton Mifflin Company.

Saskatchewan Education. (1999). *Teaching students with autism: A guide for educators.* www.sasked.gov.sk.ca/branches/curr/special_ed/sepub.shtml.

Saskatchewan Education. (2000). *Directions for diversity: Enhancing supports to children and youth with diverse needs.* Final report of the Saskatchewan Special Education Review Committee. Regina, SK: Government of Saskatchewan.

Schnoes, C., Reid, R., Wagner, M., & Marder, C. (2006). ADHD among students receiving special education services: A national survey. *Exceptional Children, 72*(4), 483-496.

Schwartz, I.S., Staub, D., Peck, C.A., & Gallucci, C. (2006). Peer relationships. In M. Snell & F. Brown (Eds.), *Instruction of students with severe disabilities* (pp. 375-404). Upper Saddle River, NJ: Pearson Education, Inc.

Scott, J., Clark, C., & Brady, M. (2000). *Students with autism.* San Diego: Singular Publishing Group.

Scruggs, T.E., & Mastropieri, M.A. (1996). Teacher perceptions of mainstreaming/inclusion, 1958-1995: A research synthesis. *Exceptional Children, 63*(1), 59-74.

Shavinina, L.V. (1999). The psychological essence of the child prodigy phenomenon: Sensitive periods and cognitive experience. *Gifted Child Quarterly, 43*(1), 25-38.

Shonkoff, J., & Meisels, S. (2000). *Handbook of early childhood intervention* (2nd ed.). New York: Cambridge University Press.

Siegel, B. (2003). *Helping children with autism learn: Treatment approaches for parents and professionals.* New York: Oxford University Press.

Siegel, L. (2000). *A review of special education in British Columbia.* Victoria, BC: British Columbia Ministry of Education.

Siegle, D., & McCoach, D.B. (2005). Making a difference: Motivating gifted students who are not achieving. *Teaching Exceptional Children, 38*(1), 22-27.

Silberman, R.K., Bruce, S.M., & Nelson, C. (2004). Children with sensory impairments. In F. Orelove, D. Sobsey, & R. Silberman (Eds.), *Educating children with multiple disabilities: A collaborative approach* (pp. 425-528). Baltimore, Maryland: Paul H. Brookes Publishing Company.

Silka, V.R., & Hauser, M.J. (1997). Psychiatric assessment of the person with mental retardation. *Psychiatric Annals, 27*(3). www.psychiatry.com/mr/assessment.html.

Silverman, L.K. (Ed.). (1993). *Counseling the gifted and talented.* Denver: Love.

Simonton, D.K. (2005). Giftedness and genetics: The emergenic-epigenetic model and its implications. *Journal for the Education of the Gifted, 28* (3/4), 270-286.

Smith, T.E., Polloway, E.A., Patton, J.R., & Dowdy, C. (1998). *Teaching students with special needs* (2nd ed.). Boston, MA: Allyn and Bacon.

Snow, R.E. (1994). Aptitude development and talent achievement. In N. Colangelo, S.G. Assouline, & D.L. Ambroson (Eds.), *Talent development: Volume II* (pp. 101-122). Dayton, Ohio: Ohio Psychology Press.

Stephens, K.R., & Karnes, F.A. (2001). Product development for gifted students. In F.A. Karnes & S.M. Bean (Eds.), *Methods and materials for teaching the gifted and talented* (pp. 181-211). Texas: Prufrock Press Inc.

Sternberg, R.J., & Grigorenko, E.L. (2003). Teaching for successful intelligence: Principles, procedures, and practices. *Journal for the Education of the Gifted, 27*(2/3), 207-226.

Strock, M. (2004). *Autism Spectrum Disorders (Pervasive Developmental Disorders).* NIH Publication No. NIH-04-5511, National Institute of Mental Health, National Institutes of Health, U.S. Department of Health and Human Services, Bethesda, MD. www.nimh.nih.gov/publicat/autism.cfm.

Sugai, G., & Horner, R. (1999). Discipline and behavioural support: Preferred processes and practices. *Effective School Practices, 17,* 10-22.

Taylor, G.R., & Harrington, F. (2001). Incidence of exceptionality. In G.R. Taylor (Ed.), *Educational interventions and services for children with exceptionalities* (2nd ed.) (pp. 3-13). Springfield, IL: Charles C. Thomas Publisher.

Taylor, R.L., Richards, S.B., & Brady, M.P. (2005). *Mental retardation: Historical perspectives, current practices, and future directions.* Boston: Pearson Education, Inc.

Thomas, A. & Chess, S. (1977). *Temperament and development.* New York, NY: Bruner/Mazel.

Toppelberg, C.O., & Shapiro, T. (2000). Language disorders: A 10-year research update review. *Journal of the American Academy of Child & Adolescent Psychiatry, 39*(2), 143-152.

Turecki, S. (2000). *The difficult child.* New York, NY: Bantam Books.

U.S. Department of Education. (2000a). *A guide to the individualized education program.* Washington, DC: Office of Special Education and Rehabilitative Services.

U.S. Department of Education. (2000b). *Twenty-second annual report to Congress on the implementation of the Individuals with Disabilities Act.* Washington, DC: Office of Special Education Programs.

U.S. Department of Education. (2002). *Twenty-third annual report to Congress on the implementation of the Individuals with Disabilities Act* (p. AA3). Washington, DC: Author.

U.S. National Research Council. (2001). *Educating children with autism.* Committee on Educational Interventions for Children with Autism. Division of Behavioral and Social Sciences and Education. Washington, DC: National Academy Press.

VanTassel-Baska, J. (1997). What matters in curriculum for gifted learners: Reflections on theory, research, and practice. In N. Colangelo & G.A. Davis (Eds.), *Handbook of gifted education* (pp. 126-135). Boston: Allyn and Bacon.

VanTassel-Baska, J., & Brown, E.F. (2001). An analysis of gifted education curriculum models. In F.A. Karnes & S.M. Bean (Eds.), *Methods and materials for teaching the gifted and talented* (pp. 93-132). Texas: Prufrock Press Inc.

Vygotsky, L.S. (1978a). *Mind and society: The development of higher mental processes.* Cambridge, MA: Harvard University Press.

Vygotsky, L.S. (1978b). *Mind in society: The development of higher psychological processes.* (M. Cole, V. John-Steiner, S. Scribner & E. Souberman, Eds.). Cambridge, MA: Harvard University Press.

Wahlberg, T. (2001). Cognitive theories and symptomology of autism. In T. Wahlberg, F. Obiakor, S. Burkhardt, & A.F. Rotatori (Eds.), *Autistic spectrum disorders: Educational and clinical interventions* (pp. 3-18). New York: JAI Press.

Weinstein, C.S. (1997). *Secondary classroom management.* New York, NY: McGraw-Hill.

Wenke, D., Frensch, P.A., & Funke, J. (2005). Complex problem solving and intelligence: Empirical relation and causal direction. In R.J. Sternberg & J.E. Pretz (Eds.), *Cognition and intelligence: Identifying the mechanisms of the mind* (pp. 160-187). Cambridge, England: Cambridge University Press.

Werts, M.G., Mamlin, N., & Pogoloff, S.M. (2002). Knowing what to expect: Introducing preservice teachers to IEP meetings. *Teacher Education & Special Education, 25*(4), 413-418.

Whelan, R. (1995). Emotional disturbance. In E.L. Meyen & T. Skirtic (Eds.), *Special education and student disability: An introduction* (pp. 271-336). Denver, CO: Love.

Whitaker, S.D. (2003). Needs of beginning special education teachers: Implications for teacher education. *Teacher Education & Special Education, 26*(2), 106-117.

Willows, D.M. (1998). Visual processes in learning disabilities. In B. Wong (Ed.), *Learning about learning disabilities* (2nd ed.) (pp. 203-236). San Diego: Academic Press.

Winders, P.C. (2003). The goal and opportunity of physical therapy for children with Down syndrome. *Down Syndrome Quarterly.* Granville, OH: Denison University. www.denison.edu/collaborations/dsq/windersphysicaltherapy.html.

Wishart, J. (1998). *Cognitive development in young children with Down syndrome: Developmental strengths, developmental weaknesses.* Burnaby, BC: Down Syndrome Research Foundation and Resource Centre. www.he.net/~altonweb/cs/downsyndrome/index.htm?page=wishart.html.

Woloshyn, V., Bennett, S., & Berrill, D. (2003). Working with students who have learning disabilities – teacher candidates speak out: Issues and concerns in preservice education and professional development. *Exceptionality Education Canada, 13*(1), 7-28.

Woolfolk-Hoy, A., & Weinstein, C.S. (2006). Student and teacher perspectives on classroom management. In C.M. Evertson & C.S. Weinstein (Eds.), *Handbook of classroom management: Research, practice and contemporary issues* (pp. 181-222). Mahwah, NJ: Lawrence Erlbaum Associates, Publishers.

Ysseldyke, J., & Olsen, K. (1999). Putting alternate assessments into practice: What to measure and possible sources of data. *Exceptional Children, 65*(2), 175-186.

Zwaigenbaum, L., Bryson, S., Rogers, T., Roberts, W., Brian, J., & Szatmari, P. (2005). Behavioral manifestations of autism in the first year of life. *International Journal of Developmental Neuroscience, 23*, 143-152.

Credits

Text Credits

Chapter 4

p. 59 Excerpted from Brophy, J. (2006). History of research on classroom management. In C.M. Evertson & C. S. Weinstein (Eds.), *Handbook of classroom management: Research, practice and contemporary issues* (pp. 17–46). Mahwah, NJ: Lawrence Erlbaum Associates, Publishers.

pp. 68–69 Excerpted from Johnson, F.L., & Edmunds, A.L. (2006). *From chaos to control: Understanding and responding to the behaviors of students with exceptionalities.* London, ON: The Althouse Press.

p. 72 Excerpted from Johnson, F.L., & Edmunds, A.L. (2006). *From chaos to control: Understanding and responding to the behaviors of students with exceptionalities.* London, ON: The Althouse Press, p. 58–59.

Chapter 5

p. 98 Excerpted from Learning Disabilities Association of Canada, http:www.idac-taac.ca.

p. 103 Excerpted from Learning Disabilities Association of Canada, http:www.idac-taac.ca.

p. 108 Excerpted from Lerner, J.W., & Kline, F. (2006). *Learning disabilities and related disorders.* Boston: Houghton Mifflin Company. Page 16, Table 1.2

pp. 113–115 Excerpted from Lerner, J.W., & Kline, F. (2006). *Learning disabilities and related disorders.* Boston: Houghton Mifflin Company. Page 497 (math), 402 (reading), 464 (writing).

p. 121 Excerpted from Conte, R. (1998). Attention disorders. In B. Wong (Ed.), *Learning about learning disabilities* (2nd ed.) (pp. 67–105). San Diego: Academic Press.

p. 123 Excerpted from The International Dyslexia Association, www.interdys.org.

p. 126 Goldberg, R.J., Higgins, E.L., Rasking, M.H., & Herman, K.L. (2003). Predictors of success in individuals with learning disabilities: A qualitative analysis of a 20-year longitudinal study. *Learning Disabilities Research & Practice,* 18(4), 222–236. Page 230. Reprinted with permission from Blackwell Publishers.

Chapter 6

pp. 141–142 Reprinted with permission from the *Diagnostic and Statistical Manual of Mental Disorders,* Fourth Edition, Text Revision (Copyright 2000). American Psychiatric Association.

pp. 152–153 Copyright © Province of British Columbia. All rights reserved. Reprinted with permission of the Province of British Columbia. www.ipp.gov.bc.ca.

pp. 153–154 Copyright © 2005 Jossey-Bass. Reprinted with permission of John Wiley & Sons, Inc.

Chapter 7

pp. 184–186 Excerpted from Coleman, L.J., & Cross, T.L. (2001). Adapted from "Teacher Identification of Superior Students," by J. S. Renzulli, R. H. Hartman, and C. M. Callahan, 1971, *Exceptional Children,* 38, pp. 211–214, 243–248. Copyright 1971 by the Council for Exceptional Children.

pp. 186–187 Excerpted from Edmunds, A.L, & Edmunds, G.A. (2005). Sensitivity: A double-edged sword for the pre-adolescent and adolescent gifted child. *Roeper Review,* 27(2), 69–77.

pp. 189–190 Excerpted from Lindsey (1980) as cited in Coleman, L.J., & Cross, T.L. (2001). *Being gifted in school: An introduction to development, guidance, and teaching.* Texas: Prufrock Press Inc. From Lindsey, M. (1980). *Training teachers of the gifted and talented.* New York: Teachers College Press.

p. 192 From Colangelo, Nicholas & Gary Davis, *Handbook of Gifted Education,* 3e. Published by Allyn and Bacon, Boston, MA. Copyright © 2003 by Pearson Education. Reprinted by permission of the publisher.

pp. 195–196 Excerpted from Siegle, D., & McCoach, D.B. (2005). Making a difference: Motivating gifted students who are not achieving. *Teaching Exceptional Children,* 38(1), 22–27.

pp. 197–198 Excerpted from Neilsen (2002) as cited in Nielsen, M.E., & Higgins, L.D. (2005). The eye of the storm: Services and programs for twice-exceptional learners. *Teaching Exceptional Children,* 38(1), 8–15.

Chapter 9

pp. 268–270 Adapted from Saskatchewan Education, www.sasked.gov.sk.ca/branches/curr/special_ed/sepub.shtml. *Teaching Students with Autism: A Guide for Educators* (Instructional Approaches and Classroom Management, p.19–25).

Chapter 10

p. 293 Excerpted from Avenues, www.avenuesforamc.com/index.htm. Pamphlet: *What causes AMC?* http://www.avenuesforamc.com/publications/pamphlet.htm#3.

Photographs

Chapter 1

p. 8 Photograph of Emily Eaton, used with permission from Carol and Clayton Eaton.

Chapter 2

p. 14 © Bob Krist/Corbis.

Chapter 3

p. 39 © Royalty Free/Corbis.
p. 43 © Bob Rowan; Progressive Image/Corbis.
p. 52 © Dan Forer/Beateworks/Corbis.
p. 53 © Bob Rowan; Progressive Image/Corbis.

Chapter 4

p. 58 Banana Stock/PictureQuest.
p. 74 Alison Derry.

Chapter 5

p. 115 © Adriane Moll/zefa/Corbis.

Chapter 7

p. 181 © Photodisc/PunchStock.

Chapter 8

p. 238 © Mika/zefa/Corbis.

Chapter 9

p. 261 © Randy Faris/Corbis.
p. 265 © Fabio Cardoso/zefa/Corbis.

Chapter 10

p. 295 © Owen Franken/Corbis.

Chapter 11

p. 316 © Helen King/Corbis.

Index